TOTAL INNOVATION MANAGEMENT

Theory and Practice

Series on Innovation and Operations Management for Chinese Enterprises

Print ISSN: 2591-7188
Online ISSN: 2591-7196

Editor: Xiaobo Wu *(School of Management, Zhejiang University, China)*

Published:

Vol. 7: *Total Innovation Management: Theory and Practice*
by Qingrui Xu

Vol. 6: *Global Manufacturing and Secondary Innovation in China: Latecomer's Advantages*
by Xiaobo Wu

Vol. 5: *R&D Investment of Multinational Corporations and China's Independent Innovation*
by Wen Xiao, Jiadong Pan and Gaobang Lin

Vol. 4: *The Theory and Policies of Mutual Benefit and Win-Win Strategy: Research on Sustainable Development of China's Open Economy*
by Lixin Yu and Wanling Chen

Vol. 3: *The Internationalization of Technological Innovation for Chinese Enterprises*
by Jin Chen

Vol. 2: *Basic Research and Industrial Innovation in China*
by Xielin Liu, Yubing He and Peng Cheng

Vol. 1: *Independent Innovation in China: Theory and Cases*
by Huibo Zhong and Jiasu Lei

Series on Innovation and Operations Management for Chinese Enterprises – Vol. 7

TOTAL INNOVATION MANAGEMENT

Theory and Practice

Qingrui XU
Zhejiang University, China

World Scientific

ZHEJIANG UNIVERSITY PRESS
浙江大学出版社

Published by

World Scientific Publishing Co. Pte. Ltd.
5 Toh Tuck Link, Singapore 596224
USA office: 27 Warren Street, Suite 401-402, Hackensack, NJ 07601
UK office: 57 Shelton Street, Covent Garden, London WC2H 9HE

and

Zhejiang University Press
No. 148, Tianmushan Road
Xixi Campus of Zhejiang University
Hangzhou 310028, China

Library of Congress Cataloging-in-Publication Data
Names: Xu, Qingrui, author.
Title: Total innovation management : theory and practice / Qingrui Xu, Zhejiang University, China.
Description: Hackensack, NJ : World Scientific, [2022] | Includes bibliographical references.
Identifiers: LCCN 2021043720 | ISBN 9789811230981 (hardcover) |
ISBN 9789811233210 (ebook) | ISBN 9789811233227 (ebook other)
Subjects: LCSH: Management--Technological innovations. | Information technology--Management.
Classification: LCC HD30.2 .X78 2022 | DDC 658.4/038--dc23/eng/20211006
LC record available at https://lccn.loc.gov/2021043720

British Library Cataloguing-in-Publication Data
A catalogue record for this book is available from the British Library.

This edition is jointly published by World Scientific Publishing Co. Pte. Ltd. and Zhejiang University Press. This edition is distributed worldwide by World Scientific Publishing Co. Pte. Ltd, except China.

Typeset by Zhejiang University Press

Printed in China

Preface

Total Innovation: The Only Way towards Innovation-oriented Enterprises

In the National Conference on Science & Technology held in 2006, "indigenous innovation" was set as a basic state policy and was required by the central government to be given a high priority in scientific and technological work. The then Chinese President Hu Jintao emphasized the importance of accelerating China's capability for indigenous innovation and to consider the capability of scientific and technological innovation as the decisive factor for the development of national scientific and technological undertakings and the core of national competitiveness and important assurance of national security.

To drive the advancements of science and technology and further lead the comprehensive and sustainable development of the national economy and society relying on indigenous innovation, innovation-oriented enterprises still have a long way to go. Only by making every economic cell of society, namely the enterprise, an innovation-oriented enterprise can the whole region become an innovation-oriented city, an innovation-oriented province or even an innovation-oriented country. This book is the research report of the "Construction of Theory and Formation Mechanism of Total Innovation Management (TIM)" (Program No. 70372018), a program funded by the National Natural Science Foundation of China. This program aims to discuss and analyze, under the general trend of indigenous innovation, how enterprises construct indigenous innovation capability through TIM and to offer enterprises theoretical foundations and practical guidance to develop themselves towards indigenous innovation.

The research results are not only the results of a three-year long research but also a reflection of the cumulative experience of our research center in the field of technology innovation for nearly 40 years. In the field of technology innovation, we have experienced three distinct phases, namely:

Secondary Innovation	Portfolio Innovation	Total Innovation
1970s to 1980s	Mid-1980s to mid-1990s	Mid-1990s to present

Secondary innovation refers to the re-innovation based on the digestion and absorption of introduced technology. Portfolio innovation and integration innovation are similar but essentially the same. Not limited to the integration of technology, portfolio innovation also includes the combination and integration of technology and non-technology innovation. The former (combination of technology innovation) includes the combination of product innovation with process innovation and the combination of significant innovation with incremental innovation; the latter (combination of technology innovation with non-technology innovation) includes the combination of technology innovation with organization and culture innovation, the combination of independent innovation with cooperative innovation, etc. Portfolio innovation is not only a project portfolio but also the strategic thinking and guidelines over project portfolio. In practice, portfolio innovation will lead enterprises to get out of the impasse of isolated technology innovation and move towards the combination of technology innovation with organization innovation, culture innovation and system innovation.

Total innovation greatly carries forward portfolio innovation by integrating technology innovation with innovation in terms of culture, system and management (non-technology innovation) in a more systematic and broader field. It not only combines the innovation of an enterprise in various aspects into a systematic and comprehensive innovation, but also, integrated with all-involvement innovation and all time-space innovation, forms a continuous and three-dimensional (i.e. three "ALL", all-element, all-involvement and all time-space) innovation paradigm that bases itself on all-involvement innovation and combines all innovation resources. Relying on the vitality of all-involvement innovation and through comprehensive and continuous innovation, it forms the holistic innovation force with strong competitive advantages, stimulates the leapfrog development of the core competence of enterprise and enables enterprise to develop itself towards the innovation-oriented path twice or three times as fast as ordinary enterprises.

Total innovation is the main characteristic of an innovation-based enterprise. Creating an innovation-oriented enterprise by constructing a total innovation system is the approach that successful foreign enterprises use to move towards excellence and also the only way that Chinese enterprises have to take to become innovation-oriented enterprises that leapfrog in development.

Rather than being limited to the innovation program, this research is built on the application and integration of research results of other programs. For instance, during the process of the "Research on the Basic Rules and Models of Business Management of State-owned Enterprises in China", a key program sponsored by the National Natural Science Foundation of China, we have discovered and revealed one of the basic rules of business management, the "Rule of Total Innovation", which can be expressed as the "strategy-oriented and technology innovation-centered rule of total innovation".

This book consists of five parts: Part One "Background and Theories", includes practices and theoretical basis of TIM; Part Two "Connotation and System Framework of TIM", includes four chapters, namely, "System Framework of TIM", "All-Element Innovation", "All-Involvement Innovation" and "All Time-Space Innovation"; Part Three "Formation and Mechanisms of TIM", includes synergy mechanism, learning mechanism and leadership mechanism; Part Four "Innovation Benefits of TIM"; and Part Five "Practice Cases", includes three cases of successful Chinese and foreign enterprises.

This research has been strongly supported by academic and business circles, benefits from the cooperative study with Prof. Li Mingfang from the University of California and Dr. Michael Menke, HP Technology & Strategy Consultant, and improved with the valuable suggestions of Dr. G. Farris (Editor-in-Chief of IEEE Transactions on Engineering Management) et al. on the interim research results. Besides, the achievements of this research cannot be separated from the active involvement and joint efforts of our strategic partners, including Ms. Yang Mianmian (President of Haier Group), Dr. Yu Zida (Vice President of Haier Group), Dr. Cui Jian (President of Baosteel Research Institute) and Dr. Mao Wuxing of Potevio Institute of Technology. Last but not least, I'd like to express my sincere gratitude to all members of our team, especially Prof. Chen Jin, Prof. Zheng Gang, Associate Professor Zhao Xiaoqing, Dr. Liu Jingjiang and all doctoral and postgraduate students, including Xie Zhangshu, Liang Xinru, Zhu Jianzhong, Wu Zhiyan, Zhu Ling, Jin Xin, Shui Chanqing, Jiang Jian, Xu Jing, Wang Haiwei and Wang Shuangying (visiting scholar). My grateful thanks also to Ms. Wang Lihua, my executive assistant, as well as Mr. Wang Kai, for their remarkable efforts on this book's editing. Some mistakes undoubtedly exist in this book because of the limitation of my knowledge. Any suggestion and advice will be sincerely appreciated.

Xu Qingrui,
Director of the Research Center of Innovation & Development
(RCID), Zhejiang University
Academician of the Chinese Academy of Engineering

List of Common Abbreviations

ATIM	Architecture for Total Innovation Management
BPR	Business Process Re-engineering
CTI	Competence of Total Innovation
DRAM	Dynamic Random Access Memory
ERP	Enterprise Resource Planning
ISA	Innovation System Architecture
ISO	International Standard Organization
JIT	Just in Time
OEC	Overall Every Control and Clear
OECD	Organization for Economic Cooperation and Development
PCT	Patent Cooperation Treaty
PDM	Product Data Management
RCID	Research Center of Innovation & Development, Zhejiang University
SBU	Strategic Business Unit
TIM	Total Innovation Management
TQM	Total Quality Management
WTO	World Trade Organization

Contents

Part One

Background and Theories

Chapter 1

Practical and Theoretical Background of Total Innovation Management

As the only thing that is constant today is change, innovation has increasingly become an invaluable source and power for the survival and development of enterprises. It has drawn attention from a great number of scholars and entrepreneurs. With the continuous development of relevant theories and practices, the contents and methods of innovation management have become increasingly complex and gradually formed a management model featuring total innovation.

1.1 Practical background of research

Since the mid-1950s, innovation and transformation have increasingly become one of the most active and attractive fields in academic and commercial circles. With the rapid development of information technology, global localization of market competition and individualized customization of customer demands, business environment has undergone fundamental changes. On the one hand, enterprises have to stand up to severe challenges. The vertical, horizontal, external and geographic boundaries are increasingly overlapping with one another. Correspondingly, core enterprises and their upstream and downstream counterparts have formed a symbiotic business ecosystem on a larger scale. For this reason, in a business ecosystem, the pattern is no longer competition between individual enterprises but between enterprise alliances. Only fast, flexible, innovation-oriented and alliance-based organizations can obtain sustained competitive advantages and high innovation rents at the time of chaos. On the other hand, the complex and fast-changing hypercompetitive environment continuously challenges the existing innovation management practices. Confronted with an increasingly non-linear complexity of interactions among all internal elements and between internal elements and the external environment, the traditional innovation management model is no longer applicable. Therefore, in the modern environment of a knowledge-based economy, it is necessary to go beyond the linear approach of Newton's classical mechanics. It is important to break through the framework of a single theory and use interdisciplinary theories and methods in conducting research on the model of innovation management in a network environment.

1.1.1 Increasingly complex competitive environments of the new century require enterprises to implement total innovation

Since the 1990s, as the trend of economic globalization and networking becomes prevalent, a tide of new scientific and technological revolutions featuring the universal application of IT technologies and the Internet has led to a fundamental reform of the environment for survival and development, operating objectives and models of enterprises. In the networking environment, the information interaction capability has been greatly improved, thus enabling information to break through space-time limitations and providing enterprises with good material and technical support for the implementation of total innovation management (TIM). It is embodied in the following aspects: on the one hand, information can be distributed and transferred among different regions, functional departments and positions, and all employees within an organization, thus providing employees involved in research, development, production, manufacturing and management with information and relevant knowledge necessary for implementing total innovation. On the other hand, information can be sufficiently shared with external suppliers, consumers, partners and competitors at a lower cost, thus technically supporting the innovation based on rapid and continuous integration of internal and external resources of an enterprise, even its global resources. According to statistics, the quantity of transverse technologies generated through technical, and license and patent transactions is ever increasing. At the same time, with economic globalization and the vigorous development of e-business and networking transactions, the boundaries of enterprises become increasingly blurred. The emergence of organizational structures like strategic alliance and virtual team enables the boundaries of enterprises to extend beyond the regional, industrial and even national limitations. It stimulates the globalization of research, development, manufacturing and marketing. Many transnational enterprises (such as Microsoft) have established R&D centers all over the world to integrate global scientific and technological resources for innovation.

Since the start of the 21st century, enterprises have had to implement total innovation to adapt to the increasingly complex and competitive environment. In light of the increasingly individualized consumer demands and time-based competition, shortened life and R&D cycle of a product, emergence of new technologies and threats from competitors, more and more enterprises discovered that the sustained competitive advantages cannot be maintained if they only rely on high production efficiency, quality and flexibility. To remain competitive in the market, enterprises have to respond to the overall demands of consumers faster than their competitors, alter the existing innovation management modes, realize the synergy effects between technology and non-technology elements, and fully mobilize employees from all departments such as production, manufacturing, marketing and services to innovate whenever and wherever possible. Only in such a manner can enterprises improve the efficiency of developing new products, continuously expand their market shares and obtain great profits. A research report of HP shows the following: Supposing the time from idea to market for a new product introduction is five years, if R&D is delayed for half a year, the profits will be decreased by 50%. Those companies that implement time-based sustained innovation management can respond to consumer demands at least 60% faster, grow three to four times faster, and obtain at least twice the profits (Stalk & Hout, 1990).

1.1.2 All-round enterprise innovation practices need the support and guidance of new advanced theories

Strengthening innovation and improving the innovation capability have already become a matter of urgency for the economic development of China. To cope with the challenges confronted by Chinese firms, it is necessary to strengthen the systematic and total innovation activities, taking technological innovation as the basis for the synergy among other factors like market, organization, and culture. Only then can the management of total innovation be strengthened.

Some Chinese and foreign enterprises leading in innovation, such as Haier, HP and 3M, are actively adapting to the changing environment and implementing total innovation to a different extent. In recent years, to improve core competitiveness, Haier Group has implemented and achieved remarkable results in total innovation, which takes value creation and value increase as their goals, technological innovation as the core, the innovation in market, organization and cultural system as the support, and business process innovation as the guarantee. The performance of technological innovation is fully improved due to the synergy and support of non-technology factors. The speed of new product development is greatly increased and the development cycle is significantly shortened. Now, on average 1.3 new products are developed and 2.5 patents are declared every working day. In recent years, Baosteel, through the "Enterprise System Innovation" (ESI) program, has promoted the total innovation of all undertakings and achieved remarkable results as well. The new endeavors independently explored by such leading enterprises need to be further summarized, refined and promoted.

The implementation of total innovation needs a set of scientific and effective innovation management theories as guidance. Restricted by the prevailing conditions, traditional innovation management theories, lacking an understanding of the drastic changes of the modern environment and the increasingly complex innovation process, cannot provide enterprises with a scientific and effective innovation management paradigm to guide practices under the new circumstances. Therefore, based on the summary of innovation theories and practices in the world and the characteristics of market environment, this study establishes and analyzes total innovation management (TIM). It is a three-dimensional synergy innovation model of "Three All", i.e. all-element, all-involvement and all time-space factors. Such a strategy-oriented innovation model aims to create and increase value and enrich and develop innovation management theories pertaining to the new age, and provide Chinese enterprises with theoretical guidance on the implementation of scientific and effective total innovation, and on how to be adapted for the changes of competitive environment.

Case Study

Haier's All-round Innovation — Construction of Capital for Future Competition

Indigenous innovation has already gained momentum in the development of enterprises. For Haier, however, indigenous innovation is embodied in system innovation, i.e. all-round innovation and all-process innovation. In other words, innovation is a system. Only with the continuous innovation of enterprise can an indigenous innovation system be built, thus forming a mechanism of total innovation to guarantee the driving force for innovation at any moment. Only in such a manner, can enterprises have capital for sound development, external competitions and to remain strong in the future.

In the 40 years after the reform and opening up, facing the increasingly distinct and new environment and needs for survival, especially due to economic globalization, Haier's innovation impulse has constantly been evoked. For more than 30 years, starting from small innovations, Haier has undertaken a difficult but unflinching process of innovation. The whole process of Haier's growth is covered mostly by innovation. From the continuous conflicts of development philosophies, overturn of management models, construction of talent mechanism, pursuit of proprietary technologies, enrichment of corporate culture, exploration of core values to the continuous pursuit of proprietary brands, Haier has reformed each cell with an everlasting innovation spirit and driving force. This is the largest source of wealth for Haier to maintain sustained development. Therefore, to establish the philosophy of all-round innovation, i.e. being dedicated to building the overall development capacity, and the philosophy of all-process innovation, i.e. being dedicated to forming a mechanism of continuous innovation, is the foundation for sustainable development of an enterprise and systematic basis for strengthening and maintaining the indigenous innovation capability of an enterprise.

In short, the all-round system innovation, the market-oriented indigenous innovation, the flat organizational structure and development model and the globalized brand strategy are experiences Haier obtained over 30 years of development and also the core strategy of Haier's future development.[①]

① Source: Zhang Ruimin, All-round innovation constructs the capital for future competition, http://tech.sina.com.cn/it/2006-08-29/12301109132.shtml, China Electronics News, 2006-08-29

1.2 Development of innovation theories: From technological innovation to total innovation

In 1912, American scholar Schumpeter first put forward the concept of "innovation". He defined "innovation" as a new combination of production factors made by the entrepreneur. He thought innovation was the critical driving force of economic growth. Schumpeter's concept of innovation involved production innovation, process innovation, market innovation, use of new raw materials, combining materials in new ways and organizational innovation. Schumpeter paved the way for research in innovation theory. After him, many scholars shifted the focus of innovation research from economic growth at the macro level to enterprise innovation management at the micro level to illuminate the "black box" of innovation within firms. Reviewing the main research on innovation management helps identify five phases, outlined as follows.

1.2.1 Phase one: Research on individual innovation (1940s to 1950s)

It was in the 1940s that systematic research on innovation of enterprises at the micro level began to take place. Influenced by Schumpeter's theory of innovation, research during the 1940s and 1950s was based on the theory of the "entrepreneur as the driving force of innovation" and mainly studied the specific innovation process, the success factors affecting innovation, and the driving forces of innovation (Rothwell et al.,1974). In this beginning phase, the basic problems of innovation were still unsettled and research focused on the separate components. Research on innovation management during this phase was characterized with single, linear and endogenous models. Schumpeter's definition tended to consider innovation at individual levels at the early stage and tended to emphasize the role of the firm. In spite of such a shift, Schumpeter generally associated innovation space with the firm. Such a philosophy had a broad impact for quite a long time and most researchers considered it as a self-evident assumption.

1.2.2 Phase two: Research on organizational promotion (1960s to 1970s)

As the theoretical research on innovation advanced, academic studies looked more closely at specialized fields of innovation. Building on the theoretical outcomes of the first phase, the second phase of innovation research mainly studied the internal sources of innovation within organizations and focused on how to attain the objective of innovation and promote innovation in organizations through effective management of R&D activities. In fact, research during the second phase mainly studied the R&D department and its activities as well as the important role of organizations themselves in the innovation process. The main contributions in this research phase were from J. Abernathy and M. Utterback. In particular, the "U-A" pattern of J. Abernathy and M. Utterback divided the evolutionary pattern of product innovation, process innovation and industrial organization into three stages: stage of fluidity, stage of transition and stage of stability.

1.2.3 Phase three: Research on outsider involvement (1970s)

Research in the third phase looked at the firm level, emphasized the important role of users in the innovation process and considered users as an important external source of innovation. The main advocate of this idea was Eric von Hippel (1988), who put forward the concept of "User as Innovator" and then "Lead User". Today, more attention is paid to the idea of users as innovation sources. For example, Stephen M. Shapiro (2001) thought that firms should invite users into the process of R&D and marketing in a co-innovation partnership. He advanced the method of "lead user," and developed the methods of finding innovation sources in "defected users" and "potential users."

The essence of the second and third research phases is on the driving force of innovation. The second research phase emphasized internal promotion of innovation and the third research phase emphasized interactive promotion of internal (R&D) and external sources (users). Impacted by the environment, the perspective of these two phases on the driving forces and sources of innovation is mechanistic and linear, and is based on the philosophy of Newton's classical mechanics.

1.2.4 Phase four: Research on portfolio, integrated and systematic innovation (1980s to 1990s)

The first three research phases of innovation theory focused not on the interactive mechanisms and relationships among the components of innovation, but on individual innovation processes, activities and components, which are the individual components in the five innovation forms cited by Schumpeter. Beginning in the 1980s, when organizations had to set more ambitious goals for innovation effectiveness in order to adapt to changing situations, the limitations of traditional theories of patterns of innovation became more apparent. Based on a systematic view, some scholars shifted the research focus from individual components in the innovation system to the interactive relationships of these components, thereby arriving at the portfolio innovation theory. For example, the research of Rothwell and Rosenberg further revealed the dynamic, integrated and comprehensive process of innovation. The innovation model developed by Rosenberg mainly focused on technological innovation, but it had already revealed that the innovation is a process of several factors interacting with each other. The research and practice of portfolio innovation theory went through four stages: products portfolio innovation, technology portfolio innovation, portfolios of various innovation elements and portfolio innovation based on core capabilities. Portfolio innovation theory is currently the predominant innovation management pattern in both China and foreign countries, and involves at least five portfolio forms: coordination between product innovation and process innovation, coordination between radical innovation and incremental innovation, coordination between implicit and explicit innovation benefits, coordination between technological innovation and organizational culture innovation, and coordination between independent internal innovation and cooperative external innovation (Wang & Xu, 1993; Xu et al., 1997). Edwards Roberts (1999) proved the interactive relationship between technological innovation and organizational innovation. Similarly, Hardy and Dougherty (1996), through empirical case studies, revealed that an enterprise's sustained product innovation competence is affected by organizational process and architecture. During the fourth research phase of innovation study, driven by portfolio innovation theory at the end of the 20th century, innovation theory further evolved into integrated and systematic innovation theory. The representative scholars of integrated innovation theory are Marco Iansiti, H. K. Tang, et al. In 1998, American scholar Iansiti put forward the concept of technology integration. Some scholars pointed out that the integration of various elements in technological innovation played an important role in guaranteeing the effect of integrated innovation (Tang, 1998; Tidd, Bessant & Pavitt, 2001; Jiang & Chen, 2000; Cao et al., 2001). Integrated innovation stresses the creative integration of existing innovative elements, which demonstrates, to a certain degree, a systematic way of thinking. The representative scholar of innovation system theory is Robert Tucker. Many scholars have done research on the concept of enterprise innovation systems (Padmore, et al., 1998; Chen, 2003). Janszen (2000) saw enterprise innovation as a complex self-adaptive system (CAS). Peters (2002) pointed out that to improve the performance of innovation, it is necessary to change from "framework thinking" to "linear thinking", i.e. emphasizing the relationship among all elements within the system. Tucker (2002) proposed five principles of innovative management, including the principle that innovation should be comprehensive, involving R&D and other departments; that innovation should seek new opportunities organizationally, systematically and continually; and that innovation must involve every member of the organization, among others. All of these principles embody a systematic and comprehensive way of thinking.

Although breaking away from the previous linear thinking pattern and pointing out the significant effects of the matching and interaction between each subsystem and component in the performance of innovation systems, the system-theory-based innovation theories that were developed in the fourth phase failed to carry out ecology-based analysis of the subjectivity and time-space effect of innovation as a social process and the combination of specific innovation systems.

1.2.5 Phase five: Research on total innovation management (21st century)

In the 21st century, innovation theories are developing toward a higher level and many scholars are conducting innovation theory research based on the ecosystem theory. The focus of this research phase is total innovation management, defined as innovation by anyone at any time in all processes, among different functions and around the world. In recent years, researchers increasingly emphasize the idea of inspiring each employee's creativity and making everyone an innovator (Tucker, 2002; Peters, 2002; Shapiro, 2001; Wheatley, 2001). Shapiro (2001) indicated that enterprises should try to realize 24/7 (7 days a week, 24 hours a day) innovation in order to respond in a timely fashion to the needs of customers. Some scholars think the emergence of new organization forms such as outsourcing and strategic alliance have advanced the globalization of R&D, manufacture, and marketing (Chowdhury, 2003; Lian & Ma, 2001; Chen, 2003). The aim of the fifth phase of development of innovation theories is to realize all-round innovation. However, current research at the fifth phase is still fragmentary, nonsystematic and discontinuous (Tucker, 2002). It needs to be further methodized and systematized. The development course of innovation theory can be briefly summarized as shown in Table 1-1.

Table 1-1 Development course of enterprise innovation theory

Phase	Main contentions	Main contributors	Theory foundation	Practical problems solved
First phase (1940s–1950s)	Individual innovation Linear and endogenous innovation process; Success factor in innovation	(Marquis, 1969) (Rothwell, 1974) (Freeman, 1974)	Newton classical mechanism	Development of new technologies and creativity of individuals
Second phase (1960s–1970s)	Organizational promotion R&D management Internal sources; Linear process model of innovation	(Roberts, 1988) (Utterback, 1994)	Newton classical mechanism	Application of new technologies and effect of organizational promotion
Third phase (1970s)	Outside sources involved; Linear process of users as innovators	(von Hippel, 1998)	Newton classical mechanism	External promotion of technolo gical innovation and user involvement

continued

Phase	Main contentions	Main contributors	Theory foundation	Practical problems solved
Fourth phase (1980s–1990s)	Chain-linked & coupling process model; Parallel (integrated) innovation process model; Portfolio innovation; Integrated innovation; System innovation	(Rothwell, 1992) (Xu, 1996) (Guo, 1997) (Chen, 2000) (Wu, 1990) (Kim, 1995)	System theory; Nonlinear science; Complexity theory	Synergy between systematic technological innovation and non-technology factors
Fifth phase (21st century)	Total innovation	(Xu, 2001, 2002) (Shapiro, 2001) (Bean, 2002) (Robert, 2002) (Tucker, 2002)	Ecosystem theory; Complexity theory	Interactive relationship between innovation as a social process and human as the innovation subject under the electronic and network environment

1.3 Presentation of research questions

From a practical point of view, on the one hand, more and more enterprises have discovered that they cannot satisfy customers' increasingly individualized demands and maintain sustained advantages in market competition by only relying on high production efficiency, quality and flexibility. Instead, technological innovations can help them get out of difficulties and achieve outstanding operating performance. On the other hand, environmental turbulence, fierce competition and change of customer demands force enterprises to carry out all-round competitions, and respond to customers' all-round demands faster than competitors. It requires not only technological innovation but also all-round, systematic and continuous innovation based on technological innovation. Leading enterprises are realizing that the ultimate performance of technological innovation is increasingly dependent on the innovations of all departments and all elements within the enterprise and the effective synergy among different elements.

From a theoretical point of view, modern innovation management theories are continuously developing towards the all-round, systematic and ecological direction. However, most mainstream research today focuses on technological innovation and technology elements, ignoring the impact of organizational, cultural and other non-technology factors on the process and performance of innovation; there is a lack of research on the synergic mechanism between non-technology factors and technological innovation. More importantly, most modern research still focuses on a certain aspect or dimension of innovation and lacks systematic and comprehensive thinking, which should incorporate the framework of complexity theory and take the new developments of the 21st century into consideration. The basic cause of such shortcomings is that for a long time, the research and thought processes of some scholars were influenced by classical Newtonian mechanics. They conducted research on technological innovation from linear and mechanical perspectives rather than from the perspective of the complexity theory which complies with the increasingly complex changes of environment and innovation process.

In the modern economic environment, to strengthen innovation and to improve enterprises' indigenous innovation capability has already become a necessity. To solve the challenges faced by innovation in China, enterprises have to strengthen innovation activities in a systematic and comprehensive way, and carry out total innovation and strengthen the management of total innovation, which focuses on technological innovation and bases itself on the synergy and coordination among other elements like organization, culture and system. Therefore, the presentation of a new generation innovation management represented by TIM is an irresistible trend.

TIM is a revolutionary paradigm rather than a simple induction. It has key differences with the traditional paradigm of innovation management in terms of theoretical foundation, strategies, architecture, elements, time-space scope and management style. In particular, it has broken through the original time-space domain and the innovation framework restricted to R&D development and R&D personnel, and highlighted the importance of an all-involvement, all-element and all time-space innovation.

Following the logical thinking of "Why to apply TIM", "What is TIM" and "How to form and realize TIM", this book emphasizes on the systematic and in-depth research on theoretic architecture, systematic construction and forming mechanism of TIM based on the theory of complex self-adaptive system and the innovation management theory. It strives to highlight the depth, creativity and practical application of theory. This book mainly focuses on the following five issues: (1) Theoretical and practical background of TIM; (2) Connotation and system framework of TIM; (3) Mechanism and model of interaction and synergy among different innovation elements (technology and non-technology); (4) The architecture and formation process and mechanism of TIM; (5) The way to strengthen and consolidate all-involvement innovation as the foundation of TIM.

Chapter 2

Main Theoretical Basis of Total Innovation Management

Any theory has its own theoretical basis and starts from a certain theoretical premise. Significantly different from the previous innovation management theory, total innovation management (TIM) shifts the research perspective from individual innovation elements and innovation system components to the whole innovation system and the relationship among all elements of the innovation system. It reveals the complexity, synergy, dynamics and ecosystem of the innovation process. Based on ecosystem theory, humanism theory, synergy theory, complexity system theory, open innovation theory, distributed innovation theory and modularity theory, the total innovation theory breaks through the previous linear thinking mode of innovation, considers enterprise innovation system as a complex innovation system and highlights the interaction among all elements within the innovation system.

2.1 Practical background of research

2.1.1 Principles of ecosystem theory

Ecology is a very young science, but the thoughts of human beings on the ecosystem have a long history. For example, ancient Chinese philosophy vividly embodies the thoughts of ecosystem wisdom in the Book of Changes, the theory of Yin & Yang and five elements, and the theory that man is an integral part of nature. The ancient theories of traditional Chinese medicine even considered the human body and the natural environment as a whole and ascribed physical illnesses to the imbalance between the two.

The word "ecology" originates from Greek word "Oikoslogos", which consists of two roots, "oikos" and "logos". The former means "house" or "habitat"; the latter means "discourse" or "research". Ecology is deemed as the "research of habitat". In the Chinese dictionary, it means the science that deals with the relations of organisms to one another and to their physical surroundings. American ecologist Odum even pointed out that ecology is the science on the integrality of human and environment. In general, ecology is the science that deals with the relations of organisms or groups of organisms to their physical surroundings (Kong et al., 2003). The system theory is an integral perspective of analysis, which studies the relationship among different elements on the whole and is broadly applied in theoretical research of different disciplines. Generally, system theories can be categorized into the mechanical system theory and the ecological system theory, according to the differences between research subjects. The former is mainly applied in natural science, focusing more on the material world; the latter is more applied in social science, mainly emphasizing the interaction between human and environment. As early as in 1921, Park and Burgess, in their book *Introduction to the Science of Sociology*, put forward the concept of human ecology for the first time. In 1935, a British scholar named Bews wrote a book titled *Human Ecology*, which established the status of ecosystem theory in social science. Thereafter, different branches of social science began to use ecosystem theories, giving birth to social, educational, administrative and urban ecosystems (Kong et al., 2003).

The ecosystem theory that deals with the relationship between nonhuman organisms and the environment has little bearing on this research. This research is mainly trying to shed light on innovation management, based on the relationship between humans and the organizational environment. From the above analysis, the focus of the ecosystem theory can be deemed as the coordination between humans and organizations and between organizations and environment, and it has three characteristics: (1) It emphasizes the principles of the diversity of subjects; (2) It focuses on the principles of the interaction between humans and organizations; (3) It focuses on the principles of the open connections between organizations and the external environment.

2.1.2 Ecosystem principles of innovation management

The ecosystem principles of innovation management can be traced back to the concept of "enterprise lifecycle", which was put forward by Mason Haire in 1959 and gradually developed into the theory of organizational life cycle. Such theory personalized organizations and argued that the development of enterprises also complies with the growth curve in biology. By using ecological viewpoints, it explained the stagnation and demise of enterprises, for example, and pointed out that the cause of such development is inadequate enterprise management, i.e. the management of an enterprise probably restricted the range of its development. Since the 1950s and 1960s, innovation has been increasingly valued in both theoretical research and in practice. It is widely believed that the success of enterprise innovation requires cooperation among different functions and employees and the coordination between the creativity of employees and the construction of innovation environment within the organization. Just as Ralph Katz (1997) said, a great number of research studies and practices prove that the failure of innovation is no longer caused by simple technical reasons but more by complex interactions among technical staff, trans-department employees and incentive mechanisms. Therefore, in innovation management, much more attention should be given to the coordination between humans and factors like organizational environment. The relationship between human and organizational environment involved in innovation management increasingly becomes the research focus for scholars. The principles of ecosystem are widely recognized and studied in the application of innovation management and break the traditional innovation management theories in three respects, as shown in Figure 2-1.

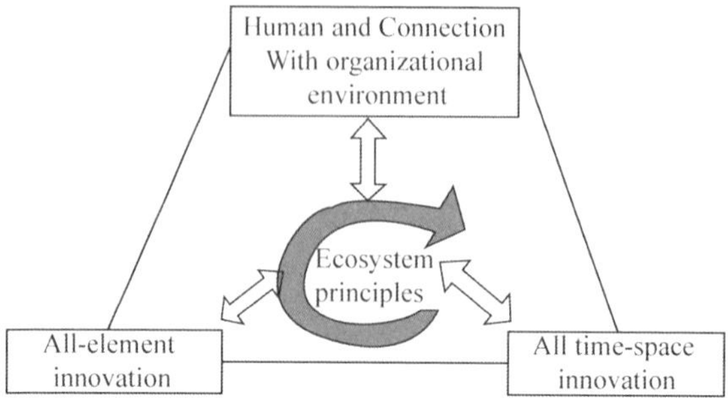

Figure 2-1 System framework of the ecosystem principles of innovation

(I) Ecosystem principles of innovation break the traditional and mechanical innovation theory and emphasize the function of human as well as the ecosystem by connecting human and the organizational environment.

On the one hand, TIM emphasizes that innovation activities are the foundation for the success of enterprise innovation. Innovation itself is a process of knowledge creation and application. Human beings are carriers of knowledge and also the initiators in the whole process of innovation. Human resources are the first resource of innovation and also the pillar upon which enterprises construct more sustained competitive advantages. As early as the 1980s, Philip Sadler, in the preface he wrote for Parker's book *Innovation Management* (Parker, 2001), pointed out that innovation may be the most difficult management task. It's partly because that in spite of the scope of the organization, for innovation to succeed, it is necessary to release the creativity, imagination, vision, decision-making ability and entrepreneurship of most people and a few very gifted individuals rather than a few advantages the enterprise holds. "Human beings are the most valuable assets of our organization"; "All we have are human resources". Such slogans are well known. From the perspective of the value of organizational innovation, innovation is the combination of the innovative decision-making behaviors of employees at all levels (Tornatzky, Eveland & Boylan, 1990). The acquisition of such value must be able to activate and manage the potential creativity of every employee and transform it to an approach to promote enterprise innovation (Tucker, 2002). According to Porter's technical analysis of enterprise value chain, technologies are involved in every value activity of enterprise (such as logistics, marketing, operation, service, enterprise infrastructure, human resource management, technical development and purchasing), while innovation has a practical impact on any activity and accordingly on the creation of enterprise value. Therefore, only by enhancing the subject of human input in innovation, fully mobilizing employees' innovation vigor and improving employees' innovation capability, can enterprises successfully carry out innovation, improve innovation performance and realize the best operating performance.

On the other hand, the most obvious characteristic of the ecosystem principles of innovation management is to emphasize the ecosystem theory that connects innovation environment with humans. The representative treatise on the theory was *An Evolutionary Theory of Economic Change* (1997) written by Nelson and Winter, who conducted research on the evolution of the economic system based on the theory of evolution and Schumpeter's innovation theories. During the analysis of organizational capability and behavior, they formed the ecological viewpoint on the interaction between innovation environment and humans: "It is true that some sort of stable accommodation between the requirements of organizational functioning and the motivations of all organization members is a necessary concomitant of routine operation". Thereafter, more scholars adopted the thoughts of innovation evolvement and reached a consensus that the creation of innovation environment must be conducive to motivating the creative behavior of humans and that environmental change and the human behavior must be linked. *Technological Innovation as an Evolutionary Process* written by Ziman (2000) compiled 21 classical articles that analyzed technology innovation from the perspective of the ecological evolution theory. Most of them studied the environmental elements related to the innovation behavior of humans, such as innovation as a cultural practice, institutionalized innovation, innovative enterprise and organization. As for practices, Gundling (2000) has investigated and analyzed 3M, "the most creative company in the world", for more than 10 years, and concluded that the most outstanding "gift" enabling 3M to fully motivate and improve the innovation energy of all employees is the creation of an overall working environment where many new factors stimulate each other.

As to the two aspects mentioned above, recent research further emphasizes innovation as a dependent variable, which is decided by factors at the levels of humans, organizations and the environment. They include innovation behaviors and methods at the individual and collective levels and the arrangement of innovation at the organizational level (Anderson, De Dreu & Nijstad, 2004; Janssen, Vliert & West, 2004). Among others, Kaufmann (1988) and Anderson, De Dreu and Nijstad (2004) separately summarized the characteristics of innovation and relevant influencing factors on subjectivity at different periods and provided a full-view schematic diagram for subsequent research. The former penned a book named *Innovation: A Cross-Disciplinary Perspective*, which summarized relevant research studies and the activities and characteristics of innovation on different levels (Table 2-1); the latter believed that current innovation fields have already greatly expanded, strengthened on innovation of subjects on different levels, and reviewed and summarized the research on the innovation characteristics of subjects on different levels and their influencing factors from 1969 to 2002 (Table 2-2).

Table 2-1 Gronhaug and Kaufmann's induction of the innovation of subjects on different levels

	Level			
	Individual	**Work group**	**Organizational**	**Social**
Cre-ativity	Creative individual; •Characteris-tics •Working method •Process •Behavior •Skill •Measure; Discover prob-lems; Solve prob-lems; Motive and creativity; Cognitive style; Creative skills; Creative envi-ronment	Creative work group •Solution •Skill; Characteristics of work group; Stimulate/obstruct innovation; Generate ideas	Management and innovation; Innovation activi-ties; Innovation within organization; Structural cha-racteristics and innovation; Creative em-ployees within organization; Roles of creative employees; Organizational construction	Innovation and suspension of innovation; Technological change; Discover problematic resources and innovation; Spillover effect Entrepreneur function; Patent; Market structure
Focus: adapt-ability	Discover prob-lems Solve prob-lems	Characteristics of work group Reform executor	Resources and adoption of inno-vation Resistance to innovation	Systematized innovation Culture and seeking cus-tomers
Diffu-sion	Bridgeman	Reform executor	Innovation facili-tator	Spillover effect Structure of relevant system
Results	Innovation on the individual level	Organizational charac-teristics Division of labor	Organizational objectives and organizational member's evalua-tion of R&D	Cut down the funding for research universities

Table 2-2 Anderson, De Dreu and Nijstad's induction of the innovation of subjects on different levels

Level of subject	Characteristics of subject	Factors influencing innovation subject
Individual	Personality	Tolerance of ambiguity; Self-confidence; Openness to experience; Unconventionality; Rule governed ; Authoritarianism; Independence; Proactivity
	Motivation	Intrinsic and extrinsic motivation; determination to succeed; personal initiative
	Cognitive ability	Above average general intellect; task-specific knowledge; divergent thinking style; ideational fluency
	Job characteristics	Autonomy; span of control; job demands; job dissatisfaction; support for innovation; mentor guidance; appropriate training
	Mood states	Negative moods
Work group	Team structure	Minority influence; cohesiveness; longevity
	Team climate	Participation; vision; norms for innovation; conflict; constructive controversy
	Team member characteristics	Heterogeneity of members; education level
	Team processes	Reflexivity; minority dissent; integration skills; decision-making model
	Leadership style	Democratic style; participative style; openness to idea proposals; leader-member exchange (LMX); expected evaluation
Organizational	Structure	Specialization; centralization; formalization; complexity; stratification; matrix principles
	Strategy	"Prospector" type; organicity
	Size	Number of employees; market share
	Resources	Annual turnover; slack resources
	Culture	Support for experimentation; tolerance of idea failure; risk-taking norms

(II) Ecosystem principles of innovation break the traditional innovation technology theory and emphasize all-element innovation including technology and non-technology elements

With the continuous development of innovation management theories and practices, the contents, modes and subjects of enterprise innovation have become increasingly diversified and systematic and gradually formed a management mode featuring total innovation. As early as the 1970s and 1980s, scholars represented by Daft put forward and developed a new model of innovation, i.e. enterprise innovation classified into technology innovation and management innovation (Daft, 1978; Damanpour & Evan, 1984), and discussed the all-element thoughts of innovation. Thereafter, many scholars conducted in-depth researches on relevant themes. For example, through empirical research, Damanpour pointed out that technology innovation and management innovation often conflict with each other. If technology innovation is stronger, management innovation would be impacted, and vice versa. Therefore, without synergy between technology innovation and management innovation, the best performance of innovation cannot be achieved (Damanpour & Gopalakrishnan, 1998).

Since the early 1980s, the research team represented by Xu Qingrui has focused on the comprehensive development of innovation. In the mid-1990s, they believed that current enterprise innovation management must be based on the accumulation and improvement of core capabilities, and focus on portfolio innovations that balance production innovation and process innovation, technology innovation and organizational culture innovation, incremental innovation and significant innovation, sustainable innovation and disruptive innovation, and dominant innovation benefits and recessive innovation benefits. The theory of portfolio innovation fully embodies the thoughts of total innovation (Xu, 2000). Tucker, in his book *Driving Growth through Innovation*, then put forward five principles of innovation management and offered an overview of total innovation models: (1) Innovation must be approached as a discipline and there must be an all-process method from "creativity to innovation" to judge the success or failure of innovation; (2) Innovation must be approached comprehensively and become a way of operating business units and functional departments on the value chain. (3) Innovation must include an organized, systematic, and continual search for new opportunities and an effective mechanism must be established in the technology and non-technology fields to carry out innovation practices; (4) Innovation must involve everyone in the organization, especially grass-roots employees; (5) Innovation must be customer-centered (Tucker, 2002). Tucker has already conducted research on some contents of TIM theory, but has not analyzed the logic relationship or constructed a system framework. Zheng Gang (2003) expanded the non-technology elements to include strategies, culture, market, organization and system, analyzed the total synergy mechanism of these five elements and put forward the measurement of all-element innovation synergy. Many scholars recognized the complexity of innovation from the perspective of enterprise, and considered it necessary to comprehensively study the interactions among elements at all dimensions related to innovation. They emphasized that, to improve the performance of innovation, enterprises must get rid of the simple thinking on isolated elements, and get the utmost out of integrated innovation and improve innovation performance through the integration of technology and non-technology elements (Iansiti & West, 1997; Jason, 2002; Radosevic, 1998; Tucker, 2002; Zhang, Chen & Xu, 1997; Xu, 2000; Peng, 2000; Jiang & Chen, 2000; Peters, 2002; Zheng, 2003; Xu, Xie & Zheng, 2004).

(III) Ecosystem principles of innovation break the traditional single time-space theory of innovation and emphasize all time-space innovation including whole process, whole value chain and integration of global resources

From the late 1980s to the early 1990s, the theory of business process redesign published by American scholars Hammer and Champy (1993) in Harvard Business Review led a global trend of business process redesign. It highlighted the transformation to the process-oriented enterprise management paradigm and provided the theoretical foundation for research on the all-process innovation and all-value chain innovation. All-process innovation mainly focuses on how enterprise realizes all-process innovation management. At the early stage, Roberts, Utterback, Rothwell, et al. focused on the technology innovation process of integrating different functions and departments (Roberts, 1999; Rothwell & Bessant, 1987; Utterback, 1994); At a later stage, scholars focused on the transformation of creativity to organizational innovation during the process of presentation to implementation of ideas (Amabile, 1996), innovative studies (Yang & Li, 2005), influencing factors within organization, innovation network within enterprise (Zhang & Wan, 2004), and evolution of innovation during the whole process of enterprise development. For example, Tushman (1998) put forward the alternating process of significant innovation and incremental innovation. Xu Qingrui, Xie Zhangshu and Zheng Gang (2004) researched the co-evolution process of innovation from technology-led innovation to system-led innovation and then to innovation jointly led by technology and system during the lifecycle of enterprise.

All-value chain innovation mainly focuses on how to realize the increase of innovation value inside and outside an enterprise. At an early stage, Porter put forward the concept of value chain within an enterprise. Chinese scholars Zhao Jianming, Si Chunlin and Tong Shi further analyzed the value network supporting technology innovation within an enterprise. At a later stage, scholars focused more on the external innovation of enterprises, mainly including users' involvement in innovation (Duggal & Revinova, 2003; Hippel, 1988; Wu & Xie, 1996), suppliers' involvement in innovation (Kamath & Liker, 1994; Xu, Jiang & Zheng, 2004), innovation value network (Sawhney & Prandelli, 2000; Amidon, 1998), internationalized innovation integrating global resources (Chell, 2001; Chen, 2003), and the transformation of innovation paradigm from closed innovation to open innovation within an enterprise (Chesbrough, 2003).

2.2 Humanism theory

2.2.1 Overview of humanism theory

(I) Fundamental view of historical materialism: "The masses of people are the creators of the history"

The fundamental view of historical materialism, "the masses of people are the creators of the history", is the theoretical basis of Mao Zedong's thoughts on the "masses" and the "mass line". Mao Zedong repeatedly pointed out that the masses of people are the creators of history. In the report named *On Coalition Government* given at the Seventh National Congress of the Communist Party of China in April 1945, Mao pointed out that "The people, and the people alone, are the motive force of world history". In an article titled "The Bankruptcy of the Idealist Conception of History" published in September 1949, he stated "Of all things in the world, people are the most precious. Under the leadership of the Communist Party, as long as there are people, every kind of miracle can be performed". In 1955, in the "Prefaces to Socialist Upsurge in China's Countryside", Mao Zedong once again pointed out that "The masses have boundless creative power". Mao Zedong's thoughts of "the masses of people are the creators of the history" include the following fundamental meanings.

Firstly, "the masses of people are the creators of the history" is a materialistic view of history. Contrary to the idealistic historical views highlighting individuals, Mao Zedong emphasized that the production, living practices and revolutionary struggles of the masses are the sources of power for social development and the masses are creators of material wealth, spiritual wealth and the motive force of historical development.

Secondly, Mao Zedong emphasized that people have infinite creativity and believed that in many circumstances, people play a dominant role and are a decisive force. Mao Zedong affirmed the functions of all tools and objects, especially the function and power of people. Mao believed that in many circumstances, people are decisive and fundamental factors. "As long as there are people, every kind of miracle can be performed". Therefore, as to war, Mao Zedong considered people, not weapons, as the decisive factor, because the richest source of power to wage a war lies in the masses of the people. As to construction, Mao Zedong emphasized that "there is strength in numbers", and he considered people as the most valuable resource for the construction of socialism and insisted on construction through mass power.

Besides, Mao Zedong deemed "the masses as the real heroes", believed the masses could liberate themselves, asked everyone to learn from the masses with an open mind, advocated the idea of "from the masses, to the masses", and proceeded to mobilize the masses to carry out various practical activities.

(II) Humanistic paradigm of management

In the early 20th century, through the "Hawthorne Experiment", Professor Mayo from Harvard University drew the conclusion that the physical working environment and benefits were not linked to the production efficiency of workers. Instead, the psychological factors and social factors of employees had the largest impact on the enthusiasm for production. Management scientists began to recognize the independent and important role of people in production. "Economic man" was promoted to "social man".

In the mid-20th century, based on the achievements of Mayo, some behaviorists carried out more in-depth and intensive research on the demands, motivations and incentives of people, humanity of organizations, informal organizations and groups. Maslow put forward the Theory of the Hierarchy of Needs, while Hertzberg proposed the Motivator-Hygiene Theory from the perspective of "what people want to get from work". Behaviorists like Maslow and Hertzberg laid stress on the role of mental incentive in production, and developed the hypothesis of humanity from "social man" to "self-actualizing man" and "complex man". The demands of people and the value of individuals gradually became the objects and factors of importance in management. From such a trend, we can discover the prototype of modern humanistic management.

In the late 20th century, with the rapid development of information technologies and innovative and high technologies, the human society accelerated its development to the information era and the era of a knowledge-driven economy. The production mode, lifestyle and ideology underwent significant changes and developed towards the realization of personal value and the embodiment of individualization and creativity. To adapt to this transition, more humanistic institutional structures, organizational models and management methods of socialized production, such as flat organization, learning-oriented teams and flexible production, emerged. The social production centered on the demands and development of people. The enterprise competition, product competition and market competition evolved to comprehensive talent competition. Human-oriented and humanistic management truly became the consensus of the public and management scientists and were applied and developed in the management practices.

(III) Human capital theory: The utmost importance of human capital in the era of a knowledge-driven economy

The rise of humanistic management theories and methods cannot be separated from people's enhanced cognition of labor within the enterprise. It is said that the foundation and development of human capital theories are the firm theoretical foundation of humanistic management.

Traditional theories believe that the three essential productive factors of enterprise, namely capital, labor force and land, can substitute for each other. And since capital is rarer and more precious than labor force, the decision-makers always give priority to the optimization of capital. However, the newly emerged human capital theories break through the shackles of traditional theories that capital is only material capital by classifying capital into human capital and material capital. Compared with investment on material capital, the investment on human capital may achieve the same and often higher return on investment since it can markedly improve the production efficiency and business management.

In 1960, American economist Schultz, known as the pioneer in human capital research, had proved with sufficient empirical evidence that: with economic modernization in all countries, the economic importance of farmland and other capital was decreasing and the importance of skills and knowledge was increasing. Traditional economic theories, which couldn't explain such phenomena, were challenged. As Schultz observed back then, except for some regions, the originally barren land in Europe boasted high productivity now; the original land in Finland whose productivity used to be lower than that of the adjacent area, the western region of the former Soviet Union, became fertile farmland; Japanese farmland, the quality of which used to be much lower than that of northern India, became very fertile. Schultz argued that such changes resulted from agricultural research, which led to the appearance of some new substitutes for farmland or land productivity enhancers. Such achievements couldn't be separated from the contributions of those who acquired advanced knowledge and skills. Schultz also noticed that in some countries where the plants and equipment were seriously destroyed during the World War II, due to the high quality of their population, the scars of war were cured soon and economic prosperity was recovered within a short term. To explain the above-mentioned phenomena, which couldn't be explained by traditional theories, Schultz introduced the concept of general capital, which not only included capital in the traditional sense but also human capital.

The human capital proposed by Schultz included the following connotations: (1) Human capital is embodied in individuals as competencies and qualities, namely knowledge, skills, qualifications, experiences and professional proficiency; (2) Seen from the perspective of economic development, human capital, especially the human capital of entrepreneurs, is scarce; (3) Human capital is the capital formed by the investment in human resources, which, in monetary form, is reflected in the increase of various expenditures on human resources, including expenditures on health, school education and on-the-job education, labor migration, etc.; (4) Just as any other capital, human resources should obtain return on investment. The economic value of human capital follows a rising trend over time; (5) The increasing economic value of human capital over time leads to its increasingly big contributions to the economic development.

The birth of the concept of human capital and the development of human capital theories enabled people to pay more attention to human factors within an enterprise and provided theoretical foundation for the generation and development of humanistic management theories and methods. With the rise of knowledge economy, enterprises gradually stepped out of the era of capital. Large scale of capital accumulation and fast-developing sciences and technologies made the capital in the traditional sense strongly liquid and substitutable and not as scarce as it used to be. Instead, human capital replaced material capital as the most important scarce resource for the development of enterprises. For this reason, in the 1980s, 20 years after the emergence of the human capital concept, humanistic management, finalized as a novel management theory and method, drew universal attention from and became accepted by a great number of enterprises.

2.2.2 Implications of the humanistic theories for research on total innovation management

(I) Human is the most active factor in innovation

Human-oriented management means that the enterprise deems human as the center and starting point during management and carries out business by rousing and mobilizing people's initiative, enthusiasm and creativity so as to realize the joint development of both the individual and the enterprise. American management guru Peter Drucker once said that the only meaningful resource of an enterprise or business is human. Management is doing things right by fully developing human resources. As the most active factor in productive forces, human creates all social wealth. It is based on such an understanding that TIM theories point out that human is the most active one among all innovation factors and all kinds of competitions in market economy are competitions of talents after all. Only by giving full play to employees can enterprises generate innovation capability and create a vigorous innovation atmosphere.

(II) Human is the source of innovative thought and the diversity of innovation originates from the extensive popular base

Innovation means diversity, while diversity originates from the extensive employee base; without the active participation of a massive number of employees, it is impossible to continuously make high-quality innovative achievements purely relying on a small number of professional researchers and developers. Only by fully rousing the enthusiasm for innovation of the masses can abundant and splendid ideas be generated and a number of innovation ideas with great potential be explored and eventually developed into new products/services which would help enterprises obtain competitiveness and economic benefits in the market.

(III) Respecting talents and the initiative of the mass is the foundation for good innovation

The basic concept of human-oriented management is to consider humans as the most fundamental and active factor in management. Human-oriented management is to consider the overall development of human as the core. Its fundamental principle is to emphasize the demands of employees and to encourage and cultivate employees. Enterprises should always insist on human-oriented core values; to respect, cultivate and encourage employees is the correct way for enterprises to treat talents. Enterprises should introduce and cultivate talents at all costs, offer employees space for growth, encourage employees to focus on on-the-job innovations, and guarantee individual creativity and motivation of employees on all levels with a corresponding institutional environment. TIM theories point out that the development of enterprise means a harmonious and joint development between individuals and the enterprise. An organization with total innovation should enable employees to realize their goals of individual growth and development, and with the resultant innovative forces of employees, jointly stimulate the innovation and development of the enterprise and achieve a win-win between individuals and the enterprise.

(IV) The starting point of total innovation management of an enterprise is to construct and improve innovative talents, including innovative managers, researchers and workers.

TIM points out that human is the most fundamental and active factor in innovation and in the era of indigenous innovation, human capital is the key for enterprises to seek development through innovation. Therefore, the starting point for enterprise to construct total innovation management system and promote TIM is to construct and continuously cultivate innovative talents. Only by building a sound system of total innovation and ensuring an effective mechanism of incentives can the abilities of talents be fully released. Since human factor is the key for indigenous innovation and sustainable development, if everyone can be provided with the space for innovation and a platform to realize self-worth and unify the value goals of the individual and the enterprise, everyone will become a valuable human resource and the enterprise will have a unique competitiveness, thus achieving the common growth of innovative talents and enterprise capital.

2.3 Synergy theory

2.3.1 What synergy means

The concept of "synergy" has a long history. Ancient eastern philosophy and western philosophy, or modern natural science and social science, all studied the harmonious development between human and nature, between human and human and between human and the whole universe. So the basic concept of "synergy" is inevitably talked about (Guo, 1988). Traditional Chinese culture also attached great importance to synergy. For example, Mencius said, "The time isn't as important as the terrain; but the terrain isn't as important as unity with the people"; Mozi believed "loving each other and benefiting each other"; Sun Tzu's *Art of War* argued that "He will win whose army is animated by the same spirit throughout all its ranks". Such viewpoints showed that the sages had already discovered the importance of synergy and cooperation between people (Guo, 1988). Famous British scientific historian Joseph Needham, who had been engaged in the research on China's for a long time believed that the yin-yang theory proposed by ancient Chinese philosopher "is seeking the perfect harmony between the two in life" (Zheng, 2003).

As a subject system, synergy is formed in an atmosphere of western culture based on individual rational analysis. Its founder, German theoretical physicist Hermann Haken, enlightened by the theory of dissipative structure, proposed the concept of "synergy" in 1973 for the first time. He used it to reflect on the harmonious cooperative relationship among the subsystems of a complex system. In 1977, he further proposed the theoretical framework of "synergetics". Besides many physical and chemical models, Haken also designed many models of ecological process, ecological group network and social phenomena, such as "public opinion model", "ecological group model", "meridian model", "population dynamic model", "predator-prey system model" and "morphogenesis model". Through a great deal of analogy analyses, Haken found that the phase transition process of a system was independent of the nature of subsystem, but it was the result of synergic movement arising from the connections between subsystems. In other words, he believed that during synergy, the joint action of many subsystems (generally belonging to interlinked categories or several different categories) generates the structure and function on a macro scale (Haken, 1976). However, people often cannot distinguish "synergy" from its synonyms like "collaboration", "cooperation", "matching", harmonizing, coordination, integration, coupling, etc. Therefore, in his doctoral dissertation centered on the concept of synergy, Zheng (2003) distinguished such phrasing (Table 2-3) and considered "synergy" as the most appropriate to analyze the complex connections in enterprise innovation.

Table 2-3 Comparison of the synonyms of synergy

Vocabulary	Chinese vocabulary	Meaning	Focus
Synergy	协同	Nonlinear and complex and interaction between subsystems to achieve the effect that cannot be realized by independent subsystem, i.e. "1+1>2"	Emphasizing the overall effect that cannot be achieved independently
Integration	集成 / 整合	Process of integrating all subsystems within an organization to finish organizational tasks	Emphasizing the consistency and integration
Cooperation, collaboration, alignment	协作、合作	Cooperating with each other to jointly finish certain tasks; two or more people work together to achieve common goals	Cooperating with each other to achieve common goals
Harmonizing	协调	Working together with each other in an appropriate way	Harmonious and appropriate
Coupling	耦合	Cooperating and combining with each other	Combining
Fit, matching	匹配	Cooperating and collocating properly	Proper
Interaction	互动	Behavior or process of interacting	Interactive

2.3.2 Application of synergy principles in innovation management

Researchers on synergy believed that under the action of externally controlled parameters, all subsystems within an open system have a competitive but cooperative relationship. When the effect of control parameters reaches a certain critical value, the system will form one or several other parameters to dominate the activities of the whole system, and further combine all parts to develop a more competitive and correlative system and to build a more orderly structure in terms of space, time and function. The most obvious characteristic is to achieve the new results or goals, which cannot be achieved by an independent subsystem, through the interaction of all subsystems. Synergy not only emphasizes cooperation, but also pursues systematic cooperation based on competition.

Competition is the basic premise and condition of synergy. For example, molecules collide with each other frequently in a system with a great deal of gas molecules; different species (or individuals of the same species) compete with each other within an ecological system; there are communications and competitions among different thoughts, methods and concepts during the forming process of thoughts and concepts. The competitions among different elements within a system are perpetual. The competitions may be strong or weak, big or small, at different phases and under different circumstances, but the perpetual difference among different elements within the system always leads to the competitions among different subsystems inside a matter or different matters. The imbalanced development is the foundation for the existence of competition (Wu, 2001). Besides, different elements within a system or different systems have different adaptive responses to the external environment and obtain different matters, information and energies, so competitions are inevitable. The existence and results of competitions will lead to a greater difference and imbalance within a system or between systems. From the perspective of the evolvement of an open system, such competitions create conditions for the self-organizing evolvement of system away from the equilibrium state and stimulate the evolvement of system from disorder to order. It offers enlightenment for innovation management that the process of technological innovation is a complex non-linear process and also a system constructed by several innovation factors (such as technology, market, culture, strategy, organization and system). Due to the significant differences in the categories and the ways that innovation factors obtain external information and energy, and due to the significant differences in their intensity, purposes and methods at different phases and under different conditions, there is bound to be competition within an enterprise for control during the process of innovation. For example, in order to hold a dominant position, different departments compete with each other to continuously increase their respective contribution to the value chain of the enterprise. In order to achieve the evolvement of system from disorder (initial stage of new product ideas) to order (commercialization of innovation results), the innovation elements will compete with each other to form one or several key elements (i.e. order parameter) which play a decisive role in stimulating innovation and promoting the evolvement of innovation system towards order.

Cooperation based on competition is the basic characteristic and objective of synergy principles. The thought of developing cooperation through communication and interaction has been confirmed in the fields of economics and sociology. Ecological research studies also show that the reason why a diversified system is more orderly than a simple system is mainly related to the diversity of subsystems. If all the subsystems are identical, competition will be extremely fierce and cruel. While single species cause a great deal of internal friction, the result is often vestigial rather than evolutionary. The synergy of different innovation elements (through functional departments) during the process of technical innovation of enterprise also requires cooperation-based interaction first. The synergy will be eventually realized through competition and cooperation. Campbell et al. (2000) also pointed out that synergy relied on the integration and coordination among different functions of an enterprise and their subsidiaries.

2.4 Conclusion

This chapter summarizes the theoretical foundations of TIM, including ecosystem theory, humanism theory and synergy theory. It is based on such theories that TIM transfers its research perspective from independent innovation element and component of innovation system to the whole innovation system and the relationship between different elements of innovation system reveals the comprehensive, complex, ecological, synergetic and dynamic process of innovation. it breaks the previous linear thinking models related to innovation, considers the enterprise innovation system as a complex innovation system and attaches importance to the interaction among different elements within the innovation system.

Part Two

Connotation and System Framework of Total Innovation Management

Chapter 3

System Framework of Total Innovation Management

3.1 Birth of the total innovation management theory

A number of scholars have been aware of the significance of total innovation for years and have done preliminary studies on it. As early as the 1970s and 1980s, some scholars had proposed and developed the innovative "Dual Core Theory" which partly reflected the ideas of total innovation. Some scholars pointed out that to realize total innovation throughout the enterprise, it is required to make innovation a capability for every employee from every department rather than an occasional activity or a passive process.

Xu et al. (2001), based on their exploration and research on the latest innovation theories in both China and foreign countries, as well as the experiences and lessons drawn from the success and failure of the operation and management of many Chinese enterprises in the mid- to late 1990s, pointed out that to adapt themselves to the changing environment, modern enterprises have to be strategy-oriented, continuously carry on total innovation centered on technological innovation, and cultivate and improve its own technological innovative capability. Besides, for the first time, they theoretically and systematically proposed the total innovation rules for the operation and management of enterprises. Such rules mainly rely on "one center and two basic points", namely taking technological innovation as the center, and combining innovation and technological innovation capabilities as two basic points. On this basis, in the Third International Symposium on Management of Technology (ISMOT, 2002) held in 2002, the new innovation management paradigm, i.e. "Total Innovation Management" (TIM), was presented and accordingly drew extensive attention and universal praises from the participants (Xu et al., 2003).

3.2 Theoretical framework of total innovation management

3.2.1 Connotation of total innovation management

Taking the training of core competencies and the improvement of sustainable competitiveness as orientation, the value creation/increase as the ultimate goal, and the organic combination and collaborative innovation of various innovation elements (such as technology, organization, market, strategy, management, culture, system, etc.) as means, TIM strives to enable everyone to innovate and everything to be innovated anytime and anywhere through effective innovation management mechanism, methods and tools (Figure 3-1).

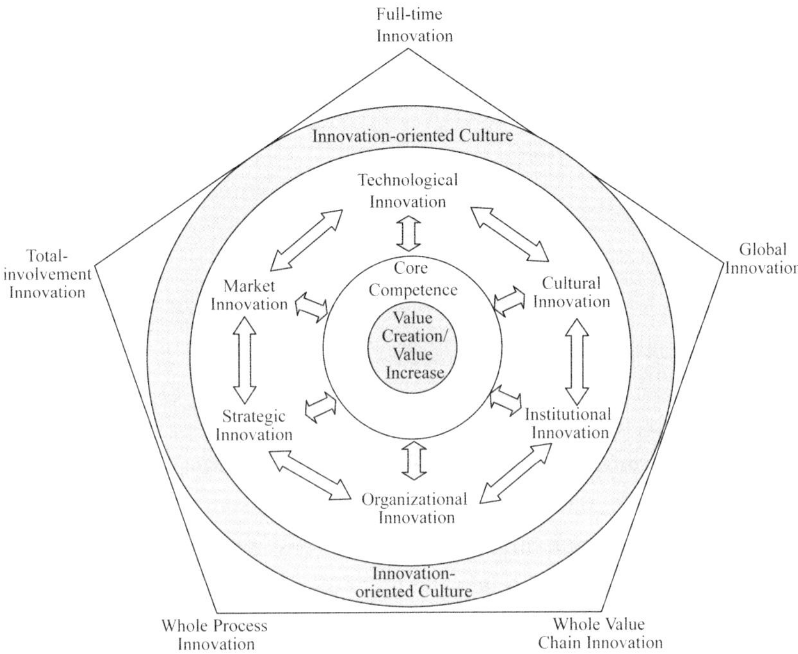

Figure 3-1 Pentagonal Model Framework of Enterprise Total Innovation Management

Source: *Xu et al., Towards Total Innovation Management* (*TIM*): *The Emerging New Trend of Innovation Management in 21st Century. Science Research Management, 2003, 5: 1-5.*

The connotation of total innovation management paradigm can be further summarized as "Three Totals & One Synergy", namely all-element innovation, all time-space innovation, all-involvement innovation and total synergy, as shown in Figure 3-2.

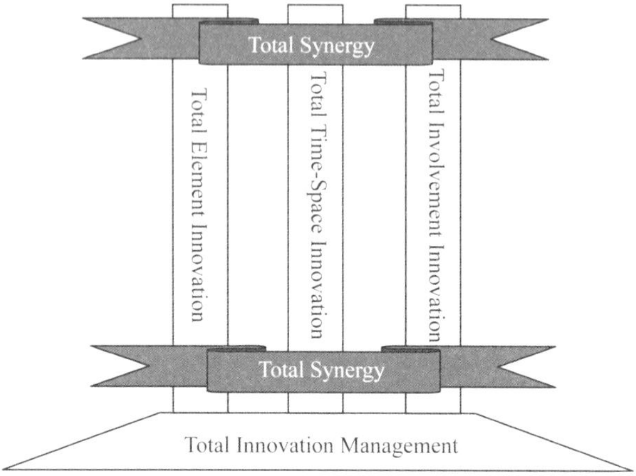

Figure 3-2 Features of Total Innovation Management: "Three Totals & One Synergy"

All-element innovation means that only with systematic view, comprehensive view and total synergy of elements closely related to the innovation performance, such as technology, strategy, culture, system and organization, can the optimal innovation performance be realized. Based on the review of domestic and foreign research on key elements influencing innovation performance, Zheng (2004) summarized six major elements, namely strategy, technology, market, culture, system and organizational element. Furthermore, the results of the empirical analysis of over 100 large and medium-size enterprises verified the significant influence of these six elements on innovation performance. Seen from the systematic and comprehensive perspective of TIM, the function of these elements cannot be separated from the all-involvement and all time-space background. On this basis, therefore, Xu and Xie (2004) proposed a TIM-based diamond model of the total synergy of all innovation elements, as shown in Figure 3-3.

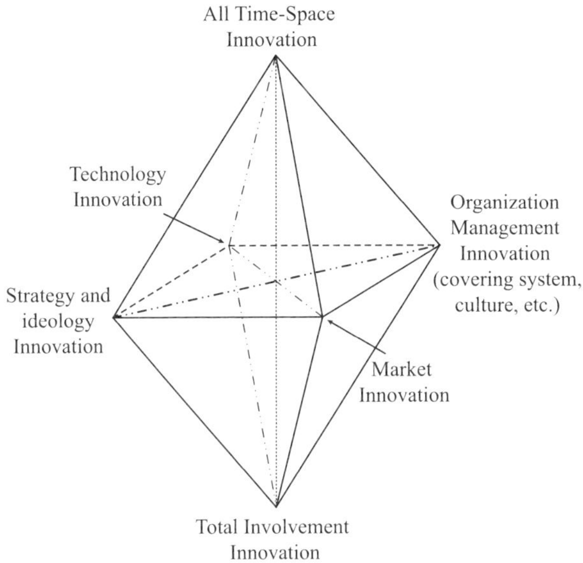

Figure 3-3 TIM Based Diamond Model of the Total Synergy of Innovation Elements

All-involvement innovation means that innovation is the joint conduct of all employees rather than the exclusive conduct of the research, development and technical personnel. From R&D personnel, sales personnel, production and manufacturing personnel to after-sales service personnel, management personnel and finance personnel, everyone may become an excellent innovator on his/her own post. In a broad sense, the all-involvement also includes users, suppliers, shareholders and other stakeholders.

Case Study 1
Geely Group Corporate Culture: "Everyone Is an Innovator"

Geely Group advocates and encourages the innovative, creative and inventive spirit of all employees. Anyone who does well in this aspect will be rewarded. In such a way, an atmosphere and a culture are created to promote the continuous advancement of innovation and invention of the whole enterprise. For example, employees from a production workshop of the powertrain company made 166 suggestions to the company in August and September, 2004 and got different material and moral rewards. Zhang Qingxian, an ordinary operator, discovered that screw tap could be used at most 200 times. He felt it was wasteful, so based on careful research and analysis, he designed a set of multi-model tap cutter sharpening equipment, which increased the screw feeding from 200 times to 800 times. Thereafter, the technology obtained a national patent and helped the company reduce the cost by 400,000 yuan per year. Zhang received the reward from the company. From January to October, 2005, more than 200 employees made over 700 innovation suggestions to the company in fields like technology, quality, management, safe production and environment, many of these suggestions were adopted by the company and effectively stimulated the progress of the company.[①]

All time-space innovation is divided into total time innovation and total space innovation (global innovation or all-region innovation). Total time innovation is an innovative strategy, an idea, an innovative concept and the organic combination of improvisational innovation, instant innovation (including rapid innovation) and continuous innovation (24/7, i.e. 24 hours a day, 7 days per week). Improvisational innovation is the flash of inspiration and solidification of creativity on certain issues; instant innovation is the just-in-time and rapid response to market demand; continuous innovation is to make innovation the eternal theme of organizational development, to innovate at all times and to set innovation as the necessary ability of all departments and employees of the company instead of it being an occasional event. Haier Group is a model of total time innovation. In "Haier Global Executives' Conference 2001", Mike, President of American Haier Trading Company, considered designing a kind of refrigerator with the upper layer being normal horizontal refrigerator and the lower layer being

① *China Business News*. Three "!" Produced by Geely, A Chinese Independent Automobile Brand drawers on a whim to respond to the complaints of American users. Having been informed of the idea of Mike, the Refrigerator Department designated four scientific researchers to work on it overnight. Through simultaneous engineering, they finished the prototype in as short as 17 hours, which amazed Mike. This refrigerator was therefore named Mike Refrigerator; in March 2001, the scientific researchers of Haier and Ericsson located at different places in the world, through a 24-hour relay by taking advantage of time difference, had released the advanced Bluetooth wireless network appliances in as short as three months, saving more than half the time when compared with traditional development modes (Data provided by Haier University, 2004).

Total space innovation (or called global innovation or all-region innovation) means that in the context of global economic integration and networking, enterprises should consider how to effectively use the innovation space (including internal and external space) and how to effectively integrate innovation resources on a global scale for their own purpose, thus realizing the internationalization and globalization of innovation, i.e. innovation at all places. It includes total value network innovation, whole process innovation, etc.

With the accelerated process of world economy integration, the trend of global innovation becomes increasingly obvious. Based on the external linkage mechanism of enterprise and the resources obtained and allocated on a global scale, global innovation is used to break the limitation of existing resources and capabilities inside the enterprise and to make the best of the external network and resources to expand, improve and build enterprise capabilities. The subject of global innovation is transnational cooperation.

Case Study 2

All Time-Space Innovation: P&G "Connect + Develop" Innovation

P&G has over 7,500 research staff members spread over nine countries and spends over U.S. 1.8 billion dollars on R&D. However, this is not the decisive factor for P&G's success in innovation. Before 2000, P&G's innovation system put more emphasis on internal competition and P&G closed the door on external creativity. Researchers were divided into groups, which competed with each other for R&D projects, funds and even attention from the leadership. Nevertheless, excessive competition led to ineffectiveness. Afterwards, P&G concluded that the prior innovation mode exclusively relying on internal staff didn't work anymore. P&G realized that its current operation revenue is U.S. 50 billion dollars and if it wants to increase this amount to U.S. 100 billion dollars, it needs to develop 500 products, with each creating an operational revenue of U.S. 100 million dollars or 50 products, with each creating an operational revenue of U.S. 1 billion dollars. It is difficult to stimulate the development of company by only relying on internal creativity. Now, the company is eager to seek external creativity.

According to P&G's estimate, about 1.5 million scientists in the global academic and industrial community have the expertise or technical skill related to P&G. Why not make use of them? Therefore, P&G proposed to change its research mode to "connect and develop": to pool the wisdom and efforts of scientists from both inside and outside of the company to expand creativity.

At present, P&G has 40 "technical entrepreneurs", whose work is, by virtue of complex search tools, to view billions of webpages, global patent databases and science literature and to find major technological breakthroughs with possible benefits to the company. P&G also joins in three Internet scientist communities. NineSigma.com links over 500,000 researchers together. The second one is InnoCentive.com, which links 70,000 scientists together. These scientists offer solutions to technical problems. P&G has also founded YourEncore.com together with Eli Lilly and Company. YourEncore.com connects retired scientists, who can provide consultations.

Besides, P&G has redefined the relationship with its suppliers. In the past, it seemed that P&G just threw contracts over the wall to them, but now they are more like an extension of P&G laboratories.

P&G says the idea of "Connect + Develop" has thoroughly changed the company's innovation process and brought some new products, including several skin care product brands like Crest Whitestrips, and Olay and Swiffer sweeper.

P&G has obtained more and more many benefits from the annual R&D budget of U.S. 1.8 billion dollars. AG Lafley, Chairman of P&G, disclosed in the recent annual report that three years ago, the R&D expenditure accounted for 4.5% of the sales volume of P&G and now the proportion has decreased to 3.5%.[②]

Total synergy refers to the all-around synergy and matching of various innovative elements (such as strategy, organization, culture, system, technology, market, etc.) under the framework of all-involvement and all time-space domain so as to realize the synergy effect of "2+2 > 5", which cannot be realized by independent elements, and to stimulate the improvement of innovation performance. The differences between "total synergy" and "synergy" in traditional sense are:

Firstly, total synergy covers more subjects with more complex interactive relationships. The concept of "synergy" in the traditional sense mostly refers to the synergy effect of "1+1 > 2" produced by the

② P&G Innovation Strategy: Outsourcing Creativity, http://searchcio.techtarget.com.cn/tips/498/1904998.shtml.2006-05-02

interaction between two or three subjects, such as the synergy between technology and market. In contrast, the "total synergy" proposed in this research covers the six key elements (strategy, organization, culture, system, technology and market) that influence innovation performance. It is comprehensive and systematic with more complex interrelations, so its total synergy effect will be more obvious.

Secondly, it emphasizes the importance of all-involvement and all time-space domain innovation. This research upholds that innovation elements can only realize the all-around total synergy within the framework of all-involvement and all time-space domain. And this is not covered by the traditional concept of "synergy".

TIM is not the generalized integration and simple extension of original innovation management theories and methods, but a revolutionary breakthrough. It has changed the original linear thinking mode of innovation management based on mechanistic concept and taken the ecological concept and complex system theory as its theoretical foundation and starting point. Seen from its theoretical foundation, objectives, strategy, structure, elements and time-space range or the management style, it has essential differences from the traditional innovation management paradigm. Especially, it has broken through original time-space domain and innovation framework restricted to R&D department and personnel according to the changes of environment, highlighted the importance of full-time innovation, globalized innovation and total-involvement innovation under the new situation, and greatly expanded the subjects, elements and time-space range of innovation. The significant difference between total innovation and traditional innovation is that it has broken the previous isolated innovation pattern, highlighted the human-oriented ecological concept of innovation and greatly expanded the elements and time-space range of innovation (Xu, Zheng & Yu, 2003).

3.2.2 Main Characteristics of Total Innovation Management

(I) Purposeful

As a new and strategic innovation paradigm in the new century, TIM has an explicit strategic objective. That is, to rely on the mass base, to integrate all innovation resources available on a global scale, to focus on the continuous improvement of the core competence of enterprises, to win sustained competitive advantage, to stimulate the continuous development of enterprises, and to create additional values for customers and stakeholders.

(II) Comprehensive

Rather than purely relying on a certain aspect or a certain element, TIM is to implement all-around innovation on all aspects of innovation, including innovation on strategy, technology, market, organization, system, thought and culture, by mobilizing and relying on the masses as well as strengthening all aspects inside or outside the enterprise.

(III) Integral

This characteristic of TIM originates from the integrality of an object, the integrality of enterprise and the integrality of innovation. The realization of any innovation activity involves various activities with inherent organic connection (such as R&D, manufacturing, marketing, supply, human resources and management) separately carried out by various employees from different departments. The deficiency of any department or employee will impact the effective implementation of the innovation activity as a whole. Therefore, innovation activity must be seen as a concerted and integral activity, that is, through effective leadership and coordination mechanism of innovation, to pull together strength from all aspects of the enterprise and to turn all resistances against innovation into a motive force.

(IV) Mass

Based on scientific and philosophical principles, human-oriented theory and ecological theory, TIM considers enterprise as an organically unified entity. In the era of open innovation, the personnel base is not restricted to the employees of an enterprise. Instead, it goes beyond the original boundary of the enterprise, which includes not only all members of the enterprise, but also community members, all stakeholders, upstream and downstream enterprises in the value chain and strategic partners of the enterprise. Great innovation vitality and potential from the public as well as the abundant diversity of employees is the inexhaustible source of innovative thoughts. Only by mobilizing and relying on the public and taking employees as the subjects of innovation can an enterprise maintain sustained and endless innovation and hold an invincible position. In light of such characteristics, TIM must base the organization and management of enterprises on the mobilization of employees and the public at all times. This is the essence that distinguishes TIM from traditional innovation paradigm.

3.3 Conclusion

This chapter introduces the framework of TIM in a systematic way. With internal interactions, the "Three All" of TIM condition, build upon and support each other. All-involvement innovation is the foundation of all-element and all time-space; all-element innovation is the organization environment and platform to stimulate and strengthen all-involvement innovation; all time-space innovation expands the time-space domains of all-involvement innovation and all-element innovation to combine innovation resources within a larger scope.

TIM is the further development of traditional innovation management and is the outcome of both the increasingly fierce market competitions and the development of innovation management theories. The differences between them are mainly embodied in the following aspects, i.e. different contents, scopes and fields of innovation, different innovation subjects, different objectives and strategies, and different models, management and assessment approaches of innovation. The connections and differences between them are shown in Table 3-1.

Table 3-1 Connections & Differences between Total Innovation Management and Traditional Innovation Management

	Traditional Innovation Management	Total Innovation Management
Content, scope and field of innovation		
Content and elements of innovation	Focus on single innovation Emphasize technology innovation and ignore other innovations	Focus on the combination and synergy of all innovative elements Emphasize total innovation
Coordination of product/ process innovation	Value product innovation more than process innovation Overemphasize the importance of product innovation	Emphasize the coordination between product innovation and process innovation
Spatial scope of innovation	Within the enterprise, emphasize self-dependence and lack enough understanding of cooperation innovation	Emphasize innovation based on the integration of global resources
Innovation speed	Low market response speed	Extremely high requirement for market response speed
Different innovation subjects		
Innovation subject	Purely emphasize the innovations from R&D department and researchers	Insist on the "subjectivity" of employees and view employees as the innovation subjects of enterprise
Innovation source	Single innovation source (internal innovation)	Multiple innovation sources, including stakeholders and entire value chain
Different objectives and strategies of innovation		
Innovation objective	Passive innovation to accomplish the superior's task	Active innovation to increase value (improve operation performance)
Relationship with core competence	Pay no attention to the interactive effect between innovation and core competence	Be centered on the cultivation of core competence and value creation
Innovation strategy	Not obvious	Not only be strategy-oriented, but also pay attention to the interaction between innovation and strategy
Model, management and assessment approaches of innovation		
Organizational form of innovation	Common line and staff organization structure	Flat, networking and process-oriented structure

continued

	Traditional Innovation Management	Total Innovation Management
Communication with other departments	Rare; Passive, driven by department interests	Very close; Active, driven by overall interests and creation of value
Project management mode	Project team built within the R&D department	Cross-functionality and cross-organization team, virtual team and blockbuster team
Assessment of innovation benefits	The assessment of innovation benefits is limited to dominant innovation benefits	Balanced consideration of dominant and recessive innovation benefits

Source: *Zheng Gang. TIM-Based Research on the Total Synergy Mechanism of All the Innovation Agents during Innovation Process. Zhejiang University Doctoral Dissertation, 2004.*

Chapter 4

All-Element Innovation

Technology innovation in China has made great progress in recent years, but there are still many problems. The underlying cause of these problems is a lack of understanding of the higher requirements for technology innovation arising from the changes of competitive environment and market demands under new circumstance. Chinese enterprises lack theoretical guidance on systematic and total innovation, and total and synergetic thoughts in innovation management. Therefore, it is necessary to conduct research on the interaction among all innovation elements during the process of innovation, and from the new perspective of total innovation so as to provide theoretical guidance and references to solve the "dilemma" and dis-synergy among innovation elements.

4.1 Analysis of main factors impacting technology innovation

There are many factors that influence the success or failure of technology innovation. Such issues had become a hot topic for research on technology innovation management theory ever since the 1950s (Werker, 2001; Olson & Eoyang, 2001; Janszen, 2002). As early as 1957, Carter and Williams, entrusted by the British Ministry of Trade, had conducted studies on the favorable and unfavorable factors for the application of scientific research in industrial products and processes. In the 1970s, the Science Policy Research Unit (SPRU) at the University of Sussex in the UK, under the leadership of Freeman, had undertaken the famous program SAPPHO (Scientific Activity Predictor from Patterns with Heuristic Origins), which tried to find the factors impacting the success of innovation by comparing 29 pairs of successful and failed innovation projects in chemical industry and scientific instrument industry.

From 1960s to 1980s, empirical research on factors impacting the success and failure of technology innovation mainly focused on the following two aspects: (1) Research on factors impacting the success and failure of technology innovation (Glove, Levy & Schwartz, 1973; Roberts & Burke, 1974; Rubinstein, 1976; Cooper, 1984; Lazo, 1965; Hopkins, 1980); (2) Comparative research on the factors of success and failure (Rothwell et al., 1974; Utterback et al., 1976; Cooper, 1979, 1985; Maidique & Zirger, 1984).

Research showed that the success of technology innovation is the result of the joint action of multiple factors. The success of innovation means that several functional departments are competent for their work and maintain good cooperative relationship with each other. Song and Parry (1996), based on the tracking studies of 788 new products manufactured by Japanese enterprises in nearly four years, discovered the success of new product development of Japanese enterprises was related to the effective integration of "R&D — manufacturing — marketing", information sharing, marketing and technology resources of an enterprise, technology capabilities, efficiency and experiences of new product development, and other factors like marketing environment. Through research on 47 new products, Montoya-Weiss and Calantone (1994) concluded that 18 factors, which were divided into to four categories, have an impact on the success of new product development.

Success of technology innovation has a strong connection with innovation of non-technology factors like market, culture, strategy and organization. The synergy of such factors plays a critical role. According to the case studies of 14 representative enterprises from both China and foreign countries, 26 factors impacting the performance of technology innovation were found. And then based on the frequency of innovation factors involved in all research studies, 21 important factors were selected. Through further induction, classification and summarization on this basis, it was eventually determined that the key factors that impact the performance of technology innovation were technology and non-technology factors like market, strategy, organization, culture and system, as shown in Table 4-1.

Table 4-1 Summary of elements impacting technology innovation

Typical enterprise / Factors	Haier	Huawei	ZTE	IBM	Intel	HP	GE	3M	Toyota	Sony	Samsung	Bao Steel	CIMC	NCPC
Leadership and strategy innovation														
Entrepreneurship	+	+	+	+	+	+	+	+	+	+	+	+	+	+
Strong leadership and support from top management	+	+	+	+	+	+	+	+	+	+	+	+	+	+
Combination of technology innovation strategy and business operation strategy	+	+	NA	+	+	+	+	NA	+	+	+	+	NA	+
Technology innovation														
Technical personnel and training	+	+	+	+	+	+	+	+	+	+	+	+	+	+
Technology and R&D capacity	+	+	+	+	+	+	+	+	+	+	+	+	+	+
Focus on external innovation sources	+	+	+	+	+	NA	+	NA	+	+	+	+	+	+
Market innovation														
Understanding of market and user demands	+	+	+	+	+	+	+	+	+	+	+	+	+	+
Marketing management	+	+	+	+	+	+	+	+	+	+	+	+	+	+
Customer service	+	+	+	+	+	+	+	+	+	+	+	+	+	+

Typical enterprise / Factors	Haier	Huawei	ZTE	IBM	Intel	HP	GE	3M	Toyota	Sony	Samsung	Bao Steel	CIMC	NCPC
Culture innovation														
Courage to take risk and tolerance of failure	+	+	+	+	+	+	+	+	+	+	+	NA	+	*
Incentive of innovation culture	+	+	+	+	+	+	+	+	+	+	+	+	+	+
System innovation														
Innovation incentive	+	+	+	+	+	+	+	+	+	+	+	+	+	+
Patent management	+	+	+	+	+	+	+	+	+	+	+	+	+	+
Organization innovation														
Flexibility and adaptability of organizational structure	+	NA	NA	+	NA	+	+	+	NA	NA	NA	NA	NA	+
Information communication, knowledge management	+	+	+	+	+	+	+	+	+	+	+	+	+	+
Cooperation with other enterprises	+	+	*	+	+	+	+	+	+	+	+	*	*	*
Synergy of elements														
R&D / market / production interface management	+	+	*	+	+	+	+	+	+	+	+	*	*	+
Synergy and matching of various elements	+	+	+	+	+	+	+	+	+	+	+	*	+	*
Management function innovation														
Innovation management	+	+	+	+	+	+	+	+	+	+	+	+	+	+
Capital and resources	+	*	+	+	+	+	+	+	+	+	+	+	+	+

Typical enterprise / Factors	Haier	Huawei	ZTE	IBM	Intel	HP	GE	3M	Toyota	Sony	Samsung	Bao Steel	CIMC	NCPC
Government support	+	+	+	+	+	+	+	+	+	+	+	+	+	+

Note: + *denotes "excellent"; * "medium"; NA "insufficient information".*
Source: *RCID Case Study Report, 2003-2006.*

Dunton (2002), in his book *The Seeds of Innovation*, summarized the top ten characteristics of innovative organizations, which include, among others, technology (they embrace new technology to strengthen their competitive advantage), culture (they welcome new ideas and approaches), market (they look to the future to anticipate the customer's future needs; they empower their customers with information and more control over the purchasing process), organization and process (they employ internal processes that support innovation), and system (they reward innovative efforts; they redefine the rules of the game and challenge complacent competitors) and the perspectives like all-involvement innovation (they encourage all employees, partners, and suppliers to take an active role in innovation) and all time-space innovation (they move quickly; they allocate resources to find, develop, and implement new ideas).

4.2 What is all-element innovation?

4.2.1 Concept of "all-element innovation"

In order to realize rapid and high-efficiency innovation in fierce competition, enterprises have to consider the synergy innovation of both technology elements and non-technology elements rather than being restricted to technology innovation. The focus of enterprise innovation should be "all-element innovation", also called "all-round innovation".

Based on the above-mentioned analysis, the elements of enterprise involved in the concept of all-element innovation are strategy, technology, organization, culture, system and market. Accordingly, the concept of "all-element innovation" is to devote itself to improving the performance of enterprise innovation with frameworks including innovation of thoughts and ideas, strategy innovation, technology innovation, organization innovation, culture innovation, system innovation, market innovation and management innovation (including innovation in terms of human resources management and financial management).

Besides, RCID research showed that the foundation for an enterprise to effectively implement all-element innovation is the active participation of all employees and all-time innovation, all-region innovation and all-process innovation. The new paradigm of total innovation management (TIM) is formed with the integration of all-element innovation, all-involvement innovation and all time-space innovation. Only with the synergy of "Three All" can an enterprise implement TIM and achieve better innovation.

Below, the connotation of each main innovation element in the all-element innovation mechanism drawn from practices and theories is defined and analyzed. The interrelations among such elements are also analyzed. The conceptual model of all-element innovation mechanism is proposed.

4.2.2 What are the main innovation elements?

(I) Strategy innovation

Different from traditional strategy management, in the all-element innovation dimension of "total innovation management", strategy innovation refers to a series of adjustments and reforms on enterprise strategies made by the enterprise to be adapted to the change of market environment and demands for self-development, including the evolutionary reform and major reforms of enterprise strategies.

Strategy innovation has connections with all time-space innovation. The enterprise strategies are changing over time and aim to participate in global competitions.

Strategy innovation also has connections with all-involvement innovation. The establishment, management and implementation of strategy require the interaction between senior managers and grass-roots employees as well as the active participation of all employees.

(II) Organization innovation

In the broad sense, organization innovation refers to organizational culture innovation, information technology innovation, process innovation and organizational structure innovation. In the narrow sense, organization innovation refers to organizational structure innovation and process innovation. Its objective is to improve an organization's capability to make quick response to customers and global market and to further improve the performance of the organization through systematic planning, implementation and effective management. The re-engineering of business processes belongs to such a category of innovation.

It mainly involves two parts: process innovation and organizational structure innovation. Process innovation is the partial upgrading or all-round reform of existing business processes to make a quick and sound response to environment and to improve performance. Organizational structure innovation refers to the change of division and coordination of labor, the setup and structure of the organization, and the coordinating and communicating methods. The reform and development of new organizational structure should maintain dynamic harmony with the organization in terms of strategy, culture, process and technology and further improve the performance of organization.

(III) Technology innovation

The objective of TIM is to improve the technology performance of an enterprise through synergy management of all elements impacting the performance of innovation, so the concept of technology innovation is a fundamental concept in the theoretical framework of TIM.

As for technological innovation, there are many definitions and research studies. According to American innovation economists and management scholars Mansfield and Roberts, technological innovation refers to the commercialized application of invention for the first time. Therefore, technological innovation is a process comprising a series of events, including the exploration, discovery, experiment, development, simulation and application of new products, new processes and new organizational structures. The process of technological innovation can be deemed as the flow and realization process of innovation elements (information, thought, material, personnel, etc.).

From continuous research on the activities of technological innovation, it is discovered that these activities have already changed from an ordinal nature to a parallel process of interaction and feedback of various activities in the fiercely competitive environment. Technological innovation not only focuses on the technologies to be innovated, but also considers the important role of organizational process, systemic process and market process.

(IV) Market innovation

There are few research studies on market innovation in both China and foreign countries. Many famous enterprises have already used such a term, but there is still no unified definition of market innovation. Most research studies on market innovation in China adopt the definition by Professor Huang Hengxue of Tsinghua University. That is, under market economy, as the main market players, enterprise innovators make efforts to develop new markets and to stimulate the research, development, organization and management for the survival and development of enterprises by introducing and realizing the commercialization and marketization of various new market elements. Although the phrase "market innovation" is not mentioned, there are a number of research studies on "marketing innovation" done by foreign researchers. However, many practitioners mainly consider marketing innovation as competing in the short term, which doesn't take the long-term market development into account.

In light of the above research studies and the non-standard market innovation practice and theoretical demands by modern enterprises, this book defines market innovation as the activities carried out by enterprises for market development and market expansion based on their business strategy as well as the marketing function implemented by their marketing subsystem (mainly including market department and marketing department) for the main body. Fundamentally speaking, market innovation consists of two parts: market development & expansion and the marketing process. Market innovation covers all contents of marketing management, including forecasting and planning of long-term demands, and all marketing activities for the expansion of a mass market.

(V) Culture innovation

First, we shall briefly look at the concept of culture innovation. Culture innovation is mostly defined by its structural connotations. For example, enterprise culture refers to the fundamental assumptions, values and external patterns of manifestation of the organization. There are many explanations of its constituents, which normally include thoughts, language, behavior, landmarks, etc.

A series of research studies themed on "the change/innovation of culture" is an important field in the research on enterprise culture. Besides, most concepts of the change/innovation of culture were generated during the organization reform of the company and they were dominant in the mid-1990s. However, many culture researchers focus on the "change of culture" rather than the "innovation of culture", while the concept of culture change plays a significantly enlightening role in the concept of culture innovation in this book.

According to previous research, the change of culture normally happens when the enterprise is confronted with the crisis of belief and values, replacement of main leaders or significant operating problems and requires fundamental changes. The process of the change of culture is mostly passive response, during which new values, system and regulations of enterprise are gradually formed through a series of processes like the replacement of main leaders, adjustment of organizational structure, reestablishment of enterprise strategies, etc. In this book, "culture innovation" examines the corporate values, employee behaviors and institutional norms matching the adjustment of enterprise strategy and the change of organizational structure and further explores the self-renewal and realization of enterprise culture.

(VI) System innovation

System is a set of social behavior rules and a service provider with economic values. When a new paradigm of enterprise innovation is formed, it is an inevitable requirement that new behavior rules come into play to cultivate and accumulate core capabilities and effectively adapt to the internal and external demands of an organization. Besides, such behavior rules have to create market values more than the operating cost. Otherwise, no enterprise will implement such rules.

The success of many innovation-based enterprises overseas, like 3M, HP, Samsung, Sony, and a few advanced Chinese enterprises, like Haier, Huawei, Baosteel and ZTE, in TIM has proved that by implementing TIM, they can effectively integrate internal and external resources, optimize the benefit of resource utility, improve core capabilities, and create and distribute more values to customers, enterprises, employees and stakeholders. It means that TIM can become a system of enterprise innovation management which provides the stakeholders of enterprise with greater economic value.

From the perspective of the system, TIM will surely enable enterprises to correct previous mistakes, like taking into account only simple innovation and ignoring overall innovation, focusing on decentralized innovation and lacking integrated innovation, putting exclusive emphasis on internal resources and neglecting the thinking models and behavioral patterns to use external resources. Accordingly, it will help innovation occupy a strategic position in the organization, expand the range of innovation activities to every employee, every moment, place and process, and arrange innovation activities to optimize the efficiency of resource utilization. Moreover, the planning mode and operational polices of the organization will also be established by focusing on innovation awareness, innovation motive, innovation capability, innovation efficiency and innovation speed. Its purpose is to strengthen the core capabilities and increase the value of an enterprise. Through the understanding of the system, TIM is the arrangement of behavioral rules of innovation activities within the framework of an enterprise based on the understanding of the external environment, integration and deployment of various innovation elements within the enterprise, and the affirmation of interaction between innovation and strategy. It is the source to improve innovation performance and core competitiveness and the inevitable choice for innovation of an enterprise.

Therefore, according to the demands of enterprise innovation, this book presents an institutional system of TIM: the organic integration between endogenous institutional system and exogenous institutional system.

Total innovation features the synergy of organizational elements, the matching of resources, and the comprehensive, socially adaptive, operative and functional innovation. It aims to continuously integrate various resources and optimize the benefit of resource utility. The institutional system based on TIM must be designed to embody such features and according to behavioral rules of total innovation, by specifying, among other things, who stimulate and implement innovation, who benefit from innovation, how to innovate, when to innovate and how to coordinate innovation. It will form the common belief of total innovation and establish the constraints and incentives of such a belief throughout the enterprise. As an institutional arrangement, total innovation will specify and directly influence the cost and efficiency of its design and operation. Hence, such systems, mainly the culture system, property right protection system, organizational system, motivational system and personnel system, will be called the endogenous institutional systems of TIM.

On the other hand, in a broad sense, TIM is also an arrangement of the institutional structure of business operation. The efficiency of its operation also depends on the functional sophistication of other institutional arrangements (mainly some external institutional arrangements), such as social and political systems, economic systems, national and regional innovation systems, property rights systems, etc. Such institutional arrangements are not generated or controlled by TIM, but they can impact the effect of TIM. Therefore, they are called exogenous institutional systems of TIM.

4.3 Analysis of interaction of main innovation elements

During the process of exploring the connotations and definitions of innovation elements, the composition and structure of innovation elements impacting TIM are listed respectively, as shown in Table 4-2. The complex interactions among innovation elements will be further discussed in the next section and Part Five based on practical cases.

Table 4-2 Interaction among main innovation elements

Innovation element	Composition	Interaction	
Concept innovation	Major reform of concepts and thoughts	Initiating strategy innovation, laying conceptual foundation for the implementation of the innovation of all elements	Synergy with culture innovation
Strategy innovation	Progressive or significant innovation of strategies	All time-space positioning of strategy innovation	All involvement of strategy management
Organization innovation	Organizational process innovation capability, organizational structure innovation	Matching the innovation of organizational culture	
Technology innovation	Technology innovation process, technology innovation performance,and technology innovation strategy	Synergy among main processes of technology innovation (technology, production, market)	Matching the organizational structure and institutional guarantee
Market innovation	Market development, marketing process	Information support and demand positioning of technology innovation	Matching the strategy innovation and institutional guarantee
Culture innovation	Change of basic assumptions, values, employee behavior characteristics, and institutional norms	Matching the enterprise innovation	Impact on organization innovation
System innovation	Endogenous institutional system and exogenous institutional system.	Culture system, property right protection system, organizational system, motivational system and personnel system	Synergy with culture innovation

4.4 Internal relations and interactive models among innovation elements

In light of its multiple dimensions and borrowing Haken's definition, synergy can be expressed as the interactive model and mechanism between different elements of a system, between elements and the system and between system and system. The effect of synergy of "2+2 > 5" combining overall effect and partial effect will often be realized by building an orderly structure. Synergy is the fundamental approach to realize the self-organizing process of a system.

Looking at the synergy of all elements, the links between different elements have hierarchical relations due to the different levels of management. Horizontal links exist on the same level (for example, the necessity for horizontal synergy between technology and market exists on the level of operation; the horizontal links between different elements of organization, management and culture exist on the level of management; the horizontal links among strategic elements and ideological elements exist on an even higher level), while vertical links exist between different levels. Based on vertical analysis, certain synergy rules exist among different elements at the organizational level. Due to the different properties of elements, their positions and roles in the all-element interaction process are different. In general, the links and interactions among all elements have many levels. According to the roles of different elements in the development of enterprises, the elements can be divided into three levels: strategic thoughts, management system and operation. The interactive synergy of all-element innovation can be specifically expressed as: taking the interaction between technology innovation and market innovation as the starting point, the interaction among multiple elements on the management level supports (stabilizes) the interaction and synergy between technology and the market, while the strategy innovation and ideological innovation provides the interaction and synergy of the former two with a long-term strategic orientation.

4.4.1 Links and interaction between technology innovation and market innovation

Innovation is a complex system. All innovation behaviors have the self-organizing characteristic to a certain degree. Since any economic activity is carried out under the market environment and any technological innovation has to prove its success through market, both market innovation and technological innovation play a critical role in the enterprise.

Through case studies of famous Chinese enterprises, we discover that the foremost condition for success in innovation is to obtain sound synergy and interaction between technological innovation and market innovation. Market innovation is the long-term and main source of motivation of technological innovation, while technological innovation is an important approach to satisfy market demands and realize market innovation. For example, through market investigations, Haier discovered that a market for mini washing machine existed in summer, so it provided the R&D of mini washing machine with definite product requirements and market orientation. The successful R&D of the third washing method, dual-power technology, enabled Haier to develop a series of washing machines with high cleaning rate and no damaging of clothing. Such products featured advanced technologies and achieved high rate of profits. Haier made a great success in both market benefits and reputation.

As the enterprise behavior system is on the same level of value chain, technological innovation and market innovation have closely tied information, resource and value delivering links between each other and play an important role in the interaction of all-element innovation of the enterprise. Only through proper interaction between technological innovation and market innovation can enterprises seek better development through innovation. This section discusses the interaction between market elements and technology elements first. Due to the strong links between market innovation and technological innovation, enterprises have to grasp the two at the same time and attach sufficient importance to both. However, since market innovation and technological innovation are not identical but contradictory to each other to a certain degree, when an enterprise cannot carry out innovation activities in a comprehensive and systematical way, it will be stuck in a dilemma. Following the analysis of the positive interactions between market element innovation and technology element innovation, this section conducts an in-depth analysis of the contradictions between market innovation and technological innovation and thus underlines the importance of the interaction of innovation elements on the level of management system. That is, constructing well-found management system platform and providing technological innovation and market innovation with strong interactive support.

(I) Mechanism of the effect of market innovation upon technological innovation

The objective of technological innovation is to offer new products to the society or to apply new processes in production. Starting with R&D and ending with market realization, technological innovation is the process of transforming scientific and technological achievements into practical productive forces.

Due to fierce market competition and continuously changing demands in the market economy, to seek survival and development, enterprises have to devote themselves to adopting new technologies to reduce the cost and improve the quality of existing products, maintain or enlarge market share or develop new products and markets. According to market rules, however, the fiercer the market competition is, the more aggressively enterprises tend to expand new markets. Market competition is the most direct and effective motive for technological innovation, as technological innovation is a basic approach to satisfy market demands and the only road to win market share.

The relationship between market innovation and technology innovation is bidirectional. On the one hand, market demands determine the content and direction of technology innovation. On the other hand, enterprises use technology innovation to expand market, create demands and form a virtuous circle through market initiation. The mechanism of the effect of market demands upon technology innovation will be elaborated from the form, approach and realization process of market demands promoting technology innovation below.

(II) Forms of marketing innovation promoting technology

There are multiple market innovations that promote enterprise innovation. As for the different types of market innovation, their manifestation patterns, ways to deliver information to enterprises and promote business operation and innovation, and subsequent innovation processes, all have different features. Generally speaking, market innovation can be classified according to the following aspects.

In terms of market conditions, they can be classified into present market demands and potential market demands. As for present market demands, enterprises can accurately grasp market information, acquire knowledge from markets, determine new product positioning, carry out technological innovation, organize sales and occupy markets. As for potential market demands, enterprises can acquire less information, which is not accurate enough and belongs to potentially useful information.

In terms of market trend, they can be classified into present market demands and future market demands. Enterprises should not only firmly grasp present market demands and use original technologies to occupy markets, but also introduce new technologies and expand their own market shares through new products; as for future market demands, enterprises need to establish an appropriate innovation strategy and take initiative based on forecasting and analysis. From the limited information provided by market, they can be classified into conscious market demands and unconscious market demands.

As shown in Figure 4-1, confronted with different types of market demands, enterprises should carry out technology innovations from different points of penetration. Such classification is overlapping but not isolated. It means that present market demands may also be the market demands for means of consumption or market demands for means of production. Therefore, at the conceptual phase of an innovation, comprehensive demands from different perspectives should be taken into consideration to discover new opportunities, conceive innovations and confirm the possibility of innovation.

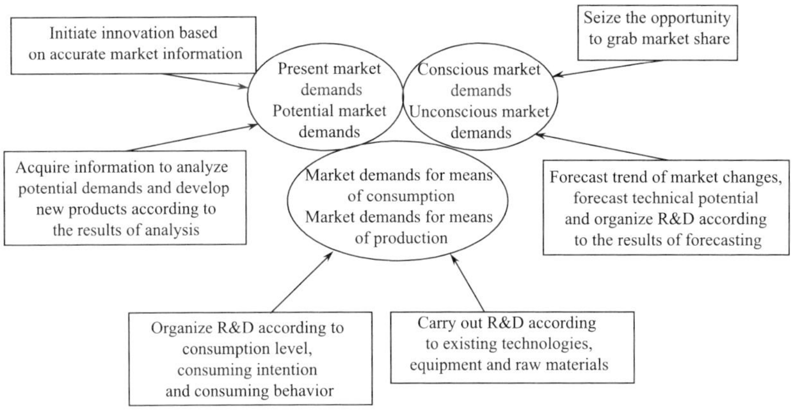

Figure 4-1 Market innovation promoting technology innovation

(III) Approaches of market innovation promoting technology innovation

Market innovation can provide an enterprise with concepts and opportunities of technological innovation, but this is the representational form of market innovation promoting enterprise innovation. To create new profit growth points and to induce overall innovation strategy and internal innovation motivation are the fundamental approaches to promote enterprise innovation.

Through the market, enterprises can understand user demands. Through certain specific products or certain new developments, enterprises can find innovative thinking, improve original products or develop new products to satisfy user demands, or apply value-function method to satisfy users' functional demands. Every kind of market demand can provide enterprise with an innovation opportunity. With the economic development, market demands become increasingly diversified and volatile. When existing products in the markets cannot satisfy users' new consumption requirements, enterprises need to develop new products to cater to users. This is a good opportunity for the innovation and development of an enterprise.

To satisfy every emerging demand, enterprises may carry out several innovations. This requires enterprises to implement sustainable innovation, be involved in the competition on a larger scale and establish market-based and technological-innovation-centered business operation strategies. With the aid of technological innovation, enterprises may satisfy market demands and realize better development. Enterprises may gain profits from technological innovation, generate internal impetus for continuous innovation and further seize all market opportunities for sustainable innovation.

4.4.2 Influence of technological innovation on market innovation

The main driving force of technological innovation originates from the market, which is the basic starting point and final destination of technology innovation. The most important element of technological innovation is having a market effect. New technologies and achievements derived from technological innovation will eventually be commercialized and returned to the market. Technological innovation and market innovation are not mutually exclusive, but they penetrate, connect, and supplement each other to form an organic whole. Technological innovation cannot be separated from the effective support of marketing, cannot surpass or lag behind the practical level of market demands and cannot ignore market purchasers' bearing capacity or future trend. The success of marketing and the satisfaction of market demands cannot be separated from the contributions of technological innovation.

Technological innovation is market-oriented which transforms scientific and technological potential into marketing advantages. The innovation department should cooperate with the marketing department, which will also play an active role in the innovation process, such as taking part in the determination of an innovation objective, screening of new product ideas and establishment of innovation budgets; working together with the technology department to write market demand reports and product manuals and provide user training and aftersales services, reporting users' feedback on new products and competitor's situations to the technology department; investigating and forecasting market demands of technology projects under development and reporting the results back to the technology department; determining the target market, market orientation, launching time and corresponding product strategies, price strategies, promotion strategies and service strategies of new products; further guaranteeing the successful marketing of innovative products.

The process of technology innovation is not just the change of technology. Since product innovation leads to the process of technology innovation, product innovation must be accompanied by market innovation

(I) Technology innovation can change the technology trajectory and lifecycle of products

The lifecycle of a product refers to the period of time from its launch to its elimination and production. It can be divided into introduction stage, growth stage, mature stage and decline stage. For enterprises, true technology innovation will maintain the periodical and sustained development trend of the lifecycle of products, and take shortening the period of digestion and absorption and dynamically introducing technologies as the premise. Driven by technology innovation, when a product is at its late mature stage, the lifecycle of a new product begins. It will make it easier for enterprises to maintain relatively stable market shares and accordingly create benefits and profits.

(II) Technology innovation also means the innovation of marketing philosophy

Technology innovation is not a pure technological concept. It is also a modernized marketing philosophy. Since new products emerge endlessly due to the increasingly shortened market lifecycle of products arising from technology development, enterprises cannot keep pace with changing consumer demands only by developing and selling products to suit consumers' demands. To adapt to such changes, enterprises must try to induce and create customer demands instead of simply satisfying customer demands. Enterprises must carry out market-oriented innovation, consider market demands and social demands as the basic starting point of technology innovation and implement the marketing concepts in the whole process of innovation.

(III) Technology innovation requires the innovation of marketing objectives

The dynamic imbalance of technology innovation leads to fierce competition among enterprises. While establishing the marketing objectives of products, it is necessary to give priority to innovative products and strengthen the development of new products; while establishing market objectives, technology-leading enterprises should strive to gain a foothold in the high-tech market first; while establishing profit objectives, it is necessary to focus on the value created by technology innovation; while establishing development objectives, it is necessary to set the introduction of technology innovation talents as an objective.

(IV) Technology innovation requires the organic coordination of marketing strategies and tactics

The success of new products in a market requires a series of effective marketing methods; it means that technology innovation also requires a series of supporting market innovation measures, including the strategy innovation of target market, the strategy innovation of market positioning and the strategy innovation of products, processing, sales promotion and distribution, rather than innovation of an individual activity or process.

4.4.3 Effect of element innovation of a management system on the synergy between market innovation and technology innovation

The synergy between technology innovation and market innovation is the foundation of enterprise innovation. Only by establishing good interaction between technology element innovation and market element innovation can enterprises seek long-term development through innovation. If the interaction between the two is relatively low, a series of problems between market innovation and technology innovation may emerge and lead to the failure of innovation.

In a competitive era where the macro environment of enterprises undertakes dramatic changes, the fundamental logic of business management also undertakes fundamental changes. From seeking stable efficiency advantages to making timely responses to the change of environment, innovation becomes the foundation for enterprises to seek survival and development in the changing environment. In particular, technology innovation and market innovation play a particularly important role in short-term competition and long-term development of enterprises.

The change of environment is all-around, but generally speaking, the survival and development of an enterprise can be ascribed to one issue: the balance between profits from short-term competition and profits from long-term capability development. The change of environment poses a significant challenge against the profits of enterprises originating from short-term competition. Due to market competition many enterprises have little time to attend to other things, so there is a serious problem here: most enterprises pay excessive attention to the innovation of market elements and when they are shackled by the concept of short-term competition, they ignore the cultivation of core technology capabilities and long-term development.

Market innovation and technology innovation have certain positive connections between each other, but in many cases, there are also some contradictions between them. Under modern circumstances, many enterprises pay excessive attention to the innovation of market elements and overly seek market innovation, seek to make timely responses to the change of environment and gain competitive advantages. In the long run, however, due to such one-sided emphasis on market innovation, enterprises exclusively focus on the R&D of application technologies and ignore the planning of manpower and material input on core technologies which plays an important role in long-term development. Accordingly, enterprises often decline rapidly in case of significant changes in industry and market and cannot maintain sustained development.

(I) It tends to form a thinking paradigm which exclusively focuses on the current market — overly emphasizing the economic benefits brought by market demands and accordingly causing a bias toward short-term benefits against long-term development .

In the development of market-oriented applications and the R&D of core technologies, the development of applied technologies features immediate effect, rich short-term profits, lower cost and lower risk, while the R&D of core technologies are just the opposite. If enterprises overly emphasize market innovation and focus on the current market and market demands, it is possible to gain certain profits in a short term and thus form a thinking paradigm which exclusively focuses on the current market: overly emphasizing the economic benefits brought by market demands, attaching importance to short-term profits and ignoring the long-term development of an enterprise.

As many scholars pointed out in their research, undue market orientation has negative impact on product innovation, because enterprises tend to develop "trendy" products with competitiveness at present. Market-oriented enterprises mainly focus on the current demands which can be clearly expressed by customers, so they will probably miss the opportunities for developing new products which customers cannot clearly express. In other words, if enterprises overly emphasize customer orientation, they will only focus on the tiny reform and improvement of products. Therefore, some scholars believe that enterprises should not seek market orientation during the process of product innovation, because it will cause nearsightedness. Market-oriented technology innovation has proved to be very effective for a short term, but it cannot maintain the development and competitiveness of an enterprise in the long term.

(II) It tends to be caught in the outdated technology paradigm — overly emphasizing the development of application-oriented products based on existing technologies and accordingly causing the lack of core technologies and products and an outdated technology paradigm.

Technology paradigm is a group of principles, rules, methods, standards and habits to deal with specific problems which are commonly followed by designers, engineers and managers. Technology paradigm specifies the direction and connotation of technological progress. The change process of technology paradigm is a slow, incremental, covert and dynamic process. In the context of rapid development of the global economy, if enterprises overly emphasize market demands and existing technological foundation, they will be exposed to the risk of being stuck in the laggard technology paradigm.

Some scholars point out that over-emphasis on market innovation will lead to adaptive organization learning. Market-oriented enterprises attach importance to the changes of environment and make responses based on their hypothesis of future customer demands and market competitions. Therefore, market-oriented technology innovation mainly relies on the previous experiences of enterprises. Since market orientation is not sufficient to encourage enterprises to take a risk, enterprises which overly emphasize market innovation often focus on the expansion and improvement of their own technological foundation. They cannot implement disruptive technology R&D. Eventually, in case of significant changes of the market, they cannot keep pace with the development of technologies.

(III) It tends to form rigid innovation mechanism — carrying out technology innovation purely in accordance with market demands, establishing the R&D management system focusing on the R&D of applied technologies, and restraining the R&D of core technologies

Innovation is a system project, which needs to mobilize various resources, involve multiple departments of the enterprises, and requires enterprises to coordinate the organizational structure, system and culture. If the internal organizational structure is suitable for technological R&D, it will greatly decrease the cost of innovation and accelerate the speed of innovation. If the internal organizational structure is not suitable for certain type of technological R&D, it will be difficult to succeed in such R&D.

If enterprises overly focus on the innovation of market elements, they will attach great importance to the technology innovation based on market demands, focus on technology innovation to reduce cost and improve production efficiency, and accordingly establish the organizational structure of traditional hierarchy. The organizational structure of traditional hierarchy is suitable for the R&D of application-oriented technologies but not that of core and disruptive technologies.

The organizational structure has structural inertia, so it cannot be changed in a short time. Organizational ecology theory believes that due to the existence of structural inertia, existing organizations have a restricted scope of behavioral choices. To a certain degree, it makes it impossible for organizations to find the "optimal solution", so they cannot adjust themselves fast enough to be adapted to the continuous changes of a competitive environment. To seek efficiency and speed, enterprises tend to simplify their routine. They simplify the organizational functions or organizational capabilities based on the achieved success and ignore other possibilities. If the technology paradigm remains unchanged, such structural simplification is effective. When industrial technologies undergo significant changes and new technology paradigm is generated, such organizational structure will be confronted with an adaptive crisis. Therefore, the over-emphasis on market innovation induces enterprises to establish organizational structure that matches the development of application-oriented technologies. Such organizational structure restrains the R&D of core technologies to a certain degree and eventually leads to the insufficient technological accumulation and inability to support the sustained development.

4.4.4 Importance of innovation on management system and innovation synergy on operation

Seen from the discussions above, technology element innovation and market element innovation are the key for enterprises to survive in fierce competitions. Besides, there is close interaction between the two. Technology innovation and market innovation are not mutually exclusive, but they penetrate, connect, and supplement each other to form an organic whole. Technology innovation cannot be separated from the effective support of marketing, cannot surpass or lag behind the practical level of market demands and cannot ignore customers' purchasing capacity or future trend. The success of marketing and satisfaction of market demands cannot be separated from the contributions of technology innovation. Furthermore, market innovation itself is built on a great number of technology innovations. Enterprises must attach importance to both technology innovation and market innovation.

As discussed above, the non-synergy or low synergy between technology element innovation and market element innovation may cause a series of problems. However, how to guarantee the high degree synergy between the two? The synergy between technology innovation and market innovation is not only the interaction between the two. It requires the synergy built on a complete management system. Without the support from the innovation of organization elements (such as human resource management innovation, financial management innovation, system innovation, organization innovation and culture innovation), the synergy between technology innovation and market innovation cannot be maintained for long and various above-mentioned problems may probably occur. Therefore, the synergy of all-element innovation requires the total synergy among human resource management innovation, financial management innovation, system innovation, organization innovation and culture innovation, the establishment of a sound organizational management system platform and the support for synergy innovation of both technology and market elements.

Cases

Table 4-3 and Table 4-4 show the analysis of interaction between market innovation and technology innovation at IBM and Huawei Technologies.

Table 4-3 Analysis of IBM management system element innovation promoting the synergy and interaction between market innovation and technology innovation

Master variables	Dependent variables	Effect of master variables on dependent variables	Source
Culture innovation	Market innovation	IBM basic principle 2: customer first, customer-oriented and market-driven	(Zhou, 2002)
	Technology innovation	IBM basic principle 1: respecting individuals, respecting talents, pursuing excellence	(Zhou, 2002)
System innovation	Technology innovation	For those who have made a success in innovation, IBM awarded them with "IBM Membership", and offered them sufficient time (up to 5 years) and fund (necessary material support) for innovation activities.	(Guo, 2006)
	Culture innovation	In the middle 1990's, IBM took measures to execute its strategic planning and implement the performance-based salary system, which helped IBM change its bureaucratic system to a high performance culture.	(Guo, 2006)
Organization innovation	Market innovation	Gerstner resolutely streamlined organs, eliminated the middle management level, merged plants, reduced the staff and cancelled the lifetime employment system. He changed IBM's traditional operation pattern which was all-inclusive and self-contained.	(Waterman, 2004)
	Technology innovation	Gerstner established 12 industrial sales units, broke the regional boundary, and carried out professional counterpart liaison based on the professions like finance, education, sanitation and commerce. In this way, IBM greatly strengthened the knowledge base, enabled employees to discuss the technological transformations as an expert and created better conditions for technology innovation.	(Waterman, 2004)

Table 4-4 Instances of Huawei management system element innovation promoting the synergy and interaction between market innovation and technology innovation

Master variables	Dependent variables	Effect of master variables on dependent variables	Source
Culture innovation	Market innovation, technology innovation	With the appearance of increasingly complex technologies and interdisciplinary efforts, technology innovation relied more and more on the collective wisdom. With the expansion of enterprise and market, marketing also relied on the power of team. Huawei's technology research, development and marketing were carried out by teams. Therefore, Ren Zhengfei specially emphasized collective efforts and collective heroism.	(Cheng & Liu, 2005)
System innovation	Market innovation	Huawei said the objectives to establish these joint ventures were "consolidating market, expanding market and occupying market by establishing interest communities; replacing business relationship with interest relationship; replacing direct sales with business operation." Huawei believed that for salesmen, sales commission was a way to stimulate and improve their enthusiasm for short-term profits, but it could make no contribution to the long-term stable relationship. However, normal customer relationship and long-term customer relationship were the trump card of Huawei. Therefore, Huawei explicitly banned the sales commission.	(Cheng & Liu, 2004) (Cheng & Liu, 2004)
	Technology innovation	At first, Huawei established a characteristic training system according to the business demands and the features of talent growth. During the process of product development, Huawei always abided by the standard international methods of software engineering design, which enabled the development and design of software to get rid of its dependence on talents.	(Cheng & Liu, 2004) (Cheng & Liu, 2005)
Organization innovation	Market innovation	Another objective why Huawei introduced Mercer to adjust its organizational structure was to establish an internationally compatible marketing system (including company level subsystem, regional subsystem, product subsystem and key account subsystem) and to be adapted to the increasingly evident demands for consultation-based marketing in international market and even local market.	(Guo & Zhang, 2004)
	Technology innovation	Through process reformation, Huawei had achieved remarkable results: half of the time and 30% cost for new product development was saved.	(Hua & Wu, 2003)

4.4.5 Guiding effect of strategy innovation and thought innovation promoting the synergy between technology innovation and market innovation

Innovation on the level of management system provides technology innovation and market innovation with a strong platform for organization and management, but this synergy platform is not sufficient for long-term and future synergy. Especially in such an age of hyper-competition, without long-term strategic consideration, the competitive advantages arising from the synergy between technology innovation and market innovation will disappear soon, and enterprises cannot maintain development through innovation.

Therefore, strategy innovation and thought innovation play an important and strategic role in the all-element innovation of enterprise. Only on such a basis can enterprises build complete management system platforms and guarantee the synergy between technology innovation and market innovation on long-term objectives.

(I) Thought innovation is the forerunner of all-element innovation

Thought and ideas are the forerunner of innovation, the internal motivation of innovation, and the premise and foundation of successful innovation. Therefore, the research on innovation cannot be separated from a basic issue, i.e. the relationship between cognition and practices. In other words, it is about how to guide innovation practices with the correct ideas and how to guarantee the success in innovation.

The foremost factor of all-element innovation is thought innovation, which is the source of all innovation, as innovation is the conscious and purposeful behavior of enterprises based on the demands for business management. The theories of management are the conceptual knowledge of management activities. In essence, ideology innovation is continuously generating, improving and enhancing the conceptual knowledge of management activities. It is an inexhaustible source to stimulate the innovation of other elements and improve the performance of business operation. Thought innovation is the forerunner of strategy innovation, technology innovation, market innovation and system innovation. With outdated thoughts and old-fashioned ideas, enterprises will make nothing from other innovations.

Thought is the forerunner of behavior. From both macro and micro levels, all reforms and achievements in history start with liberating ideas and changing mindset. The successful management of an enterprise relies on the scientific allocation of material, financial and human resources. Material resources and financial resources are static and cannot change their own form of existence, but the effect of human resources mainly originates from people's cognitive ability. In this sense, thought innovation plays a critical and guiding role in the all-element innovation of an enterprise.

The innovation of management thought plays a decisive role in the survival and development of enterprises. The development of enterprise and the change of economic form cannot be separated from the continuous ideological emancipation and the continuous upgrading of concept. To succeed in sustainable operation, enterprises have to keep innovating, which starts with the innovation of management philosophy.

Compared with specific behaviors during work, management thought is more indirect and general. It is people's perception on how a business is operated. It plays a significant and guiding role in what employees say and do. The guiding role of thought innovation in the innovation actions of an enterprise is mainly reflected in the following three aspects.

1. Thought innovation can expand the understanding of innovation

source

Innovation source refers to the basic question of who the innovator is or where the innovation concept comes from. For example, people always think that the product innovation is realized by the product manufacturer, but practices prove that there is a variety of innovation sources. Product manufacturers are no doubt the important innovation source of product innovation. In some fields, however, product users or material suppliers may be important innovation sources. The change of such concept plays a significant role in guiding the management of enterprise strategy, the management of innovation and the management of R&D.

2. The significance of thought innovation is embodied in the process of strategic decision-making and strategy implementation

Strategic decision-making and strategy implementation are core issues in business management. Strategic decisions are always formed under the guidance of certain thoughts and concepts. Any decision of an enterprise reflects its business management philosophy to varying degrees. Under the guidance of different thoughts and concepts, different strategic decisions are made. The maturity of concept also determines the maturity of strategic decision. For example, the diversity in the concept of core capabilities also leads to the diversity in different strategic decisions. Some emphasize technology innovation (like Gree), some emphasize marketing innovation (like Little Swan) and some emphasize all-round innovation (like Haier Group) and management innovation (like Baosteel). In spite of the diversity in the industrial nature, scale and growth of enterprises, the management thought plays an influencing role in the decision-making process.

3. Thought innovation has decisive influence on the formation of enterprise culture

Behavioral characteristics are an important component of enterprise culture. Enterprise culture plays a regulating, normalizing and guiding role in the behaviors of enterprises. It is the internal condition for enterprise behaviors to take place. The innovation of management thought has comprehensive and deep influence on enterprise behaviors. The innovation activities of enterprises require the managers to make progress in thought and strategy, carry out additional innovation of organizational structure and system, guarantee the implementation of new technologies and new methods throughout the organization, make it possible to carry out innovation, and eventually provide new products and services through management and functional activities like decision-making, planning, directing, organizing, coordinating and controlling.

Case Study

Huaiwei and Ren Zhengfei: Traditional Chinese Thought, Mao Zedong Thought and All-Element Innovation

Ren Zhengfei does a good job in creatively applying the war and army building theories of Mao Zedong Thought to business management practices, creating many Huawei characteristics. The basic tactics in Mao Zedong's military theories include the guerrilla warfare principles of "When the enemy advances, withdraw; when he stops, harass; when he tires, strike; when he retreats, pursue". Such thoughts are widely applied in Huawei and have become the guiding principles of market and technology innovation.

Ren Zhengfei's strategic thoughts and management thoughts are deeply rooted within Huawei. Pushed by such forward-looking thoughts, employees of Huawei deeply understand the thinking and direction of the company's development, jointly producing market innovations and technology innovations with Huawei characteristics. For example, Huawei has established the market strategy of "using the rural areas to encircle the cities and gradually occupying the cities", starting with the rural market and gradually encircling urban cities. Furthermore, Huawei put forward the famous "pressure principle": on the key elements of success and the selected strategic growth points, through more intense allocation of resources than that of its main competitors, Huawei has integrated and concentrated the human, material and financial resources to find breakthroughs. ①

(II) Strategy innovation plays a decisive role in the innovation on management system and operation

The comprehensiveness of TIM means that during the process of innovation, enterprises have to change the old innovation paradigm, as it attaches too much importance to decentralized innovation and lacks system integration innovation, it focuses too much on simple innovation and ignores the comprehensive innovation, it emphasizes the integration of internal resources and ignores the utilization of external resources, and it pays attention exclusively to the innovation of professionals but overlooks the innovation potential of average employees. They should establish the strategic position of innovation in the organization and make great efforts to create and increase enterprise values and continuously improve core capabilities. Meanwhile, since TIM involves the all-round innovation of all departments and employees in the enterprise and pays attention to innovation based on the utilization of external innovation resources and cooperation with users, universities, research institutions and other enterprises and even competitors, the input resources on innovation and the transaction costs for implementation and coordination are greatly increased.

Therefore, the all-element innovation of TIM is actually a novel innovation management paradigm led by strategy innovation and thought innovation. In other words, with enterprise strategies and strategic thoughts as the base and starting point, it emphasizes the interaction between innovation and strategy, generates the strategy-based comprehensive arrangements that integrate the all-element, all-involvement and all time-space innovation activities, and realizes the

① Cheng D & Liu L, *Inside Huawei*. Beijing: Contemporary China Publishing House, 2004 continuous improvement, increase and creation of core capabilities and values, thus satisfying the demands for the implementation of new strategy and achieving the new objectives more effectively.

The dominant strategic position of TIM within an organization is embodied in the following aspects:

1. It determines all-element innovation

Strategies, which attach importance to the establishment of an enterprise's objectives and the allocation of resources, not only determine the direction of technology development and the R&D of specific products, but also specify the organizational structure of labor division, the processes and norms to coordinate different business units, and the corporate culture to achieve the consistency of employees' behavior. As Chandler argued, strategy determines structure and structure follows strategy. Mintzberg then put forward a more comprehensive viewpoint that the development of strategy and the design of structure support each other and jointly support the organization. As they lead and follow each other, only when the organization has grown to a new height can they advance side by side.

TIM strengthens the interaction between innovation and strategy. Therefore, based on further understanding of the strategy determining the all-element innovation in TIM, innovation is a strategic activity of enterprise where both technology and non-technology innovation must be included in the strategic framework. All-element innovation will surely be able to improve technology and innovation capabilities, realize the optimal resource allocation and integrated effect, and hence satisfy the demands for the establishment and realization of enterprise strategies.

2. Strategy innovation guides all-involvement innovation

Each employee in the enterprise is the subject of TIM and the participant in the establishment and realization of enterprise strategies.

Once adjusted, the strategies will redirect the innovation activities of all employees to satisfy the demands of new strategies. Meanwhile, only by decomposing the overall objective to each employee, distributing the resources and powers required for the implementation of strategies to each employee, and making each employee a subject of strategy implementation can a new and novel atmosphere and objectives of all-involvement innovation be created. In such a way, it will not only complete individual tasks, but also stimulate the realization of strategic objectives.

3. It helps explore all time-space innovation under the guidance of strategy innovation

The establishment and implementation of strategies will surely reflect the value propositions of an enterprise in a certain time-space scope. For example, through a dozen years of development, Haier Group and ZTE gradually shifted the scope to realize value propositions from domestic market to global market, and realized the internationalized development from product export to market expansion, which were the reflections of enterprise strategies in the time-space scope of implementation. At present, due to the increasingly volatile competitive environment and the intensified uncertainty, enterprise strategies become more flexible. The implementation of strategies must be continuously adjusted with the shift of time and space. The frequent changes of enterprise strategies will surely require employees to effectively integrate internal and external resources at any time and place, i.e. carrying out all time-space innovation, so as to satisfy the new demands of strategy development.

Table 4-5 and Table 4-6 provide instances of the interaction between strategy innovation and innovation of other elements of IBM and Huawei.

Table 4-5 Interaction between strategy innovation and innovation of other elements of Huawei

Master variables	Dependent variables	Effect of master variables on dependent variables	Source
Strategy innovation	Culture innovation	The cultural construction must be carried out in line with the enterprise strategies, such as "customer-oriented culture", "high performance culture", "integrity culture", "team culture", "professional dedication culture", "continuous improvement", "cost consciousness", etc.	(Zhao, 2005)
	Market innovation	(After stepping into the high speed development stage with the development of independent products as the main profit-making model) the sales mode of Huawei must change as well and the technology and service played an increasingly significant role in the sales.	(Cheng & Liu, 2005)
	Technology innovation	In 1992, the market environment faced by Huawei was: massive demand and limited supply. The barrier to expand supply was technology. Once domestic manufacturers realized technological progress and entered the market at low cost, the profit space of telecommunication market was revealed.	(Cheng & Liu, 2004)
	System innovation	Establishing improved training system, building learning-based enterprise and serving the market expansion were important constituent parts of Huawei's strategies.	(Zhao, 2005)
	Organization innovation	To guarantee the sustainable development in the field of technologies, Huawei emphasized the cooperation with global peers in terms of technologies, manufacturing and market development. Up to now, Huawei has already cooperated with many companies, such as 5Com, Siemens, NEC, Panasonic, Intel, Motorola, Lucent, SUN and IBM, in R&D and market expansion. Huawei established COSMOBIC Technology with NEC and Panasonic and established TD-SCDMA with Siemens. Besides maintaining the technological advancement through cooperation, Huawei moved its research institutions to foreign countries and established overseas research institutions in Dallas (the U.S.), Bangalore (India), Stockholm (Sweden) and Moscow (Russia).	(Hu, 2005)

Table 4-6 Interaction between strategy innovation and innovation of other elements of IBM

Master variables	Dependent variables	Effect of master variables on dependent variables	Source
Strategy innovation	Culture innovation	To create conditions for the transformation of IBM and guarantee the successful implementation of strategies, it was necessary to reinterpret the original culture of IBM.	(Gerstner, 2004)
	Market innovation	Be customer-oriented and make IBM a market-driven company	(Gerstner, 2004)
	Technology innovation	Waston Jr. advocated that the perforating machine was outdated and the company would focus on computer	(Waterman, 2004)
	System innovation	Each employee of IBM had to make his own "individual performance promise"– decomposing the overall strategy of IBM to the tasks of individuals.	(Guo, 2006)
	Organization innovation	After reorganization, regional business units established strategy-centered leadership system. IBM Japan, the strategic core in Asia Pacific, was established. One of the primary tasks to implement reform was to change the internal structure of basic rights of IBM	(Zhong, 2002) (Gerstner, 2004)

4.4.6 Presentation of all-element & multi-level interaction mechanisms

This section analyzes the interactions between market innovation and technology innovation and tries to answer the following questions: how to solve the contradictory relationship between market innovation and technology innovation, how to make the synergy between the two effectively, and how to achieve short-term profits from competition and long-term development of competencies, realize value increase and value creation and develop flexible responses to adapt to the environment through the synergy between technology and market innovation? In fact, only by TIM can the synergy and innovation of multiple elements be comprehensively and systematically realized to solve the contradictions between market and technology innovation, fully stimulate the joint innovation of two elements and seek the consistency between short-term economic benefits and long-term development objectives.

Therefore, TIM becomes the inexorable trend of innovation management. Enterprises clearly recognize that innovation behaviors are complex and systematic, so they have to carry out TIM of all innovation elements. TIM emphasizes that the synergy between technology element innovation and market element innovation is the key point of the all-element synergy of innovation management. Based on the synergy and interaction between these elements, a multi-level, all-element and vertical synergy mechanism and model is constructed and formed, as shown in Figure 4-2.

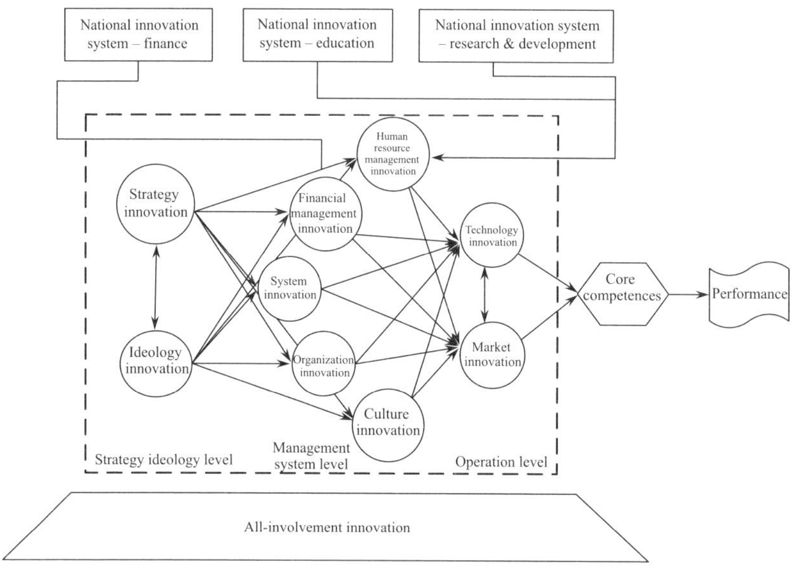

Figure 4-2 Multi-level and all-element interaction mechanism

The multi-level, all-element and vertical synergy mechanism classifies the all-element innovation in the practices of TIM into three levels: strategy innovation and ideology innovation on the first level; human resource management innovation, financial management innovation, system innovation, organization innovation and culture innovation on the second level; technology innovation and market innovation on the third level. Among them, consisting of technology elements and market elements, the third level is the main source of core capabilities and the core of all-element innovation and synergy. The strategy elements and ideology elements on the first level play an important role in determining and guiding high-level objectives in the practices of overall innovation of the organization. Innovation of multiple elements on the second level is a key process as a connecting link between the one preceding and the one following. Guided by the innovation of elements on the first level, a strong management system platform to support the synergy innovation on the operation level is constructed through the synergy innovation of multiple elements like organizational system, structure and culture. Through synergy innovation on these three levels, enterprises are able to construct their own indigenous innovation capabilities, hence seeking sustainable development.

4.5 Conclusion

This chapter proposes that there are close internal connections among all innovation elements in technology innovation, clearly defines the connotations of all elements in the theory of TIM, and discusses in depth the interactions between innovations of all elements based on the diamond pattern. The necessity of the internal connections among all elements will be discussed in detail in Chapter 8. It should be noted that the process of comprehensive synergy of all innovation elements is a process of dynamic development and also a process of multi-level synergy. Such issues will be further discussed in Chapter 8. Finally, TIM is a complex ecosystem where the all-element synergy is established on the basis of all-involvement innovation. Such issues will be discussed in Chapter 5 and Chapter 15.

Chapter 5

All-Involvement Innovation

As the main body and foundation of total innovation management, this chapter will discuss the basic contents of all-involvement innovation, including: (1) Connotation and status of all-involvement innovation; (2) Background and process of all-involvement innovation; (3) Analysis of the operation of all-involvement innovation; (4) Development process of all-involvement innovation.

All-Involvement innovation is a new innovation management form for modern enterprises to cope with economic globalization. To deal with the complex and volatile economic environment and gain competitive advantages, many enterprises begin to make great efforts to implement all-involvement innovation. In fact, few enterprises can truly do well in all-involvement innovation. This book mainly conducts in-depth analysis of the organization mechanism, the mechanism of the effect of relevant management elements and other aspects of all-involvement innovation within the framework of TIM.

5.1 Background and requirements of all-involvement innovation for enterprises

5.1.1 Increasingly personalized customer demands

More and more enterprises discover that by relying only on good production efficiency, high quality and flexibility, sustained competitive advantages in the market cannot be maintained. To avoid such predicament and remain invincible in a competitive market, enterprises have to fully mobilize the creativity of every employee and enable everyone to take an active part in the innovation activities to satisfy customer demands. For example, Haier Group has established the mechanism of "everyone is an innovation SBU", i.e. everyone is an innovation strategic business unit (SBU), to accelerate the satisfaction of the personalized demands of external users. It requires everyone to be an innovator and an operator of self-innovation who is responsible for his own "market". By fully releasing potential abilities of every employee, it aims to integrate the great potential energy of development and "maintain the everlasting competitiveness and vigorous vitality in both domestic and foreign markets with fierce competitions".

5.1.2 Requirements of hypercompetitive market environment

As the price/quality-based competitions are continuously and rapidly intensifying, the emergence of new technologies and the frequent encroachment of competitors, enterprises are required to carry out all-round competitions. It not only requires employees of all departments, including production, manufacturing, R&D, marketing and service, to have strong consciousness and capability of innovation, but also emphasizes the effective and cooperative innovation of employees at different posts in all departments. Enterprises have to create effective innovation management mechanisms, methods and tools to optimize the cost structure and rapidly launch products suitable for market demands. An example is the "15% Rule" of 3M, one of the most innovative companies in the U.S. According to the rule, on having a new idea, an employee can spend 15% of his/her working time in deepening the idea, including seeking help from engineers in other fields and cooperating with fields like manufacturing, marketing, sales and after-sale service. All departments are required to make public the latest technologies in annual forums.

5.1.3 Characteristics of organization innovation in the knowledge-based economy

In the knowledge-based economy, organization innovation has to be as fast as possible. The speed of innovation becomes an important determinant to gain competitive advantages. The increase of the speed of organization innovation mainly depends on two factors. One factor is the number of individuals who are engaged in organization innovation. Individual behavior determines the behavior of organization and individual innovation determines the innovation of organization, so the increase of the number of individuals who are engaged in organization innovation is the premise to increase the speed of organizational innovation. The other factor is the speed and capability of individual innovation. Only by accelerating the speed of and improving the capability of individual innovation can the speed of organization innovation be increased. It is obvious that to seek competitive advantages in innovation, enterprises have to authorize all employees to carry out innovation and enable every employee to have the consciousness of innovation and to take part in innovation activities.

All-involvement innovation under the framework of TIM mainly requires the following transformations: (1) The transformation from relying on experts to innovate to relying on everyone to innovate. (2) The transformation from "being required to innovate" to "being willing to innovate". (3) The transformation from innovation that focuses on organizational development to innovation that focuses on the combination of organizational development and individual development. (4) The transformation from decentralized innovation of employees to the all-involvement synergy innovation. (5) The transformation from duty-based innovation to cross-duty innovation.

5.2 Process of all-involvement innovation for enterprises

In recent years, academic and business circles in both China and foreign countries are focusing on how to stimulate the enthusiasm of every employee for innovation and how to realize all-involvement innovation. Many scholars point out that innovation should be the common behavior of all employees instead of the exclusive right of researchers. From salesmen, production personnel, researchers to after-sale service personnel, managers and financial personnel, everyone may become an outstanding innovator (Tucker, 2002; Peters, 1992; Shapiro, 2002; Wheatley, 2001; Christiansen, 2000; Dundon, 2002). Dundon (2002) believed that with the complex growth of organization, leaders needed to let all employees take part in the process of seeking the approach to organization innovation. Everyone has his/her own unique creativity. The human side plays an important role in the innovation performance. Li Jian (2002) pointed out that for a specific enterprise, the innovation on the level of employees was the source of enterprise innovation. Seen from the practices of enterprises, the process of all-involvement innovation includes the following contents.

5.2.1 From total quality management to all-involvement innovation

Total quality management (TQM) is the application of the ideology of the Japan Kaizen Movement, which stated that "everyone should stimulate the development of everything at any time", in enterprises. TQM requires everyone in the organization to play an important role in the continuous development process and further proposes that everyone in the organization should be an innovator, i.e. the innovation of everyone within the organization.

5.2.2 From continuous innovation to all-involvement innovation

Famous management consultant S. M. Shapiro (2001) brought forward a novel perspective: 24/7 innovation. Due to the constantly changing market situations and fierce market competitions, to seek survival and development, enterprises have to make unremitting efforts to innovate. 24/7 innovation means that organization and its members constantly bring forward new concepts during daily work to satisfy customers' unpredictable demands. In other words, everyone in the organization should innovate at any time and at any place, just like breathing. A sign of a successful enterprise is 24/7 innovation that all employees have to maintain the status of continuous and spontaneous innovation all the time.

5.2.3 From innovation-based origination to all-involvement innovation

Every organization needs a core competence: innovation. To become the best innovator, an organization has to authorize all employees to carry out innovation. An organization needs every employee to be able to create and bring new ideas (Hartlaub, 1994). To create an innovation-based organization, two points should be kept in mind: innovation is a network rather than a node; an innovation-based organization is not created by a few intelligent people. Instead, it is the result of structural support and relationships within an organization and the joint efforts of all employees. An innovation-based organization always hopes that more people will make contributions at any time under any circumstance. Only such an organization can be called an active and capable organization. To achieve any of these results, enterprises have to create an environment where all employees can fully contribute their creative abilities. Everyone in the organization has innovation-based talent and innovation-based talent can be discovered anywhere. Innovators are not restricted to designers, engineers, advertisers or R&D personnel. When everyone in an organization is an innovator and is able to solve problems with their own creativity, the organization can achieve the maximum benefits (all-involvement organization) (Bean & Radford, 2002).

5.3 Development process of all-involvement innovation

All-involvement innovation cannot be formed overnight and enterprises may adopt different forms of all-involvement innovation at different stages of development (Figure 5-1). All-involvement innovation has different impact on the performance of enterprise at different stages of development.

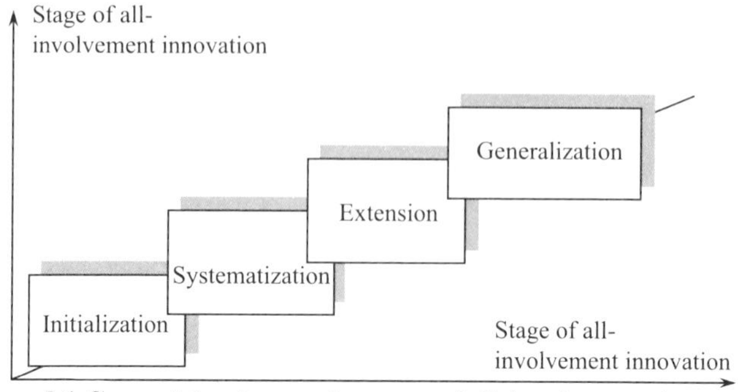

Figure 5-1 General development process of all-involvement innovation

Source: Author's compilation.

5.3.1 Initialization of all-involvement innovation

This initialization stage is the start-up stage of all-involvement innovation. With a certain understanding of all-involvement innovation, employees try to solve problems from the perspective of all the members participating in the innovation. However, while discovering problems and seeking solutions, employees cannot fully release their potential abilities and their enthusiasm for innovation is not effectively activated. Meanwhile, enterprises have established some approaches for employees to make public their ideas, but such approaches are not formal ones. Employees often try to solve problems from the perspective of all-involvement innovation after they discover such problems. It is a problem-solution pattern. Employees don't take measures to prevent problems. Besides, after the problems are solved, the activities of all-involvement innovation are often terminated in advance. No systematic and continuous activities of all-involvement innovation are formed in the enterprise. At this stage, the all-involvement activities are often scattered and unsystematic.

Employees begin to be interested in innovation activities and learn to use some new tools and technologies. They are also eager to show their capabilities in their own work and expect to achieve good results in a short time. Innovation activities at this stage are all carried out at low cost and have limited influence, just some local effect for a short time. It can improve the spirit and motivation of employees to a certain degree, but it lacks sustainability.

5.3.2 Systematization of all-involvement innovation

After initial attempts of all-involvement innovation, enterprises begin to consider how to spread the activities and enthusiasm of employees to all other employees and make innovation part of daily work rather than a one-off project. At this stage, all-involvement innovation mainly features formalization and systematization. Employees have already recognized that all-involvement innovation is an important part of enterprise and the responsibility and obligation of every employee. Enterprises have formed definite and clear values of all-involvement innovation, but they only take all-involvement innovation as the incremental improvement of employees.

Enterprises need a set of structured procedures: offering training on a regular basis, developing some methods that help and support teamwork, and considering how to manage redundant ideas. At this stage, therefore, enterprises must provide a complete set of processes to implement the activities of all-involvement innovation, such as the simplified variant of Deming's "Plan-Do-Check-Act" working cycle. Such procedures include a great deal of suggestion management systems, assessment and incentive systems, information communication systems, etc. Suggestion systems include timely responses to employees' suggestions and incentive systems include incentives for internal motivation.

Based on the preliminary attempts, enterprises promote local activities of all-involvement innovation to the whole enterprise and establish formal structures and processes to support activities of all-involvement innovation. All-involvement innovation has already become bottom-up innovation activities of employees promoted by systems. Enterprises don't only solve problems, but also set up a set of specific processes to manage all-involvement innovation and to guarantee the long-term all-involvement innovation. At this stage, enterprises are conscious of obvious activities of all-involvement innovation. Besides, some performance indexes are often measurable (such as number of participants, number of suggestions, etc.). All-involvement innovation activities at the previous two stages are restricted to little incremental improvements. Such improvements have small impacts on enterprises, but they have a large cumulative effect.

5.3.3 Extension of all-involvement innovation

At the stage of the systematization, all-involvement innovation activities of enterprises are already complete. However, such a relatively complete system still has some shortcomings. Firstly, it lacks strategic focus, which restricts its effect to the local level. Secondly, it only focuses on little incremental innovations but ignores major breakthrough innovations. At the stage of the extension, the most important characteristic is to include strategies and breakthrough innovations into the activities of all-involvement innovation. Through explicit strategies and expansion of innovation scope, enterprises have already stepped from the stage of all-involvement innovation promoted by systems to the spontaneous and routine activities of all-involvement activities.

While making great efforts to make progress from the systematization stage of all-involvement and to get rid of the lack of compelling motive, organizations begin to establish strategic plans related to all-involvement innovation. Most practices include top-down operating strategy plans and bottom-up all-involvement innovation activities which combine the discovery of problems and the problem-solving capabilities. The overall strategy of all-involvement innovation has been systematically decomposed into "bit-sized" blocks for the effective performance of employees. Such a strategy is established through in-depth discussions and sufficient communication, so everyone knows what the objectives are and why they are selected. Therefore, they can study the influence of their behavior on such objectives. Under the guidance of such a strategy, the assessment activities of all-involvement innovation are more scientific and objective and the innovation activities are closely connected with the strategic objectives. In short, the system works well and the clear strategic objectives are determined and periodically reviewed to guarantee the objectiveness of all-involvement innovation. A lot of supervision and measurement tasks are completed by specific management teams. At this point, activities of all-involvement innovation have already become part of daily work rather than special activities.

Another major characteristic of the extension of all-involvement innovation is to include major breakthrough innovations into the scope of all-involvement innovation. None of the traditional organizational forms of all-involvement innovation, such as proposal mechanism and continuous improvement, have integrated major innovations into such activities. According to traditional opinions, ordinary employees are only suitable for making little improvements on products or processes and major innovation can be only entrusted to experts. At the stage of the extension of all-involvement innovation, while experts are contributing breakthrough innovations, ordinary employees can also be involved in such major innovations. It requires expanding the training of ordinary employees and strengthening the training of their creativity and the training of some necessary tools. And it requires sufficient trust in and authorization to employees.

In the early stages, all-involvement innovation is only top-down employee behaviors and managers only provide necessary resources and system support. However, human is the most active factor of productivity. System restraints are just necessary and basic guarantees, not the ideal solution. Only by realizing the transformation from orderless management to strict system management and gradually establishing self-management can enterprises truly step onto the road of benign development. At this stage, all-involvement innovation activities are combinations of bottom-up fundamental innovation and top-down strategic guidance. All-involvement innovation is no longer blind behavior, but the guiding activities under the strategic objectives set by managers, especially senior leaders of enterprises. At this stage, all-involvement innovation activities are more objective and directional and have better performance. Besides top-down strategic guidance, all-involvement innovation at this stage extends the basic activities of incremental improvements to breakthrough innovations. All-involvement innovation has already become ubiquitous and spontaneous behavior. At this stage, therefore, the performance of innovation is more influential and often has significant impact on enterprise.

5.3.4 Generalization of all-involvement innovation

All-involvement innovation has already become spontaneous behaviors. Based on the self-promotion of employees, enterprises can loosen the strategic objectives. Enterprises only need to establish a definite overall strategy, which allows employees to take different measures of execution. The stage of all-involvement innovation based on total innovation mainly focuses on learning and coordinating. The all-involvement innovation at this stage is more comprehensive and has already become the cornerstone of total innovation. Through the combination of all-element innovation (including culture, strategy and technology innovation) and all time-space innovation and the synergy between all-involvement innovation and other innovations, enterprises at this stage have improved their innovation performance. Innovation at this stage focuses more on the cooperation between employees, attaches more importance to trans-department and trans-organization operation and relies on the collective forces of employees. Communication and learning become important abilities at this stage. Only by frequent mutual communication can employees truly understand and trust each other, maximize the collective forces and truly realize the innovation effect of "1+1 > 2". Learning is an important factor to maintain the long-term sustainability of such innovation activities. By actively acquiring resources and information, employees constantly improve their own innovation capabilities, take an active part in the innovation activities and truly achieve the state of "being willing to innovate". Through all-involvement innovation activities towards total innovation, enterprises can gain continuous competitive advantages and further make all-involvement innovation deeply rooted in enterprises.

In the analysis above, all-involvement innovation shows different characteristics at different stages (Table 5-1). At different stages, enterprises lay particular emphasis on different aspects and behavioral expressions, which have different forms and impact.

Table 5-1 Characteristics of all-involvement innovation at different stages

	Initialization	Systematization	Extension	Generalization
Focus	Problem solving	Formalization, systematization	Combination of strategic connections, major innovation and incremental innovation	Learning and synergy with other innovations
Behavioral expression	Unsystematic employee innovation behavior	Bottom-up all-involvement innovation promoted by systems	Spontaneous all-involvement innovation that integrates bottom-up and top-down innovation	All-involvement innovation synergized with employees

continued

	Initialization	Systematization	Extension	Generalization
Main forms (taking Haier for instance)	Meeting before work	TQM, OEC and rational suggestion movement	Everyone is an innovation SBU	Haier University, training network
Other main forms	Problem-sol-ving teams	Proposal system, continuous improvement, etc.	Collective wisdom and efforts, 15% Rule, technology forum, etc.	Learning- & innovation-based organization
Influence on performance	Short-term, local effect, lack of sustainability	Continuous and accumulative little effect	Significant influence	Promoting competence of total innovation and comprehensively promote innovation performance

Source: *Author's compilation*.

5.4 Effect of all-element innovation on all-involvement innovation

5.4.1 Mechanism of the effect of continuous development-based strategy upon total-involvement innovation

Continuous development requires organizations to seek continuous improvement and encourage employees to continuously study and innovate. Only by continuous innovation can enterprises satisfy market and customer demands, develop new markets and continuously stimulate and motivate employees to form and implement innovation ideas. The pursuit of continuous development generates pressure on employee innovation and offers opportunities and motivations for innovation.

To seek innovation, organizations should not be enthusiastic about short-term profits. With focus on short-term profits, organizations are unwilling to invest more in innovation and take risks, because these cannot bring short-term profits to enterprises. Enterprises which focus on short-term profits don't encourage employees to innovate because it requires offering employees certain time and space for innovation, which will surely lead to the decrease of time spent in current work, the decrease of working performance and harm enterprises' current profits. Furthermore, innovation has its intrinsic risks. Once failed, it will cause loss of profits and harm the short-term profits. On the contrary, if enterprises are not enthusiastic about short-term profits, they will offer employees certain resources for innovation activities and stimulate the enthusiasm of employees for innovation. The mechanism of the effect of continuous development on all-involvement innovation is shown in Figure 5-2.

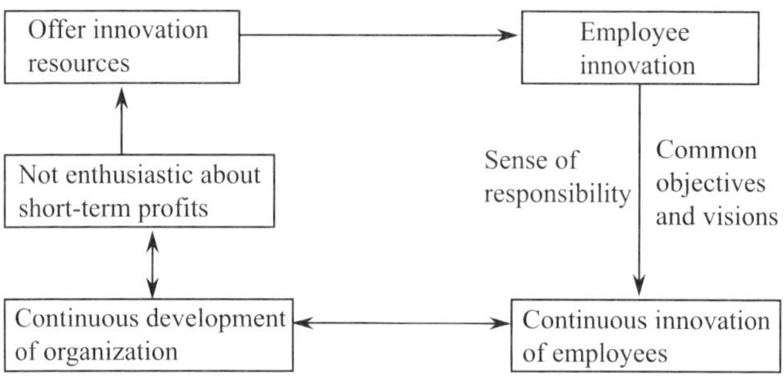

Figure 5-2 Mechanism of the effect of continuous development-based strategy upon all-involvement innovation

5.4.2 The effect of corporate culture that encourages innovation upon all-involvement innovation

The most obvious characteristic of innovation is its uncertainty or risk. It requires hard work, pioneering spirit and courage to take risks, while risks and explorations will surely lead to the occurrence of mistakes and failure. Since the future is full of uncertainties, organizations are required to encourage adventure and to tolerate failure. Only in such a way can enterprises encourage and cultivate innovators' enthusiasm for innovation in work.

During the implementation of innovation, the system guaranteed to transform innovation ideas to practical products is that enterprises should encourage people to take risks, awarding but not punishing risk takers, whether they succeed or not. Mistakes and failures may cause economic loss, but they are also experiences. Only by learning from failure can similar mistakes be avoided. In such a way, success is guaranteed next time.

Challenging work tends to stimulate employees' desire for innovation. When the work is challenging and there are sufficient opportunities for generating new solutions, people tend to make active responses. Therefore, challenging tasks can cultivate employees' initiatives for innovation.

The mechanism of the effect of encouraging risk-taking on all-involvement innovation is shown in Figure 5-3.

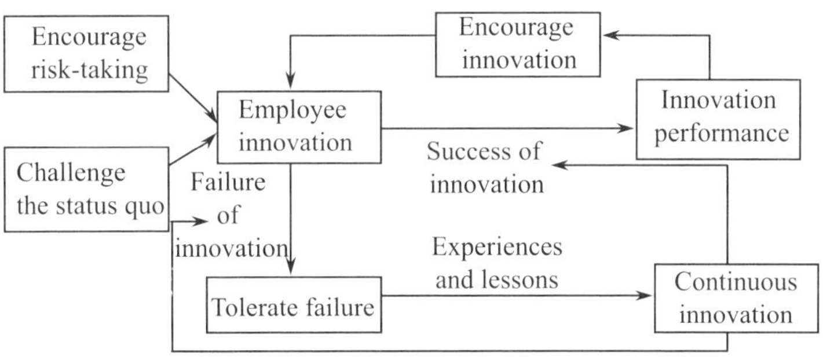

Figure 5-3 Effect of the culture that encourages risk-taking on all-involvement innovation

Source: *Author's compilation.*

5.5 Conclusion

Based on the theoretical framework of TIM, this chapter analyzes the historical background, research basis, problems, application characteristics, organization mechanism and relevant system management of all-involvement innovation. Through the examples of 3M and other companies, this chapter empirically analyzes the management elements and modes for the implementation of all-involvement innovation, provides the research on all-involvement innovation with a systematic theoretical model, and expects to provide the practical implementation of all-involvement innovation in enterprises with a guiding practical framework.

With the rise of knowledge-based economy and the tide of economic globalization, all-involvement innovation becomes a new trend of modern enterprise innovation management. But due to various problems that exist in enterprises, many enterprises fail to achieve ideal results of all-involvement innovation. One of the main reasons is the lack of explicit connections between all-element innovation and all-involvement innovation, especially the lack of internal interaction between the two. This chapter discusses the interactions between all-element innovation and all-involvement innovation, explains how to realize all-element innovation through all-involvement innovation, and emphasizes “Three All” as the close internal connections within a system as a whole.

Chapter 6

All Time-Space Innovation

All time-space innovation refers to the total innovation of enterprises implemented by integrating all time and space resources available. It is an essential part of the total innovation management (TIM) theory. All time-space innovation is an inevitable result of changing innovation environments like economic globalization, intensification of competition, individualization of demands, and the networking of values. All time-space innovation is classified into all-time innovation and all-space innovation. All-time innovation is embodied in forms like impromptu innovation, instant innovation and continuous innovation; all-space innovation is mainly embodied in all-value chain innovation, globalized innovation, etc.

6.1 All-time innovation

6.1.1 Historical background of the emergence of all-time innovation

In recent years, the competitive environment has already transformed from the industrial age to the post-industrial age (Clark, 2003; Nahm et al., 2003). In the industrial age, enterprises tend to use homogeneous labor forces and is found to compete in the homogeneous local market. In such a large and stable market, products have longer life cycles and production cost and scale economy play an important role in competition. In the post-industrial age, globalization becomes the background of competition. The wide application of information technologies leads to unprecedented change in business competition, especially the constantly accelerated information flow and the exponential growth of information accessed by individuals.

In such an era, change is the only permanent thing. The market confronted by organizations is a volatile market. The original logical foundation of obtaining competitive advantages by lowering the cost through scale economy under the premise of stable market has already been overturned.

In the 1950s, establishing large companies and obtaining a scale economy were considered a magical weapon to succeed in industrial competition. In the 1960s, with the globalized expansion of capitalism, to seek the cheapest raw material market and high-price product market on a global scale became the key weapon to obtain competitive advantages. In the 1970s, through research on the rapid rise of the Japanese industry, the foundation for competition was shifted to the quality of product. By then, the foundation for industrial competition gradually transformed from quantity-based competition to quality-based competition. In the 1980s, the trend towards speed-based competition appeared. In 1988, the concept of time-based competition (Stalk, 1988) led to a radical change in the research on the foundation for competition (Stalk & Hout, 1990; Blackburn, 1991). The strategy of time-based competition requires taking flexible production and management as the basis, accelerating the release of new products based on high quality and low cost, and making timely responses to customer demands. The key point of such competition is to reduce the time of every process, from product development, production to the final delivery to customers, to obtain competitive advantages.

The research of Arthur D. Little (1992) showed that with the rapid growth of market, if the budget cost was kept unchanged and the launch of new products was postponed by 6 months, the profits would possibly decrease by 17% to 35%. On the contrary, if new products were launched as scheduled and the development cost was increased by 50%, the profits would only decrease by 4%. Obviously, speed plays a significant role in market competition. Many enterprises have already recognized the importance of competition speed and implemented it in competitive practices.

Case Study 1
Haier

Haier believes that the rapidness of the Internet enables them to recognize that: enterprises without speed will surely be eliminated. Those enterprises which are not connected to network will be abandoned by network. Even those which are connected to network but have no competitiveness will also be abandoned. Without speed, an enterprise cannot get an order, fulfill an order or provide one-stop service. The objective of speediness is to realize "Three Zeros": zero inventory, zero distance from user and zero operating capital. ①

Kevin Rollins, vice president of DELL, once said that the biggest management challenge of DELL was to accelerate every process of business operation. Since the unit of product life cycle has already been changed from year to month, if enterprises cannot make rapid response, they will surely be eliminated. Walmart became a strong performer in its industry due to its ability to make rapid responses. Xerox was aware that slow product development would weaken its competitiveness, so it adopted the strategy of rapid innovation and reconstructed the processes to create brilliant achievements. HP used the concept of "stretching objectives" to reduce the development cycle of new products, improve quality and increase the yield by times. All such things prove that time has already become an important competitive element and played an important role in competitions.

It is thus clear that to hold an invincible position in the modern environment with fierce competition, not only rapid innovation but also systematic management of innovation knowledge is required to make organization innovation systematic and sustained. Under such premise, TIM proposes the concept of all-time innovation.

① website of Haier. http://www.haier.com/cn/haier/culture/faith5_09.asp.2006-10-05

6.1.2 Connotations and characteristics of all-time innovation

All-time innovation means that to seek continuous competitive advantages in the environment of time-based competition, enterprises take powerful measures and make full use of time resources to shorten the time of responding to customer demands and launch high-quality new products rapidly at low cost, thus satisfying customer demands and obtaining competitive advantages in market. All-time innovation is a strategy of innovation and a concept of innovation, which requires employees to maintain the consciousness of innovation at any time, have the courage to innovate and solve problems in the most appropriate way rather than sticking to convention and observing all rules and regulations.

According to the different applications of time resources, all-time innovation is mainly reflected in impromptu innovation, instant innovation and continuous innovation. Impromptu innovation is the flash of inspiration and the solidification of creativity on specific issues; instant innovation is the timely, rapid and creative solution to a certain problem; continuous innovation is to innovate in an uninterrupted way to improve the efficiency of innovation by utilizing network technologies and information technologies and effectively eliminating time difference.

Impromptu innovation is very random. By consciously accumulating creative thinking on a daily basis, it aims to improve the mode of daily behavior and make preparations for possible changes in innovation. For example, Wuxi Little Swan Group encourages its employees to write their ideas on a sticky note and put it up on an idea board. Then, such ideas are collected and systemized to pick out valuable ideas which can be put into practices. Besides, the bulletin board systems and online forums of many companies have such a function. Research in such fields is closely combined with knowledge management and especially close to research on the explicit transformation of tacit knowledge. Instant innovation features strong timeliness. When a certain change occurs, organizations have to make immediate responses to be adapted to such a change. Under normal circumstances, there is no existing method to adapt to the change, so it requires rapid innovation. It is mainly realized by a series of methods like accelerating information collection, improving efficiency of communication and improving the designing process. Continuous innovation is organizing various innovations by time and forming an innovation time network without point of discontinuity. It makes organization innovation more systematic and objectives more explicit and effectively uses the knowledge accumulated in all organization innovations.

(I) Impromptu innovation

According to the theory of impromptu innovation, innovation should not be restricted to a certain department or stage, such as an "Innovation Week". Innovation requires the organic combination between actual demands and the burst of inspiration in certain organizational contexts. Impromptu innovation may occur at any stage of the product life cycle not just at the stage of gestation or recession.

Impromptu innovation requires all members of an organization to use their creative skills at any time and better solve practical problems in a more proper way. However, impromptu innovation is not arbitrary innovation. Kao (2000) once drew an appropriate analogy with jazz.

According to Kao, jazz, like enterprises, includes a series of balancing actions. Players have to exercise according to established rules, procedures, arrangements and music scores. They have to expand forwards, upwards and outwards, so they will never be self-satisfied and self-contented. Different from classic music, Kao stated, jazz has no fatal error in improvisation. Classic music fans cannot forgive any error of the player, but no error exists in jazz, which has only unexpected notes in accordance with basic rules of harmony. Inharmonious notes or arrhythmic notes are not necessarily wrong. On the contrary, the challenge of jazz is to introduce such notes in improvisation and to bring "outside" things inside, thus improving or upgrading the vigor of music.

Firstly, impromptu innovation has to expand forward, upwards and outwards; secondly, impromptu innovation has established organizational contexts. It always occurs in specific organizational contexts and serves specific organizational objectives. Therefore, impromptu innovation has to be arranged according to certain rules and procedures. However, such rules and procedures are just instructional but not prescriptive, so, instead of ordering about impromptu innovation, they can only drive impromptu innovation and provide impromptu innovation with a space to expand forward, upwards and outwards.

At the same time, as a form of innovation, impromptu innovation is confronted with many uncertain factors. It means that impromptu innovation requires constant attempts, so failure is unavoidable. Failure can be seen as an inharmonious note in impromptu innovation. Failure may not be wrong. The challenge of impromptu innovation is to learn from failure and find a way to succeed in failure. Therefore, impromptu innovation needs a relaxed culture and atmosphere and must encourage experiments and allow failure.

Impromptu innovation relies on the collection and disposal of different kinds of information. In other words, effective impromptu innovation is built on a high-efficiency information system. Firstly, information system provides impromptu innovation with a new basis. Impromptu innovation doesn't appear out of nowhere, but it occurs based on practical demands. High-efficiency information system can provide a great deal of information, thus selecting valuable points of innovation at a high speed. Secondly, information system can stimulate information, thereby stimulating the generation of creative ideas. Only by exchanging information and constantly improving creativity can commercialized ideas be formed. Simon once pointed out that a necessary but not sufficient condition for innovation is that the appearance of creative ideas requires normal logic thinking and sufficient relevant knowledge to solve problems. Leonard and Straus (1997), in an article titled "Putting Your Company's Whole Brain to Work", point out that innovation takes place when different ideas, perceptions, and ways of processing and judging information collide. Besides, high-efficiency information system can also stimulate the spread of innovation. It is the key to the commercialization of innovation. Finally, high-efficiency information system can also collect and generate experiences and lessons from the process of innovation, accumulate all kinds of knowledge, expand the knowledge base and make preparations for possible innovation in the future.

In a word, information technology not only creates the historical background for impromptu innovation, but also makes impromptu innovation possible. Metcalfe's law states that the value of a telecommunications network is proportional to the square of the number of connected users of the system. With the increased diversity and spread of users, the power of creativity also increases exponentially. This is the intelligent basis for impromptu innovation. Only with both an intelligent basis and a sound management can impromptu innovation be put into practice.

Impromptu innovation only happens in organizations with flexible, independent and test-encouraging culture.

Firstly, in organizations which implement impromptu innovation, the leader's role is to coordinate the contradictions in impromptu innovation rather than give orders. What leaders should do is to determine organizational strategy rather than establish a specific tactical route. Leaders are often not those who are closest to the market. Although they have forward-looking strategic insights, they cannot have an insight into the changes of the market. However, only employees who are closest to market can have profound understanding of such changes, so they are really the closest to the correct answers. Leaders only need to set a good example for employees and explicitly inform organizations of strategic objectives. What GE does is that it sets a role model for employees. Leaders on all levels constantly become "heroes" one after another, setting an example for all employees and leaving employees with the decision-making power to solve problems. In the organization of impromptu innovation, innovation is neither a slogan nor a product of sudden whim at a certain moment. Instead, it is a strategic objective and what organizations depend on for existence. Employees' performance of innovation should also be listed as one of the indicators for their own performance appraisal.

Secondly, organizations should support employees' impromptu innovation in all aspects. Innovation is risky, so it might fail. Therefore, it requires organizations to encourage experiments, tolerate failure and provide sufficient resources. Impromptu innovation needs not only sufficient resources, but also plenty of time for employees to innovate. 3M offers employees 15% of working time as discretionary time, which provides a time guarantee for impromptu innovation.

Thirdly, impromptu innovation requires proper organizational structure. In traditional enterprises, the organization structure stipulates a circuitous relationship which allows dialogue and issues orders. However, information technologies abolish such an obligatory liaison route and replace it with a flexible network, which allows individuals to freely communicate with each other at any time. This is the organizational foundation for impromptu innovation.

Fourthly, impromptu innovation should be a process during which both organizations and individuals make progress together. Impromptu innovation requires employees to find and correctly utilize usable resources available in specific organizational contexts and processes. This is a process for organizations to increase asset value and a process for employees to improve their own capabilities.

Furthermore, impromptu innovation is not individual but collective, which requires teamwork. The generation of ideas requires linking different knowledge systems and inputting and applying unexpected knowledge. IT technologies can shorten the spatial distance between such liking and inputting and accelerate the realization of ideas. Due to the application of IT technologies, the communication between individuals becomes more frequent and a cross-border network always emerges in response to the needs of the times. Such a network, as an intangible network linking people, is usually formed at the right moment. For example, if a project brings together individuals from different departments within an organization, the links among such individuals will not be terminated after such a project is completed. Instead, they will often have some informal discussions. Generally speaking, such a network exists in any organization. With the development of an organization, such network relationships will become increasingly complex and the communication will become more and more frequent. In such a way, individuals who often communicate with each other will form an intangible community.

In such an intangible community, due to frequent communication, tacit understanding among individuals will be formed. Therefore, members of such a community are able to express their own thoughts without much explanation. It facilitates the mutual communication among members within the community and stimulates the generation of impromptu innovation ideas. However, such a tacit understanding may become an obstacle for communication between community members and other members of organization. To effectively implement impromptu innovation throughout the organization, it is necessary to codify such a tacit understanding, make such tacit knowledge explicit and lay an acceptable foundation within the organization, thus enabling organization members to understand and have common mental models, facilitating communication and guiding their innovation.

It should be noted that impromptu innovation is not an independent and irrelevant event. Impromptu innovation is related to various factors like knowledge of organization and individuals, values of organization, etc. Impromptu innovations occur randomly, but due to the existence of such factors, they have certain connections between each other.

Impromptu innovation occurs in certain organizational contexts. The business fields of organization determine the scope of disciplines which are involved in impromptu innovation. The value orientation of an organization plays a role as a measurement scale. Only ideas of impromptu innovation screened by an organization can be put into practice. 3M is known for its century long history of innovation. In recent years, it has been involved in diversified development in several fields, but its innovation basically focuses on the production technology of adhesive tapes which satisfy market demands. In other words, innovation is based on existing knowledge of an organization. Such knowledge is gradually accumulated during the development of an organization, thereby forming an innovation pool of the organization. When employees discover any problem during work, they combine their own knowledge and relevant information found in the pool for impromptu innovation. To ensure the sustainable development of an organization, the knowledge in the innovation pool needs to be constantly expanded and updated. The organization must constantly supplement the innovation pool with newly generated experiences and lessons of impromptu innovation, guaranteeing that challenges can be transformed to experiences and encouraging the sharing of experiences with others. A virtuous circle should be established to enable an organization to constantly accumulate knowledge during impromptu innovation and to provide strong support for future innovations.

Case Study 2
3M and Impromptu Innovation

3M is famous for creating an innovative environment for its employees. The objective of the company is: 30% of the annual sales come from new products developed in the previous four years. Its legendary innovation-oriented spirit has made 3M one of the most admirable enterprises in the U.S. for many years in succession. The atmosphere of collective coordination, regular liaison system and initiatives of employees enable innovation to come into existence at any time in 3M. When 3M was in its initial stage, the laboratory director gathered together employees every Friday afternoon, drinking coffee and making presentations of their own research plans. By far, 3M has established over a hundred subsidiaries all over China, so it is difficult to gather everyone to communicate with each other. Through meetings, interdisciplinary teams, computer network and databases, managers bring together all members. It is clearly stated in the company's tenet that: no idea for a new product will be ever stifled in the cradle. All members of the company make great efforts to establish the core values which focus on independence, reformation, individual initiatives and creativity. That's because 3M knows that it has to attempt thousands of new product ideas to maximize its success. It considers mistakes and failures as normal constituents of creation and reformation. In fact, its philosophy seems to be that "if you never make mistakes, you cannot achieve anything." However, just as what subsequent facts show, many "big mistakes" became very successful products of 3M. The birth of Post-it was attributed to a series of sudden inspirations rather than a careful plan. Old employees of 3M love to share the story of a chemist. The chemist splashed a new chemical mixture over her tennis shoes by accident. A few days later, she noticed the part of shoes splashed by such chemical mixture didn't dirty. Such chemical mixture later became Scotchgard fabric protector.②

② Gundling E, *The 3M Way to Innovation: Balancing People and Profit.* Beijing: Huaxia Publishing House, 2002

(II) Instant innovation

It is impossible to remain invincible in fierce market competition just by relying on impromptu innovation. Impromptu innovation is discretionary in a relaxed atmosphere and is suitable for idea generation. As a business behavior, it has to pay attention to the speed and effectiveness of innovation.

Enterprises may be confronted with unprecedented problems, which are often strongly time-dependent. It requires organizations to solve such problems in a better and more appropriate way within a limited time period.

Instant innovation is a kind of innovation applied at first, i.e. solving problems in a better and more appropriate way. Meanwhile, it emphasizes timeliness, which means solving problems within a limited time period. Technology takes people to a brand new time-space domain, such as the Internet Age, which requires being faster and instantaneous. Immediateness sets a still higher demand for the flexibility and reaction speed of an organization.

Instant innovation refers to the capability to make a response to and satisfy customers' demands by innovating immediately to customers' demand. Here, customers are not restricted to the service objects of an organization. They refer to the service objects of innovation in general, either the customers of the organization or members or certain departments of such an organization.

Compared with impromptu innovation, instant innovation focuses more on the implementation of innovation from the generation of ideas to the commercialization, which is often a complex process and requires more rapidness.

However, few organizations can make it. Raymond Yeh et al. (2002) believed that it was caused by the obstacles that hindered the relationships among entities like customers, employees, processes, knowledge, supply chain partners, etc. To overcome such obstacles, it is necessary to understand the transformation of value creation and delivering approaches. In the traditional concept of value chain, value is gradually accumulated along the chain. Only when products or services are finally delivered to customers, the highest value can be achieved. Value is no longer transferred in a chained mode. With the development and application of information technology in business competition and the appearance of e-commerce and virtual markets, the traditional value chain becomes interlaced and forms a complex value network. On such a network, value can be immediately created in the form of information at any point and can be easily packaged and delivered. Raymond believed that it's possible to realize instant innovation by breaking the obstacles among entities based on five principles, i.e. instant value alliance, instant study, instant adaptation, instant implementation and instant connection.

Instant value alliance believes that every transaction may win or lose customers' loyalty. Therefore, it requires offering every customer satisfying services in every business activity. That's because customer share is more important than market share. Instant value alliance means understanding and paying close attention to customers, actively inviting customers to participate in design, and forecasting customers' demands earlier.

Instant learning is embodied in the process-based knowledge management; knowledge is decomposed into easily understandable pieces, thus enabling employees to study and use them instantly.

Instant adaptation: while fully authorizing individual employees to create values for customers, they should also be integrated with the group objectives and directions as if every cell in nature is an independent individual of a whole. To realize instant adaptation, a company needs all-process management, which can enable all parts of the company to be allied with each other rather than competing with each other. It requires developing and realizing the core capabilities with a fixed objective and a trust-based corporate culture.

Instant implementation: "no contact and no boundary". To eliminate the human disturbance in operation requires companies to have two standards, that is, rapidness and zero defects. Rapidness means to be able to instantly create new process or rapidly reconfigure the existing course of work to respond to changes. Zero defects require that at any time, the results of the course of work can meet the strict demand of customers.

Instant connection: companies, suppliers, companies which produce complementary goods and customers are considered as different parts of the same ecological system. Based on mutual trust, establish strategic partnership, fulfill common obligations, reach the unified thoughts and behaviors, share information on new products, industrial development direction and market, form the consciousness of commitment to each other including risk sharing and high degree of trust, and further weaken the concept of enterprise boundaries.

The key to instant value alliance is emphasizing customer management and bringing forward the philosophy that customer share is more than important than market share. Instant connection refers to the management of suppliers and manufacturers of complementary goods. In fact, they both aim to meet the requirement of the rapidly constructing value chain, so they both can be considered as instant value chain.

Instant value chain requires organizations to adjust strategies at any time according to market changes and to form a stable, risk-sharing, trust-based and mutual-commitment-based value network together with customers, suppliers and companies which produce complementary goods, thus seeking common development, making constant progress and forming a spiraling alliance of a virtuous circle (Figure 6-1).

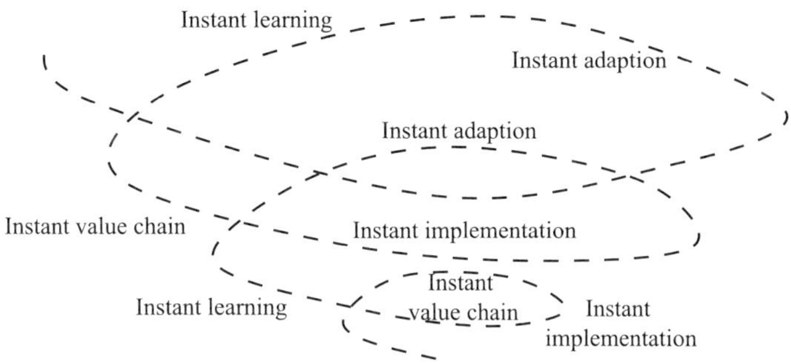

Figure 6-1 Spiraling ring of instant innovation

Case Study 3

Haier's Instant Innovation: Development of "Mike Freezer" in 17 hours

Michael Jemal (Mike), president of Haier American Trading Company, received a lot of customer feedback, saying normal freezers were too deep to pick up things conveniently. During "Haier Global Executives' Conference 2001", Mike considered designing a kind of refrigerator with the upper layer being normal horizontal refrigerator and the lower layer being drawers on a whim. Having been informed of Mike's idea, the Refrigerator Department designated four scientific researchers to work on it overnight. Through simultaneous engineering, they finished the prototype in as short as 17 hours. Furthermore, they later created the second-generation products beyond users' imagination. During the welcome banquet for the conference, when such a prototype covered by red silk appeared in the hall, loud cheers rang out continuously for a long time. Then, Ma Jian, Director of the Refrigerator Department, presented the work born out of the interaction between the business department and the engineering department, and declared to name this product after Mike. ③

③ RCID Haier University Research Data, 2003

Case Study 4

Haier's Instant Innovation: Development of "Qirong Ice Bar" in 12 Hours

On January 3, 2003, a special train carrying new products of Haier Xiaokang arrived at Wuhan, where local dealers and customers showed great interest in one of Haier Xiaokang new products, Haier Ice Bar. Especially, Liu Qirong, manager of Wuhan Industry and Trade Department Store, was so delighted with it that he could hardly bear to put it down. He thought that such an ice bar would be even better with additional ice-making function, which would enable customers to add ice while drinking wine or beverage. Therefore, Liu Qirong wrote such a suggestion on Haier Xiaokang Product Comment Card. Onsite workers of Haier thought it was a very good idea, so they submitted the card to the headquarters via fax immediately. Developers in the headquarters of Haier designed such a product overnight. After 12 hours, such a product, an ice bar with ice-making function, was born and called "Qirong Ice Bar" by developers. To enable customers to understand such a product, "Qirong Ice Bar" was directly delivered to Guangzhou by plane on the morning of January 4. When Liu Qirong was told such an ice bar was loaded on Xiaokang Special Train, he couldn't help lamenting that: "I had never imagined that you could develop a product in as short as 12 hours after I came up with a sudden idea. Now, I truly know what 'Haier speed' is and what 'satisfying users' demands' is. I'm really surprised."④

(III) Continuous innovation

Continuous innovation believes that innovation is not just an event but a time-based process. Shapiro (2001) considered continuous innovation as a blueprint for surviving and thriving in an age of change and believed that the differences between excellent enterprises and laggard enterprises originated from the diversities in continuous

④ Haier Website. http://www.haier.com/cn/service/viewl.asp?newsid=1397.2006-10-05

innovation capabilities. In the book *24/7 Innovation*, Shapiro analyzed how to realize continuous innovation from four aspects, namely strategies, technologies, processes and personnel.

Through the description of 24/7 continuous innovation, Shapiro stated that forced by the fierce competitions and constantly changing market situations, enterprises had to make endless efforts to innovate so as to seek survival and development.

TIM believes that without continuous innovation no sustained competitive advantages can be achieved. Normally, innovation behaviors have certain objectives, but the results of innovation cannot be expected. Without systematic organization, results of continuous innovation are disorderly and unsystematic. Just like a team without common objectives, even if everyone is an expert in his own field, no satisfying results will be obtained. Only when there are common objectives which are accepted by everyone can the performance of such a team be maximized.

If continuous innovation emphasizes the uninterrupted nature of innovation behaviors, the significance of sustainable innovation is that it emphasizes the sustainable development of innovation behaviors, the synergy between innovation behaviors and organizational strategies and the pooling and systematization of existing innovation, thus making them a knowledge and idea pool for subsequent innovations.

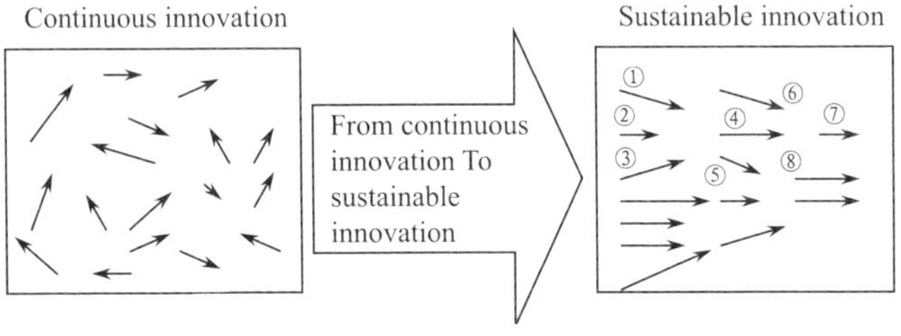

Figure 6-2 From continuous innovation to sustainable innovation

In Figure 6-2, continuous innovation will create many innovation ideas, but such ideas are scattered and cannot be banded together like strands of a rope to create sustainable competitiveness of enterprises. Different from continuous innovation, all results of sustainable innovation are "forwarding" and serve organizational strategies. Besides, the figure shows that the innovation system can be roughly classified into three stages: "1", "2" and "3" belong to the first stage; "4", "5" and "6" belong to the second stage; "7" and "8" belong to the third stage. The stages of innovation development and the stages of enterprise development are consistent. In addition to the clearly defined stages, the systematization of sustainable innovation is also embodied in the positive role of innovation at a previous stage in promoting the innovation at latter stages. For example, "4" and "5" in the figure are promoted by "1", "2" and "3", while "7" is promoted by "4" and emerging "6"; "5" and other innovations at this stage jointly promote the formation of "8".

Simply speaking, TIM believes that only sustainable innovation can effectively help enterprises obtain sustainable competitive advantages in fierce market competitions. Besides the openness like that of continuous innovation, it is also systematic, staged and predictable.

Case Study 5
Sustainable Innovation

Zhang Ruimin, CEO of Haier Group, believes that the sustainable and stable development of Haier since its foundation originates from sustainable innovation. In particular, Haier's experiences in sustainable innovation are: firstly, sustainable innovation requires sustainable and constant learning. For Haier, innovation is carried out in the constantly changing market. Such innovation requires learning and seizing opportunities at any time. Otherwise, no one can adapt to the changes of the market. Secondly, the premise to guarantee sustainable innovation is to establish a learning-based team. Innovation relies on a team, which must be pressurized and motivated to learn. Pressure is necessary for learning and innovation, and pressure comes from the innovative objectives of the team. The objective of the Haier team is to create a famous brand in the world. Finally, the self-driving force of sustainable innovation is to let every employee become the subject of indigenous innovation. Haier believes that "internationalized enterprises consist of internationalized talents". Therefore, everyone in Haier must study and innovate to become a strategic business unit of indigenous innovation. [5]

Besides, continuous innovation based on time difference has become an all time-space innovation method which is widely applied in enterprises at present. Time difference, as an objective and inevitable fact, used to bother enterprises which needed trans-meridian work contacts, but with the help of current networking and information technologies, the use of time difference has become the new method of all time-space innovation. For example, due to the 12-hour time difference between America and India, setting up a research and development center in India can guarantee the all-time operation of enterprises. In other words, when local employees in America return home, their employees in India just start working. In China, Haier's development of Bluetooth network household electric appliances is one of the successful cases.

Case Study 6
Continuous Innovation

Haier and Ericsson began to develop Bluetooth network household electric appliances in a relay since April 10, 2001. In as short as three months, they finished the first-stage development on June 10. If they followed the traditional development way, however, it would cost at least half a year. Researchers of Haier worked till 9 p.m., which was the afternoon office hour of Ericsson, i.e. 2 p.m. The research was carried

⑤ RCID Haier University Research Data, 2006

out in a relay. In Sweden, people went back home from work at 6 p.m., i.e. 1 a.m. in China. After that, researchers of both parties didn't work, but the computers could keep exchanging data, thus realizing 24-hour uninterrupted development in a relay. [6]

To sum up, all-time innovation is the organic combination of impromptu innovation, instant innovation and continuous innovation. It is the result which integrates the innovation system of organization and time, an emerging competitive resource, and an important constituent of TIM. All-time innovation is an effective method to improve the innovation performance of innovation from three aspects, namely quality, quantity and speed.

Firstly, impromptu innovation emphasizes the formation of various creative ideas at any time and place. It can be taken as the creative library of all-time innovation. As highlighted before, impromptu innovation is a process of coupling inspiration and actual demands and is often formed in an unpredictable way. The creative ideas formed by impromptu innovation may be small improvements on certain processes or products and may thoroughly overturn the technological paradigm of current products. In other words, it may be incremental innovation, significant innovation and even breakthrough innovation. The objective of research on impromptu innovation is to stimulate the generation of creative ideas and offer feasible innovation plans for the development of enterprise.

Secondly, it is to realize creative ideas. Instant innovation emphasizes the implementation of creative ideas, especially the instant implementation of various creative ideas, to shorten the lead time and acquire first-mover advantages. Even if no first-mover advantage can be obtained, it is necessary to closely follow the first movers and launch more competitive products to improve an enterprise's executive force and profit-making capacity. Instant innovation is to instantly realize the

⑥ RCID Haier University Research Data, 2006

creative ideas coming from impromptu innovation.

Finally, continuous innovation is a sequence of impromptu innovation and instant innovation throughout the enterprise and bands together impromptu innovation and instant innovation to form an innovation system, which guides the innovative direction of the enterprise and supports its sustainable development.

6.2 All-value chain innovation

6.2.1 Necessity of all-value chain innovation

As a brand-new innovation model which considers integrating innovative resources based on the value network of enterprises, all-value chain innovation includes the innovation of internal value chain and the innovation of external value chain. Internal value chain innovation refers to integrating the innovative resources from R&D, manufacturing, purchasing, marketing and finance departments, forming innovative thoughts to realize the innovation objectives, such as reducing product cost or product differentiation. External value chain innovation refers to effectively integrating innovation resources from suppliers, customers, competitors, potential entrants, universities and scientific research institutions, improving the indigenous innovation capability of enterprises, accelerating innovation speed and reducing innovation risks. This section discusses the necessity, connotations, nature, significance, characteristics and various forms of all-value chain innovation.

(I) Historical background of all-value chain innovation

In the past 30 years, competition has changed from that between individual enterprises to that between value chains. The scope of enterprise management not only covers the resources of enterprise itself, but also extends to suppliers and customers. The application of the Internet can improve both the communication among different parts of the value chain and the efficiency of value chain. What is more important, the Internet will change the structure of the value chain. Under the new economic situation, since the mid-1990s, more and more enterprises have moved to cooperative competition from confrontational competition. The strategic alliance becomes a new trend in business after the great upsurge of mergers and acquisitions. In the strategic alliance, many enterprises cooperate with each other in terms of value chain to form a value network. The value chain in every enterprise is a node in the value network. Competitive advantages are created by sharing resources inside the network, while dynamic competitive relationship is created outside the network.

Since the innovation process of modern technologies is a complex process involving multiple organizations, users, component suppliers, other governments, individuals and even relevant government organs, enterprises' environment will be taken into consideration during the process of innovation. Accordingly, innovation sources and other functional concepts like R&D, marketing and manufacturing are also expanded, while the collaboration and coordination among functional departments become more important and difficult.

In other words, the changes of a competitive environment require all-value chain innovation. The wide application of information technology makes all-value chain innovation possible.

(II) The integration of external value chain helps reduce innovation cost and risk of enterprises

The main motivations for all-value chain innovation can be summarized as given below: (1) All-value chain innovation can save the cost of technology transfers and exchanges. (2) Intra-industry and inter-industry technology spillover may happen. The spillover effect of some industrial technologies is very high. To make the "external" research and development internalized, enterprises establish cooperative research and development alliances. (3) Current high-tech innovations often rely on interdisciplinary cooperation, but few enterprises have broad knowledge. Therefore, taking full use of the knowledge of upstream and downstream enterprises, users and alliances helps reduce the risks of indigenous innovation of enterprises.

(III) The integration of external value chain helps in upgrading and improving core capabilities of an enterprise

How to build new core capabilities or improve existing core capabilities to obtain competitive advantages is a common concern in both academia and the industry. Establishing strategic and technological alliances and forming an external network is an important approach to build and improve competences (Chen, Wang & Xu, 1999). The advantages of all-value chain innovation are mainly embodied in: (1) sharing the research and development cost and spreading risks; (2) obtaining the scale advantages in research and development; (3) stimulating the flow of knowledge among enterprises and obtaining technical expertise outside enterprises; (4) establishing complementary advantages among enterprise partners; (5) rapidly obtaining new technology or markets and stimulating the upgradating and improvement of core capabilities through technical learning during the process of all-value chain innovation; and (6) enabling enterprises to concentrate on the research and development activities to improve core capabilities.

(IV) The integration of external value chain helps in expanding internal innovation sources of an enterprise

Any functional department within the internal value chain may become an innovation source. Integrating the internal value chain means expanding the internal innovation sources of enterprises. As for innovation, the research and development department generates creative ideas in terms of products and process design; the production department generates creative ideas to reduce product cost and improve differentiation; the marketing department generates creative ideas in terms of marketing and brand building; the financial department decreases the cost of final products through creative ideas in reducing capital cost.

6.2.2 Connotation and characteristics of all-value chain innovation

(I) Connotations of all-value chain innovation

The connotations of all-value chain innovation can be summarized as below: taking market and customer demands as orientation; aiming to improve enterprise performance and core capabilities /competitive competences; taking cooperative commerce, cooperative competition and multi-win principles as operating model; applying management methods, information technology, network technology and integrated technology to integrate various innovation sources in the value chain and realizing the effective planning and control of information flow, material flow, capital flow, value flow and work flow throughout the value chain; accordingly, integrating all functional departments, enterprises, customers, distributors, suppliers, service providers and strategic alliances to form a complete innovation network. Figure 6-3 is a schematic diagram of all-value chain innovation network.

The essence of all-value chain is to include the whole value chain inside and outside the enterprise into the innovation process of enterprises based on the methods of value chain analysis so as to realize the value increase and obtain core competitive advantages. The innovation process in a broad sense involves multiple departments or units to varying degrees, including the research & development department, manufacturing department, marketing department, financial department, suppliers, users, competitors and other stakeholders.

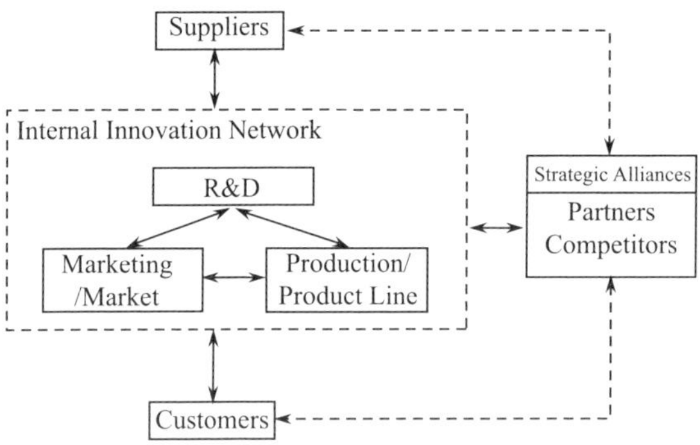

Figure 6-3 Schematic diagram of all-value chain innovation network

All-value chain innovation starts from the perspective of stakeholders, centers on the core of technology innovation, trying to obtain sustainable core capabilities and competitive advantages, and realize value creation and value increase. Different from traditional innovation activities in terms of supply chain like business process reengineering and strategic outsourcing, it includes enterprises and stakeholders related to value activities in technology innovation activities, such as inviting suppliers to participate in new product development, user-enterprise interactive innovation, R&D and strategic alliances of enterprises, etc.

(II) Characteristics of all-value chain innovation

The innovation of enterprise has always been independently undertaken and completed by the R&D department. Subsequently, with the appearance of concurrent design mode and more and more trans-department synergy innovations inside the strategic alliance of enterprises as well as inter-enterprise cooperation, it has broken the original concept that the innovation should be independently undertaken by the R&D department. In the recent 10 years, with the rise of supply chain management theories and the rapid development of network information technology, it is possible to integrate the innovation resources inside all value networks based on the thoughts of all value chain and expand it in business circles. All-value chain innovation, as a brand-new innovation model, has its unique characteristics (Figure 6-4).

In Figure 6-4, we can see that the way to describe the characteristics of innovation is the degree of stakeholders' participation in innovation and value chain integration.

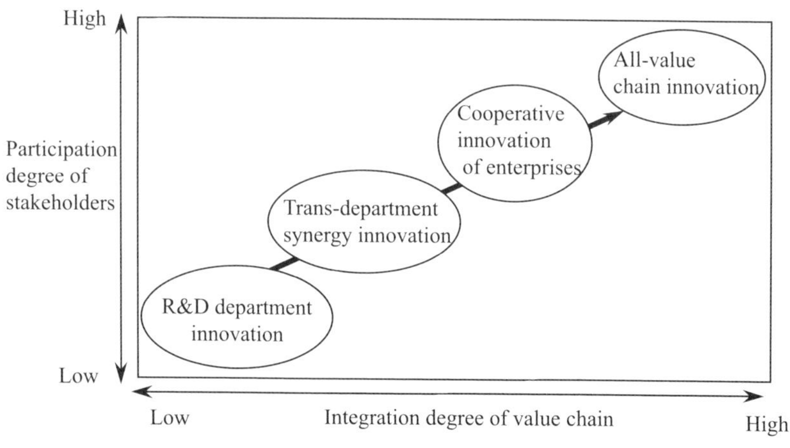

Figure 6-4 Schematic diagram of all-value chain innovation characteristics

1. Characteristic 1 of all-value chain innovation: high degree of stakeholders participating in innovation

Ansoff, the economist who coined the term "stakeholders", believed that a firm's objective should be derived by balancing the conflicting claims of the various stakeholders in the firm: managers, workers, stockholders, suppliers, vendors and customers. The degree of stakeholders participating in innovation includes the magnitude and depth of their participation in innovation. The magnitude of stakeholders participating in innovation means that enterprises include all stakeholders in the process of technology innovation. For example, enterprise shareholders determine whether to invest in new products based on factors like the technologies of new products, market risks and future returns; suppliers participate in all stages like establishing the development strategy of new products, developing new products, etc.; at the early stage of new product development, enterprises use user information, user toolbox and modular innovation to enable users to design products; forming strategic alliance with competitors or cooperative enterprises; carrying out innovation activities based on industry-university-research integration together with universities and government research institutions, etc. The depth of stakeholders participating in innovation refers to the degree to which they participate in technology innovation activities inside enterprises. Since the technology spillover existed between enterprises, moral hazards and other opportunistic behaviors may harm the cooperative innovation among enterprises; reasonable profit distribution mechanism and synergy between enterprises are very important.

2. Characteristic 2 of all-value chain innovation: high degree of value chain integration

In the customer-value-oriented market competition environment, the customer demands are volatile. Competition between enterprises no longer relies on local advantages but the system efficiency or comprehensive competition advantages based on value chain. Only by obtaining system competitive advantages can enterprises build core capabilities which the competitor cannot imitate in a short amount of time and obtain sustainable competitive advantages. The key to form system efficiency and comprehensive competitive advantages relies on the level of value chain integration, including the integration level of internal value chain, external supplier value chain, channel value chain and strategic alliances. From R&D department innovation, trans-department cooperative innovation, cooperative innovation between enterprises to all-value chain innovation, the higher the integration level of internal value chain and external value chain is, the higher the created value is.

6.2.3 Form of all-value chain innovation

Taking enterprise as boundary, value chain can be divided into internal value chain and external value chain. All-value chain is to form an organic whole through the interaction and integration between internal value chain and external value chain. As stated above, all-value chain innovation is to integrate the external value chain network into the internal technology innovation activities from the perspective of all value chain network, i.e. through the synergy and integration of innovation activities between the external value chain and internal value chain, obtaining an effect which cannot be achieved by individual activities.

Here, internal value chain innovation refers to enabling all functional departments, including purchasing, manufacturing, marketing, finance and R&D, to participate in the technology innovation activities, including participating in new product development and process innovation activities. Innovation is no longer the exclusive activity of the R&D department. It is different from the internal value chain innovation in a general sense, which refers to self-innovations along the value chain, such as adopting flexible manufacturing technologies and production methods like JIT (Just in Time). External value chain innovation refers to the upstream and downstream innovation along the value chain, strategic alliance of research and development, etc. For example, suppliers participate in developing and improving new products and processes. The main forms of all value chain innovations include suppliers participating in innovation, users participating in innovation and strategic alliance of R&D.

(I) Users participate in innovation

Professor Eric von Hippel of Massachusetts Institute of Technology (MIT) Sloan School of Management, in his book *The Sources of Innovation* in 1988, put forward the concept of "functional source of innovation", which broke through the traditional concept that technology innovation was mainly completed by manufacturers. Through a great deal of empirical research on previous innovation, Eric von Hippel discovered that there were different innovation subjects in different industries. In many industries, product users and suppliers were technology innovators.

Eric von Hippel carried out in-depth research on user innovation for a long time. As early as the 1970s, he published an article named "Customers as Innovators". Later, he put forward the concept of "lead user" innovation and developed user innovation toolbox, which enabled manufacturers to effectively integrate the thoughts of lead users into technology innovation activities inside the enterprise. Riggs and von Hippel (1994) discovered that in the industry of scientific equipment, users and manufacturers were encouraged by different incentives to innovate. Users attached importance to the significance of science, while manufacturers paid attention to the significance of commerce. Generally, innovation with high scientific significance was developed by equipment users; innovation with extremely high commercial significance was developed by manufacturers. Stefan Thaomke and Hippel, in the article named "Customers as Innovators" published in the *Harvard Business Review* in 2002, proposed that under the contexts of network environment and ICT (information communication technologies), manufacturers adopted network technologies to enable customers to participate in new product development activities.

1. Reasons why users participate in innovation

"Listen carefully to customer demands and then design new products to satisfy and even surpass customer demands." Such a principle is pursued by many industries, but now it is being confronted with challenges. At present, with increasingly rapid changes of many markets, the shortened product lifecycle requires accelerated product innovation. Product development is difficult because the customers have demand information and the product manufacturers have the solutions and it is hard to coordinate the two sides. A traditional way is that manufacturers obtain relevant information through various methods like investigating market survey and collecting industrial statistical data. However, the customer demands are mostly so complex that even customers cannot put their own demands in words. Therefore, such a process is capital-intensive and time-consuming. To fully understand customer demands often requires enormous cost and the results are always not accurate enough. Therefore, traditional product development is a tortuous and long process filled with mistakes and many attempts. Before the satisfying solution is found, manufacturers and customers must communicate with each other many times and conduct repeated tests.

Enterprises must integrate the demands and interests of customers into their product designs. Antonio J. Bailetti and Paul F. Litva (1999), based on previous research, pointed out that the problems confronted by the existing product development are: (1) the complexness and dynamics of products and environment, one of the most important tasks of developers is to how to integrate customer demands into the details of product design; (2) insufficient attention to research on the designing process. Through research on how designers integrate information generated during the designing process and information on customer demands, they discovered that the biggest obstacle that hinders the integration of R&D and marketing is the method of how researchers obtain information on customer demands.

2. Users participate in the "company-customer" interactive model of innovation

In the cooperation between customers and companies, products can be designed by using standard modules, which are provided by manufacturers. To satisfy the rigorous demands of individual users, more and more products and services adopt the form of mass customization. Mass customization requires the wide application of interaction between manufacturers and customers in the process of product development and design. With the application of a flexible production mode and new communication technology, the combination between individual preferences and mass customization becomes possible and increasingly widespread. For example, in the past, IKEA promoted low-cost strategies relying on mass production and scale economy, but now they begin to apply mass customization and provide customized kitchenware services at standard prices.

Solveig Wikstron investigated the interaction between companies and customers and pointed out that many companies often adopted the "expanded 'company-customer' interactive mode" during the process of value creation. They actively enabled customers to participate in the designing, production and marketing and played a more active role in consumption; both companies and customers participated in the destructive stage (recovery and recycle of products). At present, customers are no longer confined to market research, transaction and consumption stage; more customers are invited to participate in the designing, production and marketing. Correspondingly, companies have extended their activities to the field of customer consumption. This means the "company-customer" interaction appears in all stages of value creation.

In the models above, companies play a dominant role in designing and production and are also the main provider of information on marketing activities, but customers participate in designing and determine what information to search for. Companies offer support to consuming activities and at the destructive stage. Such interaction aims to make it easier for consumers to obtain more values.

Case Study 7
Haier Users Participating in Innovation

In recent years, Haier has organized the activity of "I design my own refrigerator", which further embodied the concept of enabling Haier users to participate in innovation. Through such an activity, Haier has received more than 1 million orders of "customized" refrigerators every year. B2X customization schemes are launched on Haier E-commerce Platform, which offers over 9,200 basic models of products like refrigerator, air-conditioner and washing machine and over 20,000 basic models for free assembly. The participation of users (or potential users) in the early design or after sales feedback of products enables products to have higher quality and be more adapted to the individualized demands of users. For example, a consumer in Harbin proposed to order a refrigerator with right-handed door and special dimensions via e-mail. As a result, relevant technological design and manufacturing were finished in 4 days and such a specially customized refrigerator was delivered to their home in a week. ⑦

(II) Suppliers participate in innovation

The rise of supply chain management in the 1990s changed the traditional view that suppliers were only component suppliers of enterprises. The supply chain management theories emphasize that manufacturers should establish strategic partnership with upstream and downstream enterprises relying on advanced information network technology and entrust such enterprises to finish some tasks, while manufacturers should concentrate their attention and resources on the

---

⑦ Rebuild a "New" Haier. *Economic Daily*, 2001-08-08

core businesses which can create special values and do better than their competitors. The final objective is to reduce the launching cost of products to the greatest extent through a systematic management model, obtain maximum benefits and achieve a "win-win" situation. Based on aforesaid thoughts, the selection basis of suppliers is no longer restricted to the factors in a traditional supply relationship, namely price and logistics. Instead, it is more important to select suppliers, who can provide high-quality products, technology innovation, product designs, data and information integration level and quality assurance, and establish strategic partnership with them by signing a long-term contract and sharing benefits. Besides, the participation of suppliers in manufacturers' technology innovation also becomes a main form of strategic partnership.

In fact, since the 1980s, many foreign suppliers began to cooperate with users (mainly manufacturers) in innovation, be more engaged in users' innovation activities and enabled "suppliers to participate in technology innovation", including enabling suppliers to participate in users' technology improvement, new product development and service innovation. For example, the late 1980s witnessed the rise of SINPD (supplier involved new product development), i.e. manufacturers involved suppliers in the new product development. Many famous transnational corporations like Boeing, Chrysler and Toyota cooperated with their suppliers in innovation on a global scale and enabled suppliers to participate in their internal technology innovation.

1. Effect of suppliers participating in innovation

Suppliers have been engaged in the practices of technology innovation in foreign countries for more than 20 years. It greatly promoted the development of manufacturing industry in developed countries like Japan and America. Theoretical research in such fields is still making progress. Although scholars have different opinions on its effect, in general, it can be concluded as given below (Xu, et al., 2004).

(1) The benefits of "suppliers participating in technology innovation" to manufacturers include: 1) the synchronized combination between suppliers and manufacturers in terms of complementary assets and the assessment of various ideas at an early stage of development, thus greatly reducing the development time; 2) reducing the risk of product development, for example the risk of discovering errors and requiring redesigning at a later stage (engineering or trial production stage) of a new product development can be reduced; 3) increasing the flexibility of new product development; 4) improving product quality by sharing technology and information and screening various schemes, decreasing development cost by avoiding waste and unnecessary mistakes, improving market adaptability and reducing market risks by sharing market and technology information with suppliers who have advanced technical know-how.

(2) The benefits of "suppliers participating in technology innovation" to suppliers include: 1) the share of information and technologies with manufacturers and the communication and interaction with engineers can improve their own technological abilities and stimulate innovation; 2) the long-term cooperation with manufacturers enables suppliers to participate in the continuous innovation activities of manufacturers; the high expectations of manufacturers or alternative pressure of suppliers will surely stimulate suppliers' constant innovation activities; 3) by signing long-term contracts, the mutual trust between the two parties and the assets specificity of manufacturers will stimulate the long-term cooperation between the two parties, guarantee the benefits of suppliers and enable suppliers to be willing to invest more on the research and development of certain manufacturers.

2. Main forms of suppliers participating in innovation

(1) Roles of partner suppliers: selecting a few first-tier suppliers as the strategic partners. Strategic suppliers will help manufacturers improve comprehensive services, including be responsible for the whole subsystem, and participate in the design of new models at the

stage of conceptualization. With stronger technical capacities than other competitors, they can provide some suggestions or solutions to realize the expected price and performance objectives of customers. They test the components of products and can even test the components of other suppliers. At the pre-concept stage, suppliers and manufacturers jointly determine the specifications of subsystem. The two parties must communicate with each other frequently during the whole cycle of the design of the complex subsystem.

(2) Roles of mature suppliers: such suppliers design and manufacture complex components. Compared with partner suppliers, they have weaker technology capabilities, so they have a smaller influence on the design of manufacturers. Such suppliers may independently develop a system, but the key indexes like performance specifications and interface requirements should be provided by manufacturers. Besides, mature suppliers are responsible for significant tests. When such test data are delivered to manufacturers, manufacturers don't need to carry out the same test. From the stage of concept to the stage of production, there exists a great deal of communication. Mature supplier relationship has little difference with partner supplier. The main difference is that the objectives of customers have greater influence on their advanced development objectives while general suppliers should establish and modify their own design objectives according to the requirements of customers.

(3) Roles of immature suppliers: immature suppliers have little influence on the design specifications of manufacturers. At the concept stage, design specifications are provided by manufacturers, while immature suppliers only provide some suggestions and are responsible for formulating the details of design and manufacturing and testing prototypes. However, customers still need to test the key performance of components to assess the performance of components. The communication is not very frequent at the concept stage and increases a lot at the prototype stage. However, the density of communication is

smaller than that of the previous two kinds of suppliers.

(4) Roles of contracted suppliers: contracted suppliers only manufacture the components designed by customers, mostly standard components or standard goods. Customers make full use of the unique manufacturing competencies of suppliers, such as the large-scale flexible manufacturing competencies. Occasionally, customers may involve suppliers in the product development. However, such cooperation seldom happens at the pre-concept stage or the concept stage. It mainly happens at the after-prototype stage, i.e. the stage of production preparations.

(III) Form strategic alliance with other stakeholders

Since the 1990s, strategic alliances among companies constantly emerge, especially featuring transnational and cross-industry strategic alliances and strategic alliances among competitors. With accelerated global technology innovation, the research and development capabilities have already become the determining factor which impacts the competitive position of enterprises. According to the different positions in the value chain, American scholar P. Lorange classified strategic alliances into three categories: associated research, resource complementation and marketing. Associated research alliance refers to the cooperation in production and R&D fields. Enterprises who participate in such alliance make full use of the comprehensive advantages of alliance, share operating resources, and cooperate with each other to jointly develop new products, new materials and new technologies. The examples of the strategic alliances based on associated research include the cooperation between Panasonic (Japan) and Intel (America) in developing DRAM technologies of 16M, the cooperation between GE (America) and three Japanese companies (replacing the original partner French Snecma) in developing new generation engine (Guo et al., 2004).

As a main form of strategic alliances, R&D strategic alliance mainly aims to enable both parties to obtain mutually beneficial technology and resources. The alliance will enable the two parties to obtain corresponding benefits in technology progress and new product development and realize the "win-win" or "multi-win" among all participants of the alliance. However, such R&D strategic alliance is generally guaranteed by signing contracts. Once the R&D task is completed, the contract will be automatically terminated. Therefore, such alliance is a weak relationship. Besides, members of the R&D strategic alliance are mostly risk type enterprises. The objective of cooperation is to obtain new technologies and to reduce the risk of capital input and the risk of project development. Such alliance is common in high-tech industries like micro-electronics, computer, bioengineering and new materials. For example, three computer giants, namely IBM, Motorola and Apple, formed an R&D strategic alliance and jointly developed Power PC microprocessor chips. The characteristic of such an alliance is that there are clear cooperative objectives and projects among the alliance bodies. Once completed, the alliance will be immediately dismissed. Under such circumstances, enterprises within an alliance concentrate their efforts in jointly creating results under limited cooperative conditions and share the achievements of cooperative projects according to certain contractual relationships.

(IV) Connections between all-value chain innovation and total innovation management

1. Relationship between all-value chain innovation and all-involvement innovation

According to Potter's technical analysis of the value chain and value system of enterprises, technologies exist not only in every value activity (such as logistics, marketing, operation, service, enterprise infrastructure construction, human resource management, technology development and purchasing) within the enterprise, but also in external value chain of enterprises. In fact, technological changes have influence on any activity and accordingly on competitions. Therefore, in fierce market competitions, only by fully arousing the enthusiasm and initiatives in innovation of all employees in departments like management, R&D, sales, production and logistics, fully exploring the innovation potential of employees and realizing all-involvement innovation can enterprises continuously and effectively improve innovation performance. The energy source of research, development, corporate management or any aspect of enterprise is "human". However, everyone has his own desire, mind and thinking mode. If employees are not fully encouraged to challenge the growing objectives, the growth of organization, the improvement of productivity and the development of industrial technologies will be surely impacted. Apart from internal employees for innovation, it is also required to make full use of the resources of suppliers on external value chain, customers, and strategic alliance partners, arouse their enthusiasm and creativity, and realize the value maximization of the whole value chain. For example, establishing innovation teams, cross-functional work teams, network work teams and so on, emphasizing cooperation, advantage complementation and information sharing among employees, and realizing the synergy innovation effect of "1+1 > 2".

2. All-value chain innovation needs cultural fusion

Fundamentally speaking, the disjointed research-production-marketing activities, difficulties to integrate industrial value chain and low system efficiency that exist in Chinese enterprises at present are corporate culture problems. Firstly, seen from the integration of internal value chain inside an enterprise, if internal employees cannot reach a consensus in the core values, if it is impossible to form the customer-value-oriented philosophy and the thinking mode focusing on the overall operation of enterprises, or if employees are used to acting independently of their own free will and lack the consciousness of cooperation and synergy, the integration of corporate culture will lack in-depth cultural support (core values). Senior managers of the enterprises often try to stimulate the integration, but employees feel confused and don't want to follow up. Then, the effect of integration will not be good enough. Secondly, seen from the integration of external resources, if the upstream and downstream enterprises cannot sufficiently communicate with each other, or if no consensus is reached by both parties on the objectives or benefits, it is hard to form trust or promises. Accordingly, the transaction cost of cooperation will be higher, and the strategic alliance and cooperative relationship cannot be truly established. Therefore, all-value chain innovation has a fundamental demand for cultural integration. To integrate value chain, enterprises must integrate culture and ideology first.

3. Relationship between all-value chain innovation and all time-space innovation

The development of network information technology makes it possible for enterprises to carry out cross-region and cross-border all time-space innovation. Many transnational enterprises establish manufacturing, R&D and purchasing bases on a global scale and create products specific to different markets. Relying on information and communication technology, enterprises integrate the upstream suppliers and downstream customers along the value chain as well as the strategic alliances distributed in different regions. To carry out all-value chain innovation within the scope of all time-space, all time-space innovation should be implemented in enterprise processes and continuous innovation of value chain.

With information and communication technology, the product designing and development system provides a method to obtain and control all members and processes in the product development project, i.e. realizing low-cost and real-time linkage and communication among main suppliers, original equipment suppliers, engineers, marketers, designers and customers on a global scale through instant messaging and web conference. Enterprises which have adopted the designing and development system have produced higher-quality products which can satisfy customers' specific demands in shorter time. And no problems that existed in the traditional design process appear. For example, National Semiconductor in America allows its customers and supply chain partners into the product design system based on the previous circuit design for cooperation, which not only saves time and money, but also creates more appropriate end products. Another example is Haier Group's cooperation with Ericsson in April 2001. By adopting all time-space innovation and the 24-hour uninterrupted development in a relay, the two enterprises successfully developed Bluetooth network household appliances. The development of network and communication technology will greatly shorten the design and production time of every component, reduce the design and manufacturing cost of products, and shorten the development cycle of a new product from product design to product launch.

6.3 Globalized Innovation

6.3.1 Characteristics of the globalization of innovation

(I) Development process of the globalization of innovation

Since the 1950s, globalization has always been an important operation strategy of transnational enterprises. Through more than half a century of development, the globalization of enterprises has experienced market globalization starting in the 1950s and production globalization starting in the 1970s and thriving in the 1980s. In the mid-to-late 1980s, the cost advantages created by pure globalization of production were easily lost. For example, in 1984, Seagate moved its manufacturing base to Singapore. Although it led to cost reduction, Seagate also lost the source of long-term competitive advantages, especially the capabilities to develop and introduce innovative products. Finally, it led to Seagate's failure in the field of hard disk drive in the late 1980s. The integration of international economy forced many companies to reconsider the important role of technology in the development of enterprise. A company cannot survive as an "isolated techno-island". Even the most successful companies with the best management in the world, like GE, cannot obtain all necessary technologies from the inside. "Competition over cooperation" has become the main strategy of enterprise development. Therefore, globalization has stepped into the stage of innovation globalization. Since the 1990s, innovation and technology management became increasingly globalized. In some technology intensive industries, like pharmacies and electronics, in order to obtain global competitive advantages, transnational companies began establishing new research institutions overseas one after another. For example, Canon carried out innovation activities in 8 research institutions in five countries and Motorola owned 14 research institutions in seven countries.

Case Study 8
Huawei's Globalized Innovation Network

Huawei continuously improves its innovation capability based on customer demands and insists on investing at least 10% of the sales revenues in R&D. At present, Huawei has already established R&D institutions all over the world, including Stockholm in Sweden, Dallas and Silicon Valley in America, Bangalore in India, Moscow in Russia, and Shenzhen, Shanghai, Beijing, Nanjing, Xi'an, Chengdu and Wuhan in China. Through the cooperation of cross-culture teams, it has implemented the asynchronous R&D strategies on a global scale.[8]

⑧ Source: http://www.huawei.com

(II) Characteristics of the globalization of innovation at different stages

According to the characteristics of innovation at different stages, the development of innovation globalization can be roughly divided into the stage of local adaptation, the stage of local intelligence use and the stage of global networking (Chen, 2003).

The appearance of local adaptation was the inevitable result of the globalization of production. Demands were the main reasons for the development of research on local adaptation. To better expand and serve foreign markets, enterprises establish research institutions in foreign countries at this stage. It had two main missions: (1) solving the localization of processing and equipments and being adapted to local production conditions like human resources and climax; (2) investigating local markets, localizing products developed by the headquarters based on local demands and being adapted to local market conditions. Today, many transnational companies still adopt such way to establish plants overseas. For example, most research institutions established by Motorola and P&G in China belong to such a category.

With the economic development of countries all over the world, the enhancement of education and technology in the third world and unbalanced technology development on a global scale, all companies began to establish innovation institutions which used local intelligence. Especially since the 1990s, technological supply factors became the main reasons for the globalization of innovation. Supply factors aimed to more effectively use foreign technologies and technology resources of universities and other research institutions or to seek low innovation cost and improve innovation efficiency. For example, America had advantages in biotechnologies, electronic system and software; Europe had its characteristic advantages in software, communication and chemical engineering fields; Japan occupied a position in other industries like household appliances, semiconductors, low-cost manufacturing technologies, etc. (Chiesa, 1996). Technical experts formed "innovation teams" in different regions. One of the important driving forces of many companies to carry out innovations overseas was to explore the core capabilities distributed in different regions. Another important driving force was that with the improvement of science and education in the third world, there were more and more high-level scientists and engineers. Besides, the labor cost was relatively low in such regions, so local talents could be used at a low cost.

Since the 1990s, with the development of information technology and the proposal of global information superhighway, information has been widely applied in the enterprise operation and laid the technological foundation for global networking. Competitive factor is another important driving factor of global networking. Increasingly fierce international competitions made the performance and quality of product the focus of competition; the increasing product differentiation accompanied the homogenization of international markets; to penetrate into the international markets, new products faced increased time pressure and pressure introduced by markets from countries in the world; the pressure to shorten innovation time was increased and the market lifecycle of new products was extended. Global innovation organization networking was the inexorable trend of global competitions. In the 1980s, only few companies pursued such a method. It takes 10 years, 20 years and even longer to establish a technology network. Companies which work towards this direction today will obtain obvious winning advantages in the future (Perrins & Tipping, 1989).

Global networking brought new challenges to the management of innovation organizations. Global networking organization management became a new hot and difficult issue. To cope with such a new trend and seek opportunities, enterprises have to strengthen indigenous technology innovation capability, own indigenous technologies and improve core capabilities. To realize the strategic objective of becoming one of the Fortune Global 500, Chinese enterprises must have a clear cognition of such a new trend to establish policies and cope with challenges.

6.3.2 Structure of global innovation network

According to their own history, practical conditions and development strategies, different transnational companies have created innovation networks with their own characteristics. According to the characteristics of different innovation institutions and coordination methods of innovation networks, the innovation networks can be classified into star-shaped networks and cobweb-shaped networks. The typical characteristic of the star-shaped network is that it has a coordinating center, which is responsible for the backflow, processing and bypass flow of knowledge among different research institutions and coordinates the relationships among different research institutions. The typical characteristic of cobweb-shaped network is that different research institutions can directly communicate and exchange knowledge with each other, but the communication on a higher level and the coordination throughout the network is normally completed through the central research institutions. At present, the network structures mainly have the following types.

(I) Types of innovation institutions

According to the missions, innovation institutions can be divided into three types, namely technology searching type, local development type and testing & researching type (Chen, 2003).

Technology searching institutions mainly have two missions: one is to monitor the development of local technology and the other is to monitor local markets. In recent years, with the development of the Chinese economy and the increasingly strong desire to go abroad, many large enterprises, like Haier, ZTE and Huawei, have established technology monitoring institutions overseas to grasp the pulse of technology development. The same is true for large transnational companies overseas. Such technology searching institutions are generally established in the environment with advanced technologies (Chisea, 1996). For example, Huawei established such a technology searching institution in Silicon Valley, America; Ericsson established technology searching institutions in Menlo Park, California and Raleigh, North Carolina; Japanese companies established small technology searching institutions in Oxford and Cambridge, Britain and Aachen, Germany. Japanese household appliance companies made great efforts to monitor local markets and understand the taste and habits of customers. They established such institutions in some important and typical markets, allocated a few designing experts close to key users and provided market demand information for product development of other innovation institutions of the enterprises.

The main mission of local development institutions is to provide local producers and marketers distributed all over the world with technological support and to enable the innovation centers or other innovation institutions to develop products suitable for local conditions. Of course, it still carries out searchable activities and provides enterprise innovation with technology and market information. The globalization of such institutions is closely related to the globalization of production and market. They are key processes in the transformation from innovation results to economic performance on a global scale. Since the reform and opening-up, transnational companies entered the Chinese market one after another. During their transfer of production to China, they also established such research institutions in China. For example, P&G established research institutions in Guangzhou and Bell established research institutions in Shanghai.

The main mission of experiment and research institutions is to develop basic and general products and processing technologies and to provide the R&D research network throughout the company with technical support. The technology developed by such institutions can be used by other innovation institutions by various approaches. Such institutions can be classified into two types: professional research institutions and comprehensive research institutions.

Professional research institutions bear full responsibility for the global application of new products or new processes in certain technological fields. It is suitable for the following two cases: the first is small market difference, i.e. the demands of a certain market can represent global demands or markets that have no difference between each other on a global scale; the second is that companies are able and willing to concentrate innovations in a place, which can make technology activities more reasonable, eliminate repeated projects and make projects more coordinated with other innovation and operation activities of companies. Such professional research institutions feature relatively strong R&D and innovation competencies. Normally, they are located in places with certain advanced technologies, such as Silicon Valley, Route 128 and New Jersey which focus on the research on semiconductors and computer technology and Massachusetts and Berkeley which focus on the research on biotechnologies. Northern Telecom has an innovation center in North America, which undertakes most of the research of the company. When the R&D of each product or technology is completed, research institutions in different places will carry out further development on this basis, mainly localized development of software system to meet the requirements of local market communication technology.

Comprehensive research institutions are responsible for developing basic technologies or general technologies, which can be used by global innovation institutions, and providing global innovation institutions with technical supports. It is research institutions that have the strongest innovation power in the company. Mostly in the form of innovation center, it also has the function of collecting information throughout the innovation network and coordinating the whole network. For example, the research center in the headquarters of Siemens is responsible for the planning of research and the coordination of all research institutions.

(II) Star-shaped innovation network

According to the type of innovation institutions, the star-shaped innovation network can be classified into technology monitoring network, technology application network and comprehensive network.

In the technology monitoring star-shaped network, except for central research institutions which are located at the center of the network as the experiment research institutions, all other innovation institutions, as technology searching institutions, are normally located at the technology leading centers and monitor local technological progress. Many large companies in China established such a network. For example, Haier have established technology monitoring institutions in countries like America, Korea, Japan, Germany and Netherlands and hence formed a global technology monitoring network to serve the enterprise's innovation. When innovation speed becomes one of the main strategic objectives, such a structure can accelerate the process of knowledge accumulation and technology learning. For example, Japanese electronics companies (NET, Sony, Toshiba and Hitachi) have established small technology searching institutions in regions with advanced technology like America and Europe and taken full advantage of technological progress all over the world to narrow the gap with the fundamental research in Europe and America.

In the comprehensive star-shaped network, there are both technology searching institutions and local development institutions. Located at the center of the network, the central research institutions coordinate the information and activities throughout the network. Companies, which have the tradition of the centralized control of innovation, like most companies in Japan and Siemens in Germany, tend to adopt such a network. Besides, some industries with inseparable process of technology innovation, like chemical industry and pharmaceutical industry, may also adopt such a form.

(III) Cobweb-shaped innovation network

The cobweb-shaped network is applicable to the following two cases: (1) the research institutions distributed on a global scale that have the power comparable to that of central research institution. For example, Alcatel has discovered that the external research institution which it has acquired through merger has the technology capabilities equivalent to those of the headquarter research institutions (such as Telettra in Italy, Telefonica in Spain and branches of ITT Inc. in Europe), so it has adopted such an organizational form; (2) companies which have the tradition of decentralization, such as Ericsson, have always allocated its technology capabilities in a decentralized way to restrict the development of headquarter research institutions. When the company is developing new switching equipment, it adopts modular development methods. Different research institutions develop different modules of the equipment to form a collaboration network.

(IV) Management of global innovation network

To satisfy the management demands of global innovation network, companies should have clear visions, be fully aware of the global innovation trend and closely integrate the R&D strategies and the corporate strategies. To effectively establish and manage the global innovation network, the following factors should be taken into consideration: technological characteristics, external factors of network, internal factors of network, (business) opportunities and (market) constraints, coordination and management requirements, and history of innovation institutions within the company. In other words, it aims to determine the technological maturity and the degree of being integrated with the customers; coordinate the relationship between innovation and other functions and use internal resources; relying on laws and political factors, such as restriction on imports, restriction on technology export and government pressure, guarantee that the comprehensive opportunities which stretch across multiple operation or technology fields are realized; do well in coordination and management and pay attention to the overall balance. It is the key to optimize technological resources.

Once the innovation network is established, innovation should be managed from a global perspective to enable the innovation network to work in a coordinated way as an organic whole. The management of global innovation network requires strong coordination capabilities. The principal manager of the innovation network should be a global coordinator rather than a regional officer. It will be greatly helpful when the following things are completed: senior managers and senior innovation managers closely cooperate with each other to establish the overall research planning and reasonably decompose and distribute it to different research institutions; central research institutions hold a meeting every two or three years and enable scientists and engineers to be aware of the technical knowledge and competences of the company; information communication is encouraged and the innovation managers of central research institutions establish direct connections among researchers from different research institutions; central research institutions monitor the manufacturing and innovation networks from time to time to determine whether to build additional research institutions.

(V) Information technology and global innovation network

Since the 1960s, many scholars have conducted a great deal of research on the important role of communication in technology innovation. Allen's research on the relationship between the spatial distance and the frequency and quality of communication has broad influence (Allen, 1977). Based on the conclusions of all such research studies, technology innovation requires good communication. So for a global research and development network, which is widely distributed across regions and has very high requirements on the management and coordination, how can the communication problems be solved? The rapid development of information technology has provided the information communication within the management of global networking with outstanding technological means. The application of information technology in the global innovation network has the following significant benefits: resource benefits arising from the scale economy and scope economy; benefits arising from the improving of expert communication and communication on professional equipment and the decreasing of isolation; time benefits arising from the synchronism and interactivity of new information communication equipment; spatial flexibility and ability to take full advantage of scarce technical talents spread all over the world; benefits arising from better communication with functional departments like production and marketing and the management and coordination of global research and development (Howells, 1995).

The application of information technology mainly adopts three forms: "virtual team", "intangible community", and the management and coordination of innovation in different places.

"Virtual team" is to organize scientific and technical personnel spread in the research institutions in different places to form a team and to jointly develop projects. The success of the "virtual team" relies on several factors: most team members are acquainted with each other through direct contact; team members are mostly distributed in 2 to 3 places and the research project is explicitly defined before the team begins to work; application of email, remote computer login, database share, new video conference and senior workstation technology, face-to-face contact, exchange visits among team members at a certain frequency and periodic exchange visit among main members in a short term.

"Intangible community" is the development of individual computer communication network that enables researchers in different places to form a network with the research equipment. It contributes to the provision of information service through email, remote login computer, database share, new video conference, senior workstation, etc.

The management and coordination of innovation in different places means that the use of information technology is very helpful for coordinating innovation in different places, thus greatly improving the efficiency of innovation.

Confronted with the global networking of innovation, Chinese enterprises must strengthen the construction of technology innovation network. Since most Chinese enterprises have weak technology innovation competencies and a number of transnational companies come to China, Chinese enterprises should establish and implement reasonable innovation strategies. On the one hand, they should enlarge the innovation investment in China to attract and retain high level technicians and to carry out indigenous innovation. On the other hand, they should monitor the development trend of internationally advanced technologies and adopt suitable cooperative innovation strategies according to the technological trajectories and innovation cycles.

6.4 Conclusion

All time-space innovation is one of the most important aspects in the theories of TIM. This is the unique characteristic of innovation management amid highly advanced information technology, network technology and the vigorous development of knowledge-based economy. The development of information technology and network technology enables time and space to become increasingly precious resources, so enterprises can use time and space to obtain competitive advantages. It is through all time-space innovation (development of Bluetooth household alliances in a relay) that Haier exchanges time with space and greatly shortens the R&D cycle. Therefore, as one of the "Three All" of TIM theories, all time-space innovation plays an important role in guiding enterprises to improve competitiveness through total innovation.

The theory of TIM deems the all-time innovation

and all-space innovation as a whole, because there are intrinsic and inevitable connections between time and space resources. Enterprises can complete the conversion between the two by innovatively applying certain technological means. It is such a conversion that provides enterprises with precious resources which other competitors don't have and helps them stand out from the fierce competitions. Just as what Zhang Ruimin, president of Haier, said, "We can use space to eliminate time and we can also use time to shorten distance and eliminate space. Successful examples of Haier in this regard include the development of Bluetooth household alliances by using network and the establishment of R&D and production center in America. It is the uninterrupted and full cooperation among R&D and productions distributed all over the world that enables Haier to occupy a position in fierce competitions."

Part Three

Formation and Mechanisms of Total Innovation Management

Chapter 7

Formation and Mechanisms of Total Innovation Management

The first part (Chapters 1 and 2) of this book introduces the theoretical and practical background of the generation of total innovation management (TIM) and explains the basic theoretical issues about "what is TIM". The second part (Chapters 3, 4, 5 and 6) offers in-depth discussions of the theoretical framework of TIM theory and "Three All" explains the core issues about "what is TIM". Part Three (Chapters 7, 8 and 9) will focus on the practical issues of "how to stimulate enterprises to realize TIM" and offer in-depth analysis of the generation mechanism of TIM.

As a new paradigm of innovation management theory, TIM represents the new direction of innovation and is the only way to seek continuous development through indigenous innovation in the modern hypercompetitive environment. However, how to implement TIM? How can enterprises construct an internal total innovation system to realize a new innovation paradigm which integrates all-element synergy innovation, all-involvement innovation and all time-space innovation? As a complex and systematic project, the process of constructing an internal total innovation system requires not only the systematic cooperation among multiple elements in multiple fields, but also the joint efforts from the country, industry and enterprise itself. Therefore, Part Three will investigate how to construct the generation mechanism of TIM with the help of both internal and external motivations, how to stimulate enterprises to guarantee the interaction and synergy among all elements through element innovation and how to enable enterprises to be adapted to the complex and changing external competitive environment based on the theories of a complex self-adaptation system. By summarizing successful experiences in China and abroad, this part will discuss the generation mechanism of TIM from synergy mechanism, learning mechanism and leadership mechanism and try to explain the practical issues about "how to enable enterprises to realize TIM".

7.1 Basic architecture and formation of the TIM system

TIM is a complete and complex system. Its complex internal interaction can be seen from the subsystems of all-element innovation. Therefore, to construct and harmoniously operate such a system is a time-consuming process. It requires hard work and gradual accumulation to form the architecture. The successful practices of Haier, Baosteel, HP and GE in implementing TIM prove that the essence of forming all-element innovation, all-involvement innovation or all time-space innovation is a process of forming the basic architecture. Therefore, the key to research on the formation of TIM is to investigate or clarify the architecture of TIM. What is its basic architecture? This chapter will discuss such a question from the following aspects: (1) basic modules and sub-modules; (2) the ideological and cultural foundation; (3) the organizational management foundation; (4) resources and network foundation; and (5) the processes and ways of formation.

7.2 Basic modules and sub-modules of basic architecture

For any innovation, it is necessary to create and continuously maintain the innovation environment corresponding to it throughout the organization. Elaine Dundon and Alex N. Pattrakos (2001), based on extensive field research and practice, put forward an empirical model of innovation system architecture, ISA (innovation system architecture) (Figure 7-1), which identifies eight dimensions or pillars that support an architecture for sustained innovation. The eight pillars are: (1) Shared innovation vision and strategy; (2) Innovation environment support; (3) Innovation resource allocation; (4) Innovation process networks; (5) Innovation programs; (6) Innovation skills development; (7) Innovation rewards and recognition; (8) External stakeholder innovation.

Based on the summary of experiences in all factors that influence the innovation process, ISA model offers a very useful analysis approach to improve the innovation process. However, such model mainly focuses on static analysis and fails to profoundly explain the interactive mechanism and formation mechanism of all aspects that influence innovation.

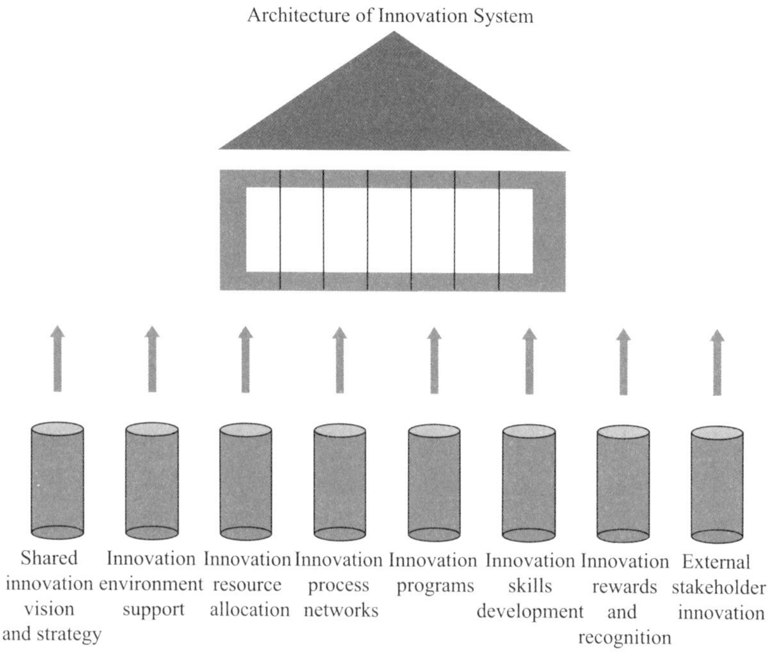

Figure 7-1 Empirical model of innovation system architecture

Source: Elaine Dundon and Alex N. Pattakos. Leading the innovation revolution: Will the real Spartacus stand up? Journal for Quality & Participation, 2001, 24(4): 48–52.

The implementation of TIM requires a solid architecture. Based on the analysis of the forming process of TIM model of Haier and other enterprises, we have refined the architecture to successfully implement TIM, which includes four basic modules and nine sub-modules. The four basic modules are: basis of ideology and culture; basis of organizational management; basis of resources; basis of network. For further in-depth analysis, these four basic modules can be divided into nine sub-modules, i.e. ideological theory, strategic objectives, innovation culture, organizational structure, basic management, human resources, technological base, innovation fund and external network. Based on the analysis of their interactive relationship, the Architecture for Total Innovation Management (ATIM) is established (Figure 7-2).

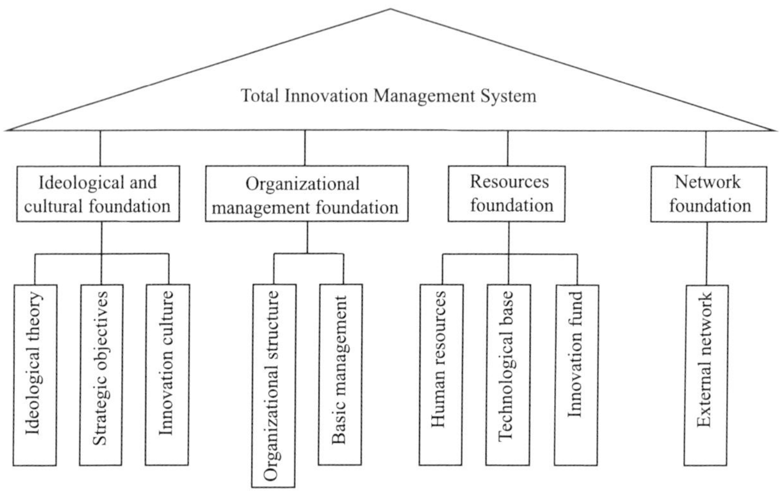

Figure 7-2 Architecture of Total Innovation Management

Based on the in-depth research on the TIM practices of Haier and other enterprises, the ATIM model explores its formation mechanism and analyzes its internal interactive mechanism. With relative independence and mutual effect, all element dimensions construct a complete supporting base system. It is the improvement and development over the previous models.

7.3 Ideological and cultural foundation

7.3.1 Ideological theory

Ideology is a set of guidelines to all behaviors. Without the ideology of innovation, the formation of all relevant systems and the construction of material environment are both "castle in the air". Innovation is risky for enterprises in some respects, so without the ideology of courage to overcome all difficulties and to climb to new heights, there will be no major breakthrough original innovation. The ideology of innovation isn't created in one stroke. It requires perseverance, the spirit of "slow work yielding fine products", and long-term planning and arrangement. It is also required to tolerate and eliminate the disturbance of all improper and utilitarian assessment methods. The formation process of Haier's brand quality ideology and culture has proved it. And it represents the awakening of the quality consciousness of Chinese enterprises and rise of the household alliance enterprises with the strongest competitive capacities in China.

Case Study 1
Smashing Defective Refrigerators: Formation of Haier's Quality Culture

In 1984, Zhang Ruimin entered Qingdao Refrigerator Factory (predecessor of Haier). In 1985, a consumer bought a refrigerator from Zhang's factory. After opening the box, the consumer found there was a scratch on the refrigerator, so he demanded an exchange. At first, the manufacturer representative thought it was a small burr and refused to exchange the product. When Zhang Ruimin learned about it, he immediately helped the consumer exchange the product and appointed someone to check all 400 refrigerators in the warehouse. It turned out that there were 76 refrigerators with different defects. Zhang gathered all employees together in the workshop and asked them how to deal with such a problem. Most employees answered that such small defects were tolerable and the best way was selling the refrigerators to employees at a lower price. At that time, the price of a refrigerator was about 1,000 yuan, which was equivalent to two years' income of an employee. Besides, refrigerators were so hard-to-get that you couldn't buy it without a refrigerator purchasing coupon, which might cost you additional 1,000 yuan. However, Zhang Ruimin said "If I allow you to sell these 76 refrigerators, it seems like I allow you to produce 760 refrigerators like them tomorrow." Therefore, he declared that all these refrigerators had to be smashed by the specific workers who produced them. He started it with the first hammering. Many employees cried bitterly when they smashed the refrigerators. In the following month, Zhang held many meetings focusing on quality improvement. After three years, Haier won the first National Quality Gold Award in the refrigerator industry in China.

Such a refrigerator-smashing event not only made Haier famous for being a quality-oriented enterprise, but also awed and convinced all employees of Haier. Through such an event, Haier has established a great image of emphasizing corporate management and product quality.[1]

Common world views and life values are the basis for creating mutual trust and connecting people within an organization. Based on the quality-oriented thoughts, Haier formed an ideological and theoretical basis of total innovation. Haier's spirit is entrepreneurship and innovation. Zhang Ruimin once said that what the Chinese enterprises pursue is the negation of negation on a philosophical level. Rather than being defeated by competitors, they should continuously deny themselves, improve themselves and transcend themselves, thus remaining invincible.

The formation of innovation ideology is closely related to the dominant ideology of enterprise leaders. Every leader has different values and attitude toward the development of enterprises. Zhang Ruimin had a far-reaching aspiration, a sense of responsibility to invigorate the enterprise to serve the country and a sense of mission to make Haier No.1 in the world. He has integrated American open innovation and individuality promotion, Japanese hard-working spirit and team spirit and traditional Chinese philosophical thoughts in a creative way and put them into practice, hence building the unique management ideological system with Haier's characteristics.

Meanwhile, Haier made great efforts to integrate the guiding role of mass media and the infection of featured activities and insisted on the promotion of Haier's values and a series of advanced concepts among all employees. It actively organized interactive learning-based team activities, created the atmosphere of learning and discussion, and instilled Haier's culture into every employee. The formation process of

① Source: RCID Haier interviews

Haier's TIM system is at first a formation process of Haier's innovative spirit and innovative culture. Coincidentally, Huawei's formation of innovation ideology is also attributed to Ren Zhengfei's unique ideology and unremitting efforts.

Case Study 2
Huawei's Innovative Concept

Ren Zhengfei has instilled into every employee a concept, "to lead or to be eliminated, there is no third way". What kind of people are most suitable for Huawei? In Ren Zhengfei's opinion, "A successful enterprise has to raise a great number of wolves. A wolf has three characters: keen sense of smell, fearlessness and bloodthirstiness, and team spirit. To expand itself, an enterprise must have these three characters. Efforts should be made to create a flexible environment, in which everyone can work hard. When new opportunities appear, a batch of leaders will naturally stand out to get a head start. Every department should have the organizational planning like a wolf pack. Not only aggressive wolves but also sharp-sighted wolves are needed."

Huawei chooses the technology intensive telecommunication industry, which has fiercer competitions than other industries. In the past, people considered innovation as an adventure. Now, the biggest risk is "not innovating". Ren Zhengfei knows very well that only by relying on its own power, can Huawei survive in the competition with other transnational groups in the Chinese market, just like a child who has just left his mother is fighting a wolf. To survive, you have to make the child a wolf as soon as possible.[2]

7.3.2 Strategic objectives

Strategic objectives are what a company plans to achieve within

② Hu Yinhua. Huawei's Wolf Culture. *Enterprise Management,* 2005 (2): 70–72 a certain period in the future. Objectives are dynamic. To adapt to the changes of external environment and the internal changes, objectives have to be continuously adjusted. Strategic objectives are systematic. Long-term objectives, short-term objectives, overall objectives and department objectives, among others, form a complete objective system of an enterprise. Without unified objectives, the enterprise cannot be banded together like strands of a rope and cannot make concerted efforts to achieve its objectives. Innovation is a risky activity for enterprises in some respects that involves many departments and employees. Without the concerted efforts of all employees, it is hard to succeed in innovation.

As an important part of an enterprise's objective system, the innovation objective plays a critical role in the development of enterprises. Since innovation is the inexhaustible driving force of enterprise development, especially in the strongly competitive market environment, innovation is particularly important.

At all stages of Haier's rapid development in more than 30 years, innovation objectives have always played a critical role in Haier's step-by-step success. From 1984 to 1991, the domestic market was immature with demand over supply. Most enterprises tried every means to increase output. However, after carefully analyzing the market situation, Haier decided that "if you do something, you have to be the best and create a famous brand." So it focused on quality and implemented the strategy of building a famous brand. By greatly strengthening the internal management, it laid a firm foundation for future development. From 1992 to 1998, Haier stepped into the second stage when Haier realized that: in fierce competition in the modern economic society, you cannot survive by fighting in isolation. Scale economy is the only way. Therefore, Haier began to implement the diversification strategy and adopted the way of low-cost expansion. By instilling new management thoughts, establishing Haier Industrial Park and liquidizing tangible assets with intangible assets, Haier has successfully realized the scale expansion. After 1999, Haier insisted on "overcoming the difficulties first" and "creating a famous export brand", began to implement the internationalization strategy and gradually established Haier's brand in the international market, thus building the good reputation of Haier. In 2004, Haier became one of the top 100 enterprises in the world, ranking 89. By the end of 2005, Haier's development got on a new stage and entered the global branding stage. It adopted the "T" model and implemented the strategy of "integrating order with personnel", which enabled every employee to have specific responsibilities and objectives and further realized the unification of corporate and individual objectives. This is also the fundamental premise to stimulate every employee's creativity and conscious innovation.

7.3.3 Innovation culture

Culture is the reflection of a company's standards, assumptions and common values. Culture is a habit and behavioral mode formed over time. The tolerant attitude can stimulate an organization and its members to realize objectives and the tolerant spirit can lead to endless ideas and resurrect a company.

The innovation ideology is good for the formation of innovation culture. Without an innovation-encouraging ideological base, no good innovation culture and no cultural atmosphere of tolerating failure can be created. It is necessary to provide the losers with opportunities to stage a comeback and the innovators with fearless courage. Especially in an enterprise, leaders should support innovation and allow failure. Aim at the best and prepare for the worst. As an exploration, innovation has uncertainties of varying degrees. Failure is inevitable. Without the policies and cultural atmosphere to allow experiments and failures, you cannot encourage people to boldly innovate and scale new heights.

Innovation is the inexhaustible driving force of Haier's sustainable development and also the soul of Haier. The motto of Haier University is: innovation, seeking truth and innovation. In the Haier Group, the word you see and hear most frequently is innovation. There are slogans, posters and cartoons created by employees about innovation anywhere, such as "the objective of innovation is to create valuable order", "the essence of innovation is creative destruction of all shackles that hinder the creation of valuable orders", etc. The concept of continuous innovation has already enjoyed popular support and is embodied in every act and move of every Haier employee.

Intel also devotes itself to creating cultural innovation and a good innovative atmosphere.

Case Study 3
Cultural Innovation at Intel

Intel was founded in 1968. In the 1970s, Intel developed the first 4004 microprocessor for personal computer in the world. In the 1980s, Intel transformed the normal chip manufacturing technique to the most efficient and the most sophisticated technique in the world. In the 1990s, guided by the innovation concept, Intel continuously improved the design of chips and significantly increased the sales volume. It was once selected by Fortune as one of ten most admired enterprises in America.

1. Six principles of Intel's corporate culture

Intel has established six principles in its corporate culture: customer service, employee satisfaction, observing disciplines, quality foremost, taking risk and result orientation. Everyone is equal in the company. Both senior manager and ordinary employees have to go to work on time. Nobody can ever enjoy special treatment: no parking lots reserved for senior managers and no special canteen for managers. Every employee has the equal opportunity to get and share rewards.

The implementation of corporate culture should be led by senior managers. Every main leader of the company should advocate the persistent and enterprising values. Intel President Barrett once said that if there is one key factor which guides us to promote the enterprise development, that factor is corporate culture. It has become part of Barrett's working routine to make an inspection tour to all factories home and abroad. People call him "global flight manager" and his accumulated air mileage is large enough to buy American West Airlines.

2. Intel's system and reform of old organizational culture

Organizational culture is a set of accumulated principles, beliefs, rites, activities and traditional habits. When a new organization member comes into a new culture for the first time, he will immediately perceive the differences between such a culture and the culture he is familiar with. However, it is hard for people who are accustomed to the old culture to actively reform such a culture. How to transform the authoritarian parenting culture and the bureaucratic culture into a cooperative and participative culture is the primary process of the cultural innovation of an enterprise.

Intel emphasizes the strategy of "breaking through old habits", "improving efficiency" and "stimulating economic growth with culture". Barrett believed that the growth of organizational culture is staged. To overcome the organizational crisis at any stage, it requires cultural transformation, which might originate from the requirements of internal mechanism.

3. Innovation consciousness and the innovation concept of an enterprise is the key to the success of an enterprise

Although more than 85% of personal computers in the world use Intel Pentium microprocessors, everyone in Intel has a sense of crisis. In order to maintain the leading position of Intel, employees of Intel begin to work at 6 am and get off work at 6 pm every day. Overtime at night is common. They have to work for at least 12 hours a day. In Intel, people who just work upon the orders of leaders have no promising future. Only those who set their wits to work, summarize experiences and have innovative spirit can keep a foothold and get promoted in Intel. Eight hours' work cannot provide enough support for innovation. Most Intel employees use their spare time to read books, do experiments, update their knowledge and present accurate experiment data to prove their new insights. Management departments on all levels encourage everyone to contribute ideas. "Friday E-mall" in silicon is filled with customers on weekends. Almost every weekend, engineers and employees of many companies go there to see the market trend, what products and patents invented by them have already been applied, what new products and new technologies appear in the market, and whether there are any new opportunities in their own scientific research field.

The realistic spirit and the principle of equality are scientific rules of Intel. Founders of Intel mostly came from Stanford University and California University at Berkeley. Their realistic spirit and principle of academic equality have significant impact on the people who followed late-comers. In Intel, ordinary employees maintain frequent communication with directors on all levels. As to major decisions, Intel implements the "system of democratic centralism". Firstly, they seek for opinions from the grass-roots staff. Once such a decision is made, the company will implement it to the letter. Normally, president and vice president of Intel don't buy first-class plane tickets and have lunch in the same canteen as the ordinary employees. The doors of their offices are often not closed for the convenience of communication with employees at any time. They become one with the masses and get to know their wishes and movements. Fully inspiring employees and encouraging employees' creativity have already become one of the main factors of Intel that attract talents from all fields. ③

③ Liu Guangming: Intel's Corporate Culture Innovation. *China Marketing Network*. 2004-10-18

7.4 Organization and management foundation

7.4.1 Organizational structure

Organizational activity cannot be finished without division of labor and cooperation. Organizational structure consists of various approaches to achieve work objectives in a collaborative way based on detailed division of labor. Organizational structure is subject to various factors. To be adapted to different strategies, technologies and competitive conditions, it is required to design and choose different organizational structures and to make dynamic adjustments to the structures. The performance of an organization largely depends on suitable organizational structure. Organizational structure is the basis for the formation of normal operation. The synergy between people needs to be ensured by organizational structure.

Innovation is a systematic and complicated process.

The failure of any process may impact the efficiency and speed of innovation. Therefore, effective organizational management is necessary. Traditional organizational structure of functional grades is good for improving organizational efficiency, but it may hinder the innovation. Only by breaking the pyramid-shaped multiple layer structure and implementing the flat structure good for the integration of leaders and the masses can the organizational shackles which restrain the creativity and initiatives of the masses be eliminated and the initiatives and vigor for innovation of the masses be aroused. If the innovation of ideological theory is the ideological basis of innovation, then organizational innovation is the organizational premise and guarantee of innovation.

The important experiences of many enterprises which have succeeded in innovation prove that their success is attributed to their organizational innovation. The business process re-engineering which Haier has carried out since the end of the 20th century has thoroughly changed the situation that functional departments directly related to the process of technology innovation lack coordination. It has restructured the unified process of technology creation into fragmented and multilayer organization structure, adopted the process-based organizational structure, constructed the business process based on market chain, and changed the mutual relationship between different departments and different working positions from the hierarchical and administrative management relationship to market relationship; the input, output and profit & loss of every department and every working position (every employee) should be settled every day, thus enabling every employee to face the market and become an "independent" operator. Haier calls it "Everyone is an innovation SBU (Strategic business unit)". When everyone becomes an operator, it will greatly stimulate employees' innovation initiatives and creativity.

During the evolution of Haier's TIM, its organizational structure has constantly adjusted to adapt to the changes of the innovation environment. It is mainly divided into three stages: (1) Stage of functional hierarchy (1984–1991). In the first stage, by promoting total quality management, Haier established a famous brand of refrigerators. At this initial stage, due to the small scale and weak management of the enterprise, its dominant organizational structure was functional hierarchy. (2) Stage of business unit system (1992–1998). With the constantly expanding enterprise scale and the increasingly complex management system, the original linear functional system could no longer meet the requirements. The coordination between different companies and the balancing between different departments became more and more important. To realize the integrated and effective management of production, supply and sales and to be geared to international standards, the business unit system was applied and it held a dominant position. (3) Stage of process-based network structure. Since 1999, to create a world-famous brand, Haier has established a strategic objective to become one of Fortune 500 in early 21st century. At this stage, to compete with world first class enterprises, Haier, relying on modern information and communication technology, started its market chain based business process re-engineering (BPR), which was a revolutionary reform of the organization. At present, Haier has already realized the flat organizational structure and process-oriented network structure, which attaches great importance to both tasks and results and realizes a zero-distance contact with market and customers.

7.4.2 Basic management

Basic management is the cornerstone of an enterprise's normal operation. The experiences of many enterprises prove that a necessary condition for the success of an enterprise is effective basic management. Based on the analysis of the reasons for the failure of an enterprise, faults in work, dereliction of duty, safety and quality accidents, all such problems are caused by ineffective and inadequate basic management. Basic management is hard and painstaking. It requires persistence, adjustment of enterprise objectives based on market changes and dynamic optimization: dogmatism should be eliminated.

In a knowledge-driven economy, to systemize learning and to build a learning-based organization have become an important part of basic management.

The miracles created by Haier are inseparable from its strong basic management. The "slope-ball theory" is the basis of Haier's management. It compares the position of the enterprise in the market to a ball on a slope. Subject to the pressure coming from market competition and internal employees' laziness, it will slide downwards if there is no braking force. To maintain the enterprise's position on the slope (market) without sliding, it needs to strengthen the braking force through internal basic management. Many management modes, management mechanisms, management methods and management procedures are derived from it.

Haier insists on implementing OEC management. O stands for "overall"; E stands for "everyone", "everyday" and "everything"; C stands for "control" and "clear". The management mode consists of objective system, daily control, clearance system, and incentive mechanism. The essence of OEC is continuous improvement through strict and meticulous process management. The OEC mode also includes concepts like "being people oriented" and extensive participation of everyone. Furthermore, "daily control and clearance" and "improving by 1% every day" also represents continuous improvement and innovation at any time. Accordingly, it helps Haier form the innovation concept of "Everyone is an innovation SBU".

Haier's basic management has experienced three stages of transformation, i.e. from disorder to orderliness, from orderliness to system, and from system to height. By improving sound quality assurance system, Haier built a strong team of entrepreneurs and managers, extracted complete, replicable and transplantable enterprise management text, improved its advanced and innovative operation philosophy, formed the corporate culture based on the professional ethics and the spirit to serve the country, enhanced the intangible value of the Haier brand, and laid the foundation for the implementation of diversification strategy.

7.5 Resources and network foundation

7.5.1 Human resources

People are the primary resources. Leaders, managers, technicians and ordinary employees are the most precious assets of the enterprise. Competitors can duplicate technologies and products, but nobody can find two people with exactly the same passion and motivation. In the rapidly changing and increasingly complex world today, well trained and energetic people play a critical role in innovation, development and implementation of strategies. Individual creativity is the source of continuous innovation. Nowadays, innovation is no longer the "specialty" of professional technicians. Everyone should become an innovator. It is necessary to cultivate innovation-oriented technicians, managers and employees.

As the most important innovation resources, human

resources, especially knowledge workers, play an important role in innovation. They are the subjects of innovation in an enterprise. The knowledge workers within an enterprise include researchers, engineers, technicians, senior technicians and relevant managers, who play important roles in the process of innovation. As the policymaker and executor of innovation strategy, leaders and senior managers play dominant roles in leading and promoting innovation of an enterprise. An advanced strategic objective and direction can motivate all knowledge workers and ordinary employees to make concerted efforts to realize unified innovation objectives. Knowledge workers are the main force in the process of indigenous innovation. In particular, high-level talents in the research and development department can grasp the key technologies. They are the core force of innovation and construct the foundation for the core capabilities of an enterprise. The training and reasonable utilization of such talents impacts the success and failure of innovation. In order to make full use of such talents, we have to firstly respect their innovation insights and build a platform for them to develop their abilities. Secondly, we need to establish system and culture innovation, offer moral incentives and material rewards and create a flexible environment and atmosphere, stimulate them to be fearless of danger and difficulty, to take risks and to break through the difficulties and obstacles during the process of innovation.

Haier's success is, in the final analysis, the success in the development and utilization of human resources. Haier believes that the foundation of the enterprise development is the realization of individual values. The individual development of employees originates from the advancement of the team as a whole. Haier has created a mechanism for employees to seek common development with the enterprise. While realizing and affirming the value of every employee, it also creates values. "Everyone is a talent and trusts each other" is the unique philosophy of Haier. Haier insists on "cultivating talents before building a brand", it follows the theory of "learning ball (on talent development)" and emphasizes the incentive of talents. Managers have to be controlled in their positions. They cannot be promoted without competition and they have to shift work at the end of their tenure. Haier implements the incentive system of "coexistence and dynamic conversion of three kinds of workers" and the "up-down" promotion mechanism. Today, with global networking and internationalization, Haier begins to make efforts to integrate international talent resources. By building corporate culture and improving the attractiveness and cohesive force, Haier has gathered talents from all over the world. It is the talent mechanism of Haier that enables Haier to move smoothly towards the internationalization.

Like the Haier Group, the Hisense Group is also one of the leading enterprises in Chinese household appliance and information industry. They pay great attention to making full use of scientific and technological talents, attracting and retaining outstanding talents and taking effective methods.

7.5.2 Technological facilities

To achieve technology innovation, sufficient material resources are necessary. Ideas cannot be transformed to goods and enterprises will lose in the changing competition. In the knowledge-based society, information and communication technology are very important.

To implement innovation, scientific experiments and trial production bases are essential. A large part of the R&D investment is used for research and experiment. R&D personnel have to be provided with modern scientific instrument and equipment for the repeated experiments of innovation schemes. Only with continuous experiments and persistent accumulation of scientific and technological knowledge can new thoughts and results of indigenous innovation be created.

If experiment equipment and trial production bases are important material basis of innovation, technology information flow is the mental nourishment of innovation. Science and technology in essence are information processing. Scientific and technological systems include a technology innovation system, which can constantly absorb, digest, transmit and exchange information and generate new information. In an information society and a knowledge-based economy, information and knowledge have already become resources as important as talents, funds and material resources. To implement effective innovation, it is necessary to effectively organize technology and market information flow, and grasp and process the rapidly changing dynamic information.

To rapidly, timely and effectively obtain and integrate all useful information resources that impact innovation decision-making and absorption of innovation, strengthening the construction of information network is an important and foundational work. The internal, external, domestic and international information network should all be constructed. In the context of knowledge-based economy where information and knowledge are accelerated by the unprecedented division of labor and professionalization, the knowledge required by innovation is widely spread all over the world. Since innovation has already been a distributed status, only by adopting open organizing methods and integrating the best resources found on a global scale can unique innovative schemes be produced. Therefore, networking is definitely not dispensable, but it's the only way for enterprises to seek survival and development through indigenous innovation.

Information-based work has contributed greatly to the successful implementation of innovation in Haier. Without the strong support of information, all previous efforts made by Haier in innovation and development would be wasted. Haier's successful research and development of Bluetooth network household alliances is a good example. To accelerate the R&D cycle, Haier and Ericsson cooperated with each other to maintain development in relay. Researchers of Haier worked till 9 p.m., which was the afternoon office hour of Ericsson, i.e. 2 p.m. The research was continued by researchers of Ericsson in a relay. Through the Internet, they realized 24-hour uninterrupted research and development and greatly improved the efficiency of research and development. In as short as three months, Haier had successfully developed the Bluetooth network household alliances. If the traditional linear development mode were adopted, it might take at least six months. Without the support of information network technology, it was an impossible task.

7.5.3 Innovation fund

Innovation is always a long and tough process. It requires extraordinary perseverance, long-term vision, persistent spirit, and continuous and enormous input of human, physical and financial resources.

Funding is an important factor for innovation. From the generation of idea to the commercialization, all innovation processes need the support of innovation funds. Without fund support, even the most creative ideas may end up with nothing. To cultivate and train talents and carry out continuous innovation, enterprises have to make stable and sufficient investment in innovation and gradually increase the fund input according to the demands and possibilities. All Chinese enterprises which have made great achievements in innovation feature continuous investment in innovation. For example, communication enterprises like ZTE and Huawei invest 10% of their sales income in research and development. Haier Group, as a household appliance manufacturer, invests 6%, higher than that of foreign enterprises in the same industry. Through the increase of R&D investment, the skills and competences of researchers can be cultivated and improved during the process of research and development. According to an analogue test we have conducted on the relationship between the increase of core capabilities and investment, if an enterprise's independent accumulation rate of fund is lower than 20%, it is hard to improve its core capabilities. Only when such a rate reaches 25% to 30%, can its core capabilities be steadily enhanced.

Insufficient fund for scientific research is a common issue in

Chinese enterprises. However, Haier considers the sufficiency of fund for scientific research as a primary task. As to the use of funds, Haier has established a principle of giving priority to the investment in scientific research. On the one hand, it guarantees the proportion of annual R&D investment increases year by year. On the other hand, it makes intensive and enlarged investment in the key and generic technologies within the group. In 1998, the R&D investment of Haier was 738 million yuan, accounting for 4.6% of the annual sale income; in 2004, the R&D investment was nearly 610 million yuan, accounting for 6% of the business volume. Haier maintain a higher level of R&D investment, which creates favorable conditions for the development of new products.

7.5.4 External network

Enterprises have to establish harmonious relationships with their customers, suppliers, research institutions, competitors, relevant government institutions and natural environment. The government has strong influence on the innovation of enterprise. It establishes innovation policies and rules and provides innovation funds. Academic research institutions also have significant influence on innovation. In the modern world, competitors may also be partners. For example, Canon and HP have fierce competitions with each other, but they have also established long-term relationship of mutual benefits.

Through effective use of external resources, Haier has built a widely distributed external innovation network spread all over the world. Haier controls national-level scientific research institutions; forms an associated development network and information network together with professors from dozens of famous universities in China; builds a network of communication, cooperation and coordination with large companies and technical research centers in several countries and forms a technological alliance on product development. Information stations and designing offices all over the world offer strong R&D

support and enable Haier to track the most advanced technologies, thus effectively integrating indigenous innovation and external acquisition.

At the initial stage, like most Chinese enterprises in the same industry, Hisense imported advanced technologies from foreign countries. However, while introducing first-class technologies, Hisense also emphasizes the idea of associated innovation. It has strategically established close technological relationship with several famous international companies like Intel, Toshiba and Phillips as well as dozens of universities and scientific research institutions in China. It has set up technology sub-centers in Shandong University, Xi'an Jiaotong University and Silicon Valley. It has established long-term relationships with Chinese Academy of Sciences, Beijing University of Aeronautics and Astronautics and Tsinghua University. For years, Hisense's technology import-innovation expenditure rate has reached 1:5 and some projects even reached 1:15, thus greatly strengthening its self-innovating capabilities.

7.6 Interrelations among the modules within the basic architecture

The four basic modules and nine sub-modules are independent of each other, but they also connect with and impact each other. Jointly, they construct the basic architecture of TIM. Besides, different sub-modules play different roles in such an architecture.

Ideologies and theories play a dominant role. Correct outlooks of the world, life and values are the soul of all actions. The implementation of TIM in Haier cannot be separated from Zhang Ruimin, the main advocator and disseminator of corporate philosophy. A team with faith may create miracles. Relying on such a team with faith, Haier created an industrial miracle in plants with poor conditions from a low starting point and built an outstanding brand in China. Strategy is the vision of an enterprise and guides the implementation of the enterprise. At every stage, Haier always maintains explicit strategic objectives, tolerates an innovation culture and creates an atmosphere good for innovation. The all-involvement innovation cannot be separated from the innovation culture which actively encourages innovation and tolerates failure.

Reasonable organizational structure is the guarantee for the implementation of innovation and basic management is the cornerstone of all innovation work. Resources (human resources, technical facilities, innovation fund, etc.) are the basis of innovation. Without human, physical and financial resources, no innovation can succeed. External network is an essential condition of all time-space innovation.

7.7 Formation process of the basic architecture

TIM is a complex system. Its formation is a time-consuming process. The formation and consolidation of four basic modules and nine sub-modules cannot be finished overnight. Investigations on domestic and foreign successful enterprises show that normally it takes international enterprises 40 to 50 years to build a relatively complete architecture of TIM; and for outstanding Chinese enterprises, it takes over 20 years to establish the architecture, borrowing from the experience of international enterprises and leapfrogging from stage to stage.

For example, since the early 1980s, Haier Group has experienced the stage of branding, the stage of diversity and the stage of internalization and now stepped into the stage of globalization. During its development, Haier has gradually improved and consolidated its architecture, especially at the stage of diversity. The improvement of architecture has laid a firm foundation for the implementation of Haier's TIM.

7.7.1 Approaches to form total innovation management

Different enterprises and even the same enterprise at different stages may face different principal contradictions. Therefore, the approaches to realize TIM may be different. The selection of approach will impact the time when the TIM is formed. To accelerate development, it is necessary to choose the best approach.

In the synergy between technology innovation and non-technology innovation (in a broad sense), does technology or non-technology become the main element of innovation? The theory of Marxist political economy does not explicitly put forward the concept of either technology innovation or non-technology innovation, but it answers this question on the philosophic level. According to such a theory, technology innovation belongs to the category of productive forces, but non-technology innovation belongs to the category of production relations. Therefore, technology innovation is dominant and determines the contents and methods of system innovation, while the effect of non-technology innovation often restrains the development of technology. The institutional economics represented by D. North emphasized the importance of technology innovation. North thinks that the activities of technology innovation are always carried within the system framework in a certain period and non-technology innovation often determined the technology innovation. Of course, North also recognizes the decisive role of technology innovation in obtaining space for the system. The above two viewpoints analyze the effects and positions of technology innovation and non-technology innovation from the macroscopic perspective. For enterprises, the roles of technology innovation and non-technology innovation in enterprise development are constantly changing. At different stages of business operation, enterprises will form the innovation synergy model led by certain element innovation or total innovation to stimulate the development of innovation. We classify non-technology elements into market elements, management elements and so on, and accordingly classify the element innovation into four leading models, as shown in Table 7-1.

Table 7-1 Element innovation leading models with different characteristics of enterprise development

Element innovation leading model	Characteristics of enterprise development
T Model	• Enterprise stage: stage of product formation • Motive force of enterprise development: introduction of technology and indigenous development • Objective of technology innovation: improving the creation efficiency of new products or service • Resource allocation: R&D input, technology department • Innovation subjects: entrepreneurs, technicians • Supporting role of management innovation: making adaptive adjustments to daily management principles and management methods
A Model	• Enterprise stage: stage of informal information communication and structural configuration • Motive force of enterprise development: redefining management system • Objective of technology innovation: establishing stable organizational rules and effective innovation operation mechanisms • Resource allocation: operation input, employment of management consultants, etc. • Innovation subjects: entrepreneurs, external consultants • Leading role of management innovation: determining the success or failure of technology innovation
M Model	• Enterprise stage: stage of product diversity and scale production • Motive force of enterprise development: increasing the market share of products or services • Objective of technology innovation: enhancing the position in the industry with better sales performance • Resource allocation: market development • Innovation subjects: entrepreneurs, sales personnel, technicians • Leading role of management innovation: determining the direction of technology and management innovation

continued

Element innovation leading model	Characteristics of enterprise development
TIM Model	• Enterprise stage: stating that emphasizes stability and giving consideration to efficiency • Motive force of enterprise development: technology and management abilities to rapidly satisfy customer demands • Objective of technology innovation: increasing the frequency of technology and management innovation and intensifying the strength of association • Resource allocation: allocating resources to technology and management departments in a balanced way • Innovation subjects: all employees

(1) Technology innovation leading model (T Model). T-leading model means the innovation and development of an enterprise are mainly promoted by technology innovation. Decision-makers tend to allocate resources to technology innovation. The management innovation mainly aims to serve the technology innovation and increase the efficiency of product or service innovation. This period is the forming stage of products. To occupy certain market and seek continuous development, enterprises have to produce or provide products or services on a certain scale through technology innovation (including independent innovation, cooperative innovation and imitative innovation) and hence build and improve its technology system. Relevant non-technology innovation mainly consists of adaptive adjustments to daily management principles and management methods. Such a model is normally used during the initial stage of enterprise development.

(2) Administration innovation leading model (A Model). A Model means that in order to obtain development, an enterprise has to smash the original administrative framework and redefine a new administrative framework. Decision-makers tend to allocate resources to administration innovation and make great efforts to create a relatively stable and effective organizational environment and a proper

operational mechanism for technology innovation. During this period, the enterprise is at a stage of informal information communication and structural configuration. Further implementation of technology innovation activities becomes a more complex process of coordinating different departments and staff members. Hence, it causes the changes in employees' common faith and their mutual relationships, adjustments to power-responsibility-favor system and changes in connections among departments. Therefore, enterprises have to attach importance to corresponding administration innovations in terms of culture (employees' code of conduct and formation of ideology), property right and organization. During this period, the effect of administration innovation often determines the success or failure of the technology innovation. Normally, such a model exists at the incubation stage of an enterprise.

(3) Market innovation leading model (M Model). M-leading model means that the innovation development of an enterprise is mainly promoted by market innovation. Decision-makers tend to allocate resources for expanding new market and strengthening marketing management. Meanwhile, the technology innovation and administration innovation mainly aim to serve the new market, satisfy different demands of potential customers and increase the market share of products or services. During this period, the enterprise is at a stage of product diversification and scale production. To increase the overall market share of products and seek rapid development, enterprises have to implement active market strategies, take full advantages of product diversity and scale production or occupy the mass consumption market. In such a way, they realize the sales performance better than most competitors and enhance their positions in the industry. While relevant technology innovation aims to be adapted to the demand for market share, administration innovation mainly makes adaptive innovations to the daily management principles and management methods. Normally, such a model exists at the stage of rapid enterprise development when the enterprise occupies the mass consumption market.

(4) Total innovation leading model (TIM Model). TIM-leading model refers to increasing the frequency of element innovation and intensifying the strength of association and thus enabling technology innovation and non-technology innovation to play equally important roles in the business operation and to jointly lead the development of enterprise innovation. Decision-makers tend to allocate resources to technology innovation and non-technology innovation in a balanced way, thus promoting technology innovation and constantly improving the management system at the same time. During this period, the enterprise is at the stage of emphasizing both stability and efficiency. With the segmentation of product and service market and expansion of production scale and market share, the enterprise is always required to have sufficient technology innovation capabilities and complete management system to rapidly satisfy customer demands. It is hard to satisfy the development demands only relying on technology or non-technology innovation and it needs to maintain the mutual adaptability between the two. Normally, such a model exists at the late or mature stage of enterprise development.

Based on the four models of enterprise innovation, there are three approaches an enterprise may take to transform A Model to TIM Model, as shown in Figure 7-3.

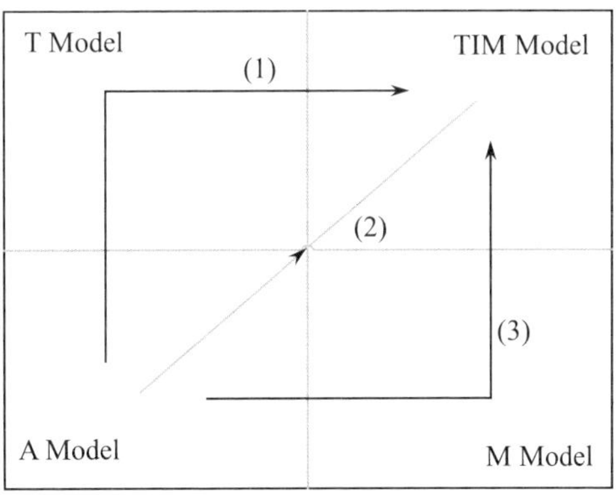

Figure 7-3 Formation pathway of total innovation management

(1) A-T-TIM: Enterprises transform from A Model to T Model and attach greater importance to the development and enhancement of technology capabilities. And then by realizing market objectives through technology innovation, they transform themselves to TIM leading model. Such an approach is suitable for enterprises with strong technology basis and strong technology innovation capabilities. For example, high-tech enterprises and many large companies abroad succeeded in their development by following such an approach.

(2) A-M-TIM: Based on consolidated management, enterprises begin to attach importance to market, achieve development by strengthening market development and marketing management, expand the enterprise scale, strengthen technology innovation and gradually move towards the TIM model. It is the approach mainly taken by some outstanding Chinese enterprises, such as Haier and Lenovo, to develop their brands. It plays an important role in guiding the growth and development of Chinese enterprises.

(3) A-TIM: Few enterprises transform directly from A Model to TIM.

7.7.2 Total innovation management competence and performance analysis

In the final analysis, the formation process of TIM architecture is the process to improve TIM competence. Based on the viewpoint of "Three All and One Synergy" of TIM and research results which reflect the systematic trend of TIM theory development and competence correlation theories, this book puts forward the framework of relationship between TIM competences and performance of technology innovation (Mao, 2006), as shown in Figure 7-4.

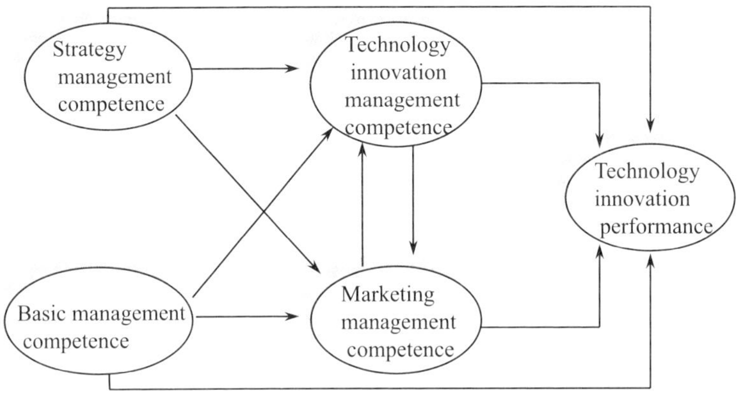

Figure 7-4 Pathway of total innovation management competences and their effect on innovation performance

Source: *Mao Wuxing. Total Innovation Management Competence of Firms: Case Study of Chinese Electronic Information Industry. Zhejiang University Doctoral Dissertation. 2006*

(1) Strategy management competence: mainly involving an enterprise's emphasis on long-term strategies and competence to establish technical strategies and match external development environment. It is the process management competence related to the overall strategies and technical strategies of the enterprises.

(2) Technology innovation management competence: mainly involving process innovation competence, R&D project management competence and R&D resource management and reserve competence, it is the management competence related to the technology innovation process in a narrow sense.

(3) Marketing management competence: mainly related to the competences to grasp and satisfy current market demands, forecast and guide the future market demands, etc.

(4) Basic management competence: mainly involving the basic

management system and the execution of technical facility innovation management, it is the business operation competence related to the innovation process.

By using the analysis framework above, this book analyzes six electronic information enterprises at home and abroad.

(I) Evolvement of TCL's total innovation management competence and performance

Since its foundation in 1981 when TCL started its innovation with communication and telephone technology, TCL has always insisted on continuous marketing and brand innovation and formed strong developing, manufacturing and sales competence of communication terminals in the 1980s. In the early 1990s, it made great efforts on system and mechanism innovation and rapidly implemented the product diversification strategy in the white consumption electronic field. In the late 1990s, it entered the field of black household appliances; in the late 1990s, it set foot in the information household appliance industry. For more than 30 years, TCL has undergone rapid and steady development. Especially since the 1990s, it has achieved an annual growth rate of 42.65% in 12 successive years and become one of the fastest growing industrial manufacturers in China.

Relying on its late-mover advantages and through the innovation of production system, TCL has formed an inimitable world-class production system, and expanded its core technology innovation competences and marketing management competences, determined the industrial strategy of diversity and gained market competitiveness. With the changes of market environment, TCL filled its capability gap through the reform of total property right system during its development, and accordingly constantly upgraded its core capabilities and established its sustainable competitive advantages in the process of market competition.

(II) Evolvement of Lenovo's total innovation management competence and performance

Lenovo is the market leader and the third largest supplier of personal computers in the world. Lenovo has the courage to bring forth new ideas and has accordingly realized many significant technological breakthroughs, including Lenovo Chinese character card and "One-Key Internet Surf". In 2003, it brought forward the affiliated application technologies of total innovation. Relying on the personal computer products with leading technologies, Lenovo had realized the largest market sales volume for eight years in succession since 1996. In May 2005, Lenovo acquired IBM Personal Computing Division and established a new Lenovo brand.

(III) Evolvement of Huawei's total innovation management competence and performance

Shenzhen Huawei Technologies Co., Ltd. (hereinafter referred to as Huawei) is specialized in the research, development, production and sales of communication network technologies and products, and devotes itself to providing telecommunication operators with fixed network, mobile network, data communication network and network solutions in the field of value added service. As one of the main suppliers in the Chinese telecommunication market, it has now successfully entered the global telecommunication market.

Huawei uses the principles of pressure to realize local breakthrough and makes great efforts to become the best in its strongest field. Winning the leadership in technology and expanding profit space, Huawei further invested the accumulated resources in the research, development and upgrading of its technologies. At present, Huawei has applied for the most patents for invention among Chinese enterprises. Even among all the enterprises in the developing countries, its number of applications for Patent Cooperation Treaty (PCT) international patents and foreign patents also comes out on top. Its trademark enjoys special protection in member countries of Paris Convention and World Trade Organization (WTO). Relying on core technologies, Huawei has already been able to directly compete with transnational companies in the global telecommunication market.

(IV) Evolvement of ZTE's total innovation management competence and performance

Founded in 1985, ZTE is now a world-leading company in the industry of comprehensive communication manufacturing and one of the fastest growing communication solution providers in recent years. On the one hand, ZTE offers a rich product line in the market through technology innovation. For example, in 1998, the product line had transformed from fixed communication network products to mobile communication network products, thus greatly expanding the product types. On the other hand, through technology innovation, ZTE has developed certain core technologies to satisfy various customer demands. Due to the success of technology innovation, the product types have been further expanded. The competitiveness and market performance of its mobile network products has already exceeded its fixed communication network products. It also successfully developed mobile system terminals. In 2004, ZTE began to step into the international market.

(V) Evolvement of Microsoft's total innovation management competence and performance

Microsoft is a company specialized in the R&D of software technologies and software products. On the one hand, it has invested large amounts of resources in the technology research and development and developed a very strong technology innovation management competence. On the other hand, relying on the unique marketing strategy of establishing industrial technical standards and holding the market at a low price, it has formed the business model of supernormal monopoly profits.

7.8 Conclusion

Considering the evolving paths of the TIM competence and performance of six electronic information enterprises at home and abroad, outstanding foreign enterprises attach extraordinary importance to technology innovation all the time. By dominating technical standards and applying for international patent protection, they seek the technological advantages and monopoly and hence obtain market monopoly and supernormal profits. The paths of their evolvement are convex. In comparison, Chinese enterprises attach more importance to market development and promote technology innovation by market, thus constantly realizing technological advancement and expanding markets. The paths of their evolvement are concave (Figure 7-5). It is consistent with the situation of Chinese enterprises which lack technology inputs at the initial stages and need to realize technology innovation by introducing, digesting and absorbing new technologies.

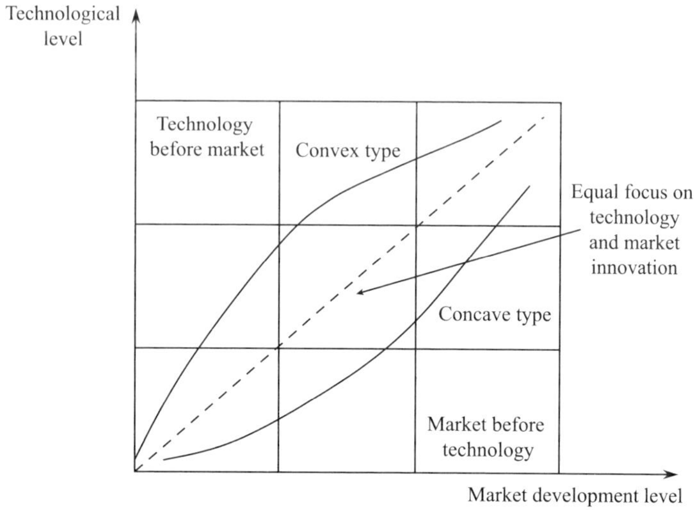

Figure 7-5 Evolving paths of total innovation management competence and performance

The differences between the two paths led to great differences between enterprises in the progress of internationalized operation. The technologically innovative products manufactured by outstanding foreign enterprises were oriented to global customers at the very beginning. Normally, it took them less than 10 years to occupy the global market and to dominate industrial technical standards. However, Huawei, the fastest among all Chinese enterprises, took about 15 years (1988-2002) to achieve such a goal.

In Figure 7-5, the ideal evolvement path is to lay equal stress on both technology and market, both technology innovation and non-technology innovation (management innovation). Taking such a path can accelerate the enterprise's development towards TIM. Therefore, it should become the direction for the globalized development of Chinese enterprises. The development of total innovation requires support from internal innovation management on all aspects.

Chapter 8

Synergy Mechanism of Total Innovation Management

The innovation of an enterprise is complex and systematic, so it requires all-element innovation. Most Chinese enterprises have already recognized the importance of total innovation management (TIM). However, the development of total innovation requires enterprises to provide various support based on internal innovation management. TIM involves a great number of widely distributed factors, so it is very difficult for enterprises to grasp the key points of management. Furthermore, since there are no mechanisms of classified management and internal connections of various innovation factors, it is hard to implement TIM in enterprises.

The internal connections and the necessity for synergy of all-element innovation have already been discussed. In Chapters 8–10, we will discuss how to concretely implement it. Therefore, based on the research on the synergy mechanism of all-element innovation, this chapter will try to construct horizontal and vertical all-element synergy mechanisms from each element of total innovation and guide enterprises to develop their technology and market synergy innovation management to TIM from the level of exercisable practices. This chapter will discuss the theoretical model and connotations of all synergy mechanism; influencing factors and approaches of all synergy innovation elements; dynamic synergy mechanism of all-element innovation; and mechanisms and models of the horizontal and vertical synergy of all elements.

8.1 Theoretical model and connotation of all synergy mechanism

8.1.1 Theories and methods of synergy and their significance

Synergetics is an interdisciplinary theory developed by Hermann Haken, a scientist of the former Federal Republic of Germany. Synergetics focuses on various systems constructed by a great number of subsystems (such as an electron, atom, cell, organ, animal and human) with completely different natures and how such subsystems cooperate to form space, time or function structure on a macro scale. Synergy in a narrow sense refers to cooperation, coordination and mutual assistance opposite to competition, but synergy in a broad sense includes both cooperation and competition (Wu, 2001). The concept of "synergy" in this research adopts its concept in a broad sense and believes that competition is a premise and necessary step to realize synergy.

The ideas of generating cooperation through communication and interaction have already been recognized in fields like economics and sociology. Ecological research also shows that the reason why evolvement of a diversified system is more orderly than that of singular system is mainly related to the differences between subsystems. If the subsystems are identical to each other, the competitions are extremely fierce and cruel. Different species in nature form a diversified system of relationships of mutual constraint and balance. However, single species may lead to a great deal of so-called internal friction. Its evolvement is often degenerated rather than evolutionary.

The synergy among different innovation elements (through functional departments) during the process of technology innovation also requires cooperation-based interaction before the final realization cooperation and synergy through competition. Campbell et al. (2000) also points out that the synergy depends on the integration and coordination among different functional departments and subordinate enterprises .

Existing research studies in China and abroad mostly focus on the synergy among enterprises or different business units within an enterprise. However, there are few research studies on synergy among innovation elements from the perspective of a system. Relevant research conducted in China and foreign countries in recent years has laid a firm foundation and offered many good trains of thought. However, existing research studies fail to differentiate and profoundly analyze the levels and the sequencing of interaction, cooperation and cross-functional integration.

8.1.2 Connotations of all synergy mechanism

Based on the conclusions of the above-mentioned theoretical analysis, especially the analysis of synergy models and processes among innovation elements, this book, from the perspective of synergetics, puts forward the first TIM model of "all synergy mechanism". Its connotation is the all-around synergy and matching of various innovative elements (such as strategy, organization, culture, system, technology, market, etc.) under the framework of all-involvement and all time-space domain so as to realize the synergy effect of "2+2 > 5", which cannot be realized by an independent element, and to stimulate the improvement of innovation performance.

The differences between "all synergy" and "synergy" in the traditional sense are: (1) "All synergy" covers more subjects with more complex interactive relationships. The concept of "synergy" in the traditional sense mostly refers to the synergy effect of "1+1 > 2" produced by the interaction between two or three subjects, such as the synergy between technology and market. In contrast, the "all synergy" proposed in this research covers six key elements (strategy, organization, culture, system, technology and market) that influence innovation performance. It is comprehensive and systematic with more complex interrelations, so its total synergy effect will be more clear. (2) It emphasizes the importance of all-involvement and all time-space domain innovation. This research upholds that innovation elements can only realize the all-around total synergy within the framework of all-involvement and all time-space domain. And this is not covered by the traditional concept of "synergy".

The analysis of "all synergy mechanism" from the perspective of TIM is based on consideration given to dimensions like all-involvement innovation and all time-space innovation, discussing the static synergy structure and dynamic synergy behavior: taking strategy innovation as the orientation, culture innovation as the basis, and technology innovation, market innovation, organization innovation and system innovation as support.

The static synergy structure is reflected in the influencing factors of and approaches to all synergy of innovation elements, measurement model of all synergy of innovation elements, etc.; dynamic synergy behavior reflects the synergy of different elements of technology innovation and non-technology innovation and its evolvement.

8.2 Influencing factors of and approaches to all synergy of innovation elements

Through the empirical research on 132 large and medium-sized industrial enterprises in China, this section summarizes the main methods and approaches to stimulate all synergy of all innovation elements (technology, strategy, market, culture, organization and system) during the process of technology innovation.

8.2.1 Strategy and leadership

1. Adopt the strategy of technology innovation which is suitable for external changes and matches the stage of enterprise development. Many studies show that in the enterprises which adopt the technology-leading strategy, the degree of overall synergy among all innovation elements is markedly higher than that in the enterprises which adopt other strategies of technology innovation.

2. Raise senior leaders' concerns. Many domestic and foreign literature reviews have shown the important role of senior leaders in stimulating synergy. This empirical research further validates this viewpoint. Practices of Chinese enterprises in recent years also show that the activities of technology innovation cannot be separated from the concerns and even personal participation of senior leaders. Many successful innovation projects are often top leadership projects. During the process of technology innovation, the lack of synergy among all-element innovation of all departments often requires the participation and decision-making of top leaders. Since the overall level of technology innovation management of Chinese enterprises and the innovation system and regulations are not perfect, the concerns of senior leaders are even more important.

8.2.2 System

1. Proper and reasonable incentive and salary system. Relevant literature review and this empirical research show that the proper and reasonable incentive and salary system play an active role in stimulating the synergy of all innovation elements during the process of technology innovation.

2. Cross-functional joint conference system. Empirical research studies show that holding cross-functional joint conference once or up to three times a month is a relatively ideal frequency for communication, which may be the best outcome of overall synergy.

3. Adopt internal marketing mechanism. Marketing may also become a means of synergy. Many successful enterprises have introduced internal marketing mechanism and used it to coordinate the relationship among different departments and different innovation elements. For example, Vincent, a former chairman of IBM, encouraged all departments, teams and groups to participate in the so-called "performance shootout" with their own design proposals and initiated

the competition of proposals. In fact, most important innovations of IBM were generated through such internal marketing competitions. P&G began to introduce and implement brand manager competition systems and mechanisms as early as 1931. They believed that only by adopting internal competitions can deterioration and clumsiness be avoided. 3M encouraged all product innovation teams and even all departments to compete with each other. In 1999, Haier carried out the business process re-engineering with "market chain" as the link. Based on the macro control of the group, Haier had transformed the business relationships between upstream and downstream processes and procedures and between different positions from the original purely administrative mechanism to equal buyer-seller relationship, service relationship and contracted relationship. Thus, it formed an order-centered business chain where the upstream and downstream procedures and positions connected and coordinated with each other. By energetically implementing "market chain", Haier could easily complete various coordination activities, which used to require a great number of human, material and financial resources and always ended up with unsatisfactory results, especially the coordination between functional departments and between innovation elements. It greatly improved the efficiency and benefits of synergy among different departments of Haier. For example, Haier had a reworking line to discover and fix defective products. Before the implementation of market chain, the production line bore little or even no responsibility for the quality of products. Therefore, there was a steady flow of defective products flowing into the reworking line, thus causing the extraordinarily heavy workload of the operators on the reworking line. By carrying out market chain mechanism, the compensation of workers on the reworking line was paid by those who were responsible for the defective product. With such a market mechanism, the reworking line was almost idle later and there was no need to employ special reworking personnel. The internal "market chain" of Haier introduced external market competition pressure into the enterprise and enabled every department to face the market directly. In such a way, everyone in the enterprise had their own customers and maintained zero distance with the market (based on RCID Haier field research).

8.2.3 Organizational structure and process

1. Stimulate the flat and flexible organizational structure. A research report of the U.S. National Science Foundation (NSF) points out that for every dollar spent on product development, small companies may invent new products four times as many as medium-sized companies and 24 times as many as large companies (Peters, 2002). It means that a compact and flexible organizational structure has significant influence on the performance of innovation. Many large and outstanding companies still make great efforts to overcome the big-enterprise-disease, improve R&D capability, adjust the organizational structure form of innovation, and advocate entrepreneurship. For example, they have built a series of high-efficiency and cross-functional teams and project teams as well as basic R&D units, which are fully empowered and are made more flexible and creative. Examples include "brand manager" system promoted by P&G and "new venture team" of 3M.

2. Innovation teams which are small in number but highly trained are the key to innovation. The NSF report showed that an ideal research team should consist of seven members (Table 8-1)

Table 8-1 Ideal sizes of cross-functional innovation research team

Representative organizations or individual scholars	Viewpoint
National Science Foundation	The ideal number is 7.
Polymer Technologies Inc.	The ideal number is 2 or 3.
HP	The ideal number is 6.
3M	The ideal number is less than 8 or 10.
Digital Equipment Corporation	The ideal number is 15 to 20.
Peters	5 to 25.

Source: Tom Peters. Theory of Innovation. Beijing: Jiuzhou Press. 2002.

3. Geographical proximity helps stimulate the synergy among departments. A research study of Allen (1977) shows that as the geographical distance increases, the effect of communication will decrease dramatically. Griffin and Hauser (1996) discovered that shortening the geographical distance between the R&D department and marketing department can help increase the information delivery between the two departments. 3M sets some R&D facilities near the operation units. In terms of office layout, it also makes every endeavor to increase the possibilities of random interactions between the R&D and market departments. Many enterprises set R&D facilities far from the location of operating departments. Somebody calls it "labs in the woods". It often works for technological breakthroughs, but it is not effective in the development and commercialization of technologies. The relationship between Bell Labs and AST is an example. Since 1925, Bell Labs created a patent almost every day and 7 members of it won the Noble Prize. For its parent company, AT&T, Bell Labs was a scientific community instead of a R&D facility. One way to cure lab-in-the-woods syndrome is: carrying out systematic personnel transfer between the R&D department and the engineering department and providing product developers with sufficient fund, capital and authorization for product development.

4. The organizational form of a cross-functional team may stimulate the synergy. Many domestic and foreign research studies and this empirical research show that adopting the organizational form of a cross-functional technology innovation team is a very effective approach to stimulate synergy among all innovation elements. Many successful innovation-based enterprises, at home and abroad, also take cross-functional teams as the main organizational form of innovation. In HP, the form of three-in-one innovation team enables manufacturing personnel and market developers (including designers) to be immersed in R&D from the initial stage of product design. Such a "three-in-one" principle is the most characteristic and positive feature of HP. 3M also has a similar principle. By involving manufacturing personnel

in the R&D of products at early stage, they have greatly strengthened the technological feasibility of new products and greatly improved the efficiency of delivering new products to the manufacturing department upon the success of R&D (Peters, 2002).

8.2.4 Culture

1. Making great efforts to build market-oriented and innovation-based culture is good for stimulating synergy and providing a flexible organizational and innovation atmosphere, which are effective for the innovation performance. Many successful companies encourage or support creative experiments of all employees as a good way to study and explore new product ideas at a low price. If such an experiment fails, it does not cause a heavy loss to the company. However, once it works, it often brings the company enormous profits. It is called “bootlegging” in GE and “scrounging” in 3M. These two companies have a long tradition of using small amounts of money and human resources to carry out all-involvement creative experiments in addition to the formal organizational system. In fact, every major breakthrough of GE in the last few decades benefited from “bootlegging” (Peters, 2002). 3M allows employees to use 15% of their working time to do creative activities according to their own interests and willingness, which has also achieved good results.

2. Stimulate employees’ mutual trust and support. Both Chinese and foreign theories and empirical research show that building the cultural atmosphere of mutual trust and support plays an important role in stimulating synergy. Our empirical research studies have further proved such a conclusion. Many innovation-based enterprises stimulate mutual understanding and trust among employees from different departments by frequently organizing exchange visits, recreational and sports activities, banquets and collective outward-bound sports.

3. The R&D department needs the assistance and cooperation of

the manufacturing department. For example, if an engineer from the HP technology department requests to use some important equipment of the production department in order to test part of a new product sample he is developing, which requires interrupting the production of an important product, most production managers in other companies will reject such a request. In HP, however, it is natural. What is most important is that members of the production department are willing to do it, because the culture of HP determines that innovation is the most important thing. This is the HP way, i.e. one needs to present the new product he is developing to everybody else and solicit opinions from them (Peters, 2002).

8.2.5 Communication and knowledge share

1. Make great efforts to stimulate the information and knowledge communication among different departments and different projects. Building a proper working environment is good for realizing free communication in different forms. For example, Corning Glass installs escalators in the newly built engineering building to increase the opportunities of face-to-face contacts; 3M organizes employee club activities for the convenience of solving problems accidentally in parties; the corporate culture of HP also emphasizes the sufficient communication among different departments. According to an employee of HP, they do not know what kind of organization is the best, but the only thing they are sure about is that they need free communication first. That is the key, which must be preserved it at all costs (Peters, 2002). HP organizes "coffee symposium" in every working area. Members of all departments can use their coffee time for informal communication. This is a tradition. In FedEx Corp, over 3,000 managers are gathered to freely communicate with each other for several days every 18 months (Peters, 2002). A senior employee left IBM for another high-tech company. After several weeks in the new company, he complained to the administrative office that there was no blackboard in the company. Without a blackboard, how could people communicate and exchange

ideas with each other? Such tools will greatly stimulate various communication activities during the process of innovation. Another company makes a pioneering and creative move to change all round tea tables for four to large and long rectangle tables. It is a great change. If small round tables are used, four people who are familiar with each other tend to sit together all the time. If large and long tables are used, they may sit around the same table with other strangers and informal communication may happen. Someone from the R&D department may meet people from the marketing, manufacturing or financial department. Just like a game of chance, increasing the opportunity for contact by a little may stimulate exchange of concepts and ideas.

2. An important idea to solve inefficient communication among different departments is to use the advanced information communication technologies and tools to stimulate the synergy among different departments, such as Internet/Intranet, Internet forum, telephone, fax, email and ERP (enterprise resource planning).

8.3 Analysis of dynamic synergy mechanism of all-element innovation

8.3.1 Review of research on the synergy of different element innovation

As innovation plays an increasingly significant role in enterprises' development and involves more and more fields, the understanding of innovation is no longer restricted to pure technology elements (including products or processes). People begin to investigate the concept of non-technology element innovation in a broad sense and accordingly conduct analysis of the connections between technology innovation and non-technology innovation. In the 1970s, R. Nelson and G. Winter, enlightened by biological evolutionary theories, built a unique theory of innovation evolution based on in-depth research on the process and mechanism of innovation. It stimulates the integration between technology innovation and non-technology innovation and led people's research on innovation theory back to the simple definition made by Schumpeter, who believed that innovation was a systematic and overall concept, including technology innovation and non-technology innovation like organization, system and management innovation. Afterwards, many scholars like Freeman (1998), Lundvall (1988) and Nelson (1988) conducted comprehensive research on technology and non-technology innovations on a national and regional scale and promoted the discussions related to the synergy of innovation. Slavo Radosevic (1998) believed that it was hard to explain the development of innovation from the perspective of R&D activities and it was necessary to understand the innovation system from the interactive evolvement of technology system and non-technology structure. Besides, he thought the technology reform mainly relied on the learning process of the organization and the process of learning was deeply impacted by the systems which regulated competition and cooperation. While investigating the portfolio innovation of enterprises from the 1980s to 1990s, Zhang, Chen & Xu (1997) believed that the innovation of enterprise should not be restricted to technology innovation and should at least include five portfolios, i.e. coordination between product innovation and process innovation, coordination between major innovation and incremental innovation, coordination between dominant innovation benefit and recessive innovation benefits, coordination between technology innovation and organizational culture innovation, and coordination between internal independent innovation and external cooperative innovation. They have fully recognized the importance of portfolio innovation of technology innovation and non-technology innovation. Many scholars (Peng, 2000; Tidd et al., 2001; Shapiro, 2001; Robert & Tucker, 2002) also acknowledged that to improve the performance of innovation, it is necessary to get rid of the simple consideration of isolated elements, emphasize the overall consideration of synergy between technology elements and non-technology elements, and improve the efficiency and performance of innovation as a whole.

However, the research above fails to recognize the dynamics of innovation synergy at different stages of enterprise development and the relevant discussions are less specific. Therefore, by using the synergetic concept of cooperation among different subsystems, this book investigates the synergy between technology innovation and non-technology innovation and its evolvement from a dynamic perspective and conducts empirical research based on the examinations of ZTE's innovation and development process.

8.3.2 Dynamic analysis of synergy mechanism (based on the case study of ZTE's dynamic synergy)

As analyzed above, during the process of interaction, all-element innovation within a system will often form one or some variables, called "order parameters", which can stimulate the integration and self-evolvement of different elements and lead the system to develop a higher and more orderly structure. For enterprises, innovation synergy can be considered as forming ordered parameters of technology innovation, non-technology innovation or both to lead the innovation development through the interactions between technology innovation subsystem and non-technology innovation subsystem. The process of its evolvement is embodied in the different forms of interactive innovations of technology elements and non-technology elements at different operation stages of enterprises. With the development of enterprise, the model of innovation synergy evolves from the innovation dominated by one element to the innovation dominated by another element. Generally speaking, it can be classified into four categories: technology innovation leading model (T Model); administration innovation leading model (A Model); market innovation leading model (M Model) and total innovation leading model (TIM Model).

Since its founding in 1985, the decision-makers of ZTE have

always insisted on technology-based development and actively explored the management and operation systems with its own characteristics in accordance with the market and economic requirements. In such a way, ZTE developed itself from a small processing factory to a large modernized high-tech enterprise. The development history of ZTE was a history of innovation and a process of orderly evolvement of the synergy of technology innovation and non-technology innovation from T Model, A Model, M Model to the TIM Model. It has experienced the following three stages.

1. Start-up stage led by technology innovation, mainly the research and development of exchangers (T Model): 1985–1992

The history of ZTE can be traced back to Zhongxing Semiconductor Co., Ltd. In June 1986, to expand the business of processing given materials and to get rid of the passive position by seeking its own products and market, the company decided to take the technology-based road and focus on the independent development of SPC exchange. Since the decision-marking level tended to distribute resources to technology innovation, all employees, especially the R&D personnel, made unremitting efforts to carry out innovation. Accordingly, they developed the ZX-60 SPC space division exchange, 500-door user SPC exchange, ZX500A SPC telephone exchange and other international and domestic leading exchange series products. Their independently developed exchange products were better than their foreign counterparts in terms of performance and price. Besides, they were more suitable for Chinese market demands and won universal praise from users and accumulated financial and material resources and technology innovation capability for further development.

2. Growing stage led by administration innovation centered on reform of property rights (A Model): 1993–1996

A core problem which bothered Chinese enterprises for a long time was the reform of property rights. As a high-tech enterprise with state-owned properties as the main body, when ZTE initially decided to drive the rapid development of enterprise with the research and development of exchange technologies, it was also restrained by property rights factors. Therefore, the company decided to carry out the reform on property rights and explore an effective approach to realize public ownership, thus building a sound administration environment for the healthy and high-speed development.

In 1993, the company decided to introduce private capital. Factory No. 691 and Shenzhen Guangyu Industrial Group in the aerospace system and a private technology enterprise, Shenzhen Zhongxing Weixian Communication Equipment Co., Ltd., jointly invested and established Shenzhen Zhongxingxin Communication Equipment Co., Ltd. Its initial registered capital was three million yuan, 51% invested by the two state-owned enterprises and 49% invested by the private enterprise "Zhongxing Weixian". To meet the economic needs of the socialist market economy, the company established a "state-owned & private-run" operation mechanism with the private technology enterprise undertaking the operation. The administration innovation with the reform of property rights as the core greatly aroused the enthusiasm of the state, collective, individuals and the masses and injected a strong development vigor into the company at its growing stage. The very year when the company was reconstructed, its independently developed 2,500-door SPC exchange was released to the market and realized sales income of 170 million yuan. It accounted for 18% in the newly increased share of rural telephone exchange market, ranking first among the products of the same type. In as short as four years after the implementation of the "state-owned & private-run" operation, the state-owned capital increased by 100 times and the net assets increased from three million yuan to 400 million yuan.

3. Rapid growing stage led by market innovation based on active marketing strategies (M Model): 1997–2003

In October 1997, Zhongxingxin Communication Equipment Co., Ltd., together with eight other companies led by Lishan Micro-electronics Corporation, jointly established a listed company: Shenzhen Zhongxing Telecommunication Equipment Corporation, which marked the start of ZTE's rapid development. With the increase in ZTE's operation, the public was optimistic about the expected profits of corporate stocks and ZTE's market value gradually increased. On November 25, 1998, *Securities Times* published an assessment and investigation report of 100 listed companies, among which ZTE ranked the first in terms of both market image and development prospect in the eyes of investment institutions and investors.

From the first half of 2001, marked by the burst of the Internet bubble and telecommunication stocks, the global telecommunication equipment industry had a sharp fall. Almost every telecommunication equipment manufacturer was affected. According to the statistical data, the market sales volume of main telecommunication equipment manufacturers on a global scale decreased by 20% on average. In 2003, except for China, the international telecommunication market was stuck in the downturn. ZTE maintained its sustained growth and further enhanced its position in the industry with sales performance better than most competitors by implementing active market strategies, making full use of diversified products and strengthening management. In 2001 and 2002, its average growth rate reached 30%. And in 2002, its order reached 16.8 billion yuan. ZTE was selected as "Enterprise of 2002 in Chinese Telecommunication Equipment Market", "Top Ten Chinese Telecommunication Enterprises with Strongest Growth Potential in 2002", and "Chinese Listed IT Company Drawing Most Attention in 2003". For three years in succession, it ranked among the top 3 of "China Securities Journal–Asian Business Top 50 Chinese IT Companies with Strongest Development Potential". The main business revenue increased from 631 million yuan in 1997 to 11.009 billion yuan in 2002, an average annual growth of 89%.

In 2003, ZTE realized the balanced growth of three core products, namely wireless product, wired product and the mobile phone.

Meanwhile, through years of hard work, the international market had its harvest time and the domestic and international markets realized the value of coordinated development. The above-mentioned three core products and two markets laid a firm foundation for the benign development of ZTM all year round.

4. Maturity stage led by total innovation (TIM Model): 2004 to present

In 2004, the global telecommunication industry got warm again. Operators began to increase their investment in the construction of telecommunication infrastructure. New telecommunication technologies were adopted more broadly. On a global scale, the construction of 3G and NGN was still ascending. Under such circumstances, ZTE continued to insist on the integrated development which coordinates market, R&D, capital, talent and management. By taking customer demands as the orientation and implementing correct market strategies and product differentiation strategies, ZTE began to step into its maturity stage. The three key strategies of "international, mobile phone and 3G" determined in early 2004 had achieved all-round breakthroughs. It benefited from the total innovation core capabilities based on the synergy between diversified technology innovation and administration innovation through years of accumulation.

On the one hand, based on adequate preparations and its original technology system and R&D capabilities, ZTE established a diversified technology innovation system and put forward the "three conversions" of the diversified technology innovation: expand the range of products from only exchange equipment to diversified products like exchange, transmission, connection, video signal and power supply; expand the target market from rural telephone network to local and municipal telephone network; expand domestic market to international market. The establishment of diversified technology innovation strategy provided a firm material basis for future technology innovation and formed a benign development of "innovation–benefit–re-innovation". At present, ZTE has developed 17 categories of communication products as independent intellectual property, including exchange, connection, substation automation and network management.

On the other hand, to ensure the successful implementation of diversified technology innovation and the high-speed growth of the company, ZTE attached great importance to non-technology innovation in terms of organization, administration and system. By far, ZTE has established complete standard and institutional systems. Such systems and standards have covered various aspects like management, R&D, production, operation and sales and provided basic code of conduct for its continuous operation of the company. From 1998 to 2002, ZTE made two major adjustments to its organizational structure, which transformed the original linear functional system (simple market business, simplex functional division and emphasis on vertical management) to the business unit system based on diversified technology innovation.The headquarters and different business units of ZTE could make their own management arrangements, which focused on development strategy, regulations and legislation, core technology research and daily product operation separately. The concrete practices included: (1) the headquarters and all functional departments concentrated on implementing brand strategies, establishing and continuously improving procedures, rules, and monitoring and inspecting various systems; they also used necessary resources to support the future development, and made full use of functional departments. (2) Setting up product business unit, ZTE laid particular emphasis on daily product operation, realizing short- and medium-term operation objectives, and improving its adaptability to market changes. The marketing business unit became the common sales platform for all product business units. In economic accounting and assessment of product business unit and marketing business unit, the development, production and marketing processes are closely integrated.

Within the new organizational framework, the company has innovated the corresponding management system, established the administration system based on electronic management, built a rich and strong network application system on the basic communication platform, supported the main internal and external businesses in terms of marketing, production, R&D, quality and management, and accordingly achieved considerable economic benefits; the use of logistics system has decreased the inventory from over 200 million in 2003 to 100 million; the electronic tracking system has improved the adoption rate of rational proposals, which enabled the company to effectively deal with over 100,000 pieces of useful advice every year and created economic profits of nearly 100 million yuan.

8.4 Evolvement and model of synergy mechanism

8.4.1 Diversity and complexity of synergy

The management and innovation of an enterprise is complex, which involves every department and even every employee of the enterprise, so synergy is diversified, complex and volatile.

It may be the synergy between different departments. For example, technology innovation, especially product innovation, cannot be separated from the full cooperation from technology or R&D department, market department and manufacturing department. If the market department doesn't investigate customer demands, the R&D department cannot develop new marketable products; if the marketing department doesn't make great efforts to promote the products, the sales of new products will be affected. Therefore, during the innovation of new products, it is necessary to coordinate the activities of R&D and market departments. Apart from synergy among different departments, in a new product development project, it also requires effectively coordinating new product designers, new process developers, production, marketing and sales personnel. Because different departments have different duties and different employees have different educational backgrounds and values, synergy will be very difficult and complex.

8.4.2 Dynamics of synergy

The diversity and complexity of an enterprise and its innovation activities determine the diversity and complexity of synergy. The complexity of innovation mechanism is also embodied in the dynamics of synergy, which is caused by the following factors.

Firstly, the changes of internal and external conditions of an enterprise lead to the changes of the contents of synergy. Accordingly, it requires applying different synergy mechanisms and methods. With the development of enterprise, its scale changes: when an enterprise has only dozens of employees, the entrepreneur can do well in the synergy by himself; when an enterprise develops into its maturity stage and has hundreds or even thousands of employees, a lot of management functions should be undertaken by different departments as it becomes extremely difficult and almost impossible for the entrepreneurs to implement effective synergy by themselves. For example, when the products of an enterprise become diversified, the development of new products requires several departments, including design, process, equipment, marketing, manufacturing and outsourcing, to share the work and cooperate with one another. The cooperation and synergy among product innovation, process innovation, equipment innovation, raw material innovation and market innovation have significant impact on the success or failure of a new product development.

Domestic and foreign experiences show that an important cause of the failure of product innovation is the insufficient synergy among different departments involved in innovation, especially the R&D, market and manufacturing departments. This is the so-called "interface" problem. The American company Xerox had its R&D department located in Palo Alto Research Center (PRAC) in California. With strong R&D capabilities, in the 1970s, it invented the principles and models of a personal computer, including display, window, mouse and program. However, due to a lack of synergy among different departments, the inventions of the R&D department could not be transformed to products or launched on the market. There were mainly two reasons. (1) The mechanism of department segmentation in a large company caused difficulties in the inter-department synergy and led to sluggish responses. Some business units were busy with existing products and were often indifferent to the new products with small sales volume and high prices. (2) At that time, Xerox had a serious defect in its organizational structure. Its central R&D department, PRAC, was independent from other departments and lacked necessary contact with other departments, which were unwilling to expand marketing channels for innovative products. Such dis-synergy between R&D and marketing was the main cause of Xerox's failure in innovation. Emulating Xerox, many large enterprises were reluctant to set up central R&D facilities and laid particular emphasis on the construction and application of business unit systems in the late 1980s. As a result, their core capabilities were impaired and even lost. That's an important reason why American enterprises in most industries, except for aerospace and computer industries, lost the competition to Japanese enterprises.

The second reason for the formation of the dynamics of synergy mechanism is the changes of external conditions, mainly social and economic conditions. As to China, due to the centralized and planned economic structure from the 1950s to the 1960s, Chinese enterprises also adopted the model of a planned economy and coordinated different departments, plants, workshops and even production technology activities and economic activities between different working procedures in a centralized way. A serious problem of such a system was that it caused disconnection between plans and reality, breeded bureaucracy, throttled the enthusiasm and innovativeness of employees and the public, and eventually led to laggard productivity, slow economic development and little improvement of people's living standards. Since the reform and opening-up, one drastic measure of the socialist economic system was to carry out market economy and rely on the mechanism of market economy to regulate and organize economic and production activities, thus realizing unprecedented fast development of productive forces, strengthening national power and significantly improving people's living standards.

The third important factor which contributes to the formation of the dynamics of synergy mechanism is the change of personnel quality. The synergy of all departments, organizations, production factors and innovation elements, in the last analysis, is the synergy of people's activities and behaviors, but people's activities and behaviors are determined by people's ideology and quality. When people take the public interest into account in whatever they do, it is easy to do well in synergy. However, if everyone only thinks about his own benefits or the benefits of a small collective, it is difficult to realize the significance of synergy. Therefore, an essential condition to realize effective synergy is to cultivate and advocate the cooperative ideology and culture of "paying attention to the interest of the whole" among all employees. For example, Haier considers culture innovation as the first step to promote innovation and development of enterprise. For more than 30 years after it was founded, Haier has insisted on the construction of corporate culture all the time and set up a special culture department to deal with such matters.

8.4.3 Evolvement model of synergy: comprehensive and integrated

The diversity, complexity and dynamics of synergy determine the comprehensive and integrated nature of synergy mechanism and its application model. Based on the best practices of domestic and foreign successful enterprises, we will discuss the characteristics and rules of synergy mechanism integration.

1. From leadership mechanism synergy to the integration of organizational mechanism synergy, leadership synergy and organizational synergy

The typical interface discussed in technology innovation is still used here because it is a key problem related to the success or failure of innovation. At the start-up stage, most innovation thoughts originate from the entrepreneurs themselves. To realize their innovation, entrepreneurs often appoint several technicians for product designs, market research and processing equipment and to separately and personally coordinate the work of different departments. When the scale of enterprise gradually increases, it will set up a technology department, market department and production department separately. Then, the problem about the interface between technology-market-manufacturing arising from the division of labor appears. In order to do well in the daily coordination among such departments, successful Chinese enterprises usually set up a department which is specialized in the development of new products under the leadership of the Chief Technology Officer (CTO). The practical experiences of Haier are to establish a technology center to administer the synergy of technology innovation in a unified way. In the first few years, after the technology center was established, Haier CEO Zhang Ruimin held a concurrent post as the director of the center. It fully reflects the combination of leadership mechanism and organization mechanism in synergy and plays an extremely important role in stimulating the successful innovation of Haier.

2. From the synergy of single function organizations to the synergy of multiple function organizations

To solve the limitations of the view of a single functional department in terms of interface and facilitate the communication among different departments during the process of innovation and development, successful enterprises mainly adopt one of the following two methods. One approach is to set up a business unit system, or so-called strategic business unit (SBU). R&D, manufacturing and marketing personnel are distributed to the SBU and maintain frequent communication between each other to satisfy the demands for synergy during innovation. The other main approach to solve interface problems is to set up a cross function team to facilitate the communication and synergy during innovation, i.e. at the initial stage of the innovation of new products and new technologies, establishing a cross function team consisting of members from R&D, marketing, market, human resource, supply and finance departments.

3. From following the planned mechanism synergy to the synergy of planned mechanism and market mechanism

With the deepening of China's reform and opening-up, the regulating mechanism of the market economy became widely known and applied. Enterprises began to apply the market regulating mechanism in internal innovation management. A successful example was Handan Steel Corporation which created the innovation management system of "breaking shackles and being market-oriented". Planning department divides the received orders to thousands of indexes and decomposes them to every employee, thus enabling every employee to be directly oriented to the market and greatly improving the initiative and the sense of responsibility of all people.

In the application of market synergy mechanism, Haier has made further progress: it has created a management system to apply market chain principles, internalized the external market effect, made employees self-operating subjects who can make independent market decisions, provided employees with individual innovation space and greatly improved the synergy efficiency among departments and working procedures.

4. From purely organizational and administrative means to the combination of leadership mechanism, learning mechanism and synergy mechanism

To adapt to the complex and volatile environment, enterprises are required to strengthen the mechanism of innovation learning and introduce the learning mechanism in synergy. One of the characteristics of organizational learning is to combine learning with corporate decisions and practical activities and to improve the decision-making capability and innovation capability of enterprises by learning.

"Regular study groups of senior managers" created and developed by Haier is a model of synergy that integrates leadership mechanism, decision-making mechanism, learning mechanism and synergy.

In the study group, leaders take the lead in learning and explaining the philosophy of management and innovation based on their experiences, jointly analyze the in-depth contradictions in the decision-making and innovation processes, and solve practical problems. Meanwhile, a lot of innovative ideas have been generated during the study and led to many major management innovations. Examples include the market-chain-based process re-engineering, the concept of "Everyone is an SBU" and so on.

8.5 Conclusion

Based on TIM, this chapter uses multidisciplinary knowledge, including innovation management theory, complexity theory and system science theory, to analyze the all synergy mechanism of innovation elements during the process of technology innovation. Featuring theoretical originality and methodological innovativeness, it enriches and develops the research on innovation management theories, further deepens the new theoretical paradigm of TIM, and helps enhance the status and influence of Chinese innovation management research at the international level. Meanwhile, taking ZTE as an example, it conducts in-depth theoretical and empirical analysis of the all synergy mechanism of innovation elements from the static and dynamic perspectives. The last section discusses the complexity, dynamics, comprehensiveness and evolvement model of synergy, introduces the best practices and experiences of Haier from the perspective of the synergy of multiple mechanisms, and provides enterprises with dynamic and specific operation frameworks and models to implement scientific and high-efficiency innovation management, improve innovation performance and win continuous competitive advantages.

In terms of practices, this chapter conducts research on the synergy mechanism from multiple perspectives, breaks through the static and general research on the synergy of all-element innovation and offers theoretical guidance and operable approaches and methods to solve the "dilemma" and dis-synergy in the technology innovation of Chinese enterprises. Furthermore, it provides enterprises with new theories, paradigms and frameworks to realize scientific and high-efficiency innovation management, improve innovation performance and win continuous competitive advantages in fierce market competition.

Chapter 9

Learning Mechanism of Total Innovation Management

With economic globalization and rapid development of scientific technologies, dynamic development has already become a main characteristic of a commercial ecosystem. Dynamic characteristics include the dynamic characteristics of market demands and technology development. Market demands are the total of customer demands and the dynamic changes of market demands are the results of the dynamic changes of customer demands. At present in China, the dynamic characteristics of market demands have already become increasingly obvious: with the rapid rise of income, people's consumption demands are not restricted to the basic life necessities and become more and more individualized. The dynamics of technology development and the dynamics of market demands are consistent with each other to a certain degree because market demand is an important motive force and source of technology development.

An obvious fact is that there are both risks and opportunities. If an organization is good at learning, it can coordinate the relationship between internal and external environment through organization learning and maintain the dynamic suitability between them. In current commercial ecosystem, organizational learning at least has the following effects on the development of organization or enterprise: understand the changes of customer demands and the composition of customers in a timely manner by organizational learning; rapidly grasp the latest industrial technologies or trend of technology development during the dynamic changes of development by organizational learning; constantly improve the management modes, values, thinking modes, fundamental assumptions and ultimate objectives of enterprises, realize the dynamic balance between internal and external environment, and win competitive advantages in increasingly fierce market competitions by organizational learning.

Since economic globalization began in the 1990s, competition of enterprises in the international market has already adopted the model of innovation competitions. Total innovation has already become the main method for enterprises to realize continuous development and win competitive advantages. Total innovation of enterprises mainly relies on the system, talents, knowledge management and innovation capabilities, but the final basis is the innovation learning to obtain dynamic innovation capabilities. At present, however, there are four kinds of problems and dilemmas which exist in the forming process of Chinese enterprises' innovation capabilities, i.e. strategic inertia problem, innovation learning dilemma, knowledge management dilemma and advantage competitions from foreign counterparts. Such problems and dilemmas prevent Chinese enterprises from forming effective approaches to innovation learning, obtaining high value-added enterprise knowledge and improving enterprises' innovation capabilities and leading to the increasingly weakened long-term market competitiveness of local Chinese enterprises. However, existing theories cannot provide Chinese enterprises with theoretical basis to solve this fundamental problem. To turn the tables, it is urgently required to study the innovation learning mechanism so as to provide Chinese enterprises with necessary theoretical basis and practical guidance.

9.1 Knowledge evolvement and innovative learning

Knowledge is the integration of three key dimensions: information, theory and experience. According to the classification of knowledge given by the Organization for Economic Cooperation and Development (OECD), knowledge can be classified into know-what, know-why, know-how and know-who. When facing the complex and volatile world, only having the information of know-what and the skills of know-how is far from enough. The more valuable forms of knowledge are know-why and know-future, as shown in Figure 9-1.

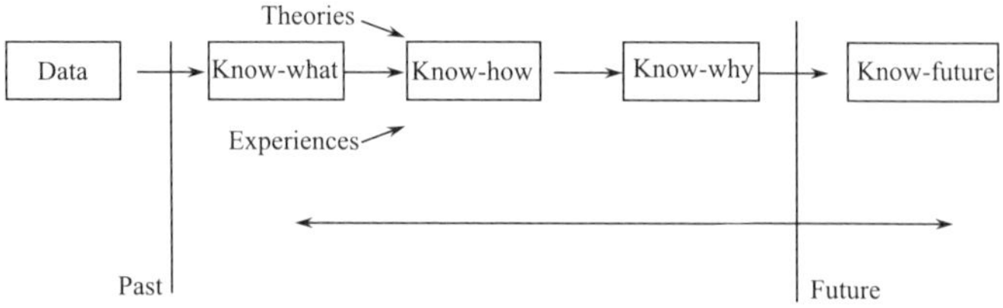

Figure 9-1 Evolvement of knowledge

The difference between understanding and wisdom is that the former is to do things right and the latter is to do right things. Another difference between know-what and know-how and between understanding and wisdom is that the former is the perception of existing and completed things and the latter is the insights into future possibilities and how to make a move.

The evolvement of knowledge is not completely emergent, because it requires repeated work and accumulation. Only by being filtered can data become useful information. Similarly, it requires long-term practices and training, from information to skills and then to understanding. However, if one devotes himself to a certain kind of work, he may develop the knowledge and capabilities corresponding to his work. But it is hard for him to acquire higher level knowledge. Some people have strong skills, but they lack systematic comprehending capacity. They can only complete certain tasks well, but they cannot understand why they do it that way and how their work may impact other parts of the organization. Therefore, knowledge at different stages needs to be acquired and obtained through different learning methods in different working environments, as shown in Table 9-1.

Table 9-1 Knowledge sequence and its connotations

Type	Connotation	Examples	Examples of acquiring approaches
Know-what	knowledge about facts	Chemical formulation, source of raw materials, usage of machine	Reading and checking database
Know-how	Capabilities, accumulated skills and knowledge to do something	Designing experiences and process of technology activities	learning by doing, learning by using, inter-organizational collaboration
Know-why	Understanding of the interactions among all key variables and in-depth understanding of the basic principles of design	Newton's laws of motion, reasons for low organizational efficiency	Knowledge integration, learning by research and development
Know-future	In-depth understanding of the development pattern of things and forecasting of possibilities of success	"4C" vision of NEC	Strategic learning and common vision

There are many models of organizational learning and classifications from different perspectives also have great differences. This book puts forward the following basic models of technology learning: programmed learning, capability learning, strategic learning and transformative learning, as shown in Table 9-2.

Table 9-2 Basic models of technology learning

Learning model	Programmed learning	Capability learning	Strategic learning	Transformative learning
Character-istics	Accumulating knowledge by repetitive work	Deepening knowledge during the pro-cess of creation	Exploring new opportunities and new technolog-ical trajectories and insights into the prospects of technology-market development	Eliminating existing thinking set and technolo-gy paradigm and being prepared to accept and open up new tracks
Learning methods	Learning by doing, learning by using,	Learning by research and development, learning by association	Technology-mar-ket positioning of enterprises and exploration of new product ideology	Learning unlearn-ing
Knowledge types	Know-what, know-how	Know-how, know-why	Know-why, know-future	/

Among them, programmed learning and capability learning have already been thoroughly researched, while strategic learning and transformative learning are seldom discussed. In fact, however, strategic learning and transformative learning play a very important role in improving technology capability. To a certain degree, their effective implementation determines whether an enterprise can develop high-level technology innovation capabilities by introducing technologies.

9.1.1 Strategic learning

Strategic learning includes not only know-what and know-how, but also know-why and know-future. It also exceeds the standards of the static efficiency of programmed learning and capability learning. In strategic learning, it is necessary to figure out what are core capabilities and why, thus providing the future efforts of organization with sufficient motive force and direction (such as seeking new organizational routines and resources) and forming the dynamic efficiency of organization. The significant changes of competitive environment make the original high-efficiency (static efficiency) capabilities valueless. Since it is no longer suitable for the new environmental conditions, enterprises must maintain the strategic learning. The true meaning of strategic learning is to continuously examine the relationship among capabilities, core capabilities and the environment, mission and internal environment of enterprises with the continuous changes of enterprises and the external environment.

During the process of new product development, strategic learning is reflected in the definition and repeated disputes of the ideology and prototype of new products. Strategic learning enables enterprises to be released from the shackles of the previous technology paradigms and to explore new designing ideas based on the underlying user demands and latest technology development. Therefore, it is embodied in the integration between technology knowledge and market demand knowledge. The creative leap arising from such integration is the essence of strategic learning.

9.1.2 Transformative learning

If strategic learning originates from new creations, transformative learning is to "destruct" the existing paradigms and thinking.

Transformative learning exists when the enterprise adjusts its major strategic focus, especially its technology paradigm, according to the significant changes of the environment. By then, the technologies and market faced by such an enterprise will undergo fundamental changes. Therefore, its existing competitive advantages will gradually disappear. And the old strategic logic will not be applicable. Enterprises will be forced to make attempts and try to understand the new competitive situation in spite of the great fuzziness and chaos. Since the technology paradigm gradually disappears, enterprises may easily get lost when they are seeking methods to get out of a predicament.

The most important characteristic of transformative learning is "unlearning". When an enterprise meets brand new problems, its previous experiences will be useless. Its linear learning method will be ineffective and even harmful.

When an enterprise faces the reform of technology or market, the core capabilities which used to bring the enterprise market advantages will probably become core rigidities (Barton, 1992). And the enterprise may overly rely on its existing capabilities and accordingly lose the dynamic capabilities to acclimatize itself to the changes of environment (Teece, Pisano & Shuen, 1997). At that time, using new technology and market knowledge and realizing the reorganization of resources through product combinations and significant organizational adjustments is a necessary approach to regain competitive advantages.

9.2 Spiral motion process of technology capabilities and evolvement of technology learning method

For enterprises in developing countries, the growth of technology capabilities will experience three stages, namely imitation, creative imitation and indigenous innovation. The accumulation of technology capabilities at every stage also experiences the transformation from external technology source to internal approaches, thus forming the three cycles of the evolvement of technology knowledge capabilities and technology learning methods, as shown in Figure 9-2.

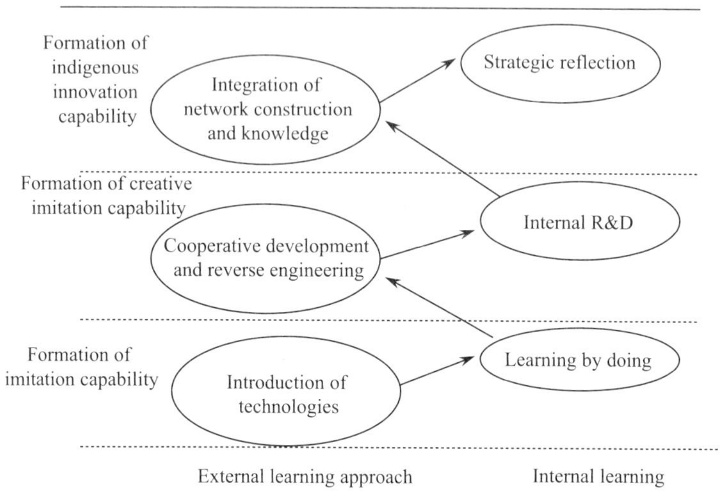

Figure 9-2 Spiral motion process of technology capabilities and evolvement of technology learning method

9.2.1 Stage of imitation

Through the introduction of technologies, enterprises begin to know advanced technologies and organizational management and hence step onto the road of mainstream technology development. However, at this time, enterprises cannot effectively use the introduced technologies and management. Only by learning in practices can they acquire the skills to make full use of technologies and build strong technology capabilities. Therefore, after the introduction of technologies, they have to digest and absorb them through internal learning by doing and learning by using. It means they have to transform the external approaches to improve capabilities to internal approaches in a timely manner.

9.2.2 Stage of creative imitation

The stage of creative imitation is to form imitation capabilities from introducing to digesting (learning by doing) and to lay a foundation for the further creative imitation. However, the absorption of production technologies cannot directly lead to the formation of innovation capabilities because the technology capabilities on these two different levels have completely different requirements for the knowledge nature of enterprises. Therefore, from imitation capability to creative imitation capability, enterprises have to experience a great leap of knowledge. For example, after having introduced technologies, many Chinese enterprises built strong imitation capabilities in as short as several years (normally three to five years). However, building further creative imitation capabilities cost them many more years (more than eight years). By far, only a few enterprises have succeeded in it.

It is difficult for an enterprise to complete such a great leap all by itself. Even if it achieves success, it must be a high-cost or time-consuming process. Therefore, internal approaches cannot help enterprises build innovation capabilities rapidly or succeed in time-based competition. Therefore, starting again from the external approach is still the shortcut to success.

Of course, the external approach at this stage is not simple introduction of technology. The knowledge to construct innovation capabilities cannot appear in the completely apparent forms like the patent and drawings of production technologies. It exists in the brains of R&D personnel, individual and organizational behavior and organizational relationship. To acquire such knowledge, the acquirer and the acquired must have close contact with each other during the development and hence understand the display forms and stimulate the transfer of such knowledge. Similarly, the R&D knowledge acquired from external sources must be absorbed before it can be fully used by enterprises. The absorbing method at this stage is internal R&D, an advanced method to digest and absorb R&D capabilities.

9.2.3 Stage of indigenous innovation

Both indigenous innovation and creative imitation are innovation, but there is an essential difference between the two. At the stage of indigenous innovation, enterprises have to go beyond the static efficiency concepts at the previous two stages, build the concept of dynamic efficiency and transform from considering its own conditions in isolation to considering its development in the industry and even in the world. Such reform of concept cannot be completed only by learning based on R&D. It requires expanding the visual field of enterprises, placing themselves in a broad environment and absorbing the most profound ideas of enterprises' development from the knowledge network.

Meanwhile, enterprises need to profoundly analyze and reflect on the development trend of industry and technology and profoundly understand the potential demands of markets and users, thus determining the future technology-market positioning and product-process technology development strategies. Therefore, enterprises must integrate the knowledge acquired via external approaches and the knowledge created by themselves. After fully absorbing the nutrients of external knowledge, enterprises should go back to its own exercises, experiences and insights and accordingly form its unique core capabilities.

Case Study 1
Hangzhou Oxygenerator Plant

In 1954, Hangzhou Oxygenerator Plant introduced equipments from Soviet Union and began to imitate them. Through the introduction and imitation of four generations' products and technologies, it had formed high-level imitation capacities in the early 1980s. Since 1985, with the support of competent departments, Hangzhou Oxygenerator Plant organized technicians from its research institutions and factories to carry out “the Seventh Five-Year” major technological breakthrough program. Through two years of development, they had developed the fifth generation product featuring the new technologies. The performance of the product reached the world leading level in the early 1980s. It indicated that the plant had already formed the creative imitation capabilities of internationally advanced products.

However, from the late 1980s to 1996, Hangzhou Oxygenerator Plant didn’t continue to devote itself to technology progress. When the new generation technologies were widely used, it failed to keep pace with the market. After 1996, in light of a great technology gap, it couldn’t come up on top. While designing and developing the sixth generation air separation units, they took a tortuous course and lost the opportunities for technology leapfrogging and indigenous innovation. Internal and external approaches of Hangzhou Oxygenerator Plant during the improvement of its technology capabilities are shown in Table 9-3 and Figure 9-3.

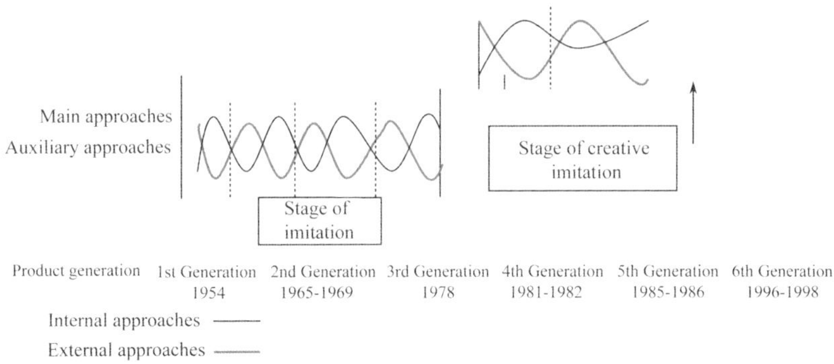

Figure 9-3 Internal and external approaches of Hangzhou Oxygenerator Plant to improve its technology capabilities

Table 9-3 Internal and external approaches of Hangzhou Oxygenerator Plant to improve its technology capabilities

	External approaches	Internal approaches
Indigenous innovation	**Not yet started**	
Stage of creative imitation ↑	From 1996 to 1998, it purchased cryogenic engineering physical property database and process simulation software from foreign countries. Meanwhile, it cooperated with Air Liquide Group and Sulzur in developing basic process design and control schemes and technologies to design, compute and control the overall process.	From 1997 to 1999, through technology monitoring and reverse engineering of equipment, it developed full distillation (hydrogen-free) oxygen generation technology, independently designed its sixth generation products, and improved its designs by comparing them with the schemes designed with the help of foreign enterprises. Finally, it designed and manufactured the sixth generation air separation equipment.
	Since 1985, it began to cooperate with Linde and other domestic and foreign enterprises and universities in designing core technology equipments like supercharged molecular sieve turboexpander.	From 1986 to 1989, it independently designed the fifth generation air separation equipment.
Stage of imitation ↑	In 1981, it introduced the normal temperature molecular sieve purification technology from Linde and centrifugal compression technology from Hitachi.	From 1981 to 1982, it developed a series of special equipments and key supporting technologies. In 1982, it independently designed and manufactured the fourth generation air separation equipment.
	In 1978, it introduced the third generation product technologies and equipments from Linde and built a joint venture with Linde.	From 1978 to 1980, via learning by doing and training, it reformed its processes, designed special equipments and established working standards.
	In 1965, it analyzed the air separation equipment imported from Japan and introduced some drawings.	By imitating and improving some components of Japanese products, in 1969, it designed and manufactured the second generation air separation equipment corresponding to the level in the 1950's.
	In 1954, it introduced the drawings of fractionating tower from the Soviet Union and carried out the disassembly and reverse engineering of air separation equipment.	It independently manufactured more than 200 sets of non-standard equipments and in 1958, it designed and manufactured the first generation air separation equipment corresponding to the level in the 1950s.

Source: *RCID research data, 2000* .

9.3 Constituents of total innovation learning mechanism and models of modular architecture

The previous two sections discussed the dynamic model of technology learning. However, technology learning is only one part of innovation learning. To establish continuous competitive advantages, enterprises have to establish a mechanism of total innovation learning, i.e. creating the system of total innovation management (TIM) by integrating strategies, system, culture, organization, processes, technologies and other factors.

The main objective of research on total innovation learning mechanism is to put forward a method to analyze how to improve total innovation capabilities and create necessary conditions for the final implementation of TIM. The basis to improve total innovation capabilities is the existing knowledge stock and relevant knowledge management, but the approach to realize innovation capability is innovation learning. Therefore, knowledge management, innovation learning and competence of total innovation are the three basic elements of total innovation learning mechanism. Secondly, it is necessary to introduce the theory of modularization to conduct necessary research on the internal structural characteristics of total innovation learning mechanism. Such modularization of an enterprise constructs the fourth element of total innovation learning mechanism. For the convenience of research, the basic concepts of the four elements of total innovation learning mechanism are briefly defined below.

Knowledge management refers to the systematic management of existing knowledge stock and the improvement of the utilization efficiency of existing knowledge. Besides, it also aims to improve the enterprises' protection and control of knowledge. The models of knowledge management include sort management, knowledge value management, knowledge distribution management, knowledge platform management and knowledge lifecycle management. On the dimension of knowledge exclusiveness, this research classifies knowledge into three categories, namely general knowledge, core knowledge and proprietary knowledge. General knowledge refers to the knowledge mastered by most enterprises in the relevant industry; core knowledge refers to the knowledge understood and mastered by only a few leading enterprises in the relevant industry, such as utility patents; proprietary knowledge refers to the exclusive knowledge owned by several enterprises, such as patent for an invention, product prototype, etc.

Innovation learning refers to the accompanied learning activities during the process innovation activities. Such learning behavior not only directly generates new knowledge flow, but also forms new capabilities. Its main approach is to improve innovation capabilities. The difference between innovation learning and total innovation capabilities is that innovation learning doesn't form overt enterprise performance directly. According to the three categories of the dimension of knowledge exclusiveness, innovation learning also has three similar corresponding categories, i.e. general, exploitation and exploratory innovation learnings. The general innovation learning generates general knowledge; the development innovation learning generates core knowledge; the exploratory innovation learning generates proprietary knowledge. The technology learning models discussed in the previous two sections can also be included in this framework. For example, programmed learning is general learning; capability learning is exploitation learning; strategic and transformative learning is exploratory learning.

Competence of total innovation refers to the competence of total innovation (CTI), i.e. the competence to integrate all existing resources and realize the performance of innovation. On a dynamic dimension, CTI can be divided into dynamic innovation capability and static innovation capability. In this research, dynamic innovation capability originates from innovation learning, while static innovation capability originates from the knowledge management of enterprises.

Figure 9-4 is the conceptual model of modularized innovation learning. On the organizational dimension, enterprise organizations can be classified into A (architecture) modular organization, M (module) modular organization and E (element) modular organization. A-modular organization is responsible for the management and coordination of enterprise architecture; M-modular organization is responsible for the functions of all modules of enterprise; E-modular organization is the minimum unit of enterprise responsible for a single and professional function. As shown in Figure 9-4, the architectural dimension and organizational dimension of the innovation learning objects maintain consistency with each other. The boxes in the center represent the objects of modularized innovation learning. For example, GA represents general architecture innovation learning and the like. By referring to the dimension of knowledge exclusiveness, innovation learning can be classified into general innovation learning, exploitation innovation learning and exploratory innovation learning (March, 1991; Mcgrath, 2001), which are not only separately corresponding to general knowledge, core knowledge and proprietary knowledge, but also maintain consistency with the innovation learning categories and innovation learning objects. Furthermore, it can be used to deeply analyze and investigate the formation, development and recession of knowledge. Among them, general innovation learning includes general architecture innovation learning, general module innovation learning and general element innovation learning. Through general innovation learning, enterprises can further decrease the daily production or operation cost, and improve the product and service quality of enterprises. Exploitation innovation learning includes core architecture innovation learning, core module innovation learning and core element innovation learning. Through general innovation learning, enterprises will continue to strengthen the competitiveness of products, technologies and operation and improve or retain profitability. Exploratory innovation learning includes proprietary architecture innovation, proprietary module innovation learning and proprietary element innovation learning. Such innovation learning aims to acquire monopoly or leading position in the relevant field or industry. Due to the uncertain factors of market, it often forms a high investment risk.

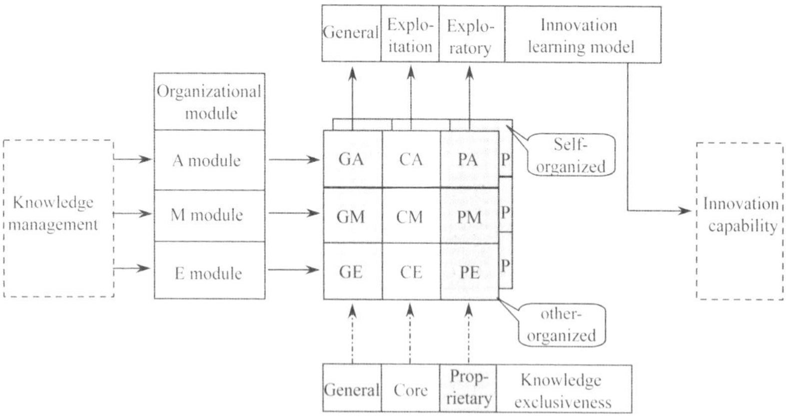

Figure 9-4 Modular architecture models of innovation learning

On the technological dimension of innovation learning objectives, the modular innovation learning architecture models shown in Figure 9-4 are applicable to both technology innovation learning and non-technology innovation learning. Besides, based on the organizational models, innovation learning can be classified into self-organized model and other-organized model. Other-organization is the innovation learning behavior organized by the enterprises, which can be also classified into general, exploitation and exploratory learnings.

Self-organized innovation learning is the spontaneous innovation learning of employees and encouraged by the enterprises. Such innovation learning exists in Shell, 3M, GE and Samsung among others. Besides, most innovation learning objects are tacit. One of the main objectives of innovation learning is to make them explicit. By far, this research has already discussed the architectures, categories and technologies of modular innovation learning architecture models and accordingly provided necessary conditions for the further research and discussion of innovation learning.

9.4 Total innovation learning mechanism

According to the innovation history of famous Chinese and foreign enterprises, the dynamic models and characteristics to improve total innovation competence through total innovation learning mechanism can be summarized as below (shown in Figure 9-5): (1) synergy model of innovation learning featuring architectural system and modular nested architecture; (2) auxiliary synergy model of inter-module innovation learning featuring innovation system, methods and sharing tools; (3) basic model of innovation learning featuring corporate universities and research centers.

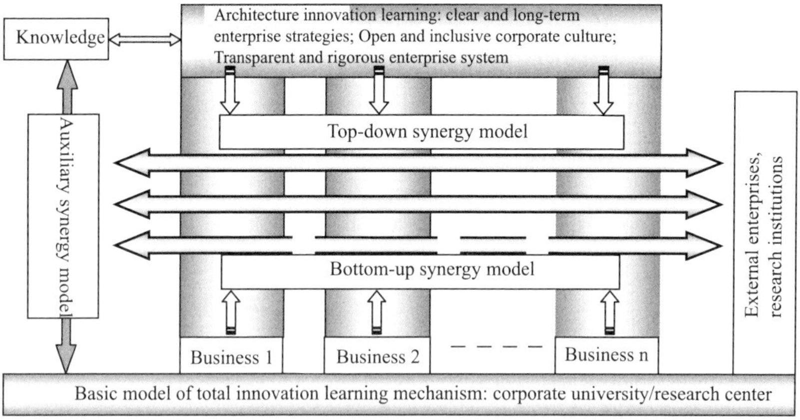

Figure 9-5 Dynamic models of total innovation learning mechanism

9.4.1 Main synergy model of total innovation learning mechanism

Learning, including strategy, culture and system of architectural system and innovation learning, is the key for enterprises' development. Of course, the strategy formed by innovation learning requires a proper cultural environment and should be implemented through the mode of institutional innovation. Besides, the nested architecture system of all business models delivers the requirements and information of architectural system, while business departments carry out the architecture innovation learning on the business level according to the requirements and information of architectural system, form proper business innovation and development strategy, culture and system, and transfer them down along the nested architecture of modules to form new business technology modular architecture, business organization modular architecture and business market modular architecture. Thus, a top-down innovation learning synergy model featuring architectural system and nested architecture of modules is formed.

Of course, through the architecture of grass-roots level models, requirements and information of innovation learning can be transferred upwards, thus enabling the upper level architecture to satisfy the demands for business or functional module development on the grass-roots level through corresponding innovation learning and to transfer such requirements and information further to other relevant business or functional modules. The objective of the innovation learning synergy is accordingly realized. In such a way, a bottom-up horizontal model of innovation learning synergy featuring architectural system and nested modular architecture is formed.

Since architectural system and nested modular architecture are the main structures of enterprises, the vertical and horizontal models of total innovation learning mechanism featuring such characteristics are the main models of innovation learning synergy. The necessary conditions for the successful implementation of such innovation learning mechanism are clear and long-term corporate strategies, open and inclusive culture and transparent and rigorous system. In other words, the architectural system of enterprises should have the self-adaptive innovation learning skill of sustainable development. Leaders should play an important role in it. Otherwise, different business modules or functional modules will work in an isolated way without effective communication.

In the increasingly fierce market competition, enterprises are required to make responses to the fleeting market opportunities through rapid innovation. The top-down synergy model of innovation learning mechanism features high efficiency, but to discover market opportunities or demands for innovation learning often requires the functional models on the grass roots level. Therefore, the synergy model of bottom-up innovation learning mechanism is especially important. However, due to the weak architectural capabilities of functional modules on the grass roots level, the innovation learning synergy with such characteristics is stuck in a way that relevant requirements and information cannot be effectively transferred. Of course, many enterprises have already developed an auxiliary horizontal model of innovation learning synergy in their own practices. Such a model will be further analyzed below.

9.4.2 Auxiliary synergy model of total innovation learning mechanism

To remedy the low efficiency of bottom-up innovation learning synergy model, some enterprises have formed characteristic auxiliary synergy model of innovation learning to improve the efficiency of innovation learning through continuous innovation learning. Examples include the brainstorming practices of GE, management by walking around of HP, best practices of Siemens, product model manager of Haier, etc.; tools like ERP (enterprise resource planning) and other innovation platforms; auxiliary innovation systems like Siemens' "Top+" innovation program. Such inter-module auxiliary innovation learning synergy model featuring innovation systems, methods and sharing tools can not only solve the internal bottom-up low efficiency synergy problems and achieve the sufficient and effective sharing of internal knowledge, but also improve the synergy efficiency of knowledge sharing and cooperative innovation learning between all business or functional models and external organizations and truly and comprehensively improve the innovation capability of enterprises.

9.4.3 Basic model of total innovation learning mechanism

Corporate universities and research centers are the organizational form and important base of traditional innovation learning and still play an important role in the innovation learning mechanism. For example, GE's Crotonville Management Campus is the non-technology innovation learning base and the place of source of GE's innovation learning. The R&D Center of GE is called the "magic house" of technology innovation. In fact, other companies like Haier, HP and Siemens have not only established their own corporate universities and technology research centers, but also maintained close connections with external academic institutions and research institutions, which play an effective role in consolidating and developing the basis of innovation learning.

9.5 Analysis of Haier's total innovation learning mechanism

Figure 9-6 shows Haier's total innovation learning model based on entrepreneurship gradually formed through continuous innovation. The figure shows that Haier has many business units, which are always changing, but such business units are mainly classified by the categories of products, such as refrigerator business unit, freezer business unit, washing machine business unit, etc. If new business units like mobile phone and PC are strong enough, all household appliance business units may be integrated. That's probably why Haier takes back many functions of the business units, such as finance, purchasing, sales, etc. Besides, current architecture also stimulates the implementation of ERP and makes it convenient for the optimization of ERP process when the organizational structure is further adjusted. Compared with large transnational companies like GE, Siemens and HP, the total of all household appliance business units shown in

Figure 9-6 is the amplification of the innovation learning model of a business group. In Figure 9-6, the top is the architectural innovation learning of enterprises. Besides the strategy innovation learning and culture innovation learning promoted by the spirit of innovation, Haier controls its innovation process and reduces the risk of innovation mainly by strict industrialized management systems, such as OEC system and the concept of "everyone is an SBU". At the bottom of the figure are the main functional departments of Haier's innovation learning. Among them, Haier Central Research Institution mainly carries out the exploratory innovation learning of internally advanced technologies, cultivates core cutting-edge and systematic system innovation capability, provides other departments with necessary technological support on product development, integrates internal and external technology R&D resources, leads and manages R&D network, and takes responsibilities for the management of product lifecycle and technology innovation flow.

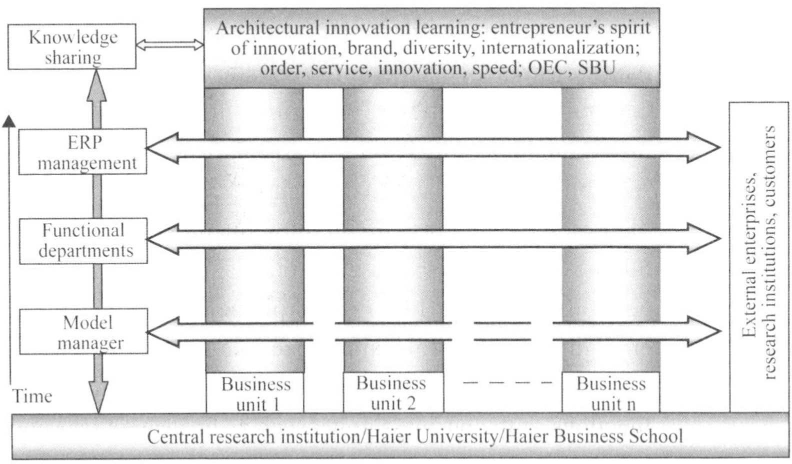

Figure 9-6 Models of Haier's total innovation learning based on entrepreneurs' spirit of innovation

Haier University and Haier Business School provide Haier employees with basic training of innovation capabilities and knowledge sharing. More importantly, it aims to improve Haier's non-technology innovation capabilities. Taking GE Management Campus as an example, it becomes the smelter of employees' ideology and the place to breed and spread Haier's innovation thoughts. The important part in Figure 9-6 is the inter-company innovation learning network of Haier to integrate external innovation learning resources, including the international resources of innovation learning. The left side is the internal innovation learning network formed by the inter-department coordination of innovation learning. Among others, "model manager" is the core of Haier's main horizontal coordination mode of technology innovation and integrated product innovation. Almost all functional departments, including R&D department, sales department, logistics department, production department, designing department and financial department, participate in product innovation. Meanwhile, ERP management platform is also used to manage the innovation process. Such a mode to coordinate product and technology innovation learning is still effectively implemented in Haier today. In such a way, Haier forms its current basic model of innovation learning at present. Seen in Figure 9-6, Haier's innovation learning model heavily relies on a strict system and hence makes Haier's innovation performance quite different.

The success of Haier's total innovation learning mechanism is attributed to its concentration on enterprise's innovation learning. The characteristic of Haier's total innovation learning mechanism is that it is led by entrepreneurs' spirit of innovation, Haier considers market as the buffer zone of the contradictions between innovators and employees through continuous architectural innovation learning of the architectural innovation system and modular innovation system and by leading the conflict of innovation to market competitions. It can not only protect both advocators and promoters of enterprise innovation, but also eliminate the negative effect of interpersonal relationship on enterprise reform and establish the innovation culture atmosphere where corporate interests are more valued than those of the individuals and small collectives. It realizes the harmonious and synergic total innovation system and enables entrepreneurs to win personal prestige and trust from employees. Besides, benefitting from entrepreneurs' continuous promotion of innovation learning, Haier improves the basic quality of its managers and grass-roots employees, lays the most important foundation for enterprise innovation and fully reflects the "human-oriented and learning-based" concept of innovation.

Haier's concrete innovation activities mainly focus on the general innovation learning and exploitation innovation learning and achieve good innovation performance, but its exploratory innovation learning plays an insignificant role in Haier's innovation practices and doesn't achieve much. Therefore, Haier's successful management experiences of innovation learning mainly originate from general innovation learning and exploitation innovation learning. It is understandable that innovation learning quite relies on strict and systematic management, because the certainty of the results of such innovation learning activities is much higher than that of exploratory innovation learning activities.

9.6 Conclusion

In the age of hyper-competition, total innovation has already become an important approach for enterprises to maintain sustainable development and win competitive advantages. However, total innovation cannot be separated from learning mechanism. Continuous innovation development eventually depends on innovation learning to acquire dynamic innovation capabilities. At present, Chinese enterprises have some problems in innovation learning, which make it impossible for Chinese enterprises to create effective innovation learning approaches, acquire high value-added enterprise knowledge, improve innovation capabilities or realize total innovation. Therefore, this chapter presents a comprehensive analysis of the learning mechanism of TIM and provides Chinese enterprises with necessary theoretical basis and practical guidance to acquire dynamic innovation capabilities through innovation learning.

Chapter 10

Leadership Mechanism of Total Innovation Management

Leaders are agents of innovation and reform. In both incremental innovation and revolutionary innovation, leaders are always considered the key factor to promote the reform of innovation leadership (Collins, Ross & Ross, 1989). Leaders are apt to attach importance to the future and provide the consciousness which goes beyond the followers' short-sighted behavior, while managers emphasize short-term objectives and make great efforts to solve the daily problems of their own departments and collective (Gardner, 1986).

At present, innovation, especially total innovation management (TIM), increasingly becomes a system project. As one of the main mechanisms to promote and coordinate system, leadership plays an important role in the practices of TIM. There are many factors which impact the organizational innovation, but we have reason to believe that leaders and their behaviors have an especially important impact on innovation (Mumford et al., 2002).

10.1 Role of leadership mechanism in promoting the total innovation of enterprises

Leadership is a key mechanism in the practices of TIM. However, how is the important role of leadership mechanism embodied in the practices of TIM? Some scholars pointed out that while assessing the effect and effectiveness of leadership mechanism, the emphasis should be laid on the key problems which are solved by the leadership mechanism during the process of innovation (Nahavandi, 2003). This section analyzes the role of leadership mechanism in stimulating the total innovation of enterprises from four aspects, namely stimulating employees' initiative for innovation, balancing technology innovation and non-technology innovation, laying ideological, cultural, resource and system foundation for total innovation, and guiding the direction of total innovation, as shown in Figure 10-1.

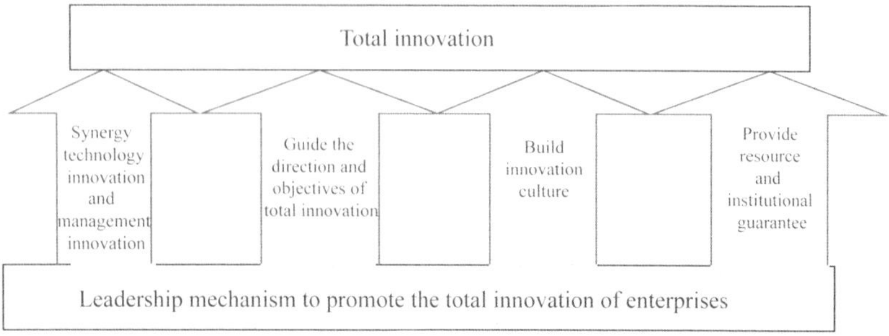

Figure 10-1 The important role of leadership in TIM practices

10.1.1 Encourage employees for total innovation

The theoretical paradigm of TIM points out that in market competition, innovation is no longer the exclusive duty of R&D personnel and technicians, but it becomes the collective behavior of all employees. Only by fully stimulating all employees' initiative and enthusiasm for innovation, exploring employees' innovation potential and realizing all-involvement innovation can leaders continuously and effectively carry out all-element innovation and all time-space innovation and improve enterprises' innovation performance. Although all-involvement innovation plays a critical role in realizing the total innovation of enterprise, very few enterprises can truly pique all employees' enthusiasm for innovation.

Case Study 1
Haier

In recent years, through internal "market chain" mechanism, Haier has enabled everyone to face the market, aroused every employee's creativity in the system and made everyone an SBU (strategic business unit) of innovation. The all-involvement innovation of Haier has achieved a significant performance level. From 1997 to 2001, Haier had totally received 136,000 rationalization proposals from employees, adopted 78,000 of them and created the economic benefits of 410 million yuan. Many parts, working procedures and products of Haier were named after the employees who innovated them, such as Baode Gasket, Mike Refrigerator, Yang Ming Separation Method, etc. ①

Sosik et al. pointed out that leaders play an important role in encouraging employees to innovate (Sosik et al., 1997; Sosik et al., 1999). On how to encourage the active innovation of employees, most researchers emphasize that leaders' support to innovation behavior are very important (Oldham & Cummings, 1996; Anderson & West, 1998; Bain et al., 2001). However, Kotter believed that measures should be taken to stimulate key personnel in the innovation system to work hard and realize expected effect. It requires leaders' "art of promotion" to make it (Kotter, 1988). Besides, Leaders must discover and use every employee's demands and requirements, further explore their potential motives and try to satisfy higher demands (Burns, 1996), and accordingly give play to every employee's innovation potential to the greatest extent.

Case Study 2
Haier

Zhang Ruimin points out that in Haier, human is the most active factor. Only by exploring the potential of every employee can enterprise become bigger, stronger and more innovative. And only by arousing the enthusiasm of everyone can Haier's continuous development be maintained. The most important task of managers in Haier is to fully arouse every employee's initiative and utilize everyone's wisdom and intelligence to contribute ideas and exert efforts for the development of Haier. ②

① Xu et al., Towards Total Innovation Management (TIM): the Emerging New Trend of Innovation Management – A Case Study of Haier Group. *Science Research Management*, 2003, 24(5)
② RCID Haier University Research Data, 2004

10.1.2 Coordinated development of technology innovation and non-technology innovation during the process of total innovation

During the process of total innovation, technology innovation and non-technology innovation connect with and stimulate each other. The transformation of technology innovation results into economic benefits must be supported by the corresponding innovation of non-technology elements like management, culture and system. Since technology innovation and non-technology innovation are closely related to each other during the innovation process, enterprises must balance technology innovation and non-technology innovation during business management and ensure the mutual effect and balanced development of the two.

The total innovation of an enterprise cannot be separated with the synergy development of technology innovation and non-technology innovation, while leaders play an important role in the synergy between the two. Senior leaders have a good and overall understanding of the enterprise and its external operations and strong capabilities to adjust all relationships within the enterprise. Only based on leaders' comprehensive judgments and systematic adjustments can the traditional paradigm which focuses on technology innovation be transformed to the new paradigm of technology and non-technology synergy innovation, and then TIM will be successfully implemented.

10.1.3 Provide good resource basis and institutional guarantee for total innovation

Stimulating all employees' creativity and coordinating multiple element innovation are two cornerstones of total innovation theory and two difficult problems in the practices of TIM. To realize all-element innovation and all-involvement innovation, practices must rely on the sound resource foundation and institutional guarantee laid by the leadership mechanism for total innovation.

Case Study 3
Haier

SBU is the basic unit of objective management. Such a unit has limited authorities and can only use limited resources. However, the way to allocate and use such resources may create different effects. In other words, such units have innovation space based on given authorities or resources.

While being interviewed by some media in Beijing, Haier CEO Zhang Ruimin expressed explicitly that Chinese enterprises must be well prepared to compete with strong foreign competitors and to meet more challenges. Haier has strengthened its integrating capabilities through business process reengineering. For either internal or external resources, and for domestic or foreign resources, only if Haier has strong integrating capabilities, can it integrate all these resources to serve itself. [3]

From a horizontal perspective, the process of total innovation involves complex business process synergy (such as synergy within a department and inter-department synergy). To improve the performance of total innovation, all-element synergy innovation is necessary. From a vertical perspective, the development and implementation of innovation often require a great deal of human resources and material resources. Therefore, only all-involvement innovation can effectively improve the performance of total innovation. As two important connotations of TIM, both all-element innovation and all-involvement innovation require the organization to provide sound resource basis and have strong

③ *Haier Weekly*, 2005-11-06

coordination capabilities. Only by improving and strengthening the leadership mechanism of TIM can the results of all-element innovation be achieved within the organization.

10.1.4 Guide the direction and objectives of total innovation

The theory of TIM points out that total innovation is the only way to adapt to the external environment and seek development opportunities (Xu et al., 2004). During this process, the proper leadership mechanism is the key to integrate external environment, internal organization and operation.

Case Study 4
Haier

For 19 years since its foundation, Haier has developed from a state-owned plant on the verge of bankruptcy to an internationally famous enterprise with 22 manufacturing bases overseas. Haier developed from a famous refrigerator brand to a famous brand in the whole household appliance industry and then the most valuable brand in China and even a world famous brand. Underlying the continuous increase in value is Haier's strategic transfer of continuous innovation: brand strategy, diversified strategy and internationalized strategy. Haier has undergone cross-industry and cross-region extension and expansion. However, every transfer of Haier's strategy is actively carried out. With profound insights into market opportunities and a global vision, Zhang Ruimin has promoted three strategic reforms conforming to the times and accordingly created the present Haier. [4]

④ *Workers' Daily*, 2004-03-09

Case Study 5
Founder

In July 1997, Wang Xuan put forward three approaches of the "internationalization of Chinese enterprises": the first approach is to cooperate with foreign enterprises to introduce technologies, occupy domestic market and exchange technologies with the market; the second approach is to introduce technologies, carry out low-cost production with sound management, and then export them to foreign markets; the third approach is to promote outstanding Chinese technologies and products to international market relying on self-owned innovation technologies.

Wang Xuan had rigorous thoughts as a scientist. Before putting forward the above conclusions, he had already conducted in-depth research and written that: at the initial stage of development, a country often has to adopt the first approach to shorten its gap with advanced international level in terms of products and management. Fujitsu was established as a joint venture with Siemens in 1935. Panasonic was established as a joint venture with Philips in 1950. Samsung was established as a joint venture with Sanyo in 1969. Daewoo was established as a joint venture with General Motors in 1967.

After conducting research on the growth models of Japanese and Korean enterprises, Wang Xuan put forward his creative idea: when Chinese enterprises are weak at the growth stage, they can adopt the first approach, "inviting a wolf into the house" and "dancing with wolf". But it may lead to two results: one is gradually transforming the first approach to the second or third approach, establishing its own technology innovation system based on external cooperation, eliminating the dependence on foreign technologies, "driving wolf away" after "dancing with wolf"; the other is being controlled by foreign counterparts, losing its own brand and power of technology R&D, giving up market but failing to acquire technologies, "being eaten by wolf" after "inviting a wolf into the house". Mr. Wang disapproved of "driving all wolves away", but advocated the mutual benefits and joint development of both parties in international cooperation. However, he asserted that "being eaten by wolf" is the tragedy of national industry.

At this stage, Mr. Wang established the internationalized strategy for Founder: "Founder Group chooses the internationalized road relying on indigenous innovation technology". Its independently developed phototypesetting system was introduced in the market in 1985 and obtained the monopoly position in domestic market in 1990. Since 1990, it began to enter the Chinese publishing industries and markets in Hong Kong, Macau and Taiwan and acquired a market share of 70% in overseas Chinese-language newspapers industry (including Southeast Asia and North America). It is based on Wang Xuan's correct internationalized strategy that Founder Japan subordinated to Founder Group could keep a foothold in Japanese market relying on innovation technologies with completely proprietary intellectual property rights. More than 300 Japanese-language famous media and newspaper organizations, including Nikkan Sports, have already adopted the Japanese-language phototypesetting system developed by Chinese people, thus fulfilling Wang Xuan's original expectation and dream – "Chinese people can gain a proper position in the international high-tech industry". ⑤

A great number of research studies show that leaders' perception of external environment has direct influence on their strategic decisions and will finally impact the innovation performance of organization (Prescott, 1986). By establishing strategies, leaders determine how to use the organizational resources and identify opportunities in the most effective way and consider whether the organization has sufficient resources to transform such opportunities to business performance.

---

⑤ Wei Xin. Truth of Innovation - Wang Xuan's Thought and Innovative Thinking. *Computer Weekly*, 2006-06

Besides, leaders are apt to attach importance to the future and provide the consciousness which goes beyond the followers' short-sighted behavior (Gardner, 1986).

Leadership mechanism is in fact a core interaction mechanism between the organization and external environment. Appropriate leadership mechanism can effectively help organizations improve their adaptive capacity to the environment through innovation, provide correct missions and strategies of total innovation, provide good strategic guidance on all-element synergy, better arouse the enthusiasm of all staff members for innovation and put forward realistic requirements on all time-space innovation.

10.2 Framework of leadership mechanism

The leadership mechanism to promote total innovation of enterprises is not a single mechanism but a complex mechanism consisting of multiple sub-mechanisms, including communication sub-mechanism, incentive sub-mechanism, culture creation sub-mechanism and decision-making sub-mechanism, as shown in Figure 10-2. The main connotation of decision-making mechanism is strategy innovation, which is to set up the general direction of total innovation by establishing strategic vision. The effect of incentive mechanism is to stimulate the enthusiasm of all employees for innovation, build an innovation platform for every employee and fully transform their knowledge wealth to economic benefits. The main effect of communication mechanism is to coordinate and solve possible problems which may appear during the process of total innovation, reform regulations and systems which may obstruct total innovation, and ensure the smooth implementation of total innovation. The main effect of culture creation mechanism is to cultivate and spread innovation culture and establish the cultural soft environment for total innovation.

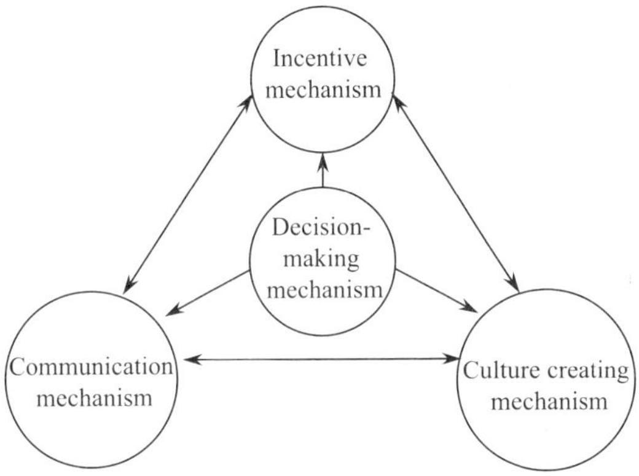

Figure 10-2 Framework of leadership mechanism

The decision-making mechanism plays a critical role. Only with the guidance of correct strategic decisions can the incentive mechanism, communication mechanism and culture creation mechanism play their roles effectively. Only through the synergy effect of these four sub-mechanisms can enterprises establish leadership mechanism to promote total innovation and ensure the successful implementation of total innovation.

10.2.1 Strategic decision mechanism

During the process of promoting the total innovation, the principal duty of leaders is to establish the strategic vision of total innovation. The strategic vision of total innovation describes the future vision which enterprises try to realize through total innovation and accordingly determines the missions, core operation philosophy and values of enterprises. To promote TIM, leaders must pass on the strategic vision to every employee through incisive and attractive short verses.

(I) Connotations and characteristics of the total innovation-oriented strategic vision

Generally speaking, the total innovation-oriented strategic vision consists of the organizational missions and values of total innovation. Normal organizational missions describe the ultimate objectives of enterprises and the characteristic measures taken to realize such objectives. The organizational missions of total innovation describe that the organization takes total innovation as the fundamental means of organizational development and the glorious vision to be realized through such means, including the specific tasks, guidelines, objectives, purposes, faith, operation principles, business definitions, etc. The organizational missions under the model of TIM often emphasize that organizational tasks are new and unprecedented products, services and experiences brought to target customers through innovation. For example, the mission of Sony is "to offer an opportunity to create and fulfill dreams to all kinds of people, including shareholders, customers, employees, and business partners. Dream in Sony!". The mission of Gemdale is "to create new living space". Under the model of TIM, innovation is not only an objective but also a means, a fundamental means to bring new products, services and experiences to customers. Therefore, organizational missions often emphasize the fundamental means of "innovation". For example, the mission of GE is "to improve living standards through science and innovation".

The values of total innovation are cherished by an organization, such as product innovation, continuous satisfaction of customers' higher requirements, etc. Leaders only emphasize the values, that the "spirit of innovation" is the core spirit cherished by the organization and only by delivering such values to all members of the enterprise can all people be clearly guided to realize the total innovation objectives.

(II) Effects of the strategic vision of total innovation on the implementation of TIM

A clear and effective strategic vision of total innovation can guide and coordinate the decentralized decisions and behaviors of decentralized people and accordingly stimulate all people to work together to realize the common objective of total innovation. The strategic vision of total innovation under the model of TIM has the following effects:

1. Embody the systematic and comprehensive nature of total innovation

Total innovation advocates a total reform of the organizational structure, culture, strategy, technology and market. It is a large and complex project and requires comprehensive and systematic thinking, planning, implementation and evaluation. Therefore, leaders need to construct a systematic and comprehensive vision, which can comprehensively and systematically convey the spiritual connotation and nature of total innovation in a terse and vigorous style and hence ensure the successful implementation of total innovation.

2. Strengthen the incentive and restraint during the implementation of total innovation

Research shows that "the juxtaposition of vision and a clear picture of current reality (where we are relative to what we want) generates what we call 'creative tension': a force to bring them together". When leaders establish the vision to serve the total innovation of enterprise and instill such vision deep into people's mind, such vision will bring all employees such "creative tension". On the one hand, it is such "creative tension" that stimulates members of the organizations to naturally generate the motive power to eliminate differences in expectations and all incompatible factors in innovation and eventually guarantee the realization of total innovation. On the other hand, it is such "creative tension" that puts pressure on members of organization to take responsibilities for the realization of the vision. Such pressure may cause certain restraints on the way organization members act and think and enable everyone to concentrate on the realization of vision. The effect of such vision ensures successful implementation of total innovation.

3. Ensure the durability of total innovation

Total innovation is a long process of evolvement. During such an arduous process, the strategic vision of total innovation can offer durable support to total innovation. Such support is mainly embodied in two aspects. The first is the persistence until the success of innovation during the process of single innovation. The strategic vision points out the development direction of organizational innovation. The second is the continuous innovation and the continuous pursuit of self-development. The success of one innovation merely means a phase achievement. Only through continuous innovation can the overall vision and organizational development be achieved to the greatest extent. Therefore, in this sense, the strategic vision of total innovation can offer persistent support on organizational innovation.

(III) How to establish and promote the organizational vision of total innovation

Developing an attractive vision is a creative activity, which cannot be generated from mechanical programs and requires leaders to have the extraordinary judging and analyzing capabilities to construct vision and deliver the connotation of vision with intuition and creativity. To establish a good vision, leaders must profoundly understand the organization (such as products, service, industrial environment, market environment and social and political environment), culture and all the members and stakeholders of the organization and have unique forward-looking insights into future development.

Establishing an organizational vision to promote total innovation is in fact the integration of two processes, namely establishing vision and instilling vision.

1. Analysis of key stakeholders

Single leader cannot have all necessary knowledge to develop a vision, so it requires the involvement of and supports from all stakeholders, which are necessary for the reform of important organizational reforms.

2. Continuous evaluation and refining of a vision

The development of a vision is an interactive and cyclic process of vision-strategy-action, rather than a simple and linear process. The implementation of a vision should be a process of continuous evaluation and refining. While continuously approaching the vision, the organization may continuously discover new possibilities and some originally impossible objectives become possible. Therefore, the establishment and implementation of vision is not a simple and linear process. It is an interactive feedback process, which impacts performance and needs to be updated and adjusted due to the changes of performance.

3. Steady preparations

Leaders should be well prepared before constructing vision. At first, it needs to encourage organization members, based on different environments and contexts. Secondly, leaders need to cultivate and create the cultural atmosphere suitable for the establishment of vision. Such culture is built on trust and encourages creativity and diversity. Thirdly, leaders need to analyze the resources and changes in the external environment of the organization in detail to determine the vision of organizational reforms.

4. Establishing an individual vision

During the implementation of TIM, it is necessary to continuously encourage members of the organization to develop their individual visions according to the organizational vision. Without individual visions, few members of the organization can comprehensively understand and be immersed in the common vision of TIM. Leaders should call upon organization members to develop individual visions which are suitable for their personal development and the planning of TIM vision. If all strong visions of organization members can be integrated, it will create a strong synergy effect and move towards the underlying objectives of individuals and organization.

5. Communication and consensus

Leaders should at first reach consensus with senior management team through high-quality communication. Reform leaders also need to carry out a series of communication and dialogue activities about the vision throughout the organization. On the one hand, it helps organization members consolidate their own visions. On the other hand, it will stimulate members to have better understanding of and provide more support on the common vision of the organization and enable members to reach a consensus on the vision. Reform leaders need to maintain a sincere attitude while carrying out "in-depth dialogue" with members. While reaching consensus with members through communication, leaders should treat others as equals, emphasize mutual respect and encourage the sharing of joys and sorrows. When a basic consensus is reached on the vision, the organization will become a "community of life". In spite of whatever obstructions, all members of organization should stay together to enjoy the joys of success or tide over the difficulties.

6. Implementation of TIM guided by the vision

Once most members of an organization understand and take an active part in the construction of individual visions and common TIM visions, the entire organization will step into a process to realize the visions of TIM. A good vision cannot only point out the development direction, but also continuously guide the sustainable development of the organization.

10.2.2 Incentive mechanism

The performance of total innovation in the final analysis relies on the abundance and application of human resources within the organization.

Incentive is a method to mobilize workers and a process of mental activities to strengthen people's will and enable them to have the internal spirit impetus to move towards the expected objectives. While investigating the employees' incentive, Professor William James of Harvard University discovered that: employees who get paid according to work can keep their job by exerting 20% to 30% of their capabilities. If they are fully encouraged, James believed they will realize 80% to 90% of their capabilities.

The incentive mechanism under the paradigm of TIM aims to arouse all members' enthusiasm for innovation and to promote and guide their innovation behavior via the strategic vision of total innovation. In other words, it is to adopt all effective methods to arouse their initiative and creativity to realize the objective of seeking development through total innovation. Therefore, establishing a rational incentive mechanism during the process of total innovation plays an important role.

(I) Main contents of total innovation-oriented incentive mechanism

The total innovation-oriented incentive mechanism innovation is mainly embodied in the following aspects:

1. Distribution mechanism of innovation enterprises: establishing the system of involving knowledge capital in profit distribution

Generally speaking, the corporate innovation on the incentive mechanism of enterprises should aim to fully arouse employees' enthusiasm for innovation. As to management talents, foreign senior managers' stock option incentive system can be used for reference to realize the consistency between the operating behavior of senior managers and the long-term objectives of enterprises, thus fully arousing the initiative and enthusiasm of management talents. As for technicians, it may take technology as capital contribution and transforming technological results to income. For innovators, certain incentive of property right should be provided based on the sufficient evaluation of innovation property right. In a word, the total innovation-oriented incentive mechanism should enable key staff members to participate in the distribution of enterprise profits relying on human capital and fully arouse their initiatives, thus realizing the objective of indigenous development of human capital.

2. Innovation-based enterprise management system: implementing human-oriented management system

To explore the knowledge capital of employees, enterprises must enable employees to recognize their own values and create a mechanism to let them voluntarily improve and develop and be willing to contribute their own human capital. It is necessary to offer employees' sufficient participation rights to arouse their initiative and enthusiasm. Therefore, the incentive mechanism of total innovation is to create a flexible working environment, provide a platform to exploit their talent, establish rules of the game, implement sufficient authorization and objective management, and endow them with certain right to control.

Case Study 6
Haier

In recent years, Haier has implemented the model manager system during the new product development process. Model managers within such a product range have sufficient decision-making power and should take full responsibilities, thus giving full play to their creativity and initiatives. Due to the internalization of responsibilities, while being confronted with difficulties, they have sufficient motive power to study consciously until the problems are solved. In the short term, it creates certain values for enterprises. In the long term, it helps build a good atmosphere for learning and improvement, not only retaining talent, but also significantly enhancing human capital.

(Source: RCID Haier University Research Data, 2004)

3. Innovation training mechanism: creating conditions for employees' self-realization

Under traditional incentive mechanism, enterprises attach importance to the salary increase and promotion, which enable employees to be greatly satisfied in terms of personal income and social respects. However, overly following traditional incentive mechanism will surely lead to the weakened effect of incentive. While the basic demands are satisfied, knowledge-based employees attach more importance to the spiritual demands and demands for self-realization. Therefore, the incentive mechanism within total innovation should also be oriented to encourage employees and develop human resources to the greatest extent. Enterprises should actively create conditions, encourage employees to conduct in-depth study and research in their own working field, provide them with opportunities to learn from and communicate with industry leaders and experts, and make more top talents stand out from the crowd.

(II) Main characteristics of total innovation incentive mechanism

In the incentive mechanism of total innovation, it needs to emphasize the organic integration of multiple incentives. A single incentive means may accomplish the very opposite. Therefore, the incentive mechanism of total innovation must emphasize the following:

1. Symbiosis and interaction between individual growth incentive and enterprise development incentive.

Based on sufficient understanding of the individual demands and career development interests of employees, enterprises should design professional careers for them. Besides, enterprises should also emphasize human capital investment on technicians, provide them with learning opportunities to receive education and improve their own skills, enable them to undertake more challenging work or promote them to more important posts, thus strengthening technicians' capabilities to realize individual objectives and competitiveness to gain occupational opportunities in the future and continuously increasing their values in human capital market.

2. Coexistence of material incentive and spiritual incentive

As the basis of corporate incentive mechanism, material incentives mainly include salary, bonus and welfare. It determines the satisfaction of employees' basic demands and is the most fundamental means of incentive. However, for high level talents, the effect of spiritual incentive is more obvious. Only by integrating material incentive and spiritual incentive and adjusting the balance between the two from individual to individual can the good effect of incentive be realized.

3. Paying equal attention to long-term and short-term incentives

During the process of total innovation, while implementing incentives, enterprises should integrate short-term incentive and long-term incentive to arouse employees' durable enthusiasm and initiatives. Short-term incentive can effectively arouse employees' initiatives in a short time and create good innovation performance. However, after the short-term effect ends, its incentive effect will probably decline fast. The long-term incentive may show effect slowly, but its effect may last longer and become stronger as time goes by. Therefore, during the process of total innovation, it is necessary to integrate long-term incentive and short-term incentive and establish effective incentive mechanism with rapid and long-lasting effect.

4. Organic integration of individual incentive and team incentive

At present, the technology intensive and intelligence intensive characteristics determine that many tasks should be completed by teams. In both new product development and improvement of technological process, teams can combine multiple advantages, skills and knowledge and emphasize individual creativities and the collaborative operations, thus making their respective advantages complementary to each other and utilize the advantages of the team as whole. Therefore, while providing incentives, enterprises must make a team incentive plan and implement the incentives targeting at the whole team. Besides, while carrying out team incentive programs, enterprises should subdivide the objects of incentives to the greatest extent and carry out individual incentives at the same time so as to realize the organic integration of individual incentive and team incentive.

5. Attaching importance to individuals' "self-incentive"

During the process of total innovation, while implementing incentives, enterprises should pay attention to the characteristics of workers, such as having strong self-esteem, valuing personal feelings and contribution, loving to accept challenging work and pursing self-growth, emphasizing "self-motivation" of individuals, carrying out effective self-supervision, self-evaluating and self-control, integrating employees' individual objectives with organizational objectives, satisfying workers' individual demands by realizing organizational objectives, and truly realizing "administering by non-interference".

6. Attaching importance to emotional incentive

Emotional incentive values employees' inside world. It is realized through two-way communication and exchange of emotion based on the plasticity, tendentiousness and stability of emotion. Inter-personnel emotional associations are taken as the means of incentive. The advantage of emotional incentive mechanism relies on its ability to eliminate employees' negative emotions, arouse employees' initiatives and generate the so-called "internal exciting force" in management.

Enterprises should not only make the best use of science and technology talents and enable them to create more values, but should also care for their work and life, and enable them to spend more time and effort in scientific research, form the sense of loyalty, belonging, identity and responsibility, and serve the enterprise whole-heartedly.

10.2.3 Coordination-communication mechanism

Coordination always plays an extremely important role in management. In essence, leader is a special form of communication and coordination. Fayol, founder of classic western organizational theories, put forward that "management is planning organization, command, coordination and control". He further pointed out that "coordination is creating harmony among all activities to facilitate the working and success of the unit". Therefore, during the process of TIM, enterprises should require all employees to cooperate with each other and make joint efforts to form an organic whole.

Malone and Crowston (1994), based on the interdisciplinary studies on coordination, established the coordination theory, which plays an important role in guiding the theories and applications in all relevant disciplines. They defined coordination as a process of managing dependencies among activities and believed that if there were no dependencies, it was unnecessary to carry out coordination. The research on the synergy mechanism of TIM system focus on the high complexity of innovation system, which makes its coordination mechanism very complex and hard to grasp. Only by summarizing the general principles and characteristics of coordination can the coordination be consciously applied in practices and guide the practices of TIM.

The coordination mechanism of TIM is completely different from the traditional one. TIM coordination mechanism requires being simple, flexible, dynamic and forward-looking and has to reflect the characteristics of total innovation, like dynamics, equality and complexity. It not only requires the coordination relying on rigid measures like an institutional system, but also needs to build firm trusting relationships, actively develop harmonious interpersonal relationships and establish the new coordination method "integrating flexible and rigid measures". The so-called "flexible coordination" means dealing with all kinds of complex problems or potential conflicts which may occur at any time by building harmonious relationships and mutual trust and relying on flexible and multi-level communication.

Compared with normal coordination mechanism, TIM coordination mechanism has the following characteristics.

1. Important effect of TIM coordination mechanism

TIM coordination mechanism plays a critical role in realizing TIM. Economist Williamson pointed out that social and economic issues are mainly to be adapted to the special time-space combined environment in a high-efficiency and rapid way. Such adaption can only be realized when the enterprise implements high quality total innovation. While facing a constantly changing environment, the core task of organization is to eliminate the threats caused by various factors and be continuously adapted to the constantly changing environment through innovation. Therefore, under such circumstances, the survival of an organization depends on the internal and external adaption process of the organization — this is the coordination mechanism of organization.

2. Coordinate the internal production and operation within the enterprise by using market mechanism

Coordinating by market mechanism means introducing market mechanism into the organization and breaking through the walls standing between employees and the market. The introduction of market mechanism delivers the market pressure to inside enterprises without any loss, thus strengthening employees' crisis awareness and sense of urgency and stimulating them to seek higher operation objectives through innovation. Under such a model, employees' behaviors are no longer coordinated by administrative measures but by the market instead. What is most critical is that the market mechanism can deliver to employees some basic principles, based on which employees are motivated to seek coordination and development.

3. Comprehensive application of several coordinating approaches

Compared with other types of synergy mechanism, TIM synergy mechanism requires applying several coordinating approaches. In the highly uncertain environment, the coordination of organization becomes more important and also more complex. In a simple and homogeneous environment, an organization may adopt more mechanical and centralized coordination mechanism, such as supervision, institutional system and process standardization. In highly uncertain environment, successful organizations always tolerate the existence of differences and have high diversities. Therefore, leaders must use meticulous integrating processes in many departments and adopt more organic, decentralized and differentiated structures. Only by comprehensively adopting several coordinating approaches can the organization be coordinated.

4. Information coordination increases, but the cost decreases

When the external environment is rapidly changing, total innovation is an important way to cope with external changes. However, a great deal of external and relevant information about multiple elements inside the enterprises lead to the increase of leaders' coordination. Therefore, in the TIM system, it needs to build a coordination mechanism of centralized coordination and decentralized disposal, which cannot only solve the increase of coordination content, but also significantly reduce the cost of coordination. Information technologies can break through time and space, promote a great deal of information communication, integrate the geographically scattered teams into a large coordination center, and improve the efficiency of coordination. While improving efficiency, the decrease of employees will reduce the cost of coordination. Meanwhile, computer technologies cannot only speed up information transfer, but also strengthen the purposefulness of information transfer, reduce the blindness of transfer and greatly save the cost.

Case Study 7
ABB

In the network operation of transnational companies, real communication and coordination focus on the application of regulations and rules rather than power. In ABB, the headquarters only retain 100 employees. The president just makes a round trip among different nodes within the company network. He doesn't order people about, but only checks the performance. The key reason why the whole network can work in an orderly and high-efficiency way relies on the control and coordination based on scientific regulations and rules. It provides all subsidiaries with strong decision-making power, but it also requires decision-makers to take responsibilities for the consequence of their decision. Therefore, it doesn't lead to the abuse of power. It allows managers of subsidiaries to have strong funds for usage power, but it doesn't lead to waste. The reason is that the company has established a scientific financial control system and corresponding regulations and rules which require each expenditure to be proved with the statement issued by external accountants and audit institutions. All actors should be responsible for their behaviors inconsistent with company regulations. In such a way, it endows all subsidiaries with the right of mutual exchange and free cooperation. Therefore, such coordination plays a significant role in improving the efficiency of the whole network.

10.2.4 Mechanism of ideological building and culture cultivation

Ideology and culture refer to the behavior standards, values and faith gradually formed during the business operation. Once they are formed in the organization, they will be delivered to new organization members through the socialization of organization, thus enabling employees to acquire the same behavior standards, values and faith rapidly and be blended into the big family of organization. The ideology and culture of enterprises deliver the behavior standards which are encouraged by the organization and accepted and followed by most employees. Such standards deeply impact the employees' thinking mode, working attitude and behavior pattern and can coordinate the harmonious relationship between employees and organization to a great extent. A proper corporate culture should encourage innovation, tolerate temporary failure, encourage employees to realize organizational objectives and encourage employees to consider the synergy among all elements from a systematic perspective.

(I) Ideological work with Chinese characteristics is the basis and premise to construct total innovation management

Ideological concept is the guide of innovation, internal motivation to carry out innovation and the basis and premise to realize successful innovation. Using Marxist theory and Mao Zedong Thought to carry out in-depth ideological work among employees and establishing a scientific outlook of the world and correct outlook on life is the foundation to promote all work and TIM.

Ideology lagging behind reality, old thoughts and bad habits are the main resistances to TIM. Therefore, to lead all employees of an enterprise to realize total innovation, the first thing is to cultivate ideology and upgrade concepts. The ideological innovation is the source of all innovations. That's because innovation is the conscious and purposeful behavior to satisfy enterprises' business management demands, while management ideology is the rational knowledge of management activities. Ideological innovation is in fact to generate, improve and enhance the rational knowledge of management activities. It is the inexhaustible source to stimulate other element innovation and improve the operation performance of enterprises. Strategy innovation, technology innovation, market innovation and system innovation are all led by ideological innovation. With laggard ideology and conservative thoughts, any other innovation of the enterprises is impossible. To realize the synergy among all elements of TIM, the most fundamental requirement is that all departments and all employees have the concept of putting the interests of the whole above everything else. Otherwise, no coordinating or incentive measures will work.

Ideological work is one of the important parts of the leadership mechanism with Chinese characteristics. The reason why some Chinese enterprises successfully implement total innovation inside is that their outstanding leaders have correctly used the successful ideological and political experiences in Chinese revolutionary traditions and made full use of them in the modern management work.

(II) Important role of leaders in building corporate culture

Leaders are originators and promoters of corporate culture and forerunners of reform. They play a significant role in positioning, creating, controlling and transforming the corporate culture during the establishment, control and development of corporate culture. Therefore, leaders become the most active factor in the dynamic model of corporate culture and have a great effect.

1. Leaders are originators of corporate culture

Through rational and smooth communication channels, leaders continuously convey their decisions, attitude and thoughts to every employee in a timely and rapid manner and make immediate responses to employees' opinions and ideas. They can strengthen the preliminary cultural concept in accordance with society, which enables the leaders and employees to reach consensus on objectives, form emotional blend and make consistent moves, it gradually becomes the common faith of all employees and forms the common values.

Leaders can also spread culture and form internal public opinion atmosphere through specific cultural activities and internal media. Besides, outstanding models in the enterprises can set positive examples for all other employees. Especially, the cultural quality, cultural accomplishment and leadership style of bosses, as non-right factors, will form great influence and emotional appeal and enable employees to take conscious actions.

2. Leaders are promoters of corporate culture

Unlike enterprises' strategy and organizational management system, corporate culture is not clearly visible and cannot achieve obvious results in a short term. But it can be spread to every corner of business management.

To make every member believe the vision and be willing to practice the common values, leaders have to practice what they preach. If common values are only verbal or written slogans and the leaders just order people about, such values cannot be accepted by employees and can never form a corporate culture. Corporate culture doesn't consist of preaching and slogans. It is embodied in behavior, daily decisions, management methods and code of conduct. Corporate culture is the practice of collective wisdom rather than what leaders advocate. Leaders should make an example for others and lead everyone to practice the corporate culture. They should have keen powers of observation and be able to analyze the psychology and objective environment of everyone, find common ground and reach consensus. Leaders play an important role in leading others to abide by the corporate culture.

3. Leaders are forerunners of corporate culture

Corporate culture is not invariable. It continuously changes and improves itself with the changes of the objective environment. When a certain value outlook is formed, it reflects the primary motivation and imagination of enterprise members. Relevant management system and working procedures established subsequently provide necessary measures and guarantees for the success of enterprises. However, with the enterprises' development, the changes of objective conditions, improvement of employees' quality and skills, and the changes of employees' demands, the original value outlook of enterprises may not be suitable for the current situations. At this time, senior leaders should question the original models based on the changes of the objective environment and respect for history and tradition and propose to transform operational philosophy and management methods, reform value outlook and develop a perfect cultural atmosphere. Such behaviors may face pressure and resistances in many ways. Leaders have to withstand the pressure and break through resistance relying on their administrative power and personal charms.

Leaders should actively promote the development and innovation of corporate culture. Through management, business decisions and strengthened information communication, they can speed up the transformation of employees' concept. If necessary, they can take compulsory measures to promote reform. It depends on the scope of change of the external environment.

Leaders are the forerunners of ideological and political work. Only if leaders do well in ideological work, can enterprises create a good ideological and political work atmosphere and everyone can pay attention to the interests of the whole, thus making all members banded together like strands of a rope.

10.3 Conclusion

Total innovation theory believes that innovation increasingly becomes a systematic project. As one of the main mechanisms of system promotion and coordination, leadership mechanism plays a very important role in the practices of TIM. In particular, it plays a leading and critical role in constructing the ideological and cultural basis of TIM and in cultivating people. Although many elements in the organization can impact the organizational innovation, we have reasons to believe that leaders and their behaviors have especially important influence. Therefore, as one of the three main mechanisms to promote the formation of total innovation, leadership mechanism has significant effect on the formation of total innovation. This chapter firstly discusses the roles of leadership mechanism in stimulating the total innovation process and then separately explains the four sub-mechanisms (strategic decision mechanism, incentive mechanism, coordination-communication mechanism and ideology and culture building mechanism) of leadership mechanism. In such a way, it fully elaborates the process and mechanism of how leaders stimulate the formation of total innovation within an enterprise.

Part Four

Innovation Benefits of Total Innovation Management

Chapter 11

Analysis on the Innovation Benefits of Total Innovation Management

11.1 Shortcomings of existing innovation benefit evaluation and TIM perspectives

11.1.1 Shortcomings of studies on innovation benefit evaluation

Innovation benefit evaluation is a method to supervise and manage the effect and efficiency of enterprises' innovation (including technology and management system innovation; normally, the focus is technology innovation). The systematic analysis and comprehensive evaluation of innovation benefit help enterprises recognize their own technology innovation status, make rational innovation decisions, analyze main factors that impact innovation benefits, correctly measure the effect of implementation, analyze the utilization efficiency of technology innovation resources, and reduce innovation risks, thus enabling enterprises to gradually improve their innovation systems, adopt effective technology innovation strategies, improve competitive advantages and obtain the best economic and social benefits. The objective of innovation benefit evaluation is not only summarizing and evaluating the innovation activities, but more importantly, serving the present and guiding the future. The innovation benefit evaluation should serve the innovation activities and play a guiding role in the innovation activities. Therefore, scientific and rational enterprise innovation benefit evaluation will directly impact the effect of technology innovation and the efficiency of management innovation and be related to the survival and development of enterprises.

The innovation benefit is affected by multiple factors, but the direct determinants are the input and output of innovation and the management of innovation. Many practical cases show that same innovation input may not obtain the same results. The main cause is the differences in innovation management. Innovation is a complex process and involves several functional departments like market investigation, R&D, production, sales and service. To improve the benefits of innovation, it needs to properly coordinate different departments, including the setup, information management and incentive mechanisms of organizations. Most enterprises don't have a set of complete or effective innovation management mechanism, which is usually the key influencing factor of enterprise innovation benefits. As a new innovation management paradigm, total innovation management (TIM) is the all-involvement innovation, all time-space innovation and all-element innovation, which includes the innovation of enterprise strategy, technology, system, culture, organization, market and management. However, domestic and foreign scholars' understanding of innovation benefit mainly focuses on the input-output efficiency and results, but ignores the innovation process and many other influencing factors of innovation benefit, such as management, strategy, culture and system. Therefore, existing innovation benefit evaluation can no longer satisfy the demand of TIM. To be specific, it has the following shortcomings (Chen & Chen, 2006).

(I) Overly emphasize the technology innovation resource input, but fail to correctly reflect the output of innovation

The current system overly emphasizes the R&D resource input. In fact, R&D resources are the input instead of innovation output. It is closely related to the changes of technology, but it cannot measure the benefit of technology innovation. Besides, in the environment of open innovation, R&D resources cannot include all efforts that enterprises have made in terms of technology innovation. For example, the benefits of "learning by doing" and the application of user knowledge, supplier knowledge and competitor knowledge cannot be fully reflected through the index of R&D resources input. Overly emphasizing R&D resources input cannot reflect the benefit of technology innovation. Furthermore, it may also cause the one-sided recognition and misunderstanding of decision-makers in enterprises. In open innovation environment, senior leaders must thoroughly change the one-sided viewpoint that R&D is innovation, make full use of and integrate the internal and external innovation resources, and improve the technology innovation capabilities and innovation benefits.

(II) Measure technology innovation only based on patent data and ignore other important indexes

Many scholars often use patent data to measure the technology innovation of an enterprise within a certain period, but patent data is not a suitable index of innovation output. Invention is not certainly technology innovation. Only the invention which has been successfully commercialized and led to obvious economic benefits is technology innovation. Many patents never lead to innovation, but only reflect the inventions which barely embody economic value. Chinese enterprises are even more special. Influenced by the passive protection and traditional concept in the past, many enterprises are often not willing to apply for patents for inventions with market prospect. They believe that applying for patent may leak their know-how, so they are not willing to publicize such inventions to protect their technology products and they are not willing to invest in setting up patent strategy department. Besides, since Chinese patent system is still developing, quite a number of enterprises don't want to apply for patent protection in order to "seize" the market. Many innovations are not corresponding to the patented inventions. Therefore, as a means of measurement, patent data can only reflect the technology capabilities but not the results of technology innovation of an enterprise. They cannot be used as the direct index of technology innovation benefit. Taking into consideration the protection of know-how at present in China, number of technical documents, number of technical know-how and number of research papers, among others, should be added as a supplement to innovation output to reflect the influence of technology innovation output on the accumulation of technology capabilities. The number of new standards established by an enterprise as a presider or a participant is an important index to measure the output of technology innovation. "The third-class enterprises sell labor; the second-class enterprises sell products; the first-class enterprises sell technologies; the first-class enterprises sell standards" gradually becomes a market consensus. The basis for the establishment of technical standards is technical strength. Only by carrying out continuous innovation, improving the quality and level of products and developing core technologies with proprietary intellectual property rights can enterprises have a say in the industrial standardization field. Without strong development strength and technology innovation strength, it is difficult to participate in the establishment of standards. By establishing first-class technical standards, enterprises can control the leading edge of technology development and firmly seize the initiative in technology development. It will help enterprises take a leading position in domestic and foreign market competitions. Therefore, the number of industrial standards established by an enterprise reflects the benefits of technology innovation of an enterprise and functions as an important symbol of first-class core competitiveness.

(III) Focus on product technology innovation, but fail to reflect the benefit of process technology innovation

Existing technology benefit evaluation index system mainly focuses on product technology innovation, but fails to reflect the process technology innovation benefits. Commonly used indexes to reflect innovation benefits include: number of new products, sales volume of new products, opportunities to earn foreign exchange through export and profit rate of new products. However, such indexes can only reflect the benefits of product technology innovation. Process technology innovation may improve the utilization of production factors, replace the labor force with the use of capital, improve labor productivity and reduce unit product cost; process innovation may lead to the significant decrease of material consumption and energy consumption, reduce pollution, decrease noise, improve working environment and reduce harm to the environment; process innovation may improve product quality and shorten the production cycle and lead time of products. Economic benefits and social benefits arising from such technology innovations are often significant, but it is hard to measure them or acquire the original data of indexes. It is incomplete and one-sided if the technology innovation benefits measured by process innovation are ignored. Therefore, the realization of the ultimate innovation objective depends on the multiple factors and multiple processes. The innovation focus of successful enterprises is not local breakthrough but the overall arrangement of process design. For example, Haier Group and CIMC (China International Marine Containers) attach great importance to the restraining factors and processes during the innovation. Haier always devotes itself to the reconstruction of internal process, while CIMC insists on the process technology, reduction of product cost and improvement of product quality.

(IV) Existing indexes pay insufficient attention to the benefits of long-term innovation and innovation process

Technology innovation capability is a process of dynamic development and continuous development. The benefits of innovation process reflect the management level of innovation activities and represent the potential and future technology innovation benefits of an enterprise. Prevailing innovation benefit evaluation fails to play a guiding role in the management of technology innovation and fails to provide effective support for the construction of technology innovation capability and improvement of innovation mechanism and innovation culture. Good innovation performance must be guaranteed by an outstanding innovation management process. Objective technology innovation benefit evaluation should also evaluate the benefits of innovation process as a supplement to reflect the long-term development potential of technology innovation and potential innovation benefits.

11.1.2 TIM innovation benefit evaluation perspectives

As to the shortcomings of existing innovation benefit evaluation above, this section constructs a TIM innovation benefit evaluation system and integrate the short-term innovation benefits and long-term innovation benefits as well as dynamic innovation indexes and static innovation indexes based on the theories on innovation at different levels in OECD's Oslo Manual as well as the connotation of technology innovation and development trend of modern technology innovation. It aims to establish a relatively complete enterprise innovation benefit evaluation index system and provides enterprises scientific basis and theoretical guidance for correctly evaluating technology innovation benefit, more effectively implementing innovation management, improving innovation mechanism and culture and enhancing technology innovation capabilities. To be specific, TIM innovation benefit evaluation method takes the two-dimensional innovation audit proposed by Chiesa et al. (1996) as its framework and divides innovation evaluation into performance audit and process audit. Meanwhile, it also combines the Balanced Score Card performance evaluation system proposed by Kaplan and Norton (1992) and introduces non-financial evaluation indexes in three fields to cover the shortage of traditional performance evaluation which lays particular stress on financial indexes. The traditional financial indexes convey the results which are already presented (Zhao, 2006), but it doesn't tell the managers what promote the future performance and how to create new values by investing in customers, suppliers, employees and technology reforms. Balanced Score Card can retain the attention to short-term performance via financial dimension on the one hand and promote long-term financial and competitive advantages on the other hand. In other words, by examining the finance, customers, internal process, learning and growth of enterprises, it can guarantee the implementation of strategies from the systematic perspectives.

TIM innovation benefit evaluation absorbs the theoretical quintessence of both two-dimenionsal innovation audit and Balance Score Card and consists of innovation process and innovation performance. In the past, many innovation benefit evaluations only attach importance to the final performance and ignore the innovation process. However, it is far from enough by only examining the innovation performance. The research on the process of technology innovation management is also necessary. That's because good performance must be safeguarded by good management process. Finding the reasons for good performance is the key of management. Just like an iceberg, innovation performance is what is above the water and innovation process is what lies beneath the water. Only by comprehensively evaluating both parts can the whole picture be completely reflected. TIM innovation benefit evaluation completely includes the following levels: (1) core innovation process, consisting of technology acquisition, innovation information, product innovation and process innovation; (2) peripheral system of innovation, consisting of innovation strategy, organizational environment, resource supply and technology accumulation; (3) innovation performance. The overall evaluation of technology innovation performance is mainly based on the modification of design thoughts in Oslo Manual (OECD, 2000), including new product sales rate, new product profit rate, number of new products, number of new processes, number of patents, number of established standards, etc.

The framework of TIM innovation benefit evaluation is shown in Figure 11-1 and Figure 11-2.

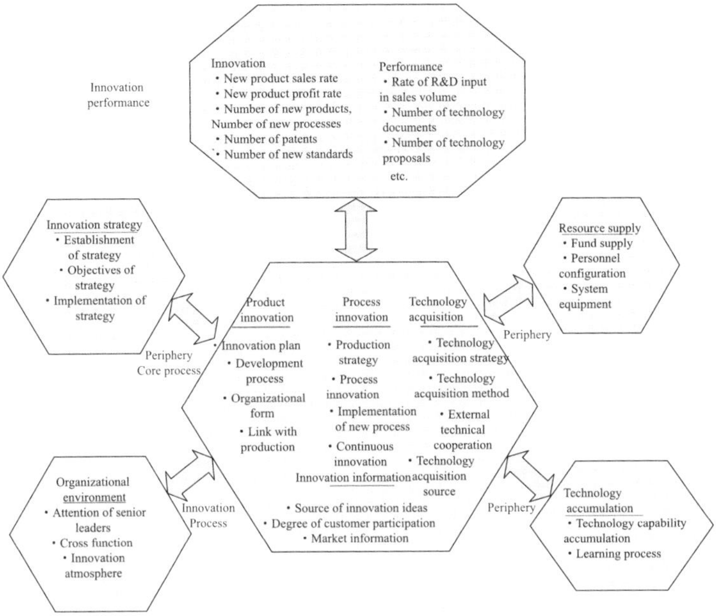

Figure 11-1 Schematic diagram of TIM innovation benefit evaluation framework

Source: *RCID Innovation Investigation Report of Haier and CIMC in 2004–2006.*

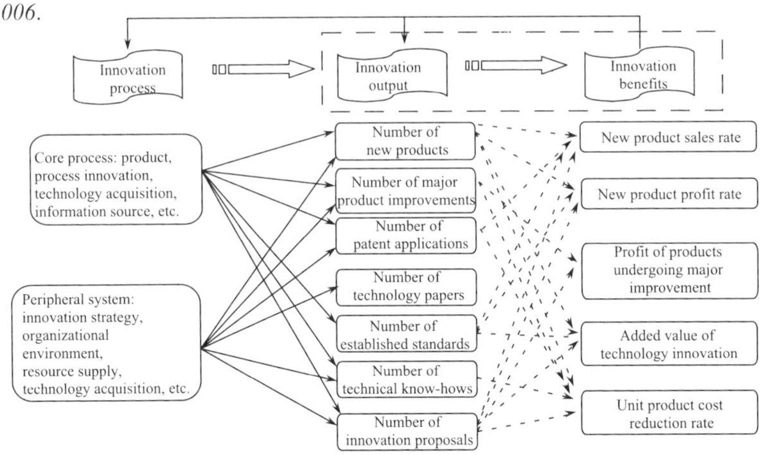

Figure 11-2 Diagram of relationship among TIM innovation benefit evaluation factors

Source: *RCID Innovation Investigation Report of Haier and CIMC in 2004–2006.*

11.2 Analysis of TIM innovation benefit evaluation factors

11.2.1 Analysis of main evaluation factors of TIM innovation benefit

(I) Innovation performance

Corresponding to the customer perspective and financial perspective of Balanced Score Card, TIM innovation benefit evaluation reflects the performance of innovation. To be specific, firstly, starting from the customer perspective means we have to figure out who our target customers are and what the value orientation of our service is. To achieve long-term financial performance, enterprises have to create products and services which are satisfactory to customers. The objective of technology innovation is to increase the economic benefits of an enterprise. Enterprises can create satisfactory products through product innovation, and decrease product cost and increase product competitiveness through process innovation. In other words, enterprises can gain market recognition and further realize its long-term financial objectives through technology innovation. Secondly, the financial perspective shows whether the implementation of strategy whose indexes have already been set and refined from all other perspectives can lead to the improvement of final results. All improvements of an enterprise should be directed towards the financial objectives. While evaluating the benefits of technology innovation, the financial indexes eventually embody the contribution of technology innovation to enterprise and reflect the current operation status to a certain degree. The main indexes to be examined should include return on investment, asset-liability ratio, main business income increasing rate, sales income increasing rate, net profit increasing rate, market value and economic added economic value. Therefore, compared with the customer perspective and financial perspective, the innovation performance indexes mainly include number of new products, new product sales rate, number of major product (process) improvements, number of patent applications, number of invention patent applications, innovation product unit cost reduction rate, production efficiency improvement rate, number of technical know-hows, number of innovation proposals, new product profit rate, energy saving index value and environmental improvement index value.

(II) Core innovation process

Corresponding to the internal process perspective of Balanced Score Card, TIM innovation benefit evaluation reflects the core process of innovation, i.e. identifying or creating the key process which is able to continuously increase the value for customers and shareholders. It has overcome the shortcoming of traditional benefit evaluation which stays in a certain department. Just reforming such indexes can only help organizations seek survival, but it cannot help them form unique competitive advantages. Therefore, to realize financial benefits and to attract and retain customers, enterprises have to rely on their internal procedures, decisions and behaviors eventually. The process of internal operation consists of a series of activities from determining customer demands, developing products and services items satisfactory to customers, manufacturing and selling products and services, to providing after-sales services. Such an innovation process is the control and coordination of all factors, including capital, personal, decisions, organization, mechanism, etc. The management of innovation process is to determine how to improve technology innovation. It mainly examines the ratio between internal innovation fund and external innovation fund, technology leaders, number of technology gatekeepers, technology innovation input/sales volume, industry-university-research cooperation innovation input, number of innovation technicians/employees, personnel training fee/innovation input, innovation information source, etc.

(III) Peripheral system of innovation

The learning and growing perspectives of the Balance Score Card construct the peripheral system of innovation. Learning and growing are enhancers to realize other objectives. The indexes set from this perspective are used to bridge the gap between reality and objective and accordingly guarantee the sustainable benefits in the future. To avoid the short-term behavior, enterprises should emphasize the importance of sustainable supporting conditions, attach importance to the analysis of the gap between existing capabilities and potential capabilities to satisfy demands, focus on the synergy among all internal and external factors, and fill the gap through balanced development of innovation strategy, organizational environment, resource supply and technology accumulation. Indexes for investigation on this level include: innovation intention and sense of responsibility of leaders, innovation incentive mechanism, organizational innovation culture and atmosphere, forecasting and evaluation capabilities of technology innovation, establishment and implementation effect of innovation strategy, level of technical equipment, and quantity of R&D institutions built in other regions.

11.2.2 Construction of TIM innovation benefit evaluation index system

TIM innovation benefit evaluation index system is shown in Table 11-1.

Category		No.	Index	Dimension weight (%)	Index weight (%)	Reference value S	Actual value X	Score X/S
Innovation performance (key indexes)	Direct benefit	1	New product sales rate					
		2	New product profit rate					
	Indirect benefit 1	1	Number of new products					
		2	Number of major product (process) improvements					
		3	Number of established new standards					
		4	Innovation product unit cost reduction rate					
		5	Production efficiency improvement rate					
		6	Energy saving index value					
		7	Environmental improvement index value					
	Indirect benefit 2	1	Number of patent applications					
		2	Number of invention patent applications					
		3	Number of technical know-hows					
		4	Number of innovation proposals					
		5	Number of technology papers					

continued

Category		No.	Index	Dimension weight (%)	Index weight (%)	Reference value S	Actual value X	Score X/S
Innovation process benefits (auxiliary indexes)	Core innovation process	1	Ratio between internal and external innovation fund					
		2	Technology leaders, number of technology gatekeepers					
		3	Brand value					
		4	Innovation information source					
		5	Personnel training fee/innovation input					
		6	Technology innovation input/sales volume					
		7	Industry-university-research cooperation innovation input					
		8	Number of innovation technicians/employees					
	Peripheral system of innovation	1	Innovation intention and sense of responsibility of leaders					
		2	Innovation incentive mechanism					
		3	Organizational innovation culture and atmosphere					

continued

Category		No.	Index	Dimension weight (%)	Index weight (%)	Reference value S	Actual value X	Score X/S
Innovation process benefits (auxiliary indexes)	Peripheral system of innovation	4	Forecasting and evaluation capabilities of technology innovation					
		5	Establishment and implementation effect of innovation strategy					
		6	Level of technical equipment					
		7	Quantity of R&D institutions built in other regions					

Source: *RCID Innovation Investigation Report of Haier and CIMC in 2004–2006.*

11.3 Case Study of TIM innovation benefits

11.3.1 Analysis of Haier's TIM innovation benefits

Since 1999, to adapt to the new economy, satisfy the demands for fierce comprehensive competitions, accelerate the market response to satisfy customers' individualized demands, and improve innovation performance, Haier has gradually carried out TIM with process reengineering innovation as forerunner, all-involvement innovation and all time-space innovation as main characteristics and effective synergy among strategy, organization, culture and technology innovations as basis and has achieved remarkable results, as shown in Figure 11-3.

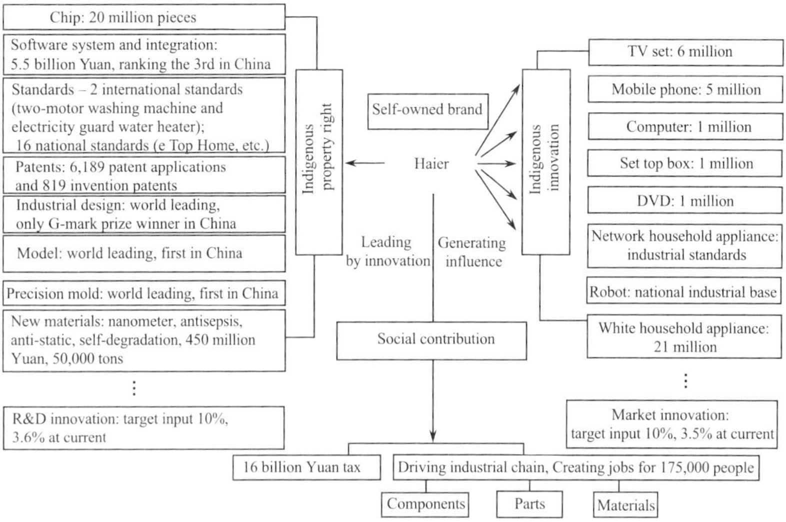

Figure 11-3 Overall diagram of Haier's innovation benefits

Source: Haier Chairwoman Yang Mianmian's speech in the opening ceremony of Zhejiang University & Haier Innovation Management Joint Research Center: "Build an innovation-based enterprise with indigenous innovation: innovation and development of Haier", Sept. 18, 2006, Hangzhou, Zhejiang.

(I) Innovation performance and benefits

(1) It has greatly accelerated R&D and innovation: in 2005, 1.8 new products were released and 2.8 patent applications were filed every working day. At present, it has totally applied for 6,189 patents, including 819 invention patents, ranking the first in China.

(2) It has greatly accelerated the responses to market. After implementing TIM, the lead time of refrigerator was decreased from 9.5 days to 6.5 days, decreasing 32% on average; the customer response time of different departments was decreased from 36 days to 10 days; domestic procurement cycle was decreased from 10 days to 3 days; the order processing time was decreased from 7 days to 1 day.

(3) It has significantly reduced the cost of production and operation and comprehensively improved the whole-process operating efficiency. Through whole-process innovation, the business process has been geared to first-class international companies, thus greatly enhancing Haier's international competitiveness. The area of warehouse for finished products was decreased from 290,000m^2 to 210,000m^2. Assuming the warehousing fee for each square meter is 0.3 yuan per day, it saved 9 million yuan warehousing fee per year. The purchasing fee was decreased by 4%. By cutting the unqualified international suppliers, Haier decreased the purchasing cost by 24 million yuan.

(4) In 2005, the annual business volume of Haier reached 103.9 billion yuan, about 20,000 times as high as that 10 years ago, and its value of exports reached U.S. 1 billion dollars. For 22 years since its foundation, it has maintained the average growth rate of 63% and paid taxes of 10 billion yuan.

(II) Innovation process benefits

(1) Growth of brand value. With the implementation of internationalized strategy, Haier's reputation overseas became better and better. According to the investigation of Euromonitor, an authoritative consumption market investigating and analyzing institution in the world, in 2005, Haier ranked the fourth among white goods manufacturers in the world and the market share of Haier refrigerators in global refrigerator brand market ranked the first in the world. In the list of World Top 500 Brands made by World Brand Lab, Haier ranked the 89th due to its continuously increased investment overseas, higher degree of internationalization and rise of brand awareness in the world. On August 30, 2005, in the "China Top Ten World Class Brands" published by British Financial Times, Haier ranked the first. All such facts proved that: the international competitiveness of Haier achieved the first level in the world.

(2) It accumulated core competences. Through TIM, on the one hand, Haier integrated global science and technology resources and used them for innovation. On the other hand, Haier seized every opportunity to cultivate its own indigenous innovation capabilities to ensure the continuous competitiveness. Besides, through TIM, Haier could satisfy users' individualized demands faster than its competitors and accordingly strengthened its core competences, as shown in Figure 11-4.

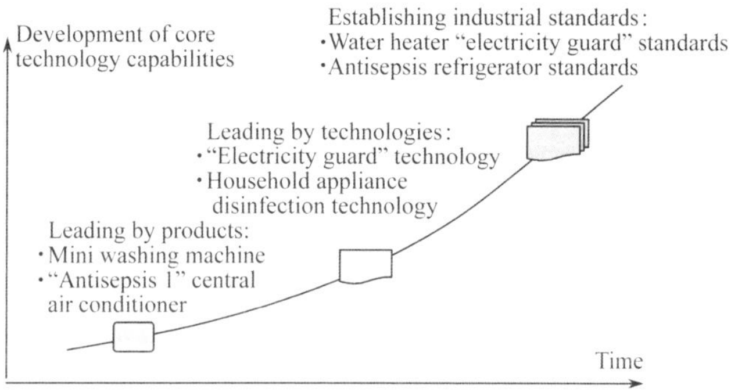

Figure 11-4 Development of Haier's core technology competences

(3) More cooperation with external research institutions. Haier has set up 15 R&D centers, 6 design departments and 10 science and technology outlets in Europe, North America and Asia-Pacific region, thus forming a global information network. Haier has abandoned the closed, linear and low-efficiency development method and creatively implemented the parallel development based on the integration of global technology and intelligence resources. Haier's network household appliance series, which made quite a splash in Domotechnica 2001, integrated the technical designs of Japanese and American experts and the color designs of French fashion designers. Different kinds of design and development are carried out synchronously, thus greatly accelerating the innovation.

(4) Haier, by joining hands with 28 companies with first-class technology in America, Japan and Germany, has established Haier

Central Research Institute. Besides, it has set up 10 international first-class advanced technology labs on environment, electromagnetic compatibility, etc. and established 48 scientific research and development entities in China and foreign countries by making use of global technology resources. The application of such advanced technologies and cooperation with international first-class scientific R&D institutions enabled Haier to realize the transformation of scientific and technological achievements by using the most advanced technology innovation means.

11.3.2 Analysis of CIMC's TIM innovation benefits

Founded in 1980, China International Marine Containers (CIMC) was one of the earliest sino-foreign joint ventures in Shenzhen Special Economic Zone and also one of the earliest four container manufacturers in China. At the very beginning, CIMC was only an unimpressive small container manufacturer. Its brand awareness was a far cry from large container manufacturers in Korea and Japan and its scale was even smaller that many container manufacturers in China. Through 26 years of tremendous development, especially in recent 10 years, CIMC has already transformed from a traditional product manufacturer to a strong play in global container manufacturing industry and the only manufacturer and supplier who can provide dry cargo containers, refrigerated containers, tank containers and special containers in the world. Now, it has also successfully entered the field of road transport vehicles. With 6 product fields, 24 product series and over 1,000 product varieties, CIMC is a leading manufacturer with international competitiveness in world container industry. Since 1996, CIMC had maintained the largest output and sales volume of containers in the world and an international market share of 50% for several years. In 2005, the sales income of CIMC exceeded 30 billion yuan. With more than 40 wholly-owned subsidiaries and holding subsidiaries in China and foreign countries, 34,000 employees and a container market share of over 50%, it has steadily seized the top position in world container industry.

For 26 years, besides the significant position of its products in terms of production, sales volume and market, CIMC has also achieved its excellence in innovation. CIMC has always given top priority to the technology development and innovation management, continuously strengthened indigenous innovation capabilities and led the value increase and industrial upgrading with technology innovation. Relying on such development strategy which is much better than that of many traditional manufacturing enterprises, CIMC has basically grasped the core technologies of the industry and became an industry leader by leading the technology development direction of world container industry. After 1996, CIMC began to implement the strategy of technology-led development and insisted on the three-in-one indigenous innovation route of introduction-absorption-re-innovation, integration innovation and original innovation, thus gradually grasping the core designs of components and key technologies of products and creating numbers of new products like safe and intelligent containers, environmentally friendly wood floor and water-based paint, energy saving welding machine, ice chest green foaming agent and indigenous innovation vehicle model.

(I) Innovation performance

(1) The sales income and profits rate of innovation products have a substantial growth, as shown in Figure 11-5.

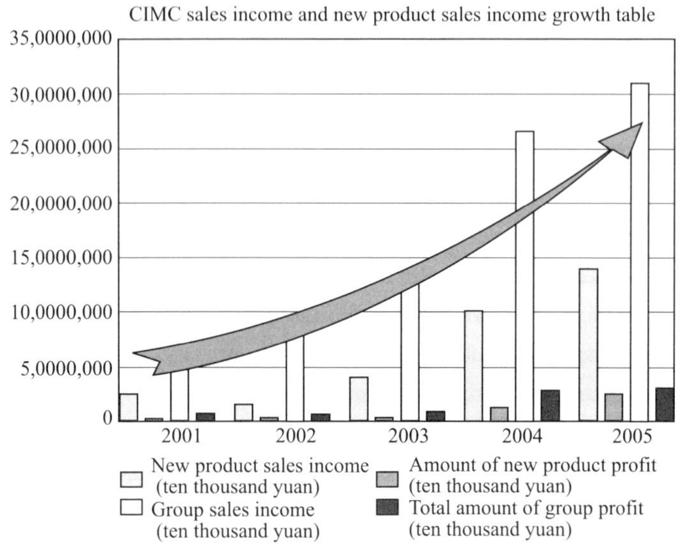

Figure 11-5 Increase of sales income of profit rate of CIMC's innovation products

Source: CIMC Vice President Wu Fapei's speech in the opening ceremony of Zhejiang University & CIMC Innovation Management Joint Research Center: "Implement indigenous innovation strategy and build a leading position in global industry", Sept. 19, 2006, Hangzhou, Zhejiang.

(2) As to product development, CIMC has independently developed many new products with proprietary intellectual property rights and established the all-round competitive advantages with both standard dry cargo containers for low-end products and special vehicles for high-end products through TIM. It is the only container manufacturer in the world who can provide all kinds of products. The representative products include intelligent container, environmentally friendly container, environmentally friendly cryogenic storage container, cyclopentane foaming agent, intelligent tank container and tank truck, A380 boarding bridge products, eucalyptus wood board, etc.

(3) As to patents and standards, by far CIMC has already applied for more than 850 independent patents, including 240 invention patents

and 80 applications overseas. Besides, it has all core technologies in six major product fields. CIMC takes an active part in establishing (revising) national laws, regulations and standards and reestablishing national industrial standards. At present, it has totally taken a part in the establishment of 36 international, national and industrial standards in 6 product fields. Among them, 9 standards have already been accepted as national and industrial standards. Furthermore, it is the only representative of Chinese enterprises who participated in the establishment of international standards of container industry.

(4) As to its position in industry, total innovation enables CMIC to rise rapidly and have a dialogue with international leading enterprises. In 1994, CIMC was just a passive make-to-order plant. In 2006, CIMC became the container supplier with largest sales volume in the world and the dominant power which led the technology development direction of world container industry.

(II) Innovation process benefits

(1) Brand value. When many Chinese manufacturing enterprises were still struggling for survival in fierce price war, CIMC had constantly strengthened its competitive advantages with continuous and high-quality total innovation activities and developed from a small Chinese container manufacturer to a magnate in the world container manufacturing industry. Data show that CIMC brought its superiority as a “world factory” into full play relying on its outstanding production and production activities and realized the leap-type transformation from a market follower to an industrial frontrunner through high-quality total innovation activities. For five years in succession, CIMC was listed by Fortune (China) as one of “Top 100 Listed Companies in China” and ranked the 3rd in the “Top 100 Listed Companies with Strongest Competitiveness in China in 2005” published by Global Competitive Organization. In 2005, CIMC President Mai Boliang was selected as one of “Top 25 Most Influential Business Leaders in China” published

by Fortune. In 2005, CIMC ranked the 28th in the "Top 500 Most Valuable Brands in China in 2005" selected by World Brand Lab and ranked the 55th in the "Top 150 Asian Companies" selected by Business Week. At present, CIMC has already become a "one-stop and full life circle" service provider which provides the design, manufacturing and maintenance of all kinds of products. In the fields of dry cargo containers, refrigerated containers, special containers, tank storing and shipping equipment and road transport vehicles, CIMC stands at the leading edge of global industrial development. What is more important, CIMC has already gasped the technical leadership in the development of container products and fundamentally consolidated its competitiveness. Now, it is developing itself towards a leading enterprise in global container industry.

(2) Effective human resources management system and incentive system. In terms of the construction of human resource teams, it has consciously encouraged technicians to bring forth new ideas and create excellent innovation atmosphere for all employees by introducing broadband salary system, two-way processional development road and planning of professional development. By organizing annual innovation meetings, "3+1" innovation project, programs for technological breakthroughs, technical excellence center and other innovation activities, it arouses the employees' enthusiasm for innovation and rewards technicians' achievements of major innovations.

(3) Technology innovation based on external cooperation and independent development. Based on the careful analysis of CIMC's innovation approach in 26 years, it is clear that every result of the major technology innovation of CIMC has undergone the clear route from imitation, learning to independent development. The refrigerated container business of CIMC is a classic case. In 1995, CIMC decided to produce standard refrigerated containers to expand its business, while the material used for refrigerated container contained 95% aluminum. At that time, Japan seized all core technologies about aluminum

refrigerated containers and Germany seized all core technologies about stainless steel refrigerated containers. To choose Japanese technologies or German technologies, such a decision would have a significant impact on CIMC's future market competitiveness. Through careful industrial and technological analysis, CIMC accurately estimated that the refrigerated containers would surely develop towards steel containers. Therefore, CIMC got rid of the traditional thinking mode and chose to buy German proprietary technologies instead of Japanese aluminum container technologies which were much more popular then. Afterwards, CIMC began to produce steel refrigerated containers in Shanghai. By 2000, CIMC had not only digested and absorbed German proprietary technologies, but also had several proprietary patents. By authorizing such patents to other manufacturers, it collected about three million yuan patent royalty every year. At present, CIMC has the world largest refrigerated container product base and become the technology leader in global refrigerated container industry.

(4) CIMC also attaches great importance to researches on key technologies and generic technologies, actively cooperates with universities, research institutions, suppliers and customers on basic research and gradually drives the technological advancement and value increase of the whole industrial chain with researches on advanced technologies. Based on the researches on and innovation of basic material technologies, environmental protection technologies as well as the development of radio-frequency technique, container wood floor materials, composite materials, environment friendly foaming agent, environment friendly paint, welding technologies, energy saving technologies and waste gas treatment technologies, CIMC has constantly improved its technology capabilities and implemented the responsibilities and duties of a Chinese enterprise. Aiming at intelligence, safety, environmental protection, high efficiency and energy conservation, CIMC actively explores and constantly releases new research results and drives the technological advancement and value increase of whole industrial chain based on the researches on

advanced technologies.

(5) Organization innovation: distributed R&D management and organization system. Organization innovation is the important guarantee for the implementation of TIM. Innovation-based enterprises require flat and network organizational structure, which has to be adjusted in good time according to the innovation requirements. Taking into consideration that its subsidiaries are distributed in different regions and even different countries, CIMC has carried out bold innovation on its organizational pattern, established distributed innovation system with characteristic "centralized market and distributed R&D and manufacturing", and included the enterprises without technology sub-centers into the technology development system of the group through sharing and joint research and development of manufacturing technologies and achievement of product technologies.

(6) Distributed innovation system requires rapid and convenient sharing and exchange of innovation achievements, enables the sufficient flow of innovation resources and interaction among different enterprises, and makes use of the synergy resource advantages to the greatest extent. In this way, over 1,000 technical experts and R&D engineers distributed all over the world can realize the sharing and complementation of objectives and resources and improve the overall competitiveness of the group. CIMC actively uses modernized information technologies as the guarantee for technology innovation and R&D. Among others, through the product data management (PDM) system synchronously built by technology center and group ERP, CIMC has established a product R&D synergy platform between enterprises and sub-centers, thus realizing the integration of computer-aided technologies as well as the integration of PDM and ERP and guaranteeing the high-efficiency of operation of R&D and production models. CAE computer center established in 2003 provides all enterprises with strong support for the improvement of product reliability. The upgrading of R&D and IT tools have improved the product development efficiency, shortened

the product development period, established standard and high-efficiency quality assurance system and customer-centered internal operation system of rapid response, and improved its competitiveness in international market.

11.3.3 Analysis of Baosteel's TIM innovation benefits

Shanghai Baosteel Group Corporation (hereinafter referred to as Baosteel) is a large iron and steel conglomerate set up on November 17, 1998, with the former Baoshan Iron and Steel (Group) Corporation as the core, and absorbing the former Shanghai Metallurgical Holding Group Corporation and the former Shanghai Meishan Group Co., Ltd. Now, Baosteel is one of the most profitable steel enterprises in the world enjoying international competence, and its annual production capacity is about 20 million tons. Baosteel produces high demand products in the domestic and international market.

Since its foundation, Baosteel follows its "premium products" strategy and aims to become the prime research and development base for new processes, new technologies and new materials in China's iron and steel industry. Baosteel's premium products include automobile steel, oil and gas exploitation and transportation steel, stainless steel household electric appliance steel, transportation facilities steel, silicon steel, boiler and pressure vessel steel, food and beverage packing steel, metal production steel, special material steel, high-grade construction steel. Baosteel aims to become the prime R&D base for new processes, new technologies and new materials in China's iron and steel industry. Baosteel follows a strategy of "one main industry of exceptional quality with appropriate and relevant diversified trades". Besides its main steel business, Baosteel also engages in diversified industries such as trade, finance, engineering & equipment manufacturing, information, coal chemical industry, deep processing of steel products and recycling. Baosteel conducts internationalized operation. Its global network, including 20 overseas and domestic trading companies, has taken shape. Baosteel cooperates and establishes joint ventures with international steel giants; it has made strategic alliances worldwide to achieve win-win result on the basis of mutual benefit.

Baosteel has committed itself to clean production and paid great attention to environmental protection to make a green Baosteel. Baoshan Iron & Steel Co., Ltd. is the first enterprise among the domestic metallurgical circle to get the ISO14001 certificate. Its greenbelt covers 42.71% of total plant area, and its air quality in the plant area has reached the standard of a state-level scenic spot.

(I) Innovation performance

(1) Sustainable growth of performance. In 2004, it produced 21.41 million tons steel, realizing a year-on-year increase of 7.8%; it sold 22.50 tons commercial steel materials, realizing a year-on-year increase of 9.8%; it achieved the consolidated sales revenue of 161.8 billion yuan, realizing a year-on-year increase of 34.4%; it achieved the consolidated revenue of 21.9 billion yuan, realizing a year-on-year increase of 66.3%; the sales price of steel per ton was significantly increased. The benefits of high added-value products became increasingly obvious. The sustainable growth was realized. As shown in Figure 11-6.

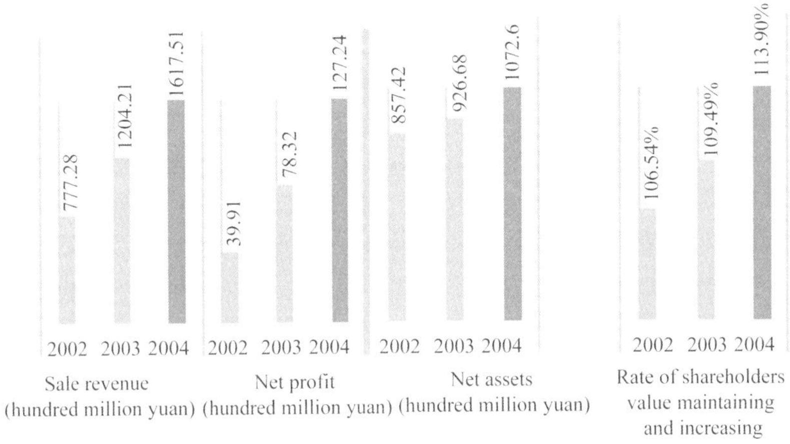

Figure 11-6 Diagram of the sustained growth of Baosteel's innovation performance

Source: *2004 Annual Report of Shanghai Baosteel Group Corporation.*

(2) The unit product cost significantly decreased. At present, the high-end steel products Baosteel feature the lowest price in the world. Low cost is one of Baosteel's advantages. It is mainly embodied in the following aspects: The first aspect is the labor cost advantages. The labor productivity of Baosteel is at the international leading level, so it has the low labor cost advantages. The second aspect is the obvious scale effect. Except for primary rolling, all other working procedures of Baosteel are at full-load production, thus realizing the full scale effect. The third aspect is the low energy cost. Baosteel has world leading energy recovery rate (negative energy steelmaking, world first gas turbine electric generator) and scientific and reasonable plant configuration. Almost all its energy media are produced by itself, thus forming Baosteel's low energy cost advantages. The fourth aspect is the low consumption cost. Baosteel has good capital reputation, stable supply chain and coastal location, which greatly reduce its purchasing cost. Plus the advanced consumption indexes, it has already become Baosteel's low consumption cost advantages (Fan et al., 2006).

(3) The patents have significantly improved the enterprise's technology innovation level and core competences. By the end of 2005, Baosteel has in total applied for 2,141 patents, 1,036 of which have been granted, and has 3,339 items of technical know-how. It has also applied for 8 PCT international patents, 2 of which have already been granted. It has 29 trademarks registered in the Trademark Office of the State Bureau for Industrial and Commercial Administration and 35 foreign registered trademarks. In recent years, over 70 patented technologies of Baosteel have won gold or silver prizes in international invention exposition or Chinese patent technology exposition. 70% of its patented technologies have been put into effect and promoted. Relying on such a large scale of stocked intellectual properties, Baosteel's technology trading business rises with its technology trading volume increasing rapidly. By far, it has totally signed technology trading contracts valuing 250 million yuan. After reorganization, Baosteel's number of applied patents and authorized technical know-how items has undergone a rapid annual increase of 20%. From "introduction, digestion, tracking and innovation" to "independence, openness, integration and innovation", Baosteel has formed unique intellectual property features during the practices of technology innovation practices. In recent years, to encourage technicians to protect and implement its application of patents for technology innovation, Baosteel has established the technicians' Technology Innovation Mileage Accumulation (TIMA) program, which sorts patents, technical know-hows and values they create in internal implementation and technology trading by different weights and takes intellectual properties as a scale to measure technicians technology innovation capabilities and contribution degree. By promoting "TIMA" program, it has greatly activated technicians' internal demands for intellectual properties. In 2004, the proportion of patents applied by technicians was increased to 74% from 61% in 2003.

(II) Innovation process benefits

(1) Brand growth. On December 6, 2004, Standard and Poor's

announced that it was raising Baosteel's credit rating from "BBB" to "BBB+" with a "stable" outlook. In July 2005, Baosteel ranked 309th in "2004 World Top 500 Companies" selected by Fortune. It became one of the first enterprises in Chinese competitive industry and manufacturing industry which continued to hold a post in "World Fortune 500".

(2) Energy conservation and energy consumption reduction. Since the construction of its plant, Baosteel has made it a top priority to maintain a balance between manufacturing efficiency and environmental protection. The company has deployed the most advanced production facilities and environmental equipment in order to reduce pollution at the source. It has also continuously upgraded its technology to reduce consumption of resources and energies during production. In 2004, total energy consumption per ton of steel was 675 kg and water consumption per ton of steel was 4.08 m^3, in line with international standards and only 1/4 of average domestic level. Researches to develop better products are ongoing. The company launched the project to develop non-chrome fingerprint-free products, and successfully co-developed the CT-308T9H paint with a Japanese partner. Both parties would share and apply for the related patent. In 2004, the company released its first ever environmental impact report to the public, providing an objective and systematic overview on clean production, policies, implementation and management for high anti-pollution standards.

(3) Environmental protection. Baosteel implements strict environmental management, comprehensively promotes clean production and ISO14001 environmental management system, and aims to establish an eco-type iron and steel enterprise. After its environmental management system was established in accordance with ISO14001 standards, Baosteel continues to develop its environmental management through periodic planning, implementation, inspection and improvement. All its indexes of environmental protection have already reached the first level in the world and it has been certified as a "National

Environmentally Friendly Corporation". According to the objective of building an eco-type iron and steel enterprise, all it subsidiaries also insist on the road of sustainable development. In terms of product structure adjustment, administration of pollution and greening construction, they have all made great efforts for large-scale planning and reconstruction. In 2004, Baosteel stopped one of its converter and a steelmaking production line in advance, thus greatly decreasing the emission of dust and smoke and greatly improving the environmental quality in surrounding areas. Meanwhile, it has also demolished many old buildings for the construction of greenery and created outstanding ecological environment with beautiful view. Baosteel adopts advanced and low-pollution production technologies and advanced and mature environmental protection technologies in its new and reconstruction projects. During the production, it has also enlarged the input in environmental protection and strictly controlled the generation, disposal and emission of all pollutants.

(4) Rapid enhancement of core competences. Through technology innovation, Baosteel has already formed its core technology chain with internationally leading process technologies and production equipment. Its steadily decreased cost of molten iron, molten iron purity control, thickness controlling precision of hot rolling, shape and thickness controlling precision of cold rolling and design of steel pipe hole pattern have all reached advanced level in the world. A number of its preceding researches, like thin-strip casting, nanotechnology, spray-up process and electromagnetic metallurgy, have also made headway.

(5) Development of key process technologies has achieved remarkable results. Baosteel has successfully developed new mining technology of pillarless sublevel caving with high sublevel and large drive interval and improved the high phosphorus ore beneficiation technologies. Its researches on low-cost ore blending, coal blending and blast furnace coal injection have also achieved remarkable results. With the increasingly improved clean steel production technologies and

vacuum refining technologies, its pipeline steel, interstitial free steel and petroleum pipeline have also undergone rapid development.

(6) Further improvement of automation technologies. By applying automated technologies, the steel rolling system of Baosteel has continuously improved its product precision and evenness, creating conditions for the production of high-end products. Integrated technologies have made breakthrough progress. The converter dephosphorizing reconstruction project has been completed and put into operation, thus providing strong technology and equipment support for the production of ultra-low phosphorus steel and pipeline steel as well as high quality wide and thick plates. It has laid a foundation for the steel plant to reach world class level. It has successfully developed Manufacturing Execution System (MES) and several key technologies, which are consistent with national situations and in line with international standards. It has formed MES product software with completely proprietary intellectual property rights.

(7) Rapid development of production technologies. Baosteel has carried out researches on general application technologies, like the forming technology, welding technology, rust protection and coating technologies, and special technologies like tin plate, electrical steel plate, oil well pipe, boiler pipe and wire rod. Preliminary results have been achieved.

(8) Continuous improvement of scientific research conditions. Baosteel has already established laboratories on tailored blank laser welding, thermal spraying and electrical steel as well as large scale smelting unit, steel rolling pilot plant test unit and thin-strip casting test unit (first stage). Besides, it is now building continuous casting test (routine) platform and dioxin laboratory and also makes preparations for the construction galvanization/continuous annealing test unit.

11.4 Conclusion

Following the previous three chapters which discuss "how TIM works", this chapter mainly focuses on "how to evaluate TIM". It brings forward an applicable index system for the benefit evaluation of TIM and analyzes the innovation benefits of TIM based on the case studies of Haier, CIMC and Baosteel. Innovation benefit evaluation doesn't only aim to summarize and evaluate the past innovation activities. What is more important is that it aims to serve and guide the future. TIM cannot be accomplished in an action and it is not invariable. The innovation benefit evaluation of TIM plays an important role in guiding enterprises to evaluate their realization of TIM and how to continuously develop and improve their total innovations.

Part Five

Cases

Chapter 12

Haier Group

12.1 Profile of Haier

Haier Group is the fourth largest white household appliances manufacturer in the world and the No.1 electronic information manufacturer in China. With more than 240 legal entities, it has established localized design centers, manufacturing bases and trading companies in over 30 countries in the world. The total number of its employees all over the world is more than 50,000. It focuses on the development of four pillar industries, namely science and technology, industry, trade and finance. In 2005, Haier achieved a global turnover of 103.9 billion yuan (12.8 billion U.S. dollars). For 22 years since its foundation, it has maintained an average growth rate of 63% and paid taxes of 10 billion yuan.

Guided by the brand strategy established by CEO Zhang Ruimin, Haier has successively implemented a brand building strategy, diversification strategy and internationalization strategy. On December 26, 2005, Haier initiated its fourth stage of development strategy — stage of global brand strategy. With the implementation of its internationalization strategy, Haier's reputation overseas becomes better and better. According to the latest investigation by Euromonitor, an authoritative consumption market investigating and analyzing institution in the world, Haier ranked the fourth among white household appliances manufacturers in the world and the market share of Haier refrigerators in global refrigerator brand market ranked the first in the world.

What enables Haier to maintain sustained and rapid development? Zhang Ruimin believes that the rapid development of Haier Group should be attributed to the hard work of all Haier members as well as the continuous innovation and entrepreneurial spirit of Haier to satisfy users' individualized demands as soon as possible.

12.2 Development Process of Haier's Innovation

12.2.1 First stage: Brand building based on quality (1984 to 1991)

At the initial stage, by "smashing refrigerators", Haier established its guiding philosophy of "quality is life". It was very far-sighted back then. At that time, the supply of products was not adequate to the demand. Manufacturers could sell out all products they produced, so many of them only focused on yield then. Facts have proven that by 1989, many refrigerator manufacturers had been eliminated by market forces for their indifference to quality. In contrast, Haier refrigerator had undergone rapid development and won the trust of customers. In 1988, relying on its first-class product quality, Haier refrigerator won the first gold prize in the history of Chinese refrigerators. Besides, it had passed ISO9001 and many European and American certifications. In such a way, it had basically built a famous brand in China.

12.2.2 Second stage: Diversified development (1992 to 1998)

Since the 1990s, in order to become one of the Fortune 500 companies and build a world famous brand, Haier had to give top priority to scale expansion. In 1992, the turnover of Haier was only a small percentage of the turnover of the last one in the Fortune 500 list. After summarizing the successful experiences of the top 250 companies, Haier found that it was far from enough to expand its scale just relying on one product. The diversified development was necessary. Therefore, from 1992 to 1998, Haier took a road of low-cost expansion, activated "stunned fish", liquidized tangible assets with intangible assets and successfully realized the expansion of scale and diversity of products.

During its diversified development, Haier realized a perfect synergy between culture and strategy, which played a very important role in Haier's merger and acquisition. The other result of diversified development was that Haier had strengthened its technology capabilities and begun to introduce "secondary innovation" and indigenous innovation transformation.

12.2.3 Third stage: Internationalized development (1999 to 2005)

Since the middle 1990s, the trend of globalization and world economic integration has become increasingly obvious. Many transnational companies like Electrolux, Whirlpool, Siemens, GE, Panasonic and Mitsubishi entered the Chinese market one after another. As the market competitions in household appliance industry became increasingly fierce, many famous domestic brands got defeated in the competitions. Zhang Ruimin was aware of the severe market competitions. He believed that the competition with international giants was just like “dancing with wolves”. You might either defeat the wolves or be eaten by the wolves. Haier decided to “dance with wolves” and created a world famous brand. Therefore, since 1999, Haier began to make great efforts to implement the internationalization strategy, realized the brand internationalization through the internationalized management and services, gradually occupied a market share in the international market and built the good reputation of Haier. In March 2000, the government of Kershaw County, South Carolina renamed a road near Haier Industrial Park as Haier Boulevard in appreciation of the company's contribution to the local economy. It was for the first time a road in America was renamed after a Chinese brand. Haier Boulevard symbolized the rise and recognition of a Chinese brand in the world.

12.2.4 Fourth stage: Global brand (2006 to present)

In 2006, to further strengthen its competitiveness and build a world famous brand, Haier formally put forward the strategy of global brand. Generally, people adopt the standards of “10/20/30” to measure world famous brands, i.e. brand value exceeds 1 billion dollars and 20% of income and 30% of profits comes from overseas markets. At present, Haier has already met the former two standards, but still has quite a gap in the third standard. The strategic objectives of Haier at this stage: in foreign market, continuously create highly differentiated products to satisfy local demands, sell mainstream products through mainstream channels in foreign market and finally realize the high value-added profits through high differentiation.

In over 20 years during Haier’s development, due to the effective synergy among all innovation elements, Haier has greatly improved its innovation performance, accumulated and developed the core competitiveness and accordingly promoted the rapid and sustainable development (Table 12-1).

Table 12-1 Process of Haier's development and innovation and synergy among all innovation elements

Stage	I. Brand building	II. Diversification development	□. Internationalization development	IV. Globalization brand
Scope	Inside	Market expansion	Global expansion and starting a new undertaking	Integration of global resources
Time	1984–1991	1992–1998	1999–2005	2006–present
Focus	Order quality	Multiple products, scale and cost	Speed and innovation	Resources, brand and innovation
Strategy innovation (ideology innovation)	Brand strategy	Diversification strategy Seeking potential before profits Shining in the east before shining in the west	"Going out", internationalization strategy Transfer from manufacturing industry to service industry Three "1/3"	Creating global competitiveness with efficiency, and building a world class global brand
System innovation	Pre-shift system ★ Saturday senior manager training (synergy mechanism)	Coexistence and dynamic conversion of three kinds of workers Talent incentive system Rational suggestion system ▲	R&D investment system – system of development on debt Everyone is an SBU ★	Strengthening incentive system
Culture and concept innovation	To be number one (quality culture) ★ Refining and zero defect "Three eye" theory	Sincerity forever Serving the company and the country and seeking excellence Activating "stunned fish" Always trembled and always skating on thin ice	Building brand by exports Difficulties before easiness "Dancing with wolves" Competitive cooperation	Create resources and reputation on a global scale Quick decision and quick success Design market not products: new barrel theory
Management innovation	TQM Overall Every Control and Clear (OEC, 1989) ★ 6S Big Footprint ISO9001 certification	OEC management – Haier gene ★ Responsibility chain Self-management shift Mandatory management to self-management	Internal imitation of market Market chain SST End to end, zero distance from customer Self-management: 6 Sigma Management	Integrating order with personnel ★ T Model

continued

Stage	I. Brand building	II. Diversification development	□. Internationalization development	IV. Globalization brand
Organization innovation	Linear function structure	Establishing technology center with Zhang Ruimin as director ★ Business unit system ★ Combined fleet	BPR ★ Network process structure ▲ One-stop service, one-vote-to-end process	Network process structure
Market innovation	Winning market based on excellent quality	Rapid response and immediate action Only off-season thoughts, never off-season market ▲ Star services Selling reputation instead of products	Creating valuable order Fight a value was not a price war Three-in-one localized operation	Going out, going up 30% of profits coming from foreign markets Creating blue ocean with differentiation
Technology innovation	Introducing and absorbing German refrigerator technologies Imitation innovation	Secondary innovation, indigenous (cooperative) innovation ★ Difficulties in market as the subjects of innovation Creative imitation and reference as the approach of innovation	Integrate global innovation resources Internalization, advancement, integrity Full-directional innovation based total innovation management ▲	Integrating global resources and carrying out indigenous innovation Full-directional innovation based total innovation management ★

Source: *RCID Haier University Research Data on Haier University, 2006.*

Note: ★ *indicates the main element innovation at this stage;* ▲ *indicates the important innovation of synergy.*

12.3 Main innovations at all development phases of Haier

12.3.1 Main innovation at the stage of brand building: "Overall Every Control and Clear" management model to market chain

One of the most valuable assets of Haier is its "Overall Every Control and Clear" (OEC) management model innovation, which still plays an important role today. However, OEC is just a basic management mode. For the development of an enterprise, just OEC is not enough. Besides, several management measures of OEC tend to make employees screws of the large enterprise machine. This is inconsistent with the present objective of Haier, creating customer-oriented system and satisfying the market demands. The consciousness of the screw is the direct cause of "large enterprise syndrome" which leads to stiffness and lags in response.

In the era of network economy and time-based competitions, whoever satisfies the individualized demands of users fastest will become the winner. Haier hopes to explore a new model, which can enable everyone to carry out continuous innovation and to directly face the market, create valuable order fastest, realize their own values by creating values for users, make everyone energetic and prevent the "large enterprise syndrome" during the development of enterprise.

If OEC management enables Haier employees to "do things right", market chain enables employees to "do right things". The essence of Haier's market chain is to transform external market pressure to internal market pressure and to solve the contradiction between the large enterprise scale and sustainable innovation capability. In other words, it should provide every employee with the space for individualized innovation in the new economy to satisfy customers' individualized demands. The developed OEC basic management is the guarantee of daily management of market chain (Figure 12-1).

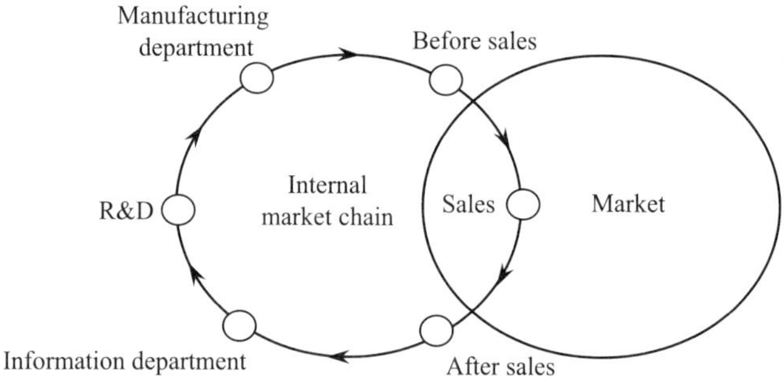

Figure 12-1 Schematic diagram of Haier's market chain

Source: *RCID Research Data of Haier University, 2004.*

12.3.2 Main innovation at the stage of diversified development

(I) Technology innovation: secondary innovation, combination between indigenous innovation and introduction

"The first one is introduced; the second one is made in China; the third one is exported; the fourth one is locally produced". From introduction, imitation to integrated innovation and indigenous innovation, Haier always insists on the main line of industry-university-research cooperation, integrates global innovation resources and makes great efforts to construct its own core competitiveness. Based on a comprehensive survey of Haier's development, it is clear that Haier has undergone the following evolvement route of technology innovation: the first step is to introduce technologies; the second step is to digest and absorb technologies and grasp independent manufacturing technologies; the third step is to carry out further innovation; the fourth step is to fully own technologies with proprietary intellectual property rights.

At present, Haier has already been engaged in white household appliances (white goods), black goods and beige goods, totally 96 major categories and 15,100 products with different specifications. Technologies and products in the sense of total innovation have already occupied the absolute position. For example, Haier's "Patriot Chip" was the first mass-produced digital television decoding chip with proprietary intellectual property rights in China. It occupied a market share of over 50% in China. Haier invented a washing machine of the fourth principle, i.e. dual-power automatic washing machine, the digital streaming media television featuring 3A high definition technologies, etc.

(II) Organization innovation: business unit system and flat structure

How to maintain the high-efficiency operation and rapid market response of enterprises at the same time? Haier believes that the organizational form is extremely important, so it constantly breaks the old, builds the new and adjusts itself to be adapted to external changes, thus always maintaining an orderly and unbalanced status. Generally, the innovation process of Haier can be divided into three stages (Figure 12-2).

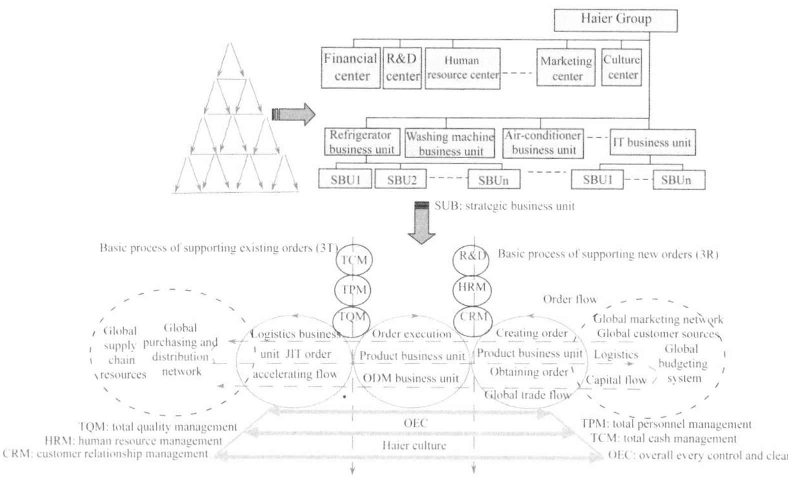

Figure 12-2 Evolvement of Haier's organizational structure innovation

Source: RCID's collection and sorting of Haier's annual reports, 2002.

1. Linear functional system (1984–1991)

At this stage, Haier used 7 years to make itself a well-known refrigerator brand. At this stage, Haier mainly implemented its total quality management through the structural organizational form of linear functional system. It complied with the environment and situation back then.

2. Business unit system (1992–1998)

At the stage of diversified development, with the increasing expansion of product and business fields and scope, the original linear functional system became ineffective. Therefore, Haier adopted the business unit system, aka "combined fleet" system.

3. Process-based flat organizational structure (1999 to present)

To further increase the market response speed and avoid "large enterprise syndrome", since 1999, Haier has further "reformed" its original organizational structure and carried out business process reengineering centered on order information flow. All work of the enterprise must focus on orders. Business process reengineering made the organizational structure more flat and information-based. By integrating global supply chain resources and global user resources, Haier formed a new operating mechanism based on order information flow to drive the logistics and capital flow. Through the establishment of process network organizational structure, Haier has basically realized the zero distance from customers and accordingly won stronger competitiveness.

(III) Culture innovation: everyone is an innovator

Haier's corporate culture is human-oriented culture, which considers a human as the most active factor in enterprise. Only by exploring the potential of every employee can the enterprise become better, bigger and more innovative. And only by involving everyone can the corporate strategy be implemented. The core of human-oriented concept is that people are born with initiatives and creativities. Human-oriented management believes the power of company not only relies on the initiatives of employees but also on the firm reliance on individual values. Zhang Ruimin believes that to establish an innovation-based enterprise, innovation should be made a habit of every employee. Only if all employees are encouraged to start from every little thing and start from changing working environment or working method, can an environment suitable for innovation be created.

From 1984, when Haier smashed 76 defective refrigerators, Haier began to seek the Haier culture of "precision and zero defects". During the process of brand building, Haier gradually formed the OEC management philosophy of "everyone is responsible for something and everything is managed by someone" and "overall every control and clear". Through strict process management, Haier has not only ensured the product quality, but also cultivated high-quality employees and reserved talents and culture capital for the diversified development and internationalized development strategy in the future. The successful realization of activating "stunned fish" and "everyone is an SBU" are the results of Haier's cultural deposits.

During years of practices, Haier has gradually formed its unique culture and atmosphere of innovation and successfully instilled the core values of innovation into the strategy, organization, system and technology innovations of the enterprise, thus constructing Haier's concept of "sustainable innovation and all-involvement innovation" for everyone from president to all business units.

12.3.3 Main innovation at the stage of internationalized development

(I) Reengineering-centered organization innovation

After 1999, to build a world famous brand, Haier established the strategic plan of becoming one of Fortune 500 companies in early 21st century. At the stage of internationalized development, Haier's production, R&D and service had to compete with first-class enterprises in the world. Relying on modern information technologies and communication technologies, Haier started its Business Process Reengineering (BPR) Project focusing on "market chain". It was a revolutionary reform of the organization. At present, Haier has already established the flat organizational structure and process-oriented network structure, which focuses on both tasks and results. It realized the importance of zero distance effect between market and customers. At every stage of process reengineering, the organizational structure of Haier was also adjusted according to the demands. For example, since 1999 when Haier began to implement business process reengineering, Haier has adjusted its organizational structure and reorganized its process over 40 times.

(II) Market innovation

During the process from brand building to internalization, Haier came up with many market innovation concepts, like "only off-season thoughts, never off-season market", "innovation is seizing the opportunities" and "fighting value war not price war". Guided by such concepts, Haier exceeded the simple "4P" Model of marketing and put forward its own market innovation method. Its essence can be expressed as "creating market and customers".

"Remake a cake". Haier didn't seize a share of original market via price war, but used technology innovation to "remake a cake", i.e. creating new market. The transparent wine cabinet of Haier obtained an "exclusive market cake" for creating the demands for free-style wine cabinets. At represent, transparent wine cabinet of Haier has occupied a share of 55% in American market of similar products and been called "a product without competitor" by American marketing master Kotler. In 2002, the sales revenue of products which satisfied the demands created by Haier accounted for over 60% of the total sales of Haier. Among other innovative products, the electricity guard water heater, 007 refrigerator, electricity guard mobile phone, dual-power washing machine, oxygen bar air-conditioner and G5 digital high definition television of Haier have separately become leading products.

Fight a value war but not a price war. Since the middle and late

1990s, household appliances were oversupplied in the market. In order to decrease excess inventory, all manufacturers competed with each other even with the prices lower than cost. The problems caused by price war were very serious. In 1998, the Chinese color TV industry as a whole suffered a great loss. By 2001, among 15 listed household appliance manufacturers in China, 9 companies suffered a loss and the largest amount of loss reached as high as 1.5 billion yuan. Haier believed that the key to the problem was not price but the failure to seize users' demands. Haier never manufactured products for inventory. It only carried out production based on valuable orders and increased the added value of products relying on innovation. Electricity guard water heater of Haier was about to become international standard for successfully solving a worldwide problem of charged earth wire. Although the price of Haier's electricity guard water heater was 100 yuan higher than the average price of similar products, it was still selling very well.

(III) Management innovation: "integrating order with personnel" and T-Model

Since 2005, Haier's T-Model featuring "integrating order with personnel" has been practiced. According to Zhang Ruimin's definition, the direct connotation of T-Model is Today, Time, Target and Team. The profound and specific supply and demand mechanism is that on specific data and time, realizing the link between enterprise's supply values and customers' demand values. T-Model is the specific form of Zhang Ruimin's management thoughts of "integrating order with personnel" at present. In a word, everyone and every department defines the time to realize its market objective as day "T" and determines the budgets before day "T" and the improvements after day "T". The development model of "integrating order with personnel" offers an innovative thinking for solving the global problem of inventory and delinquent account. It was called the management mode which "seized the global business pulse".

Haier's T-Model embodies the barrel theory: the amount of water kept in a barrel depends on the size of barrel and represents the market performance. Chinese market is just a small barrel and the world market is a big barrel. Barrel hoop ensures the close bonding of boards. Such hoop are the four elements of Haier's T Model: time, target, today and team. When all boards are connected, they don't restrict each other but form a market relationship. The bottom of the barrel represents the basic management platform.

Every board represents a node of the process. "T+" is the process until delivery to user and "T-" is all preparations for the process. These two are connected with each other, so the barrel becomes a circle. The objective of "T" is not defined by the enterprise but the market. If the market demands the delivery on the fifth day, it has to be made ready on the fifth day.

The objective of the mode of "integrating order with personnel" is to make Haier a world famous brand (Figure 12-3).

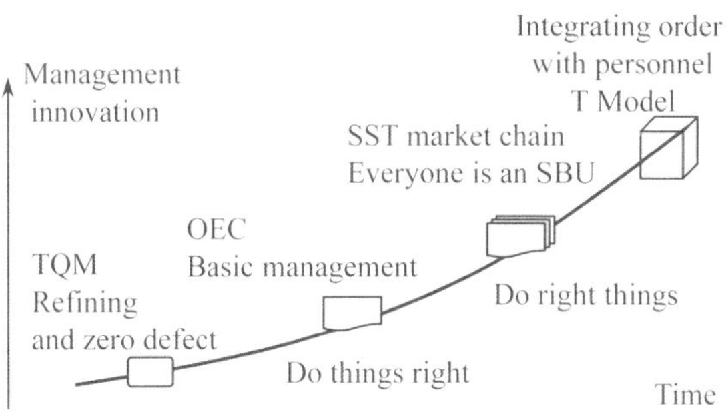

Figure 12-3 Main line of Haier's management innovation development

Source: *RCID Research Data of Haier University 2006.*

12.4 All-involvement innovation of Haier: "Everyone is an innovation SBU"

Zhang Ruimin believes that the innovation of employees is the most valuable asset of an enterprise. The nature of management is not controlling employees' behaviors, but offering innovation space for employees. In March 2001, when the market chain framework was basically formed, Haier made great efforts to promote the reform of human resource management throughout the group. It aimed to enable everyone in the group to become an operator and SBU with innovation spirit.

According to traditional enterprise management theories, an enterprise may have many kinds of products and have many channels to reach the markets, but it is hard to enable every employee to target the market. In Haier, however, "everyone is an operator" and "everyone can create valuable orders" are not just slogans.

The innovation vigor of Haier employees comes from the unique OEC management method of Haier and a complete set of effective management systems with “market chain” management mechanism as the core. Since 1999, according to the external market requirements, Haier began to innovate its management mechanism and carried out the internal “market chain” system, thus enabling every employee to face the market and have an innovation space.

The formation of Haier’s innovation mechanism of “everyone is an SBU” reflects the total innovation concept under new circumstances. By giving full play to the potential of every employee, it has formed great development potential.

12.5 All time-space innovation

(I) Globalization of Haier's innovation

Zhang Ruimin believes that an enterprise is borderless. It is borderless inside to let everyone satisfy the market and it is borderless outside to integrate global resources. By integrating global superior resources and using information stations and R&D institutions distributed all over the world, Haier has fully satisfied the individualized and diversified demands of users, realized the localized product design and enabled Haier to have strong technology innovation capabilities to compete with international companies.

Haier has set up 15 R&D centers, 6 designing departments and 10 science and technology outlets in Europe, North America and Asia-Pacific region, thus forming a global information network. Haier has abandoned the closed, linear and low-efficiency development and creatively implemented the parallel development based on the integration of global technology and intelligence resources. Haier's network household appliance series, which made quite a splash in Domotechnica 2001, integrated the technical designs of Japanese and American experts and the color designs of French fashion designers. Different kinds of design and development are carried out synchronously, thus greatly accelerating innovation.

Haier, by joining hands with 28 companies with first-class technologies in America, Japan and Germany, has established Haier Central Research Institute. Besides, it has set up 10 international first-class advanced technology labs on environment, electromagnetic compatibility, etc. and established 48 scientific research and development entities in China and foreign countries by making use of global technology resources. The application of such advanced technologies and cooperation with international first-class scientific research and development institutions enabled Haier to realize the transformation of scientific and technological achievements by using the most advanced technology innovation.

(II) All-time innovation of Haier

Haier's philosophy of speed: speed creates user resources, i.e. becoming the first-choice supplier of users by moving faster than competitors. Just as what Zhang Ruimin said, "Compared with famous transnational companies, Haier has no advantages in terms of capital, technology or scale, but Haier has a comparative advantage on speed. When dealers propose a requirement, we can meet their requirement much faster than those old transnational companies". Haier's speed objective is to realize "three zeros": zero inventories, zero distance with users and zero operation cost.

The business process reengineering with market chain as the link proposed by Haier since 1999 puts forward that: logistics eliminates space with time and trade flow eliminates time with space. It fully reflects that Haier has embodied its fast reaction and innovation in every link of the business process.

The international color TV R&D cycle is normally 9 months. However, by adopting parallel development strategy, promoting rapid and inverted triangle development strategy and implementing synchronous development, Haier MGM color TV set was introduced to the market in 3 months. At the beginning, most peers were suspicious of it, but subsequently, MDL and 2nd Generation MGM color TV sets of Haier were also launched rapidly. The facts really shocked other enterprises in the same industry.

Haier's speed concept of "immediate action" has greatly improved its flexibility and market response speed. Once upon a time, while purchasing a certain model of washing machine, a Japanese customer who wanted to have all-round cooperation with Haier said the handle of the machine didn't tally with the usage habit of Japanese women. "Next time, you should change it", he said. As a result, after 35 minutes, a technician of Haier handed over a newly hand-made handle to him. He was deeply moved. "I don't need to see it. With such innovation spirit and speed, the cooperation with Haier will surely succeed."

Haier and Ericsson began to develop the Bluetooth network household electric appliances in a relay since April 10, 2001. In as short as 3 months, they finished the first-stage development on June 10th. If they followed the traditional development way, however, it would take at least half a year. Researchers of Haier worked till 9 p.m., which was the afternoon office hour of Ericsson, i.e. 2 p.m. The research was carried out in a relay. In Sweden, people went back home from work at 6 p.m., i.e. 1 a.m. in China. After that, researchers of both parties didn't work, but the computers could keep exchanging data, thus realizing 24-hour uninterrupted development in a relay.

(III) All-value-chain innovation of Haier

Haier always attaches great importance to users' participation in innovation. Haier believes that the difficulty Haier has to overcome is the subject of innovation. The feedback of users (or potential users) after participating in the early stage product design or aftersales feedback can help Haier further improve the product quality and make it in accordance with users' individualized demands. For example, a consumer in Harbin proposed to order a refrigerator with right-handed door and special dimensions via e-mail. As a result, the relevant technological design and manufacturing were finished in 4 days and such a specially customized refrigerator was delivered to that home in a week. Besides, Haier has also integrated the value chain resources of global suppliers, dealers and shareholders into the innovation of Haier and carried out innovation together with them. For example, Mike Refrigerator, which sold well in European and American markets, originated from the creative idea of the American dealer Mike and was named after him. At present, suppliers who have participated in Haier's frontend design of products with their high and new technologies account for 32.5% of all Haier's suppliers.

By involving users, suppliers and dealers in the innovation, Haier can not only make its products in accordance with users' individualized demands, but also greatly improve the speed and cycle of innovation and decrease innovation cost. Sub-suppliers have bound their own development together with the development of Haier, not only providing Haier with high-quality and low-cost components, but also being actively involved in the front end design of Haier products. For example, the world largest motor supplier, Emerson, only supplied motors for Haier at the beginning. Now, it has invested 60 million U.S. dollars in Haier development zone to establish a motor plant.

(IV) All-process innovation of Haier

Since 1999, to avoid "large enterprise syndrome", improve the efficiency and flexibility and satisfy the demands for international competitions and network-based development, Haier has revolutionarily implemented the business process reengineering with market chain as the link, and transformed the original layered linear functional system and business unit system to flat process network structure, thus enabling its business process to be in line with the first-class international companies. Practices in recent years have proved that through process innovation, Haier has not only significantly accelerated its market response, R&D and innovation, but also reduced all costs and greatly improved Haier's international competitiveness.

12.6 Interactive relationship among all innovation elements of Haier

The interactions of all innovation elements of Haier's TIM can be concluded as given below: (1) Technology innovation is the key. Without strong indigenous technology innovation capabilities, the premise and significance of total innovation doesn't exist. (2) Strategy innovation is the direction. Strategy innovation determines the directions of both development and innovation management of Haier. (3) Market innovation is the objective. The objective of innovation is to create valuable orders. (4) Management innovation is the basis. Management innovation lays a firm managerial foundation for the development of Haier. (5) Organization innovation is the guarantee. Process reengineering improves market response, management efficiency and flexibility to satisfy market demands of large enterprises. (6) Ideology and culture innovation are the forerunners. Innovation is the soul of Haier's culture. The concept of innovation is already deeply rooted and embodied in the behavior of every member of Haier. (7) System innovation is the motive power. Through market chain salary system, all salaries of employees come from the market. Everyone has a zero-distance contact with the market and everyone is a SBU of innovation. (8) Synergy innovation as a means. Taking the organic combination and synergy of different innovation elements as a means, Haier stimulated the performance of innovation.

Table 12-2 lists the interactional relationship among all innovation elements of Haier's TIM.

Table 12-2 Examples of the interaction between innovation elements of Haier's total innovation management

Master variables	Dependent variables	Effect of element innovation (quotation)	Source
Strategy innovation	Market innovation	Haier is outstanding because it started with weak enterprise running under deficit, passed through short-term cruel competitions, constantly improved its own strength with the aim to become a global enterprise and finally realized long-term effect.	*Business Strategy and Role of Entrepreneurs* (Haier University, 2004)
	Technology innovation	Since 1999, it carried out diversified construction … and began to produce more new products.	*Business Strategy and Role of Entrepreneurs* (Haier University, 2004)
	Organization innovation	In 1999, it acquired Qingdao Air-conditioning Factory and Qingdao Refrigerator Factory. In 1992, it acquired 13 enterprises under deficit in Shandong including washing machine factories and accordingly formed Haier Group.	*Business Strategy and Role of Entrepreneurs* (Haier University, 2004)
		Implementing the subsidiary system was a main approach to realize diversification in a short time. Haier's cross-regional merger of publicly owned enterprises was far beyond the trend at that time.	*Business Strategy and Role of Entrepreneurs* (Haier University, 2004)

Master variables	Dependent variables	Effect of element innovation (quotation)	Source
		Becoming a large global enterprise is the objective of Haier. Since the foundation of Haier Group as a comprehensive household appliance manufacturer, it adopted the business unit structure system.	*Business Strategy and Role of Entrepreneurs* (Haier University, 2004)
		Its business strategies indeed changed its organizational structure and hence accumulated the capabilities to suit the business strategy.	*Business Strategy and Role of Entrepreneurs* (Haier University, 2004)
Culture innovation	Management innovation	The "Slope-ball Theory" … lead to the formation of Haier's basic "OEC management".	*Strategy Management and Corporate Culture Is the Life of an Enterprises* (Haier University, 2004)
	Market innovation	"The only market rule unchanged is changing forever" — you have to create market and users ahead of the market.	*Strategy Management and Corporate Culture Is the Life of an Enterprises* (Haier University, 2004)
Market innovation	Strategy innovation	In 1995, Haier began to provide "international star-level services" …Haier pursued for the new core of differentiation strategy.	*Business Strategy and Role of Entrepreneur* (Haier University, 2004)
	Organization innovation	Driven by the market, the technology department was separated from Haier refrigerator factory and became Qingdao Refrigeration Technology Research Center with independent accounting.	*Strategy Management and Corporate Culture Is the Life of an Enterprise* (Haier University, 2004)
	Technology innovation	The R&D tenet of Haier is that "anything that bothers users is our development subject".	*Strategy Management and Corporate Culture Is the Life of an Enterprise* (Haier University, 2004)
		Principle of market-based subjects of technology innovation: be market-oriented; Never target at improving the results of technical research and development, but aim to use the results to "create market and create users".	*Strategy Management and Corporate Culture Is the Life of an Enterprise* (Haier University, 2004)
	System innovation	"Model manager" is the "new product" generated during Haier's process reengineering. Developers should not end with the completion of product design. They should also be jointly responsible for the market sales, expenses, profits and after-sales services. The system of "one-vote-to-end process" should be carried out to realize the zero distance contact with market and operation.	(Hu, 2004)

continued

Master variables	Dependent variables	Effect of element innovation (quotation)	Source
	Management innovation	The new sales management model is integrated with ERP distribution module. From the customer manager placing an order, the production department confirming the order, the products being delivered to trading company and the trading companies delivering the products to dealers, the whole process is controlled by a unique order number.	(Hu, 2004)
Technology innovation	Strategy innovation	Principle of the internationalization of innovation objectives: starting from a high point of every technology innovation…using the existed results of international researches as the basis to establish the main direction of research.	*Strategy Management and Corporate Culture Is the Life of an Enterprise* (Haier University, 2004)
		To create a brand and popular products, it is necessary to establish the mechanism of indigenous innovation and to make the main body of technology innovation.	*Strategy Management and Corporate Culture Is the Life of an Enterprise* (Haier University, 2004)
	Market innovation	Principle of the commercialization of the results of technology innovation: follow the triangle structure principle led by technology innovation and increase the market share. … increase the market share to over 30%.	*Strategy Management and Corporate Culture Is the Life of an Enterprise* (Haier University, 2004)
		Indigenous innovation is an important approach for enterprises to participate in competitions and win dominant position.	*Strategy Management and Corporate Culture Is the Life of an Enterprise* (Haier University, 2004)
	Organization innovation	The informationalization of enterprise doesn't only refer to processing all data within an enterprise with computers. It should be system project, an information system project to closely connect enterprise with market.	(Hu, 2004)
Organization innovation	Strategy innovation	Haier established joint ventures with Mitsubishi Heavy Industries (commercial air conditioner) in 1992 and Italy Merloni (roller washing machine) in 1994 separately and adopted the practical strategy to develop itself towards a comprehensive household appliance manufacturer.	*Business Strategy and Role of Entrepreneur* (Haier University, 2004)

continued

Master variables	Dependent variables	Effect of element innovation (quotation)	Source
	System innovation	The key of "market chain" model is the implementation of thoroughly standardized procedures. The personnel evaluation adopts standardized evaluation system and assessment software or thoroughly implements the pure consequentialism to avoid subjective factors.	*Business Strategy and Role of Entrepreneur* (Haier University, 2004)
	Management innovation	As to managers, Haier takes market but not the position as the center. It is purely order-oriented in market, result-oriented in distribution and objective-oriented as a whole.	(Hu, 2004)
	Culture innovation	Running factories in America helps Haier build global corporate culture.	*Business Strategy and Role of Entrepreneur* (Haier University, 2004)
System innovation	Strategy innovation	In the early 1990's, Haier establishes a complete set of employee incentive and monitoring system. By introducing such a mechanism, it lays a firm foundation for its success in diversification.	*Business Strategy and Role of Entrepreneur* (Haier University, 2004)
	Technology innovation	Haier encourages employees to engage in technology reform and invention. It has set up "Haier Hope Prize" to encourage employees' little inventions, little reforms and rational suggestions. It has also set up "naming tool prize". The name of every employee whose invention or reformed tool helps improve the labor productivity may be used to name the tool after being submitted to and approved by the congress of workers and staff.	*Strategy Management and Corporate Culture Is the Life of an Enterprise* (Haier University, 2004)

12.7 Leadership mechanism, synergy mechanism and learning mechanism

The outstanding achievements of Haier, obviously, have something to do with Zhang Ruimin's entrepreneurship, innovation spirit and innovation capabilities activities in the past twenty years. It is his perseverance and leading by example that promoted the innovation learning of Haier and improved the overall innovation capability of Haier.

Zhang Ruimin claims that one doesn't only learn in innovation practices, he also attaches importance to the learning of innovation theories, such as the western management and strategy theories of Drucker, Michael Porter, et al. and the ancient Chinese philosophical thoughts of Lao Zi, Zhuang Zi, Sun Zi, et al. "When things have become strong, they become old", said Lao Zi, and "innovation is creative destruction" proposed by Schumpeter expressed the same innovation thoughts.

Having a thorough knowledge of both western and traditional Chinese philosophy made Zhang Ruimin a follower of both Chinese and western innovation sages. Zhang has not only a strong consciousness of market economy, but also a strong ability to control corporate culture. He is the tutor and trainer of Haier's innovation. In Haier, senior leaders led by Zhang Ruimin not only personally publicize the concept, significance and future of innovation, but also provide managers with training courses as trainers to improve the management skills and innovation capabilities on all levels. That's why Haier formed its forward-looking, effective and sustainable innovation.

Senior managers of Haier have a regular interactive training program which is held every Saturday. CEO Zhang Ruimin and Chairwoman Yang Mianmian personally lead the senior management team to discuss new management ideas, analyze problems discovered in the practices and seek solutions. This is a very effective learning mechanism and also a unique leadership and synergy mechanism. Due to their own benefits, different departments and business units may often have some contradictions and conflicts between each other. Such things are also coordinated and solved during this training program. Many major management reforms and strategic decisions of Haier came from this Saturday manager training program, such as the business process reengineering with market chain as the link implemented by Haier at the end of 1998, "everyone is an SBU" and "integrating order with personnel". The training of senior managers on Saturday enables the top decision-makers of Haier to be aware of recent events and problems of the group in time and effectively deliver their new ideas and concepts to the middle level managers. Haier's successful practices for years have been proved to be very effective in integrating leadership mechanism, learning mechanism and synergy mechanism (Figure 12-4).

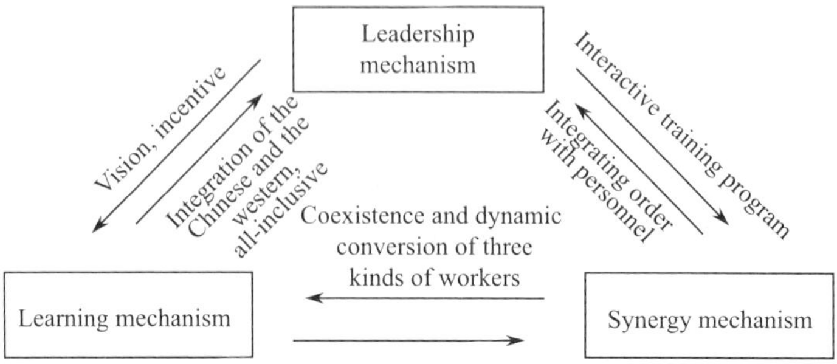

Figure 12-4 Interactions among three mechanisms

12.8 Cost benefit analysis of Haier's implementation of total innovation management

12.8.1 Preliminary performance of Haier's implementation of TIM

The implementation of TIM has achieved remarkable results and greatly improved the core competences and market competitiveness of Haier.

(1) Greatly accelerate R&D and innovation. In 2005, 1.8 new products were released and 2.8 patent applications were filed every working day. The lead time of refrigerator was decreased from 9.5 days to 6.5 days, decreasing 32% on average; the customer response time of different departments was decreased from 36 days to 10 days; domestic procurement cycle was decreased from 10 days to 3 days; the order processing time was decreased from 7 days to 1 day (Table 12-3).

Table 12-3 Improved R&D performance and market response speed

Year / Innovation index	1999	2001	2002	2003	2005
Number of products manufactured every day	1	1.3	1.5	1.8	1.8
Number of patents applied every working day	2.2	2.5	2.6	2.7	2.8
Current asset turnover rate	118 days	88 days	83 days	78 days	< 78 days
New product output rate	80%	> 80%	> 82%	> 85%	> 85%
Domestic purchasing cycle (day)	10 days	7 days	5 days	3 days	< 3 days
Order processing time	7 days	1 day	< 5 hours	< 1 hour	< 1 hour

Source: *RCID Research Data of Haier, 2006.*

(2) Increase of brand value. According to the annual report of 2005 issued by Beijing Famous Brand Evaluation Co, Ltd., Haier ranked the first in the list of "Most Valuable Brands in China" for 4 years in succession with a brand value of 70.2 billion yuan.

(3) Increase of patents. In recent years, the number of patents applied by Haier has undergone a sustained growth (Figure 12-5). By far, it has totally applied for 6,189 patents, including 819 invention patents, ranking the first in China.

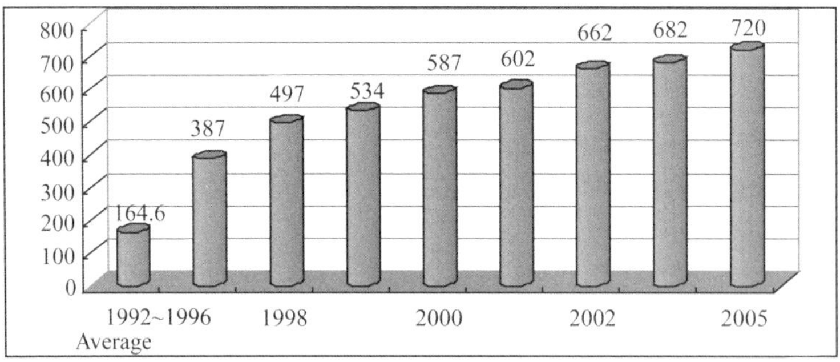

Figure 12-5 Increase of the number of patents applied by Haier

Source: *RCID Survey of Haier University, 2006.*

(4) Growth of core competences. Through TIM, on the one hand, Haier has integrated global science and technology resources and used them for innovation. On the other hand, Haier seized every opportunity to cultivate its own indigenous innovation capabilities to ensure continuous competitiveness. Besides, through TIM, Haier could satisfy users' individualized demands faster than its competitors and accordingly strengthened its core competences (Figure 12-6).

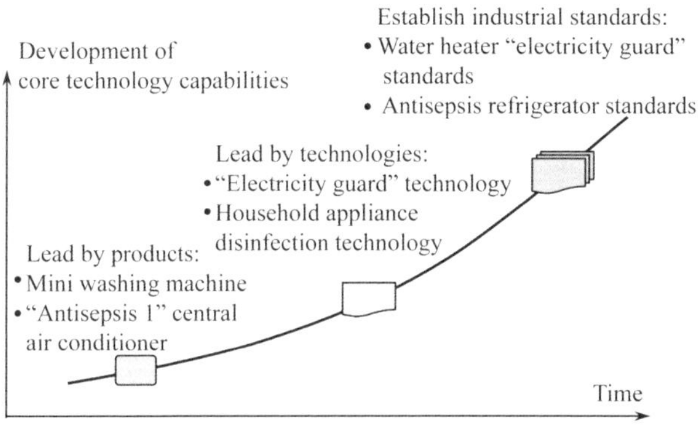

Figure 12-6 Development of Haier's core technology competences

12.8.2 Preliminary analysis of Haier's implementation of TIM

Taking the shares of listed Qingdao Haier Co., Ltd. as an example, we shall conduct a preliminary analysis of Haier's implementation of TIM, as shown in Figure 12-7.

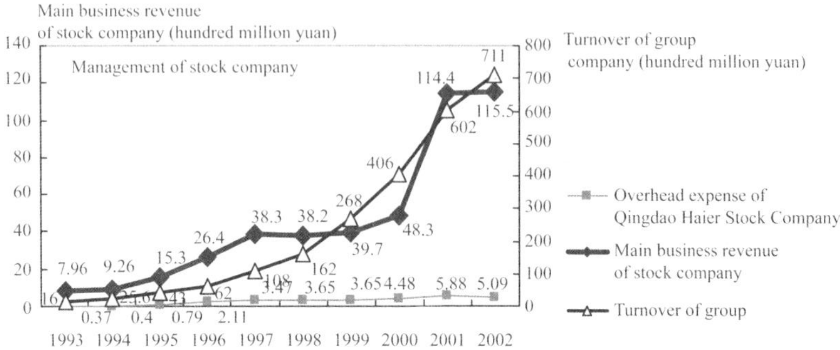

Figure 12-7 Preliminary cost analysis of Haier's implementation of total innovation management

(*Taking Qingdao Haier Stock Company as an example, data up to 2002*)

Source: *RCID's summary of the annual reports of Haier and other data, 2003.*

In Figure 12-7, overhead expense refers to the expenses incurred by the organization and management of the production operation, including the expenses incurred by the board of directors and administrative management departments during the business management of the enterprise or other expenses that should be afforded by the enterprise. Most expenses caused by the implementation of TIM can be classified as overhead expense. Therefore, the benefits and cost of TIM can be reflected in the overhead expense and main business revenue. Seen from Figure 12-7, the implementation of TIM didn't lead to significant increase of overhead cost, but the turnover increased a lot. It means Haier's implementation of TIM has generated good effects.

12.9 Conclusion

Haier Group takes innovation as its soul and characteristic. Since its foundation in 1984, Haier has developed from a collective plant on the verge of bankruptcy to the No.1 brand in China and a world famous household appliance brand through continuous implementation of total innovation, including ideology and concept innovation, strategy innovation, technology innovation, market innovation, culture innovation, organization system innovation and management innovation. Its successful experiences are worth in-depth research and learning.

12.9.1 Haier's technology innovation is built on the platform of all-round innovation

Haier's technology innovation is fully embodied in the integration of all-element innovation on the platform of all-round innovation. Through the effective use of external forces, Haier has realized the integration of independent development and cooperation-based development. It has established a large external innovation network on a global scale and formed strong supports for the scientific research system of Haier. Meanwhile, it makes great efforts to carry out mass innovation activities and lays a firm foundation for Haier's innovation by integrating the innovation of all departments and all personnel (Figure 12-8).

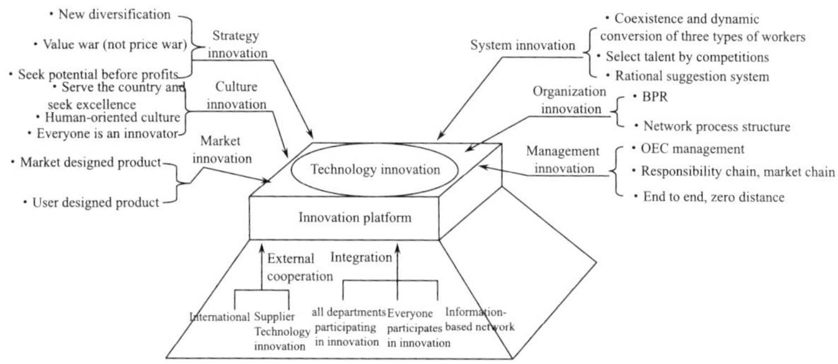

Figure 12-8 Technology innovation based on all-round innovation platform and its supporting system

Source: *Xu et al. Tao of Total Innovation*: *Case Study of Haier Group's Technology Innovation Management. Journal of Dalian University of Technology* (*Social Science Edition*), *2004.*

Such a system of innovation-based technology organization was not built over night. It is under the guidance of indigenous innovation and "market designed products" that the approach to realize such a system is gradually formed.

12.9.2 Formation of Haier's technology innovation system

In recent years, Haier has taken business strategy as the orientation and technology center as the core, satisfied users' individualized demands as soon as possible, integrated all innovation elements for technology innovation, and gradually formed a high-efficiency technology innovation system featuring benign interaction, synergy among all innovation elements and all personnel involvement. The technology innovation system of Haier aims to create valuable orders and win continuous international competitiveness. Based on the analysis framework of SPRE (strategy, process, resource and environment), it has formed an organic and harmonious entity consisting of the elements like R&D organization, interface management, human resource, capital, culture, enterprise leadership, decision-making and institutional system. (Figure 12-9)

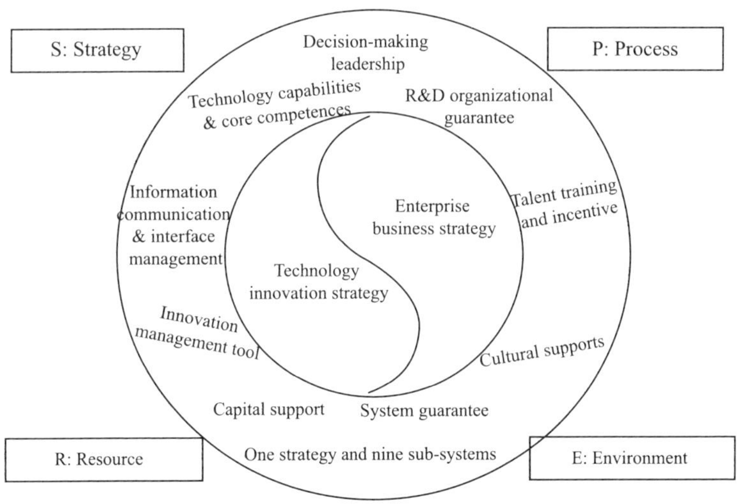

Figure 12-9 Framework of Haier's Technology Innovation System

Source: RCID Research Data of Haier University, 2006.

Haier's practices of implementing TIM have validated the theory of TIM. Some of its successful experiences are worth learning (Figure 12-10).

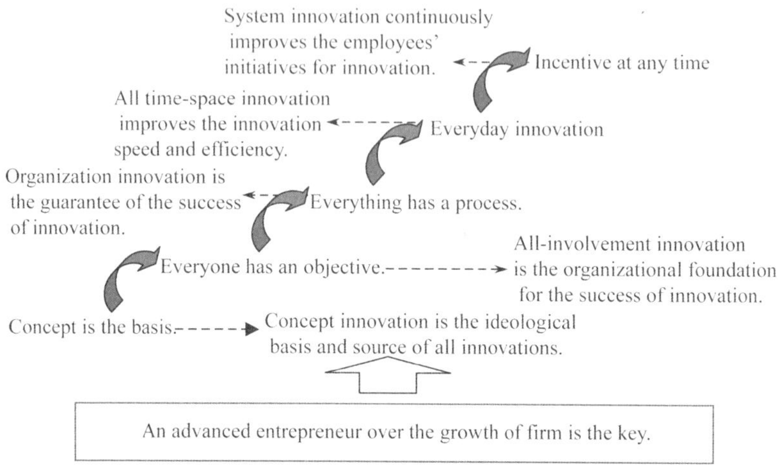

Figure 12-10 Enlightenment of Haier's implementation of total innovation management

Source: *RCID Research Data of Haier University, 2004.*

(1) Concept innovation is the basis and ideological source of all innovations; (2) All-involvement innovation and management innovation are the organizational basis and guarantee of total innovation; (3) Strategy innovation and market innovation guide the direction; (4) Innovation at any time and innovation at any place are important methods to improve innovation speed and efficiency; (5) An entrepreneur whose ideology goes beyond the development speed of the enterprise is the key to promoting Haier's innovation and development.

Chapter 13

Hewlett-Packard

In 1939, Bill Hewlett and David Packard, graduates of Stanford University integrated their product concepts and unique management styles and established Hewlett-Packard (HP) in a shabby garage in Palo Alto, California. HP, name of the company, is the initials of their family names. Interestingly enough, they tossed a coin to determine whose family name should be placed first. Hewlett was lucky, so his family name was placed in front of Packard's.

HP was world famous for its "Rules of the Garage" and technology innovation and later became a symbol of the entrepreneurship of high-tech companies in Silicon Valley. Inexhaustible motive power for innovation made HP an "evergreen tree" in Silicon Valley. HP now consists of functional departments and 4 major business groups: enterprise system group, information product group, printing & imaging system group and professional & supporting service group. In 2002, it had 140,000 employees all over the world with the annual sales revenue reaching U.S. 7.32 billion dollars.

Today, HP takes the leading position in the industry in terms of capital, technology, information, service and solutions. HP has the most complete IT product lines and covers the product services and technology supports of computer and imaging equipment. Printer, server and personal computer of HP all take the leading position in the world. Its customers are widely distributed in the sectors like telecommunication, finance, government, traffic, transportation, resource, aerospace, electronics, manufacturing and education.

13.1 History of HP's innovation

The history of HP's innovation can be divided into four stages, namely, initial stage, technology innovation stage, transition stage and strategic development stage.

13.1.1 Initial stage

It mainly refers to the 1940s and 1950s. Benefitting from low price and high quality products, HP rapidly gained a market share at its initial stage. Due to the continuous orders from the American government during the Second World War, HP rapidly expanded its scale and developed several new products. Meanwhile, founders of HP established unique enterprise management model, including "management by walking around", which facilitated close connections with the employees through random communication or formal talks. In such a way, they became aware of the concerns and viewpoints of employees and showed their trust and respect for employees. Based on the trust atmosphere of "everyone in an organization wants to do a good job", HP determined its overall objectives and allowed employees to carry out the "management by objectives" in their own professional fields. On such a basis, HP established the famous open corporate culture, which later became a model of entrepreneurial firms in Silicon Valley. It established the "open door policy", which meant that the tool cabinets and manager offices should always be unlocked. It aimed to strengthen the mutual trust and communication between employees and managers, thus creating an equal working environmental for all employees. Such a management model encouraged every employee to innovate at any time. In the 1950s, HP established its way of growth — HP Way, and got listed in 1957. At the end of the 1950s, HP started its globalized production and marketing from Europe. Due to the continuous increase of enterprise scale, the innovation of organizational structure is inevitable. Therefore, it built a structure suitable for instrument products. At the initial stage, HP established a series of employee incentive systems, such as serious illness medical insurance, pensions system and stock option incentive system, which provided system guarantees for the subsequent innovation and development.

13.1.2 Technology innovation stage

The 1960s to the 1980s witnessed the unprecedented prosperity of HP's technology innovation. It got rid of the stale and brought forth new products, including the famous electronic calculator, personal laser printer and ink-jet printer. Such products brought HP high profits and enabled it to maintain high-speed growth in the global market for over 20 years. Besides, such products helped HP accumulate a great deal of technology patents and core technology competences. Meanwhile, the organization also underwent rapid expansion. As early as in the early 1960s, it entered the Japanese market and established a joint venture named Yokogawa Hewlett-Packard (YHP). By 1963, the sales volume overseas of HP had accounted for 18% of the gross sales of HP. Western

Europe, Canada and Japan became its largest overseas markets. In the 1970s to the 1980s, led by the strategy of technology innovation, HP chose the electronic calculator as its main industry and began its globalized R&D in the 1980s. For example, the laser printer was a new product developed by HP based on Canon's laser marking technology and their strong partnership. Meanwhile, the precision RISC (Reduced Instruction Set Computer) microprocessor system structure launched by HP enabled HP to become a technology leader in the industry of computer servers.

13.1.3 Transition stage

The 1990s was the most unstable period for HP since its foundation. Firstly, the market for the electronic calculator quickly shrank and HP was anxious for a new prospect in its substitute product, i.e. personal computer. However, since the personal computer was successfully developed in the 1980s, it had always remained in obscurity in global market due to the lack of competitiveness. The main cause was that the traditional organizational structure of HP was not suitable for the personal computer industry and the competitive environment of high-speed innovation. Therefore, after the adjustment of organizational structure, HP gathered all professions related to the personal computer in a single branch and then it rapidly became the world largest PC supplier (Lynn & Akgun, 2001). Secondly, HP split its traditional instrument product department and made preparations for the strategic adjustment of organizational structure. Thirdly, the traditional leader selecting mode of HP was challenged and main senior leaders quit the senior management at this stage. By the end of the 1990s, professional manager Carleton Fiorina was appointed as the new CEO of HP. Therefore, the trust among management, employees, financial circle, directors and media was inevitably challenged. Of course, new leaders would lead HP to create new prosperity.

13.1.4 Strategic development stage

Since the 21st century, HP strictly implemented the policy to reduce business cost through public electronic purchasing platform and carried out strategic adjustment of organizational structure and product structure through the merger of Compaq, which was the largest merger in the world in 2002. The new HP consisted of four groups, namely ESG (enterprise systems group), PSG (personal systems group), IPG (imaging and printing group) and HPS (HP services). HPS was a new industry for HP and people were all optimistic about its future.

The contents of HP's total innovation management (TIM) at different stages are shown in Table 13-1.

Table 13-1 HP's total innovation management at all stages

Development stage / Focus of innovation	Initial stage (1939 to 1959)	Development stage (1960s to 1980s)	Transition stage (1990s)	Strategic development stage (2000 to present)
Strategy innovation	Self-adapting business strategy based on culture and technology innovation	Focused on the innovation and development of electronic technologies and relevant products	Entered network industry through organization innovation.	Through organization, formed an enterprise structure suitable for large and complex product innovation
Culture innovation	Open corporate culture • Trust: "everyone in an organization wants to do a good job" • Open: open door policy	No data	Self-administration culture was not suitable for the development of complex products.	Highlighted the effect of efficiency on corporate culture
System innovation	Employee incentive system that shows respect • Employees' serious illness medical insurance • Pension system • Stock option incentive system	No data	Loose enterprise system may lose the control of complex organization system.	Establishing unified system standards and strengthening encouragement mechanism

continued

Technology innovation	Electronic instruments: electronic counter, oscilloscope	Electronic calculator Computer Personal laser printer and ink-jet printer	Carried out continuous innovation of superior products and technologies (such as personal printer technology).	• Emphasized the combination innovation of traditional product functions or technologies (such as combination of personal printer and copying machine and fax machine) Innovation of computer technologies
Organization innovation	• Communication-advocated organization management • Management by walking around • Independent "objective management"	Establishing globalized R&D institution	• Simplified organizational structure • Transformed from professional labor division to business labor division.	• Completed industrial splitting and merger, established independent business department based on the category of product or industry • Completed the unified enterprise management network platform and strengthened the management efficiency and monitoring of organization
Market innovation	• Low-cost, low-price and high-quality products • At the end of the 1950s, HP started its globalized production and marketing from Europe.	Development of global market	Development of global market	Continuous development of global market
All time-space innovation	No data	Established overseas R&D center in England	No data	No data
All-involvement innovation	Encouraging employees to participate in innovation	No data	No data	No data

Source: *RCID internal data.*

13.2 HP's innovation within TIM architecture

13.2.1 Technology innovation

Product integration innovation. HP's Office Jet All-in-One Printer was a product integrating printer, faxing machine and copying machine.

Product and process combination innovation. HP DeskJet 5550 Printer adopted 6-ink-box ink-jet printing and 4800-optimized dots-per-inch technology, which significantly exceeded the traditional imaging quality and anti-color-fading capability (it can last as long as 73 years, twice as long as that of the traditional printed image).

Independent innovation. In 1951, PT developed a high frequency calculator (HP524A).

Secondary innovation. HP's innovation of the printer

was the best example of secondary innovation. In 1958, in its first acquisition, it purchased a high quality VCR manufacturer named F. L. Moseley Pasadena. This is the initial stage when HP entered the printer industry, the first step into the monitor industry. Since the 1980s, based on the successful innovation of monitoring technologies, HP had become a market leader. The presentative products were HP laser printer and DeskJet printer.

Customer innovation. For most of the time during its development, HP produces products that serve scientists and engineers. HP is a company with many scientists and engineers, so HP has realized that the designing and production of products to solve internal problems in the industry might be an external market with great potential. This was also one of the earliest methods used by HP to win "customer" input. The important role of customer demands in technology innovation was also emphasized in the book, *HP Way*.

Supplier innovation. The earliest design technology of HP's electronic calculator originated from Tom Ausben, an engineer working for a calculator manufacturer. His design was not accepted by many calculator manufacturers, but when he presented his design to HP, HP organized a research team to develop such technology together with him. A series of subsequent technology innovations made the electronic calculator one of HP's main products.

Cooperation innovation. HP and Canon achieved great success in their first cooperation on laser printer and such a cooperative relationship lasted for nearly 20 years. In the 1990s, HP began to cooperate with Intel in developing public 64-bit microprocessor technologies oriented to the computers in the 21st century. Workers of the HP laboratory spent many years seeking the upgrade of the product of PA-RISC. In 2001, it released a new process, originally named IA-64 and now called Itanium.

13.2.2 Organization and system innovation

David Packard believed that management by objectives (MBO) was the core of organization management. By clearly connecting all other objects, MBO is the best way to enable workers to flexibly achieve their objectives within the limits of their functions and powers.

The business unit system was one of HP's earliest successful paradigms of organization innovation in the late 1950s. It was more suitable for the portfolio innovation of HP's earliest inspection equipment products and stimulated the rapid growth of enterprise. It enabled small enterprises to maintain spontaneity and flexibility, respond rapidly to market demands and effectively avoid the bureaucratic malpractice in large enterprises. The business unit system worked well in production lines with clear boundaries, but it was not suitable for system machines like computer. When the organizational structure was no longer suitable for the business demands and led to bureaucratization, the development of the computer industry in the 1990s became very slow. Since the 1990s, HP began to organize flat reform and achieved results. Its share price increased from 20 dollars per share in 1990 to 70 dollars per share in 1993.

The most important organization innovation of HP was adopted in the first 20 years since its founding. In the following decades, HP only made some supplements. For example, the "open corporate culture" emphasized in the stable organizational plan helped establish a team with mutual trust and shared values among managers and employees. All such things were good for the sustainable innovation of HP.

13.2.3 Culture innovation

In the 1940s, HP gradually formed its famous "open corporate culture", a new management paradigm built by Bill Hewlett and David Packard, which ensured that a the manager or employee who raised a question would not invite adverse consequences. Thrust and integrity were the most important contents of open management.

A new management paradigm, "management by walking around (MBWA)", stimulated better communication within HP. This was HP's management in a different way, which ensured close connection with employees and their work through casual communication or formal talks. Being aware of what employees' concerns reflects the trust of and respect for employees.

At the same time, HP created a sense of identity that "everyone in an organization wants to do a good job". HP also established its "open door policy" and aimed to build mutual trust and understanding, thus enabling employees to express their thoughts, opinions and problems freely.

13.2.4 All-involvement and all time-space innovation

HP always encouraged employees to make contributions to the enterprise and made great efforts to provide employees with conditions and training for work. The motto of HP was "HP Invent", so "everyone is creator" became an important part of HP's culture. HP encouraged employees to take risks and immunized the loser from punishment. It created good conditions for "all-involvement innovation".

HP's "Rules of the Garage" strongly supported "all time-space innovation". Examples included the 9th rule "Make a contribution every day. If it doesn't contribute, it doesn't leave the garage" and the 2nd rule "Work quickly, keep the tools unlocked, work whenever" (Packard 1995).

The innovation of HP gradually caught up with the trend of globalization, including the synergy innovation among organization, customers, partners and suppliers.

According to years of experience in consultation and working experience in HP, Dr. Menke Micheal evaluated the formation and current situation of total innovation management, as shown in Table 13-2.

Table 13-2 HP's evaluation of TIM as a whole

Project	Score	Reasons
Technology and culture innovation	A+	Well done
Market and management innovation	A-	If HP could keep ahead of its competitors in some key fields which used to be ignored, it could obtain larger market share.
Strategy and portfolio innovation	B+	Nicely done, but it still restrains the development of enterprise in certain aspects.
System innovation	B	Nicely done, but it still restrains the development of enterprise in certain aspects.
Organization innovation	B-	Many reforms require further exploration; it is still required to improve the working mode on the boundary of organization.

Source: *Menke M. Total innovation management: An introduction and comparison to HP. Report PPT in Zhejiang University. Zhejiang University RCID Internal Data, 2003.*

13.3 Dynamic innovation and synergy innovation

According to the analysis of HP's history, the core of its innovation is not unchanged but is changing with the change of internal conditions, development status and external environment. It is dynamic and conforms to the logic of enterprise development. If the organizational structure lags behind the demands for enterprise development, it will hinder the growth of the enterprise. The core of innovation should be organization innovation. Otherwise, the technology innovation and market innovation cannot be fully effective and may even cause the death of enterprise. In the personal computer industry, HP was encountered with such a problem. Since the organizational structure of HP was not suitable for industrial system and rapid innovation competition, HP had been hovering on personal computer products for 15 years (Lynn & Akgün, 2001). DuPont, an American company with a history of 200 years, saved the enterprise from the verge of survival crisis through several organizational reforms. It may prove that organizational innovation is also related to the survival of an enterprise. Similarly, the strategy innovation, culture innovation, system innovation and market innovation are all related to the survival of an enterprise. Therefore, the core of enterprise innovation is dynamic rather than pure technology innovation.

Similarly, the main innovation synergy factors in every era are also dynamic and changing. The following is the analysis of innovation synergy based on the chronicles of HP.

In its early years, HP laid an important foundation for the synergy innovation, including open culture, management by objectives, system model, technology innovation orientation and pattern of market behavior. Among others, open culture and management by objectives used to be the foundation of success and were challenged when HP entered the computer industry.

Seen from the history of HP, the 1960s was the most harmonious period for HP in terms of innovation. Technology innovation was strongly supported by the enterprise system and promoted the high-speed growth of enterprise together with market innovation. Half of HP's technology capabilities in the 20th century were established during this period.

In the 1980s, with the advent of information era, HP's technology innovation of peripheral products of computer, such as personal laser printer and ink-jet printer, had achieved great success and its products became world famous. However, HP was stalled for the innovation of its personal computer products and couldn't keep up with the market trend. In the early 1990s when HP adjusted its organizational structure, it finally tapped its potential.

In the late 1990s, the calculator products of HP entered the mature period, so they had to seek other products to satisfy the demand for the growth of the enterprise. Then, HP selected the computer industry as its objective and enlarged its investment in it, but HP also discovered its bureaucratic trend of organizational structure at the same time. Therefore, HP began to establish a flat organizational structure. With the innovation of enterprise system, it achieved remarkable results.

Since the reform in the decade before was not enough to make HP a mainstream IT enterprise, strategy innovation became the core of HP's innovation in the early 21st century. HP put forward adaptive and diversified strategies. Meanwhile, it carried out organization innovation, culture innovation and system innovation, as shown in Table 13-3.

Table 13-3 HP's dynamic innovation core and main innovation synergy factors

Time	Core of innovation	Main innovation synergy factors
1940s to 1950s	Culture innovation System innovation	Organization, system, technology and market
1960s to 1980s	Technology innovation Market innovation	Technology, market and system
1990s	Organization innovation	Organization and system
21st century	Strategy innovation	Strategy, organization, culture and system

Through the analysis of HP's dynamic innovation process above, it can be discovered that the process of spontaneous formation of TIM was a self-adaptive innovation process when members of HP formed the instinct to innovate during the practices of innovation management to reach the objectives of enterprise. TIM of HP featured an open corporate culture and an internal trust atmosphere, which further stimulated the benign interaction between entrepreneur's spirit of innovation and employees' desire for innovation, built a self-adaptive total innovation learning mechanism and basically achieved the effect of synergy innovation. Such TIM model is shown in Figure 13-1.

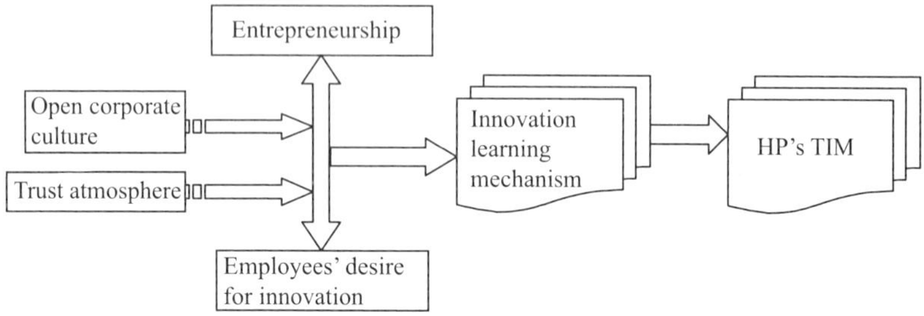

Figure 13-1 HP's TIM model of the interaction between entrepreneurs and employees

HP established the organizational structure of a self-governing business unit system suitable for innovation synergy in the 1950s. This was an organizational structure which divided the work by product modules and was suitable for simple technology innovation learning of interfaces between product modules. However, in the 1980s when HP entered the industry of computers, there were problems caused by such organizational structure, such as a great deal of coordination and decision-making work to be personally handled by the entrepreneur and complex technologies involved in the interfaces between different modules of complex computer products, greatly slowed down HP's innovation of computer products. However, the computer module technologies in the market underwent rapid development, which threw HP's computer products into great passivity in the market competitions. It was in the middle 1990s when HP was suddenly enlightened and set up an independent computer branch, which enabled HP to rise in the PC industry. Then, in the early 21st century, HP completed the reconstruction of business by the category of products, which was the common organizational structure adopted by large enterprises then and could stimulate communication, share innovation learning related to product technologies and relevant management knowledge and improve enterprises' innovation capabilities and speed. Meanwhile, it provided the scenario management of enterprise knowledge with necessary conditions, i.e. the mutual correspondence between knowledge structure and organizational structure.

By far, in the history of HP, the benign interaction among innovation elements like strategy innovation, culture innovation, market innovation, technology innovation, system innovation and organization innovation, has created an overall effect of "2+2 > 5" and accordingly improved the overall innovation performance of the company. Table 13-4 shows the analysis of the interactive relationship among different elements of all-element innovation of HP.

Table 13-4 Analysis of the interactive relationship among different elements of all-element innovation

Master variables	Dependent variables	Effect of element innovation (quotation)	Source
Strategy innovation	Culture innovation	Scrupulous consumers may discover there is a word "invent" under every logo of HP. Such a logo doesn't only reflect HP's unique innovative spirit, dependability and reputation and position in high quality design, but also represent a new motive power and the faith to make progress.	(Dafoe, 2004)
	Market innovation	HP's marketing strategy changes with different customers. For customers of personal computer, HP always insists on the retail strategy. The retailers it cooperates with to sell HP or Compaq computers include compUSA, Walmart, Sears and Radio Shack. Besides, HP also increases its sales volume through online shopping.	(Dafoe, 2004)
	Technology innovation	But right from the beginning, Bill and I knew we didn't want to be a "me-too" company merely copying products already on the market. To this day, HP continually strives to develop products that represent true advancement.	(Packard, 2001)
	Organization innovation	Our rapid growth up to 1956 had brought to light some organizational weaknesses. And with prospects for continuing growth ahead, I thought it was time to provide more structure to the company and a better delineation of goals and responsibilities.	(Packard, 2001)

continued

Master variables	Dependent variables	Effect of element innovation (quotation)	Source
Culture innovation	Strategy innovation	The establishment of such objectives and the way to realize the values of enterprise jointly laid a theoretical foundation for "HP Way", an extraordinarily important business management theory. These are the soul of HP.	(Dafoe, 2004)
	Technology innovation	To be useful in an era of worldwide competition and rapid change, new products must be developed quickly and produced efficiently with manufacturing processes and techniques that assure quality and economy.	(Packard, 2001)
Market innovation	Culture innovation	The fundamental basis for success in the operation of Hewlett-Packard is the job we do in satisfying the needs of our customers. We encourage every person in our organization to think continually about how his or her activities related to the central purpose of serving our customers. The essence of customer satisfaction at HP is our commitment to quality, a commitment that begins in our laboratories and extends into every phase of our operations.	(Packard, 2001)
	System innovation	With the number of operating divisions and their product lines steadily increasing, we gradually adopted a group structure. This involved combining, organizationally, divisions with related product lines and markets into a group headed by a group manager with a small group of staff. Each group was responsible for the coordination of divisional activities and the overall operations and financial performance of its members.	(Packard, 2001)
Technology innovation	Strategy innovation	Just as it has in the past, our growth in the future will come from new products. In 1994, we spent two billion dollars in new product development…The so-called new products, I mean products that make real contributions to technology, not products that copy what someone else has done. This must be our standard in the future just as it has been in the past.	(Packard, 2001)
	Organization innovation	In the 1960's, however, some opportunities came along for us to acquire companies whose technologies and products complemented our own.	(Packard, 2001)

continued

Master variables	Dependent variables	Effect of element innovation (quotation)	Source
System innovation	Culture innovation	Linked with the "management by walking around" is another important management practice at HP, and a basic tenet of the HP Way. It's called the "open door policy". Like MBWA, this policy is aimed at building mutual trust and understanding, and creating an environment in which people feel free to express their ideas, opinions, problems and concerns.	(Packard, 2001)
	Technology innovation	I should point out that the successful practice of management by objective is a two-way street. Manager at all levels must be sure that their people clearly understand the overall objectives and goals of the company, as well as the specific goals of their particular division or department.	(Packard, 2001)
	Market innovation	...stressed the importance of customer feedback in helping us design and develop products aimed at real customer needs.	(Packard, 2001)
	Organization innovation	During the 2 years when Carly was the CEO of HP, she deeply reformed the organizational system of company, changed the product-centered organizational structure to customer-centered structure and reduced the 83 business units down to 17.	(Packard, 2001)
Organization innovation	Culture innovation	After the merger of HP and Compaq, the advantages of the corporate culture of two companies were combined and the shortcomings were discovered and eliminated.	(Dafoe, 2004)
	Market innovation	An organizational structure, once created, should be flexible and responsive to the developing needs of the organization and changes in the marketplace.	(Packard, 2001)
	System innovation	A primary goal in setting up these divisions was to give each one considerable autonomy, creating an environment that fostered individual motivation, initiative, and creativity, and that gave a wide latitude of freedom in working toward common goals and objectives.	(Packard, 2001)

13.4 Leadership mechanism and learning mechanism within TIM

As one of the main mechanisms to promote and coordinate the system, leadership mechanism plays an important role in the practices of TIM, especially the synergy between technology innovation and management innovation, guiding the direction and objective of total innovation, building innovation culture, providing resource and system guarantee, and promoting all-involvement innovation. Table 13-5 below shows the analysis of how leadership mechanism promotes total innovation.

Table 13-5 Analysis of how leadership mechanism promoting total innovation

Master variables	Dependent variables	Mechanism of action	Source
Leadership mechanism to promote total innovation	Synergy of technology innovation and management innovation	We had come to realize that a successful new instrument had to include new technology and be practicd. This meant that the most important new instruments would combine new technology and demonstrate marketability. There were, from time to time, new development opportunities that included new technology in areas where we had no marketing capability. We sold these to firms that had the marketing ability. They reflected on our strategy to concentrate on building a group of complementary products rather than becoming involved in a lot of unrelated things. I believe this decision to focus our efforts was extremely important, not only in the early days of the company.	(Packard, 2001)
	Guiding the direction and objective of total innovation	When Bill Hewlett and I put together the initial plans for our business enterprise in 1937, we hadn't yet focused our interest and energies on the field of electronic instrumentation. What we did decide, however, was that we wanted to direct our efforts toward making important technical contributions to the advancement of science, industry, and human welfare. It was a lofty, ambitious goal.	(Packard, 2001)
	Building innovation culture	The success of HP was called "Human, Human and Human". A free, relaxed and joyful working environment arouses the enthusiasm of every employee for innovation and explores the potential of everyone.	(Packard, 2001)
	Providing resource and system guarantee, promote all-involvement innovation	The close relationships among HP people encouraged a form of participatory management that supported individual freedom and initiative while emphasizing commonness of purpose and teamwork. In the early years we were all working on the same problems. We solicited and used ideas from wherever we could get them. The net result was that each employee felt that he or she was a member of the team. As the company grew, we could no longer take teamwork for granted. We had to try to emphasize and strengthen it. That's one of the reasons we didn't single out divisions or groups that were doing particularly well. And why benefits such as profit sharing are provided not to selected individuals or groups but to all eligible employees. It's imperative that there be a strong spirit of helpfulness and cooperation among all elements of the company and that this spirit be recognized and respected as a cornerstone of the HP Way. A primary goal in setting up these divisions was to	(Packard, 2001)

continued

Master variables	Dependent variables	Mechanism of action	Source
Strategic thinking	Formation of indigenous innovation capability	give each division considerable autonomy, creating an environment that fostered individual motivation, initiative and creativity, and that gave wide latitude of freedom in working toward common goals and objectives. We wanted to avoid bureaucracy and to be sure that problem-solving decisions be made as close as possible to the level where the problem occurred. We also wanted each division to retain and nurture the kind of intimacy, the caring for people, and the ease of communication that were characteristic of the company when it was smaller.	(Packard, 2001)
Network construction and knowledge integration			(Packard, 2001)
Internal research and development	Formation of creative imitation capability		(Packard, 2001)
Cooperative development and research			(Packard, 2001)
Learning by doing	Formation of imitation capability		(Packard, 2001)
Introduction of technology			(Packard, 2001)

Only by relying on the innovation learning of dynamic innovation capabilities can enterprises form effective innovation learning approaches, acquire high value-added enterprise knowledge, strengthen their own competitiveness learning mechanism and realize the objective of sustainable development. Table 13-6 below shows the analysis of how learning mechanism promoted HP's capabilities

Table 13-6 Analysis of how learning mechanism promoting HP's capabilities

Master variables	Dependent variables	Content of action	Source
Strategic thinking	Formation of indigenous innovation capability	But right from the beginning, Bill and I knew we didn't want to be a "me-too" company merely copying products already on the market. To this day, HP continually strives to develop products that represent true advancement.	(Packard, 2001)
Network construction and knowledge integration		We started a monthly publication in 1949 called the HP Journal...The HP Journal described the technology used in the development of important new products. Although this information was useful to our competitors, we thought the benefits outweighed this disadvantage.	(Packard, 2001)
Internal research and development	Formation of creative imitation capability	With my experience at GE and with Charlie's help, I was quite capable of making the vacuum-tube models to test Russ Varian's theories. When one thinks of HP contributions, one usually thinks of innovative products. But it's important to point out that over the years we have attempted to make contributions as well in the form of new manufacturing methods and techniques. These manufacturing innovations often make state-of-the-art product contributions possible.	(Packard, 2001)
Cooperative development and research		He assured us, however, that competition was a good thing and it was better to have two companies introducing a new product, especially if it incorporated new technology, because that made it all the more credible to the customer. After that meeting, Eastham and his General Radio colleagues continued to be helpful to us, and although we were competitors, we also became good friends.	(Packard, 2001)
Learning by doing	Formation of imitation capability	I enjoyed athletics and learned some lessons that were helpful in managing HP...teamwork becomes very important...Given equally good players and good teamwork, the team with the strongest will to win will prevail.	(Packard, 2001)
Introduction of technology		I enjoyed my experience at GE. I was able to learn many things that later proved helpful when we started our own business, and I also developed close friendships with some individuals who would later make their own mark in electronics.	(Packard, 2001)

The relationship among all-element synergy mechanism, leadership mechanism and learning mechanism can be shown in Figure 13-2 and Table 13-7.

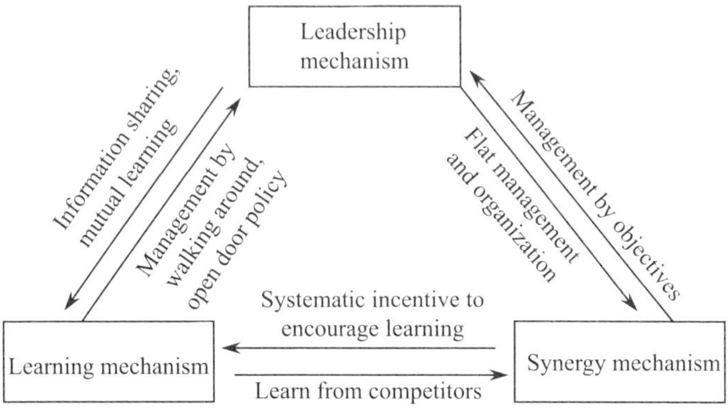

Figure 13-2 Analysis of how leadership mechanism promotes total innovation

Table 13-7 Analysis of connections among leadership mechanism, learning mechanism and synergy mechanism

Master variables	Dependent variables	Example of interaction between mechanism	Source
Leadership mechanism	Learning mechanism	We started a monthly publication in 1949 called the *HP Journal*...The *HP Journal* described the technology used in the development of important new products. Although this information was useful to our competitors, we thought the benefits outweighed this disadvantage.	(Packard, 2001)
	Synergy mechanism	Towards such direction of reform, HP put forward the strategy of electronic service, and adjusted and reformed the organizational structure & working procedures, examination & incentive system, and corporate culture & code of conduct.	(Dafoe, 2004)
Learning mechanism	Leadership mechanism	Linked with the "management by walking around" is another important management practice at HP, and a basic tenet of the HP Way. It's called the "open door policy". Like MBWA, this policy is aimed at building mutual trust and understanding, and creating an environment in which people feel free to express their ideas, opinions, problems and concerns.	(Packard, 2001)
	Synergy mechanism	To be useful in an era of worldwide competition and rapid change, new products must be developed quickly and produced efficiently with manufacturing processes and techniques that assure quality and economy.	(Packard, 2001)

continued

Master variables	Dependent variables	Example of interaction between mechanism	Source
Synergy mechanism	Learning mechanism	After the merger of HP and Compaq, the advantages of the corporate culture of two companies were combined and the shortcomings were discovered and eliminated.	(Dafoe, 2004)
	Leadership mechanism	Manager of HP at all levels attach great importance to the knowledge management. Every manager of HP realizes that to form effective plans, they must have good knowledge management and share experiences and knowledge with all employees.	(Dafoe, 2004)

The development of HP has seldom been restrained by external factors. With unique talent advantages and strong innovation capabilities inside the enterprise, the only thing that obstructs HP's development is its achievements and advantages in the past. The gradual formation of TIM model is the solution of HP to exceed the past. The TIM model of HP doesn't only have the core dynamics of innovation and the diversification of innovation synergy, but also feature the unique interaction between entrepreneurs' innovation spirit and employees' innovation desire based on openness, diversification and trust. After the first generation took over the leadership from the founders of HP, the uniqueness of HP's TIM was challenged to a certain degree. It was confronted with challenges like the contradiction between high-efficiency control of organization and traditional atmosphere of trust, contradiction between requirement for high-speed innovation of system technologies and traditional monopolistic innovation, contradiction between closed culture of organization control and the openness of traditional innovation culture, and the influence of the change of power distribution mechanism and remuneration mechanism on the innovation mechanism of an enterprise. To solve such a series of contradictions required the wisdom and capabilities of new successors. It will also have significant influence on the evolvement of HP's TIM model.

In a word, HP has already formed a new and systematic model of total innovation synergy based on the traditional culture of innovation. There may be many uncertain factors on the road ahead, but just as what HP did at the initial stage, HP has constructed a new and complete innovation system. They are now expecting to attract many leaders who are capable of expanding total innovation. The only thing they are waiting for is the development opportunities for new product technologies.

13.5 Conclusion

This chapter divides the development process of HP into four stages, i.e. initial stage, technology innovation stage, transition stage and strategic development stage. Through the in-depth analysis of the contents of TIM at these four stages under the framework of TIM, it points out the development of HP from a "garage" to an "evergreen tree" in Silicon Valley famous for its technology innovation and open corporate culture profits from technology innovation, strategy innovation, culture innovation, organization innovation and system innovation in the atmosphere of total innovation. Besides, the core of HP's innovation is not unchanged but dynamic. The main innovation synergy factors in different eras are also changing. Finally, it carefully analyzes the interactions between element innovation in all-element innovation, how leadership promotes total innovation, how learning mechanism promotes the improvement of capabilities, and the connections among leadership mechanism, learning mechanism and synergy mechanism. The conclusion is that HP has already formed a new and systematic model of total innovation synergy based on the traditional corporate culture of innovation.

Chapter 14

Samsung

Samsung Group, the largest Korean trading group, is an umbrella organization for a 26-company conglomerate, with 300 juridical persons and offices in nearly 70 countries and areas worldwide. The group has 196,000 employees.

Through more than 80 years of development, over 30 enterprises belonging to Samsung Group, 16 enterprises have invested in China, such as Samsung Electronics, Samsung SDI, Samsung Electro-Mechanics, Samsung Corning, Samsung Network, Samsung Life, Samsung Fire & Marine Insurance, Samsung Securities and Samsung C&T. They are involved in many fields like electronics, finance, trading, heavy industry, construction, chemical industry, clothing, wool textile and advertisement. Main products of Samsung which operate in China include: communication and office products like mobile phones, laser printers, and monitors; core components like semiconductors; AV products like rear-projection large screen televisions, DVDs and home theatres; optoelectronic products like digital cameras; white household appliances like large side by side refrigerators, central air-conditioners and chest-type air-conditioners, as shown in Table 14-1.

Table 14-1 Business of Subsidiaries of Samsung Group

Group company	Field	Business scope
Business group	Information and communication	Computer, communication devices, home electronics
	Machine and equipment	Transportation equipment, industrial machine and equipment, general machine, machinery equipment
	Steel and metal	Steel sheet, galvanized steel sheet, stainless steel, nonferrous metals and precious metal
	Chemistry	Petrochemical products, synthetic resin, organic chemistry, inorganic chemistry, fine chemistry, rubber materials and products, paper materials and products
	Energy, mineral and food	Cooper, oil and gas, coal and food
E&C group	Construction	Construction projects, factory construction, SOC projects, residential real estate
Retail division	Retail	Samsung shopping center, Samsung online mart, Utoo Park

continued

Group company	Field	Business scope
Next-generation strategic business	Trading	Comprehensive services, beefing up trilateral trade operation, development of Chinese market, brand expansion and brand authorizing
	Construction &Trading	Cultivating 5 iconic products and 3 next-generation business fields, promoting the core capabilities of engineering construction, building comprehensive real estate service system

14.1 Analysis of the three development phases of Samsung's total innovation management

Founded in 1938, Samsung Group has now become the largest enterprise group in Korea. During its 80 years of development with the political and economic changes of Korea and the development of global science, technology and economy, Samsung, as a family enterprise, has undergone the administration of two generations and developed itself from a small trading company to a large group with international influence, and from a manufacturer purely relying on the introduction and imitation of technologies to a technologically leading enterprise with independent R&D capabilities. It has already achieved great success. Due to its strong power and sound operation, it is now called the "great white shark in Korea" (Yang, 2005). The development of Samsung can be divided into three stages, namely, the stage of foundation and development dominated by technology innovation, the stage of reconstructing new undertaking dominated by strategic adjustment and the stage of integrated development dominated by total innovation.

14.1.1 Stage of foundation and development (1938 to the early and middle 1980s)

On March 1, 1938, founding chairman Byung-chull Lee started a business named Samsung Sanghoe in Taegu, Korea, with 30,000 won (about RMB 180 yuan according to recent exchange rate).

(I) Strategy innovation: No.1 in Korea

At the very beginning of Samsung Sanghoe, Lee's trading company exported dried fish, vegetables and fruit to Beijing and to China's Northeast. But in just over a decade, Samsung would have its own small mills and sales operation, the foundation of what would become the modern global corporation that still bears the Samsung name today. In the operation afterwards, Samsung always insisted on the strategy of diversification and aimed at becoming the No.1 enterprise in Korea. Just as Byung-chull Lee said in his autobiography, "To be the first" means Samsung should press forward with indomitable will and try to be the best. Its sugar mill is the first modernized and large scale manufacturing enterprise in Korea. In the future, in whatever field, the company must take the lead in Korea and make contribution to the prosperity of the country and affluence of the people.

In November 1948, Chairman Lee moved Samsung's offices to Seoul and founded the Samsung Corporation, which marked the beginning of Samsung's entry into full-scale international trade. The corporation became one of Korea's top seven trading firms in as short as one year and the largest trading company in Korea by early 1950. After the 1950s when the Korean War ended, a thousand things waited to be done in Korea. Being fully aware of the social and economic development in Korea back then, Samsung made great efforts to promote the diversification strategy of the enterprise. First, Samsung established Cheil Sugar (known today as Jeil Jedang) in 1953, which began domestically manufacturing products that substituted for previously imported goods. The next year, Samsung set up Cheil Industries, initiating a new era of fabrics made in Korea. After the implementation of diversification strategy for half a century, Samsung began to operate diversified products in almost all fields, from biscuit and cake, to automobile, plane, petrochemical industry, shipbuilding, aviation, finance, electronics and communication, thereby covering everything. Especially, the two industries determined in Samsung's diversification strategy led to the present pattern of Samsung's industrial development: one is the electronic industry and the other is the semiconductor industry.

(II) Culture and system innovation: Culture and system of orderliness

Born in a famer's family, Byung-chull Lee studied in a private school run by his grandfather and was greatly influenced by Confucian culture, which laid a foundation for his future business philosophy, the family culture that emphasizes orderliness and humanity.

Before Kun-hee Lee took office, Samsung formed a concept of hierarchy and subordination, which was incompatible with the innovation culture advocated by Kun-hee Lee. For example, in Samsung, there was even a game of drinking "loyalty wine". Subordinates put socks and shoes into the wine jar and drank such "loyalty wine" in their superiors' presence to show their loyalty to the superior leaders. Within the enterprise, there formed a sectarian relationship based on school, blood relationship and region. Such a culture had many disadvantages. Firstly, the enterprise was divided into too many departments, which led to low efficiency. Secondly, there were many inexplicit power-responsibility-favor relations. Thirdly, the enterprise followed a concept of obedience and loyalty, which was bad for employees, especially the grass-roots level employees. Fourthly, it was difficult for talents with different cultural or regional backgrounds to blend in Samsung and it hindered Samsung's internationalization. Meanwhile, the concept of obedience was also embodied in the mode of competition adopted by Byung-chull Lee, which only offered the winner opportunities. For example, Jong-yong Yun, who used to be the director of VCR business unit of Samsung Electronics, left Samsung for its competitor, Hyundai Electronics, in the middle 1980s. That's because at the initial stage, VCR suffered the uncertainties of technologies and high unqualified rate. Therefore, Jong-yong Yun was fired by Byung-chull Lee. Such a philosophy arose in Kun-hee Lee's outstanding operating capability, but it also restrained the creativity of employees. Byung-chull Lee even had to deal with the decorative materials of building by himself.

Deeply influenced by Confucian culture, Byung-chull Lee emphasized the concept of hierarchy and subordination on the one hand, and insisted on the human-oriented concept and attached great importance to employees' rational pursuit. For Byung-chull Lee, "to plant a tree, you have to find one who is good at planting tree with a sincere attitude. Sometimes, you also need help from others, so you have to know if you can get such help. You must get hold of the capabilities and suitability of those available."

Developing itself from a small trading company to a large group with international influence, the success of Samsung cannot be separated from its respect for employees and human-oriented operating philosophy of seeking the common development of enterprise and employees. Samsung believed that "every employee has his own dream and the company has its development objective. The company should give employees some enlightenment and guidance, work hard together with the employees, and make employees feel proud of working for the company. They shall share the joys of success at the end". Therefore, members of Samsung call themselves Samsungers. This is unique in

Korean companies and directly reflects the human-oriented philosophy of Samsung. Such human-oriented philosophy was directly embodied in a series of human resource management systems of Samsung. As early as the 1930s to the 1940s, when the corporate atmosphere was relatively old-fashioned, Samsung established the system of letting employees participate in the investment and profit sharing as well as the bonus system in addition to employees' normal salary system. In the 1950s, when most Korean companies recruited employees through school, family and relative relationships, Samsung released its first public recruitment advertisement. In 1957, Samsung established the first public recruitment system in Korea. Even the two sons of Byung-chull Lee failed to enter Samsung through the examinations.

(III) Technology innovation: Imitation innovation

In 1983 when Samsung entered the DRAM (Dynamic Random Access Memory) market, due to the technology and resource limitations, Samsung decided to introduce technologies and DRAM designs from American companies Micron and Zytrex and chip production technologies from Sharp. Therefore, by recruiting Korean scientists and engineers who worked in America and appointing employees in America and Japan to study, Samsung established a DRAM design and technological breakthrough team in both Silicon Valley and Korea. Researchers in America mainly collected information and learnt the latest semiconductor designing technologies in America; the team in Korea mainly carried out production and R&D by imitating the technologies of American and Japanese enterprises. Meanwhile, it cooperated with the production department in Korea to solve some problems during the production. Two working teams in Silicon Valley and Korea impacted each other through training, joint research and consultation and made sufficient preparations for the digestion of VLSI (very large-scale integration) technology introduced from an American company.

After the successful development and operation of large scale production system of 4K, 16K, 64K and 256K DRAM, in September

1985, although Samsung could purchase designing technologies from American enterprises, Samsung's R&D team decided to develop 1M DRAM. Such an R&D task was still distributed to the two technology development teams in America and Korea. The domestic R&D team in Korea completed the design of circuit in March 1986 and manufactured feasible molds in June 1986, thus shortening the gap from 2 years in developing 256K DRAM to 1 year in developing 1M DRAM. In about 3 months, the working group in Silicon Valley had successfully developed 1M DRAM, which indicated the transfer of R&D center of Samsung from California to Korea and the successful transformation of Samsung from imitation innovation to indigenous innovation.

(IV) Organization innovation: Strict hierarchy

At this stage, the organizational structure of Samsung features strict hierarchy (as shown in Figure 14-1) and a great number of divisions. A typical embodiment of such strict hierarchy was the setting of a secretarial pool, which had the power only second to the president and directly took orders from Byung-chull Lee. The secretarial pool directly monitored the operation of all business units, reported to Byung-chull Lee and made significant decisions on the management, personnel and structural adjustment. One of the major disadvantages of secretarial pool was that the responsible person from the secretarial pool overly controled the operation of business unit, but they didn't understand the onsite situation and bore no responsibilities.

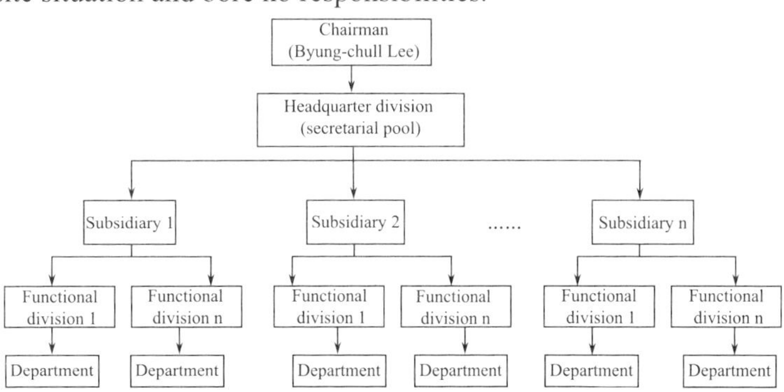

Figure 14-1 Hierarchical organizational structure of Samsung

14.1.2 Stage of reconstructing new undertaking featuring business reorganization (1988 to 1993)

The death of Byung-chull Lee on November 19, 1987, brought a change of generations. Kun-hee Lee, the third son of the founder, took his place and assured the continuation of his father's work. In 1988, on the fiftieth anniversary of Samsung, Kun-hee Lee claimed to restructure old businesses and enter new ones with the aim of becoming one of the world's top companies in the 21st century. During the process of reconstructing a new undertaking, Samsung actively adjusted its business structure and began to expand its business to new fields. To become one of the top five electronic enterprises in the world, Samsung integrated its electronic company, semiconductor company and communication company into Samsung Electronics. In the late 1980s, Samsung devoted itself to the electronic industry and heavy industry, and gained a reputation in the high-tech field.

At the stage of reconstructing a new undertaking, Samsung mainly focused on the business reorganization and structural adjustment. According to the existing problem of having no clear objectives, Samsung cleared up the businesses which didn't go well or had no promising future and strengthened its investment in R&D.

At this stage, the corporate culture, organization and system of Samsung mainly followed the management style of Byung-chull Lee, but Kun-hee Lee began to realize the problems. Since the early 1990s, Kun-hee Lee began to form the new operation philosophy and ordered the subordinates to change and reform. The main methods adopted by Kun-hee Lee include: adopting the single chairman system that Kun-hee Lee was solely responsible for the development of the company; building a core team, among others, Jong-yong Yun (general manager of Samsung Electronics), later a strongly supporter and core member when Kun-hee Lee promoted new management movement; Road

Show (starting in March 1993, Kun-hee Lee went on a four-month long journey from Los Angeles, Frankfurt, Osaka, Tokyo to London, took over 1,800 directors to foreign countries and discussed with them for over 500 hours). During the discussions overseas, Kun-hee Lee constantly instilled the reform thoughts into the directors and laid an ideological foundation for the successful reform of Samsung.

14.1.3 Stage of integrated development (1993 to present)

(I) New strategy to become a world first-class enterprise

Based on the understanding and forecasting of the world market, Samsung put forward the objective to become a first-class enterprise in the 21st century and attached importance to the implementation of new business development strategy, quality strategy and internationalization strategy.

Firstly, it established the "selective and centralized" business development strategy. Since 1988 when Samsung proposed "reconstructing a new undertaking", according to the existing problem of having no clear objectives, Samsung cleared up the businesses which didn't go well or had no promising future and strengthened its investment in R&D in the business that had bright prospects. On such a basis, it also carried out active business structure adjustments and began to expand its business to new fields. The number of companies belonging to Samsung was decreased from 50 to 24 in 1998. The total sales volume of the cut-off department was 2.5 billion U.S. dollars, mainly in the food, textile and service industry.

Secondly, it established a quality strategy. In the new strategy, Samsung aimed at obtaining several world class products and services and considered quality as the life of an enterprise and defective products as the "cancer" which destroyed the organization. To realize such an objective, Samsung devoted itself to improving product quality, human resource quality and operation quality. As for the strengthening of quality, Samsung Electronics and Samsung Electro-Mechanics implemented the "line-stopping" mechanism. When a disqualified product was discovered during the process of production, the whole production line would be stopped until the problem was solved. In order to improve the quality of Samsung services, Samsung Human Resource Development Institution gave lectures to all service personnel of Samsung. Shilla Hotel of Samsung Group also provided the employees of Samsung Life, Samsung Securities and Samsung Credit Card with etiquette training courses. In terms of operation, Samsung began to implement new business management since 1993. The company aimed to strengthen employees' innovation consciousness and capabilities of employees and to increase production efficiency through the reforms of culture, organization and system. According to the investigation on the effect of the "new business management" in 1 year, 88% of the respondents believed they were moving towards the right direction and 73% of the respondents thought the productivity was effectively improved in the previous year.

Thirdly, it established an internationalization strategy. According to Samsung's guidelines of "carrying out production in the places where there are markets", since the late 1980s, Samsung established production and R&D departments in Southeast Asia and America. In spite of a late start, it has now established nearly 300 corporate bodies and offices in nearly 70 countries and regions with a total of 196,000 employees. The specific internationalization strategies included: establishing overseas head company system and building three head companies in Japan, America and Europe separately; implementing unified raw material purchasing and distribution system overseas; establishing overseas investment system with joint venture as the core; building complete after-sales service network on a global scale.

(II) Human-oriented innovation ideology

Developing itself from a small trading company to a large group with international influence, the success of Samsung cannot be separated from its respect for employees and human-oriented operating philosophy of seeking the common development of enterprise and employees. It is embodied in the following aspects:

Firstly, Samsung always drove its growth with the development of talents. Just as what Kun-hee Lee said, the competitiveness and value of Samsung mainly depended on the number of the outstanding talents. The core personnel should be given proper incentives, entrusted with important duties and offered a good atmosphere to tap their potential. The development of Samsung was attributed to the contributions of a great number of high-quality employees. At present, Samsung Group has 180,000 employees, including 12,000 doctors. Among 48,000 managers, except 25,000 employees with professional title of production skill, 25% of the rest have bachelor or doctor's degree.

Secondly, the operating philosophy of Samsung attached great importance to the respect for people. On the international website of Samsung Group, the company clearly emphasized that the cornerstone of its operation values is the respect for people. In a narrow sense, strongly advocating the "respect for people" refers to respecting employees. And in a broad sense, it includes the respect for customers, society and even the whole human race. To realize such a philosophy, Samsung provided employees with fair treatment and created a good atmosphere and space for employees to develop themselves. By developing better products, Samsung aims at improving people's quality of life and to make the life of people more comfortable and convenient.

To improve the quality of employees and enable them to be better integrated into society, Samsung spent about 1% of its sales income in human resources development and spent 100 million dollars in employee training. Meanwhile, Samsung set up human resource development center in Seoul to be responsible for the education and training of employees. It had dozens of training centers and thousands of trainers. The second and third steps of personnel training were to provide employees with proper business skills and enable them to play to their strengths in proper positions. At the same time, Samsung always insisted on "employee's welfare first". For example, Samsung set up a unique organization, CDC (career development center), which helped employees with opportunities for new job or new career and guaranteed the livelihood of retired employees of Samsung.

Thirdly, it encouraged continuous self-innovation. In 1993, in the annual meeting of Samsung held in Frankfurt, Kun-hee Lee announced to carry out "new business" reform, the core concept of which was: change. This was a reforming movement aiming to realize the transformation from "business based on quantity" to "business based on operation" and the reform towards a first-class enterprise through the positive changes of individual employees and the whole enterprise. The concluding remark of this meeting was "Change everything but your wife and children", which drew universal attention from the world. Samsung mainly encouraged two aspects of innovations: first is continuous innovation. Just as what Kun-hee Lee said to the employees, "It is not hard to change once, but it is hard to stick with change. Every day, we insist on changing a little bit. Never go back. If you cannot change yourself, you cannot change anything. All such things cannot happen overnight. Please remember that a firm will is the key for success". In fact, the success of Samsung today is attributed to its corporate atmosphere of innovating forever and continuously seeking improvement. On the other hand, innovation must start from yourself. Samsung believes that every change starts from itself. If it doesn't change, nothing will change. If it changes, even if nobody else changes, it will create positive effect. Besides, in the opinion of Kun-hee Lee, such innovation was voluntary. "If only you really want to change and want to show your capabilities; when you discover that the change is successful and you are full of energy, when everyone around you see the achievements of your reform, such reform can go on."

(III) Realize independent technology innovation

The most typical and universally researched and promoted case of Samsung's realization of independent technology innovation was the process of Samsung developing its technologies from imitation to innovation in the semiconductor industry.

Samsung's indigenous innovation of DRAM started from the R&D of 16M in 1990. Samsung had advanced technologies at that time. As to the development of 64M, Samsung was faster than Hyundai and LG. In the second half of 1994, Samsung became the world largest supplier of 64M DRAM commercial prototype and supplied products to super large customers like HP, IBM and Sun Corporation. From then to now, Samsung has become a world leader in the development and design of DRAM (The innovation process of DRAM from imitation to innovation is shown in Table 14-2).

Table 14-2 Innovation process of DRAM from imitation to innovation

Type of DRAM	64K	256K	1M	4M	16M	64M	256M	1G	4G
Leading time of Samsung (year)	-4.5	-3	-2	-0.5	0	2.5	2.5	3.5	-

Source: *Samsung international website. http://www.samsungcorp.com.*

After the successful development of 64K DRAM and 256K DRAM, the company has accumulated considerable knowledge on the design and production of semiconductors and was able to independently design the whole production process of 1M DRAM and above. Then, the company shifted the focus on large scale production of new products. For this purpose, Samsung built a cross-functional team of technology and production, combined the product R&D and the design of production, equipment and process, effectively reduced the cost of production and significantly shortened the time of productization. In March 1996, Samsung built a SLIM (short cycle time and low inventory in manufacturing) team on an annual basis, which ended in 2001. This team consisted of seven groups with employees coming from the manufacturing department, photo engineering department, total productivity department, production control and system technology departments of Samsung Electronics and employees coming from Leachman and Associate (L&A). By establishing an online database supporting SLIM and electronic data differences (including natural period, process time and equipment condition table), the team can immediately dispose of the industrialized project and data interface. Main activities and important results of SLIM team are shown in Table 14-3.

Table 14-3 Main activities and important results of SLIM team

Time	Team activities	Main results
1996. 3~ 1997. 2	Building a SLIM team based production line 4 and 5	The cycle time per layer of production line 4 and 5 was reduced by 4.5 and 2 respectively.
1997. 3~ 1998.2	Building a SLIM team based production line 6 and 7	The cycle time per layer of production line 4 and 5 was reduced by 1.5 and 1.6 respectively; The cycle time per layer of production line 6 and 7 was reduced by 3.4 and 2.5 respectively.
1998. 3~ 1999.2	Building a SLIM team based production line 2, 3 and 8	The cycle time per layer of production line 4 and 5 was reduced to 1.3 and 1.6 respectively.
1999. 3~ 2000.3	Building a team based on EDS and integrated testing	The on-time delivery of EDS increased from 70% to 96%; the on-time delivery of testing increasing from 74% to 98% .
2000. 4~ 2001.6	Emphasizing the time arrangement of imitation and the maintenance and use of equipment, and planning the use of new equipment	/

Source: *Robert C L et al. SLIM: short cycle time and low inventory in manufacturing at Samsung Electronics. Linthicum. 2002, 32 (1), 61–79.*

Meanwhile, Samsung had significantly improved its indigenous design and innovation capabilities. Taking Samsung Electronics as an example, it has won several IDEA (Industrial Design Excellence Awards) awards and become the company that won the most awards for several years in succession. These proved that the design capabilities of Samsung have already reached the world level. In 2003, Samsung obtained 1,313 patents in America, ranking ninth among all enterprises in the world.

(IV) Build the team-based organizational structure

The organizational structure of Samsung Group is shown in Figure 14-2.

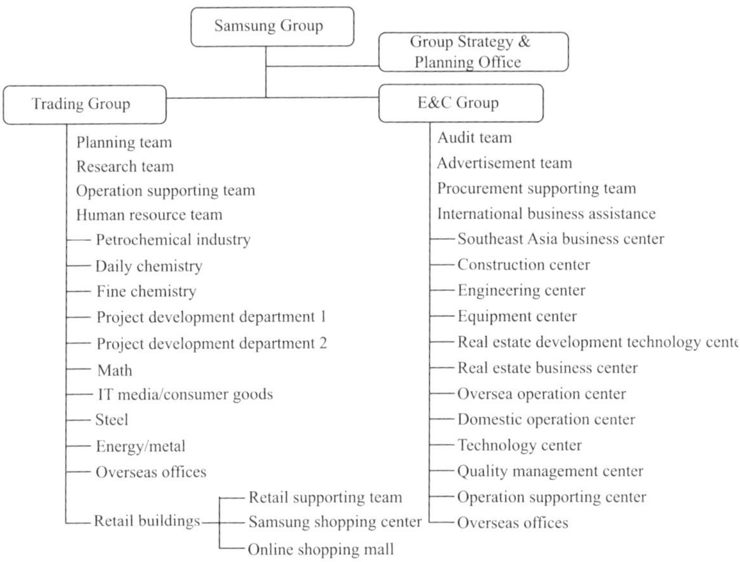

Figure 14-2 Organizational structure of Samsung Group

Source: Samsung international website. http://www.samsungcorp.com.

In 1985, Samsung began to realize that the original hierarchical structure of organization and overly divided departments prevented employees of Samsung from carrying out indigenous and cooperative innovation. After Samsung implemented the "new business" management, in 1995, the company used teamwork experiences on the successful development of DRAM for reference, thoroughly abandoned the hierarchical structure of the organization (as shown in Figure 14-3) and established the organizational form with team as the basic unit (as shown in Figure 14-4). As to the production and quality problems, Samsung often formed a quality improvement team consisting of researchers, designers and production personnel and even involved the sales representatives, consumers and suppliers into the process of production planning so as to catch up with and surpass first-class enterprises. Meanwhile, team was also widely used to solve management problems. For example, in 1997, Samsung hired outstanding talents overseas to form a future strategy team, which consisted of 25 MBAs, all from top universities in the world. When Samsung Electronics, Samsung Life and Samsung Securities were confronted with some problems which were not proper for asking external assistance, the future strategy team would work to establish and implement relevant plans until the problems were solved.

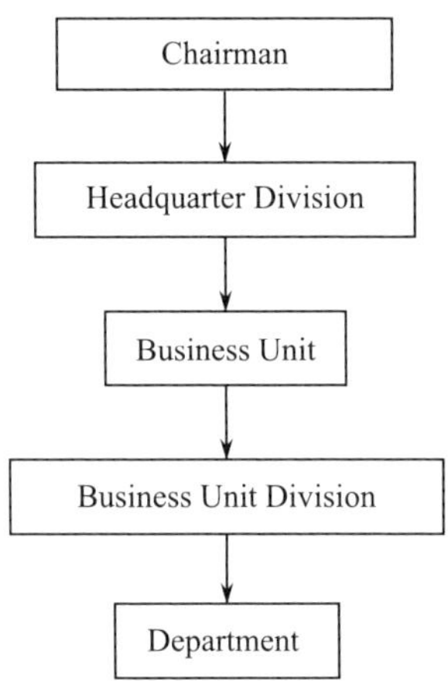

Figure 14-3 Samsung's organizational form in 1990

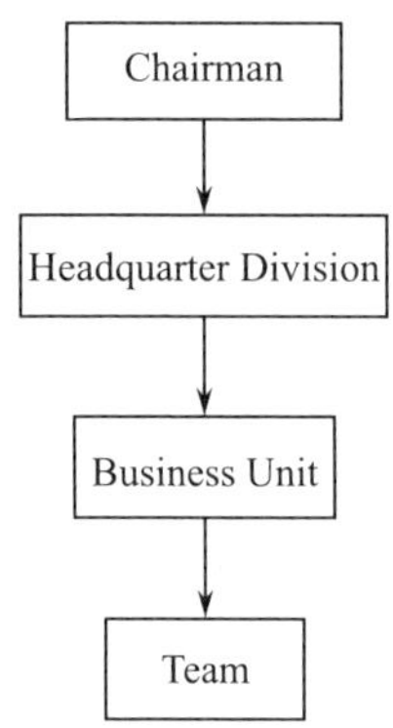

Figure 14-4 Samsung's organizational form in 1995

The new organizational form expanded the span of management, greatly reduced the number of managers, improved the management efficiency of the organization and strengthened the employees' decision-making power for innovation.

(V) Institutional system that embodies the recognition of employees' innovation values

In order to support the "new business" management of Samsung and encourage employees' continuous self-innovation, the company promoted a series of new measures, including the employee innovation incentive system, human resource management system and the well-known Seven-to-Four working system. Such system innovations fully reflected Samsung's recognition of employees' innovation values and the corporate culture and philosophy of respecting employees.

1. Employee innovation incentive system

Samsung cherished every talent and was willing to award such talents, especially those creative technology talents. The company provided professional technicians with favorable treatment, caring for them in life and encouraging them to discover and solve problems in work. For example, Samsung China set up "Proposal Award" every month to encourage those who had wonderful proposals and executors would receive the awards directly from the general manager on monthly meetings. Employees who won such an award several times may get promoted and participate in training program overseas. Meanwhile, Samsung strongly disagreed on the concept to restrain those who didn't follow the traditional rules. Just as Kun-hee Lee said, "I like those who cause trouble". To support the employees' indigenous innovation, Samsung encouraged employees to form innovation teams freely. The team members had full autonomy to do whatever research activities as they pleased. The research was carried out by individuals in their spare time. Once the research was recognized by the company, they would be provided with the funds and instruments by the company and obtain corresponding awards.

To further encourage employees' innovation, Samsung introduced the Seven-to-Four working system in 1993, i.e. starting work at 7 a.m. and leaving at 4 p.m. Such system was even called an epoch-making breakthrough following the Nine-to-Five eight hour working system founded by Bosch in 1906 (Hong, 2003). Clearly, Samsung adopted the Seven-to-Four working system to enable employees to have more time to learn and improve their innovation capabilities. Firstly, such a system could improve working efficiency. Employees of Samsung could use more time in the afternoon to participate in health management, foreign language training and club activities to develop their capabilities. Besides, it could help them avoid the rush hours and save time. Secondly, such innovation would set an example for employees' innovation. It showed that the company hoped the employees could have more time to improve themselves. In Korea, after work at 6 or 7 p.m., employees probably went to the restaurant for dinner and then went home. They had little time to learn. Thirdly, in addition to such a system, the company had also carried out some other supporting reforms to encourage employee innovation. For example, after having introducing Seven-to-Four working system, Kun-hee Lee then decided to provide employees with 50% discounted foreign language studying programs and other education courses offered by Samsung international and regional experts, Samsung Techno-MBA, 21st Century Leadership Program and 21st Century CEO Program.

2. Human resource management system

The human resource management of Samsung Group took the lead in publicly recruiting graduates in campus in Korea. To provide employee innovation with good external environment, Samsung established the institutional systems suitable for employee innovation at all processes of human resource management. During the recruitment, the company implemented an open, fair and equal recruitment system and attracted innovation-based talents on a global scale. During the training, the company emphasized the cultivation of innovation-based talents. For example, the company implemented a 3-year "regional expert program". The program was special for 400 employees who had have over 3 years working experiences in Samsung. Samsung gave a lot of money to them and sent them to foreign countries for a long period. For the following 12 months, these people stayed in foreign countries and did whatever they wanted. Then, they returned to Korea and worked for several years before they were sent back to their own countries, and then they are expected to promote the products of Samsung there. For this three-year plan, the company spent 100 million dollars in training 2,000 young managers. As to the remuneration, Samsung promoted the evaluation system and remuneration system based on capabilities and performance. As to the employee configuration, selection and promotion, the company broke through the promotion system based on the length of service and constructed diversified career channels featuring the coexistence of position system and professional title system. Besides, Samsung also implemented the "three-matching" system to select new employees, i.e. examining whether the candidates' personality matched the corporate culture of Samsung, whether the candidates' character matched the position they were applying for and whether the candidates' personality matched the working style of their direct supervisors. During the daily management, it required all employees to work together with innovation-based talents and respect the personality of such talents. The company also had a special policy to further develop the capabilities of the top 5% A-level talents and enable them to have more diversified professional capabilities. Therefore, the company established a "CEO" School, which was founded in September 1993 and aimed to provide all 850 managers within the group with a 6-month reeducation, three months in Korea and three months in foreign countries. The latter mainly focused on foreign language study.

14.2 Analysis of TIM features at all development phases of Samsung's innovation

Through the innovation-based operation of two generations of leaders as well as the joint efforts of all employees, especially after the company began to implement "new business" management in 1993, Samsung Group made great efforts to implement TIM and enabled Samsung to develop itself from a large family consortium in Korea to a top international enterprise in the world. According to the analysis of different stages above, the TIM of Samsung became increasingly comprehensive with more innovation elements and innovation subjects. The innovation was extended to every employee and to every field in the world. The characteristics of Samsung's TIM at each stage are shown in Table 14-4.

Table 14-4 Analysis of Samsung Group's TIM all-element innovation at different stages

	Stage of foundation and development 1938-1987	Background of reform	Stage of reconstructing new undertaking 1987-1993	Background of reform	Stage of integrated development 1993 to present
Strategy innovation	No.1 in Korea Increase of quantity	1. Byung-chull Lee, founder of Samsung, passed away on Nov. 19, 1987. 2. Kun-hee Lee, son of Byung-chull with international vision and innovative spirit took over the position as the chairman. 3. In the 1970s and 1980s, the competitive weakness of Korean companies in Japanese, American and European market with low cost, low price and low quality became increasingly obvious.	Its business mainly focused on four core sectors, namely electronics, machinery, chemical industry and finance.	In 1993, Samsung held its annual meeting in Frankfurt and announced to implement "new business". Kun-hee Lee began to make the plan for Samsung to become No.1 in the world since early 1990. Fukuda event: it revealed the shortcomings of Samsung Electronics in product development, like insufficient attention to quality and bureaucracy.	The strategic objective to be No.1 in the world • Quality-led strategy (product quality, human resource quality and operation quality) • Internationalization strategy (carried out production wherever there was a market and strengthen Chinese market strategy) • "Selective and centralized" business development strategy (Samsung decreased the number of its subsidiaries from 50 in 1988 to 24 in 1998)
Culture innovation	Confusion culture Orderliness-based (subordination and obedience) Human-oriented (talent first, rational pursuit)		• Enlightened subordinates to innovate • Road show overseas		Created innovation-based culture • Change everything but wife and children • Human-oriented concept featuring the joint development of employees and organization ("Samsunger", valued employees' contributions, emphasized the respect for people, "employees welfare first") • Encouraged innovation (innovation trust, everyone is the boss)
Technology innovation	Imitation innovation Introduction of technology and production based on imitation DRAM Technology from America (Silicon Valley) and Process from Japan (Sharp)		Initially realized the indigenous innovation Initially realized the indigenous development of 1MB DRAM		Realized indigenous innovation • DRAM realized the indigenous innovation and became world leading; Samsung developed the first 1GB DRAM in the world in 1996 and released 1GB DRAM first in 1999. • Strengthened the combination of product and process innovation (built SLIM team)

Organization innovation	Strict hierarchy secretarial pool		Cultivated a core team		Took team as organizational form • CEO's span of management increased from 17 people to 25 people; the proportion of grass-roots employees increased from about 70% to 80% • Simplified the organization and distributed power • Distributed duties to vice presidents • "Technology Valley", "Newton Program", "Top " of Samsung C&T,
System innovation	Characteristic human resource system and Korean system of company politics • Employees participated in investment and profit sharing. • First public recruitment advertisement • Established the first personnel system to recruit employees publicly in Korea • Drink "loyalty wine"		• Single chairman system • Kun-hee Lee planned the reform and consciously weakened the power of secretarial pool.		Reflected the respect and recognition of employee innovation Implemented human resource management system good for innovation, and strengthened the cultivation of top 5% A-level talents Seven-to-Four working system Supporting system of Seven-to-Four (Samsung international and regional experts, Samsung TechnoMBA, 21st Century Leadership Program and 21st Century CEO Program.)
All-involvement innovation	Innovation of entrepreneur and technicians • Operation innovation of Byung-chull Lee • DRAM development teams in America and Korea		Innovation of entrepreneurs and technicians Management innovation of Kun-hee Lee		Every employee is the boss. • Management innovation of Kun-hee Lee • "Technology Valley" teams like those who cause trouble.
All time-space innovation	Appropriate innovation in Korea		Global operation Built production and R&D departments in Southeast Asia and America since the late 1980's		Global operation Established global environment research center in 1993 Established headquarters in America, Europe and China separately in 1995 Established global strategy group in 1997 Three enterprises of Samsung Group were among the Fortune 500 in 2003.

14.3 Evaluation of Samsung's TIM models at different phases

According to the in-depth analysis of contents and characteristics of Samsung's TIM at all stages above as well as the business performance of Samsung at all stages, this section will evaluate Samsung's TIM on different dimensions. "5" is the full score and "1" is the least innovative. Taking all dimensions of TIM at the stage of foundation and development as benchmark (1 point), and comparing all dimensions at the other two stages with these to get the corresponding scores. The higher the score is, the more innovative the enterprise is. The specific conclusions are shown in Table 14-5 and Figure 14-5.

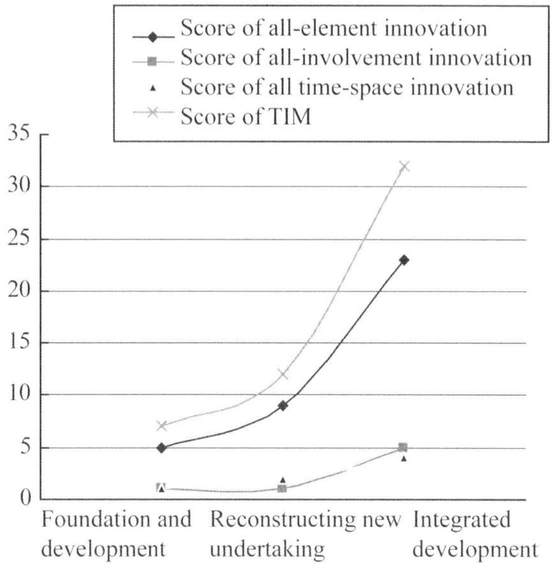

Figure 14-5 Score of different dimensions of Samsung's TIM at different stages

Table 14-5 Score of different dimensions of Samsung's TIM at different stages

Different dimensions of TIM	Stage of foundation and development	Stage of reconstructing new undertaking	Stage of integrated development
	Score	Score	Score
Strategy innovation	1	3	5
Culture innovation	1	2	4
Technology innovation	1	2	5
Organization innovation	1	1	4
System innovation	1	1	5
All-element innovation	5	9	23
All-involvement innovation	1	1	5
All time-space innovation	1	2	4
Total score of TIM	7	12	32

According to the conclusions of Samsung's TIM at all stages shown in the table above, it is clear that Samsung emphasizes the comprehensive development of innovation operation. Especially after the "new management" was proposed, all dimensions of TIM showed good development momentum. Samsung had particularly made great improvements in terms of strategy, culture, technology, organization and system. The continuous improvement of Samsung's TIM also led to direct economic benefits for the company. In 2003, the turnover of Samsung Group was about U.S. 96.5 billion dollars and its brand value was as high as U.S. 10.86 billion dollars, ranking 25th in the top 100 brands in the world and becoming the fast growing brand for two years in succession. Three enterprises of Samsung Group appeared on the list of Fortune 500 in 2003. Samsung Electronics ranked the 59th, Samsung C&T ranked 115th and Samsung Life ranked 236th. The flagship company of the group, Samsung Electronics ranked third in the Top 100 IT Companies in 2003 selected by *Business Week*. It has increasingly become an industrial forerunner and its influence has already surpassed many traditional magnates in the industry. At present, Samsung has nearly 20 products with the largest market share in the world. According to the statistics of Dataquest (March 2004), the products of Samsung which occupied the largest market share in world included DRAM (29%), SDRAM (26.9%), FLASH (21%) and DDI (18.8%), which showed the strong technology power of Samsung in the international market. Meanwhile, Samsung had significantly improved its indigenous design and innovation capabilities. Taking Samsung Electronics as an example, it has won several IDEA (Industrial Design Excellence Awards) awards and become the company that won the most awards for several years in succession. These prove that the design capabilities of Samsung have already reached the world level. In 2003, Samsung obtained 1,313 patents in America, ranking ninth among all enterprises in the world.

14.4 Interactions among Samsung's total innovation management elements and mechanisms

The fundamental cause of Samsung's transformation from a small company, which produced low price products by imitation, to a first-class group is embodied in its process of TIM. Its innovation elements have become increasingly comprehensive, closely connected and benignly interactive. The mutual relationships among main innovation elements of Samsung are shown in Figure 14-6 and Table 14-6.

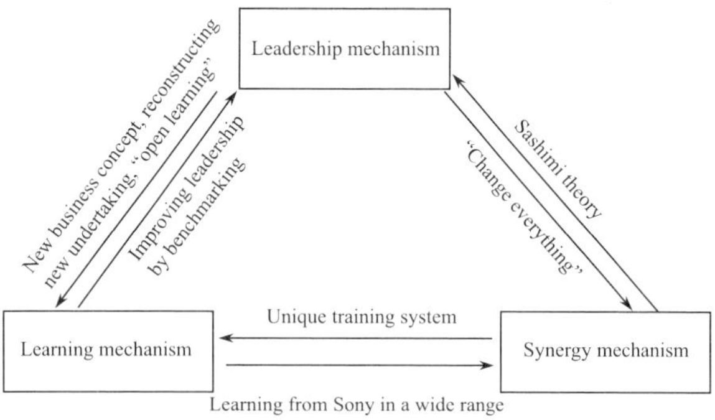

Figure 14-6 Schematic diagram of the relationships among leadership mechanism, learning mechanism and synergy mechanism

Table 14-6 Interactions among innovation elements of all-element innovation

Master variables	Dependent variables	Effect of element innovation (quotation)	Source
Strategy innovation	Culture innovation	International first class strategy enabled Samsung to construct a corporate culture in accordance with the new development form of enterprise – "marking contributions to the human society and coexisting with customers". In 1993, the annual meeting of Samsung held in Frankfurt, Kun-hee Lee announced to carry out "new business" reform, the core concept of "change". This was a reforming movement aiming to realize the transformation from "business based on quantity" to "business based on operation" and the reform towards a world first-class enterprise through the positive changes of individual employees and the whole enterprise.	(Guo, 2004) (Yang, 2005)
	Technology innovation	Kun-hee Lee pointed out that "we have to make our best to seize the scientific and technological fields demanded by the next century". The development strategy ahead of time enabled Samsung to win many first places in the sophisticated industries.	(Fu, 1994)
	System innovation	Samsung controlled the unqualified rate of product above the standards of Japanese companies and ensured the best quality-first operation in the world. The company carried out decisive reforms of organization and personnel, which was mainly embodied in the quality-led strategy.	(Hong, 2003)
	Organization innovation	With the strategic transformation of Samsung in China (from manufacturing center to market center), the R&D resources of Samsung also began to be led to China. By far, Samsung has already established several R&D institutions and design centers for semiconductor, communication, multi-media and software in China.	(Zhou, 2004)
Culture innovation	Strategy innovation	Samsung realized the crisis of operation and decided to change the operating way of wining competitiveness by quantity to the way of "quality-based operation".	(Yang, 2005)
	Market innovation	The customer-oriented concept enabled Samsung's product design to be more comfortable and convenient for consumers. The first mobile phone brand of Samsung, "Anycall", was a very popular design.	(Jiang and Wen, 2004)
	Technology innovation	With the strengthened global consciousness, a "tide of green goods" appeared in Western Europe first. Samsung seized such an opportunity and developed high-tech products like "green beeper" and "biological TV".	(Guo, 2004)
	System innovation	Guided by Lee's spirit of "I like those who cause trouble", Samsung established the corresponding incentive system and linked the constructive suggestions, inventions and research results directly with personal benefits.	(Jiang and Wen, 2004)
	Organization innovation	Guided by Lee's spirit of "I like those who cause trouble", Samsung established a great number of interest groups.	(Jiang and Wen, 2004)

Market innovation	Strategy innovation	The "sashimi" theory of product marketing emphasized the strategy that Samsung products should be launched to market much faster than those of its competitors.	(Jiang and Wen, 2004)
	Culture innovation	Samsung is filled with a sense of urgency that "time is money and efficiency is life".	(Jiang and Wen, 2004)
	Technology innovation	Averagely, Samsung needs 5 months to transform a concept to products; while 6 years ago, it needed 14 months.	(Jiang and Wen, 2004)
	Organization innovation	Fewer bureaucratic hierarchies during the decision-making process of new product development, budget and marketing plan accelerated Samsung's decision-making efficiency.	(Jiang and Wen, 2004)
Technology innovation	System innovation	Introduction of Seven-to-Four working system	(Fan, 2006)
	Organization innovation	In March 1996, Samsung built a SLIM (short cycle time and low inventory in manufacturing) team. As to the production and quality problems, Samsung often formed a quality improvement team consisting of researchers, designers and production personnel and even involved the sales representatives, consumers and suppliers in the process of production planning so as to catch up with and surpass world first-class enterprises. To support the employees' indigenous innovation, Samsung encouraged employees to form innovation teams freely. The team member had full autonomy to do whatever research activities as they want.	(Leachman et al, 2002)
System innovation	Technology innovation	Samsung Group invested 10% of its annual sales revenue into the research and development.	(Ning and Luo, 1996)
	Culture innovation	The introduction of Seven-to-Four working system enabled Samsung to simplify the contents of report and improve meeting culture.	(Hong, 2003)
	Organization innovation	Seven-to-Four working system led to the dramatic change inside Samsung. An environment for free speech was formed and the business decision-making power was decentralized.	(Hong, 2003)
Organization innovation	Culture innovation	The projects similar to "Technology Valley" including the "Newton Project", Samsung C&T and "Top Gun" of Samsung Electronics. Such informal teams created a good innovation atmosphere within Samsung Group.	/

The leadership of Samsung represented by Byung-chull Lee and Kun-hee Lee played an important role in the growth of Samsung. The effect of its leadership mechanism is mainly embodied in coordinating technology innovation and management innovation, guiding the direction and objective of total innovation, building innovation culture, carrying out organization innovation, and providing resource and system guarantees. The analysis of the effect of Samsung's leadership mechanism on innovation factors is shown in Table 14-7.

Table 14-7 Analysis of the influence of leadership mechanism on innovation elements

Master variables	Dependent variables	Influence (quotation)	Source
Leadership mechanism to promote total innovation	Synergy of technology innovation and management innovation	During the process of Samsung Electronics developing towards a super company in the world, many comprehensive factors played a role. However, underneath the complex surface, experts reach a consensus that the great success of Samsung should be firstly attributed to the outstanding leadership of Kun-hee Lee. Rolf H. Carson once said "the capabilities of a leader determine the destiny of an enterprise". Most management experts agree. Therefore, to avoid absolute exclusionism on strategic cooperation is the principle of Samsung to cooperate with other companies. And one strategy of Samsung is to cooperate with outstanding companies in all fields.	(Jin, 2003)
	Guiding the direction and objective of total innovation	Let's become one of the top enterprises in the world in our generation. I'd like to exert all my energies to realize such a lofty objective. On the 50th anniversary of Samsung in 1988, Kun-hee Lee announced the "new undertaking" of the group and set up the goal of Samsung's development as becoming one of top enterprises in the world. Kun-hee Lee pointed out that it was necessary to thoroughly change the bad habit of "seeking the quantity of companies rather the quality". A senior officer of Samsung said, "the new business concept of surviving by changes was widely accepted at last. That was different from other companies". "The new business concept couldn't be implemented due to the social contexts at first, but the domestic financial crisis helped."	(Jin, 2003)
	Building innovation culture	In 1996, Kun-hee Lee made an exciting decision. He began to avoid the imitation of products. Under the pressure of Chinese manufacturers' lost cost, Kun-hee Lee warned all employees of Samsung: innovate, or die. For 14 years, Samsung had always been engaged in social and public welfare. It reflected the operation philosophy of Kun-hee Lee. He often said to his trusted followers that "I hope Samsung may become a first-class company and help employees live a life as rich as those in developed countries". "Enterprises which don't make contributions to the society cannot survive". He also emphasized that we should understand the significance of social services from the overall concept of survival strategy and consider it as part of our operation.	(Jin, 2003)
	Organization innovation, providing resource and system guarantee	The competitiveness of Samsung Electronics comes from its stable triangular frame structure: Chairman Kun-hee Lee is at the peak of the triangle and responsible for guiding the direction of operation and setting up strategic objectives; the division of structural adjustment is responsible for helping Chairman and the chief executives implement strategic decisions; the chief executives are responsible for the specific direction, i.e. how to carry out practical operation activities.	(Jin, 2003)

During the process of building effective organization learning mechanism to improve the human resource competitiveness and strengthen the organization funds, Samsung has undergone several stages, like imitation, formation of creative imitation capabilities and formation of independent innovation capabilities. The analysis of its learning mechanism promoting the improvement of capabilities as well as interactions among the various mechanisms is shown in Table 14-8 and Table 14-9.

Table 14-8 Analysis of learning mechanism promoting the improvement of capabilities

Master variables	Dependent variables	Influence (quotation)	Source
Strategic thinking	Formation of indigenous innovation capability	On the 50th anniversary of Samsung in 1988, Kun-hee Lee announced the "new undertaking" of the group and set up the goal of Samsung's development as becoming one of top enterprises in the world. Kun-hee Lee pointed out that it was necessary to thoroughly change the bad habit of "seeking the quantity of companies rather the quality".	(Yang, 2005)
Network construction and knowledge integration		"So I like going to developed countries to learn advanced technologies or bring technicians and their technologies back home. I feel I have done a good work at this aspect."	(Jin, 2003)
Internal research and development	Formation of creative imitation capability	Every year, Samsung sends about 200 talents to learn advanced technologies from research institutions overseas. Samsung has really made a large investment. The head of Samsung Advanced Institute of Technology emphasized that "such advanced technologies are the soil for Samsung to survive in the future 5 to 10 years". Setting up research institutions just for the training of R&D technologies was never seen before in Korea. In 1990, Kun-hee Lee announced the "new undertaking" and set up such research institution at the same time. It aimed to correspond to the long-term strategy of the company. Besides, Samsung has also set up a complete system. Samsung Electronics considers intellectual property as the most valuable asset. For a long time, it has continuously enlarged its investment in R&D. It has 17,000 R&D staff members, accounting for over 30% among all employees (48,000). Besides, it has set up R&D centers in America, Japan, Britain, India and Russia separately, with a total of about 700 R&D staff members.	(Jin, 2003)

continued

Master variables	Dependent variables	Influence (quotation)	Source
Coopera-tive devel-opment and research		Kun-hee Lee emphasized that "Samsung will still cooperate with Sony in various fields, so don't goad Sony". Therefore, to avoid absolute exclusionism on strategic cooperation is the principle of Samsung to cooperate with other companies. And one strategy of Samsung is to cooperate with outstanding companies in all fields. According to the head of Business Planning Department, Samsung expected to "realize its goal of becoming top enterprise in the world through strong-strong collaboration". In the past, the complementary cooperation relationship was widely accepted. However, confronted with the fierce competitions at present, you have to cooperate with the strongest company to survive and realize the common development objectives. To learn the advanced experiences and strengths of top companies, Samsung had made great efforts. It held seminars once to twice per year and invited CEOs of Sony, Toshiba and other large companies to exchange ideas with the leaders of Samsung.	(Jin, 2003)
Learning by doing	Formation of imitation capability	As to such a failure, he has summarized four pieces of experiences, which are the cornerstone of his operation philosophy: 1. To run an enterprise, you must have insights into the trend of domestic and foreign changes and make great efforts to be adapted to such a trend; 2. You have to calmly evaluate your own capabilities and never do things beyond your capabilities. 3. Don't be engaged in speculative activities with fluke mind. 4. Cultivate your intuitive judgment capability and countermeasure research capability. While implementing Plan A, you also have to make Plan B and Plan C. When you discover the implementation of Plan A is inconsistent with the general trend, you must make a prompt decision and resort to Plan B or Plan C.	(Yang, 2005)
Introduc-tion of technology		At the end of the 1960s, Japan Sanyo Electric taught Samsung electronic technologies for the first time.	(Jin, 2003)

Table 14-9 Interactions among leadership mechanism, learning mechanism and synergy mechanism

Master variables	Dependent variables	Interactions between mechanisms	Source
Leadership mechanism	Learning mechanism	After determining the "new business" concept, "open learning" became an important cultural feature of Samsung. Samsung learnt from companies which grasp know-how in different fields and set up example companies to learn from for all departments. Setting up research institutions just for the training of R&D technologies was never seen before in Korea. In 1990, Kun-hee Lee announced the "new undertaking" and set up such research institution at the same time. It aimed to correspond to the long-term strategy of the company. Besides, Samsung has also set up a complete system. "So I like going to developed countries to learn advanced technologies or "bring technicians and their technologies back home."	(Jin, 2003)
Learning mechanism	Leadership mechanism	Brizentrro software package can effectively plan, adjust and control all operation resources of the enterprise... It reflects the advanced management of Samsung to a certain degree and is also the final result of continuous learning by benchmarking of Samsung.	(Chen, 2005)
	Synergy mechanism	Guided by the strong guidance of such an objective, Samsung learnt from Sony in all fields like brand, product, technology and design. It has continuously cultivated its learning capabilities and made great efforts to absorb the advantages of Sony.	(Chen, 2005)
Synergy mechanism	Learning mechanism	Through years of development, Samsung has formed a complete set of unique training system.	(Yang, 2005)
	Leadership mechanism	To prevent its products from becoming "leftover sashimi", Samsung Electronics adopted the strategy to continuously build new rules and overturn old rules.	(Yang, 2005)

14.5 Conclusion

Through the in-depth analysis of the contents and characteristics of TIM of Samsung at the stage of foundation and development, the stage of reconstructing new undertaking and the stage of integrated development, this chapter points out during 80 years' development, Samsung has developed itself from a small trading company to a large group with international influence and from the manufacturing enterprise that purely relied on the introduction and imitation of technologies to a technologically leading enterprise with the ability for independent R&D. All such great achievements are closely related to Samsung's strategy of insisting on human-oriented development. The success of Samsung's all-involvement process was attributed to the good atmosphere of organization innovation created by the total innovation of technology, strategy, culture, organization and system, which included realizing independent technology innovation, establishing the strategic objective to become No.1 in the world, building innovation-based culture, forming a team-based organizational structure and recognizing employees' innovation values.

This chapter also carries out a semi-quantitative analysis of Samsung's TIM on different dimensions at different stages, which intuitively shows the rapid development of Samsung on all aspects is closely related to the continuous improvement of its total innovation since 1993 when Samsung implemented TIM. Finally, it analyzes the interactions among all elements of total innovation, the influence of leadership mechanism on innovation elements, the improvement of capabilities promoted by learning mechanisms and the interactions among leadership, synergy and learning mechanisms.

Chapter 15

Conclusion

We are now in an era full of reforms. Knowledge has already become the main source and motive power of economic development. The revolution of new science and technology represented by information stimulates the rapid development of economic globalization. The construction and universal application of global information network will play a significant role in the revolution of modern social and industrial structure and the organizational structure of enterprise. Technology innovation increasingly becomes the key for stimulating economic growth and improving scientific and technological competitiveness (Porter, 1990; Hitt et al., 1997).

As a new paradigm of innovation management, total innovation management (TIM), based on the principles of humanism, ecology theory, open innovation theory, distributed innovation theory and principles of complex system, deeply analyzes the cases of successful enterprises both in China and abroad and extracts a technology-centered systematic model of all-involvement, all time-space and total innovation with innovation based on the synergy of technology and non-technology element innovation. TIM is the logical requirement of theoretical development of innovation management under new circumstances and an inevitable choice of innovation-based enterprises to realize value creation and to continuously improve their core competences and competitiveness.

15.1 Necessity of TIM

15.1.1 Demand for the reform of objective environment

The network environment which takes computer network as the material and technological foundation leads to dramatic changes of connecting relationships and methods of information. Internet and e-Commerce enable consumers to obtain more and more information at the fastest speed. The horizons of consumers become extraordinarily broad and the time-space restraints on the selection of goods are greatly reduced. The living standards of people have improved a lot, so their demands for goods become more individualized. The fierce market competitions raise higher requirements for the quality, supply speed and prices of products.

Confronted with the increasingly individualized

demands of customers and increasingly fierce competitions in the market, more and more enterprises realize that: in light of the increasingly individualized customer demand and time-based competition, more and more enterprises discover that only by relying on good production efficiency, high quality and flexibility, the sustained competitive advantages in market cannot be maintained. They have satisfied customers' comprehensive demands faster than their competitors. It not only requires technology innovation, but also the systematic, comprehensive and sustained innovation.

Meanwhile, advanced enterprises realize that: the final performance of technology innovation increasingly depends on the effective synergy among different departments and innovation elements. The rapid exchange and sharing of information under network environment make all-round innovation possible. To maintain sustainable competitive advantages in fierce market competitions, enterprises have to make full use of the effective access, rapid delivery, high-level sharing, frequent exchange and application of information, integrate the innovation capabilities of every employee at any time and place and improve the overall capabilities of an organization.

15.1.2 Demand for the development of innovation theories

In 1912, Schumpeter put forward the concept of "innovation" and defined "innovation" as the construction of new production function and a new combination of factors of production, including product, market and organization. After that, the systematic research on innovation management were continuously enriched and developed. It has been developed from the in-depth research on single element innovation, i.e. the research on technology innovation (represented by Mansfield and Schwartz) or non-technology innovation (represented by North), to the preliminary research on the complex and systematic innovation, which mainly focuses on the relationship between different element innovations, including portfolio innovation (Xu et al., 1997), integration innovation (Iansiti and West, 1997; Tang, 1998; Tidd et al., 2001; Jiang and Chen, 2000; Cao et al., 2001) and system innovation (Nelson and Winter, 1997; Peters, 2002; Radosevic, 1998).

With the continuous development of innovation management theories, research on many influencing factors of innovation has gained more and more depth. Gradually, a systematic thinking mode has formed. Research on innovation has no longer been restricted to pure innovation of technology or non-technology elements (including organization, system, strategy and culture), but begin to conduct an analysis of the connections among several innovation elements based on a systematic perspective.

However, due to the restraints of prevailing conditions back then, the traditional innovation management theories lacked the insights into the drastic changes of environment and the complex process innovation at present. The research on the synergy among innovation elements is mostly restricted to the synergy between two-dimensional elements (such as technology and market, technology and organization, technology and culture, technology and strategy) or three three-dimensional elements (such as technology, organization and culture) (Zhang et al., 1997; Peng, 2000; Tidd et al., 2001). There is no system view based on total innovation, which can include the technology elements and several non-technology elements into one overall framework. Now, it still lacks in-depth research on the synergy mechanisms like the levels, process and influencing factors of synergy; it lacks the assessment models and methods with scientific quantitative analysis of the synergy of all elements; it lacks the in-depth analysis of the multidisciplinary and crossed perspectives based on the theory of complexity. It is impossible to provide enterprises with a scientific and effective innovation management paradigm to guide practices under new circumstances.

Based on the systematic view of complexity and the ecological theory, open and distributed innovation view and human-oriented theory, TIM conducts comprehensive and systematic analysis of the synergy innovation between technology and non-technology elements, and puts forward the synergy innovation of technology elements and various non-technology elements (organization, strategy, culture and system) with technology innovation (or organization management) as the center and strategy innovation as the forerunner. It is not only the grasping of current development trends of innovation management, but also the overall breakthroughs.

15.1.3 Inevitable demand of historical development

The Renaissance in Europe liberated people from the spiritual shackles of religious authority. A rational and equal cultural environment with respect for human dignity and values became the soil to encourage the perception of truth and to breed modern science. The Renaissance stimulated the development of European sciences and technologies. The innovation encourages rational questioning and creation and doesn't go for blind faith in any authority. The innovation process tolerates failure and deems failure as the mother of success. The innovation process requires the spirit of indefatigable pursuit. The innovation process requires an atmosphere for innovation culture.

TIM originates from innovation-based culture. During the process of total innovation, the synergy of different element innovations and the cooperative innovation of personnel from different departments will surely shock the original philosophy. Therefore, it is required to redefine the management behavior and thinking mode of enterprise innovation, generate new innovation concept, form the entrepreneurship-centered and innovation-based culture which advocates all-involvement innovation, encourages risk-taking and tolerates failure, and enrich and develop the specific contents and forms of innovation-based culture during the process of practices.

15.2 Connotations and nature of TIM

Based on the comprehensive and systematic view of TIM, and taking the training of core competence and the improvement of sustainable competitiveness as orientation, the value creation/increase as ultimate goal, and the organic combination and collaborative innovation of various innovation elements (such as technology, organization, market, strategy, management, culture, system, etc.) as means, TIM aims to realize the "Three All and One Synergy" through effective innovation management mechanism, methods and tools. TIM breaks through the previous model of innovation exclusively carried out by the R&D department, highlights the ecology theory of innovation based on human-oriented concept and complex system, and greatly expands the elements and time-space scope of innovation.

The key for TIM is: focusing on one central task, relying on two basic points and realizing one objective. Specially, it means taking the cultivation and enhancement of core competences of enterprise as the central task, taking the strategic orientation and the organic combination and synergy innovation of all innovation elements as two basic points, and realizing the objective of value creation/increase (improving business performance).

The basic characteristics of TIM: (1) Strategic. Taking the business strategy as basis and starting point and the cultivation and enhancement of core competences of enterprise as the central task; not only satisfying the demands for improving present operation business, but also maintaining the sustainable competitiveness by cultivating and accumulating dynamic core competences; (2) Universal. Innovation activities penetrate every process, every event, every employee and every corner; (3) People. Emphasize the dominant role of innovation in business activities and establish the compulsory code of conduct; (4) Holistic. As a system project, TIM cannot be completed without the coordination and supports from all departments and all elements. It is such a holistic nature that bands all departments and all employees of the enterprise together like strands of a rope and forms a holistic innovative force.

The essence of total innovation: to give full freedom to the innovation vigor of all employees, carry out all-round innovation, apply, explore and integrate all innovation resources on a global scale, form integrated force, constantly improve the core competences, and create the maximum value for customers. Meanwhile, it should seek profits for all stakeholders.

15.3 TIM as a bridge to innovation-oriented enterprises

15.3.1 Innovation-based enterprises

Building innovation-based enterprises through indigenous innovation is a major strategic measure to comprehensively implement the scientific outlook on development in China. To realize indigenous innovation, the enterprise must become the subject of indigenous innovation. Only if many enterprises become innovation-based enterprise can the indigenous innovation capabilities be improved to strengthen the overall innovation capabilities of the country as a whole. So what is an innovation-based enterprise? Based on the existing research, it can be concluded that: for innovation-based enterprises, innovation should become the main motive power to stimulate enterprise development and be penetrated into all aspects of enterprise. Comprehensive and all-round innovation, including strategy innovation, technology innovation, management innovation, organization innovation, culture innovation and market innovation, are the essential characteristics of innovation-based enterprises. All-involvement innovation is the foundation and innovation should be implanted in all employees' minds. Everyone should be involved in the innovation at any time, at any place and at any event.

15.3.2 Secondary innovation: Portfolio innovation (integrated) and total innovation management

The development of innovation-based enterprises in foreign countries have undergone the stages of efficiency, quality and flexibility before they finally became innovation-based. The main characteristics include: the innovation covers all aspects of technology innovation and non-technology innovation, emphasizes all involvement and attaches importance to the improvement of core competences. Chinese enterprises have different starting points, so they also have different origins of force. Based on the review of the development of Chinese enterprises since 1949, their innovation management has undergone the following five stages:

(1) First stage (early 1950s to 1958): introduction and imitation

This stage refers to the period from the three-year economic recovery to the first five-year plan when Chinese enterprises mainly learnt and introduced technical equipment from the former Soviet Union and reconstructed them to adapt to the practical demands in China. The innovation at this stage mainly focused on imitation innovation, learnt from the Stakhanovite Movement of the former Soviet Union, widely carried out the mass rational suggestion activities of “two participation, one reform and three combination”, and solved the problems that existed in the process of introduction through incremental improvement.

(2) Second stage (later 1950s to 1978): creative imitation

At this stage, as to the dogmatism and bookishness arising from the blind worship for technology innovation during learning, the "ideological emancipation movement" was carried out to eliminate all obstacles of innovation. The technology innovation develops itself from pure imitation to a self-designing stage when the imitation and innovation are combined.

(3) Third stage (1978 to early 1990s): improved secondary innovation

The model at this stage is shown in Figure 15-1.

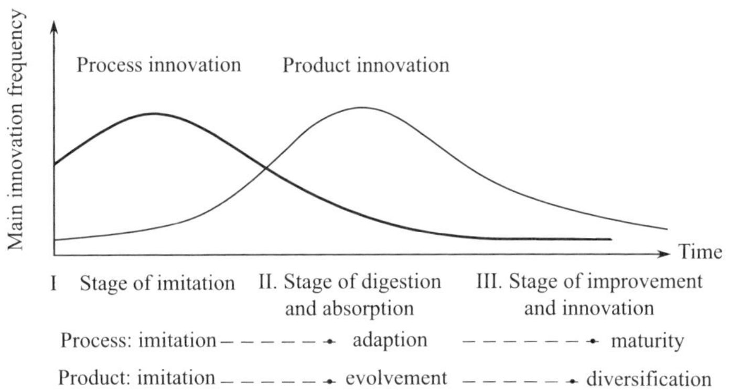

Figure 15-1 Dynamic model of secondary innovation

(4) Fourth stage (late 1980s to late 1990s): portfolio innovation constructed core competences and laid foundation for indigenous innovation

In the 1970s, the research on portfolio innovation mainly stayed with the product innovation, i.e. investigating optimal portfolio of different kinds of products to optimize the use of limited resources and maintain sustainable development. In the 1980s, enterprises began to attach importance to the relationship between product innovation and process innovation in the portfolio innovation of technologies. In the 1990s, relevant research had already gone beyond the category of technology innovation portfolio, covered the organizational innovation and culture innovation, and expanded the indigenous innovation to the stage of all-round portfolio and synergy innovation which integrated the cooperative innovation of external forces (Figure 15-2). After the mid-1990s, with further research on and practices of portfolio innovation, the core competence theory represented by Prahalad and Hamel (1990) was widely accepted and introduced to the field of portfolio innovation research.

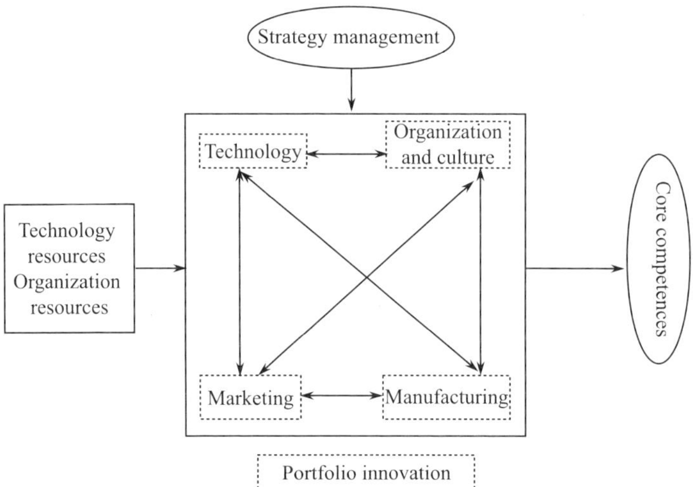

Figure 15-2 Model of portfolio innovation based on core competences

The model of portfolio innovation further enriched and developed the viewpoints of universal relations and systematic viewpoints, profoundly revealed the interaction and combination of all elements of the innovation system and the underlying rules, and reflected the development of things from simplicity to complexity and from low level to high level.

(5) Fifth stage (since early 21st century): stage of total innovation management

Continuous innovation is the only choice for enterprises to seek survival and development under new economic conditions. TIM is the new paradigm of technology innovation management in the 21st century and also the new direction of business management, as shown in Figure 15-3.

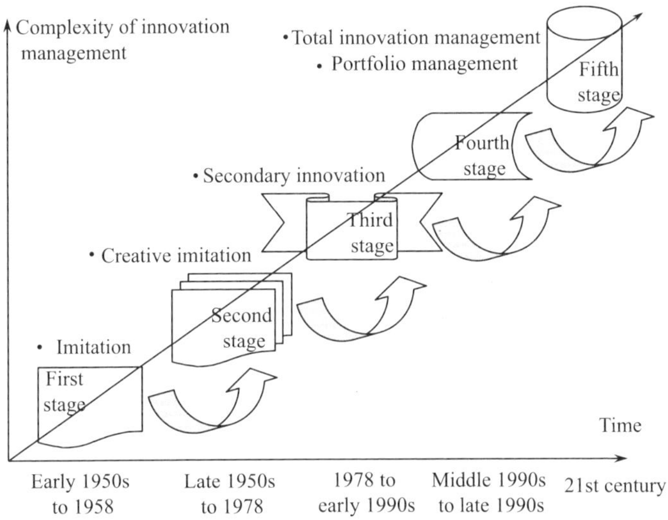

Figure 15-3 Schematic diagram of innovation management development

15.4 Construction of indigenous innovation capability through TIM

Generally speaking, the elements of technology capabilities can be decomposed into personnel capability, information capability, equipment capability and organization capability. With the development of science and technology, knowledge plays an increasingly important role in economic development. According to our research, the elements of indigenous innovation capabilities are adjusted to four dimensions, namely technical facilities, human resources, information knowledge and organization culture. To improve indigenous innovation capabilities, enterprises should deal with all these four elements and adopt corresponding measures. The structural relationship of TIM promoting the indigenous innovation capabilities is shown in Figure 15-4.

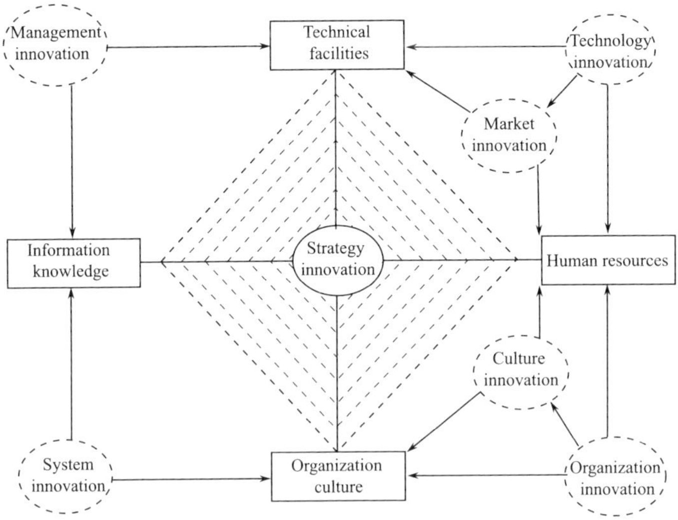

Figure 15-4 Schematic diagram of the structural relationship of total innovation management promoting the technology innovation capabilities

Seen from the figure above, strategy innovation plays a dominant role, while technology innovation stimulates the upgrading of technical facilities, cultivates technology innovation talent and improves the technology level of technicians. Meanwhile, technology innovation directly influences the technical facilities and human resources through market innovation; management innovation and system innovation stimulate the accumulation and enhancement of organization and individual knowledge and improve the efficiency of technical facilities; system innovation also stimulates the reform and adjustment of organizational culture; organization innovation influences culture innovation and also human resources. Therefore, through all-element innovation, all aspects of technology innovation are separately accumulated and comprehensively enhanced through four dimensions and nearly 20 approaches to finally construct the indigenous innovation capabilities of enterprises.

15.5 Research prospects

From the generation of TIM to further research on total innovation, it has a history of only ten years. In these ten years, RCID team has devoted itself to theoretical research and discussions as well as case studies. However, it is still far from enough. The references used in this book are mainly experiences of Chinese and foreign enterprises which have successfully realized TIM. How to realize TIM in different industries and small and medium-sized enterprises still needs further investigation. At the initial stage, theoretical research also focuses on the inevitability and constructing principles of the generation of TIM and lacks sufficient research on the realization process and principles/mechanisms of TIM. Therefore, a lot of work has to be done in terms of theoretical research. In summary, further research should be concentrated on the following aspects:

(1) Forming mechanism and model of TIM in small and medium-sized enterprises;

(2) Forming mechanism and model of TIM in different industries;

(3) Internal connections and interactions among all elements of all-element innovation;

(4) Synergy models among all innovation elements;

(5) Interactions among functional mechanisms of leadership mechanism, synergy mechanism and learning mechanism during the formation and implementation of TIM;

(6) Capability evaluation model of TIM;

(7) Effect of the implementation of TIM on the formation of indigenous innovation capabilities;

(8) Assessment of basic models of TIM benefits and the characteristics of their applications in different types of enterprises.

In other words, TIM is still a new thing under the sun and needs full support from all relevant parties. Last but not the least, I would like to express our sincere thanks to all my colleagues from academic and business circles!

Bibliography

2014 *Annual Report of Shanghai Baosteel Group Company*, http://news.baosteel.com/group/07press/pdf/annualreport/ar2004.pdf, 2006/10/08.

Afsaneh N. 2003. *The Art and Science of Leadership*. Beijing: China Machine Press.

Alchain A. & North D. 1994. *Change of Property Rights and System*. Shanghai: Shanghai Sanlian Bookstore.

Allen T. J. 1977. *Managing the Flow of Technology*. Cambridge, MA: MIT Press.

Amabile T. M. 1996. *Creativity in Context. Boulder*, CO: Westview.

Amabile T. M. 1988. A model of creativity and innovation in organizations. *Research in Organizational Behavior*. 10: 123–168.

Anderson N., De Dreu C., Nijstad B. The Routinization of Innovation Research: A Constructively Critical Review of the State-of-the-Science. *Journal of Organizational Behavior*, 2004, 25(2): 147-173.

Anderson N. R. & West M. D. 1998. Measuring climate for work group innovation: development and validation of the team climate inventory. *Journal of Organizational Behavior*. 19: 235–258.

Aoki M. & Takizawa H. 2002. Information, incentives and option value: the Silicon Valley model. *Journal of Comparative Economics*. 30 (4): 759–786.

Aoki M. 2003. *Modularity: The Nature of New Industrial Architecture*. Shanghai: Shanghai Far East Publishers.

Arora A., Gambardella A. & Rullani E. 1997. Division of labor and the locus of inventive activity. *Journal of Management & Governance*. 1 (1): 123–140.

Bailetti A. J. & Litva P. F. 1995. Integrating customer requirements into product designs. *Product Innovation Management*. 12: 3–15.

Bain P. G., Mann C. & Pirola-Merlo A. 2001. The innovation imperative: the relationships between team climate, innovation, and performance in research and development teams. *Small Group Research*. 32: 55–73.

Baldwin C. Y. & Clark K. B. 1997. Managing in an age of modularity. *Harvard Business Review*. 75 (5): 84 –93.

Baoshan Iron & Steel Co. Ltd. 2006. Use of intellectual property: Creating first class Baosteel brand. *Shanghai Business*. 5:12–15.

Bartmess A. & Cerny K. 1993. Building competitive advantage through a global network of capabilities. *California Management Review*. 35 (2): 78–103.

Bessant J. 2003. *High-involvement Innovation*. San Francisco, CA: Jossey-Bass.

Blackhurn J. D. 1991. *Time-based Competition: The Next Battleground in American Manufacturing*. Homewood: Business One Irwin.

Burgelman R. A., Kosnik T. J. & van den Poel M. 1988. Toward an inn(ed.)ovative capability audit framework. In: Burgelman R. A. & Maidique M. A. *Strategic Management of Technology and Innovation*. Homewood, IL: Irwin.

Burke W. W. 2001. *Organization Change: Theory and Practice*. London, New Delphi: Sage Publications, Inc.

Burns J. M. 1996. *Leadership*. Beijing: China Social Sciences Publishing House.

Cao Q., Wang Z. & Wang Z. 2001. *Integrated Innovation of Enterprise*. Beijing: Xuelin Press.

Campbell A. 2002. *Strategic Synergy* (2nd Edition). Beijing: China Machine Press.

Cardinal L. B. 2001. Technological innovation in the pharmaceutical industry: the use of organizational control in managing research and development. *Organizational Science*, 12: 19–36.

Carlson B., Jacobson S. & Holmén M. et al. 2002. Innovation systems: analytical and methodological issues. *Research Policy*, 31: 233–245.

Charman T. & Baron-Cohen S. 1995. Understanding photos, models, and beliefs: a test of the modularity thesis of theory of mind. *Cognitive Development*, 10 (2): 287–298.

Chell E. 2001. Entrepreneurship: globalization, innovation and development. *International Journal of Entrepreneurial Behaviour & Research*. 7 (5): 205–206.

Chen J., Wang Y. & Xu Q. 1999. Core Competence of Corporation: A Literature Review. *Science Research Management*, 20 (5): 13–20.

Chen J. & Chen Y. 2006. The Study of Indicators System on Technological Innovation Performance in Enterprises. *Management of Scientific Research*, 3: 87–91.

Chen J., Geng X. & Smith R. 1998. Technical Innovation Audit: Framework and Sino-Canada Comparison. *Management of Scientific Research*, 6: 21–29.

Chen J. 2003. *Global Innovation: International Paradigm of Technology Innovation of Enterprise*. Beijing: Economic Science Press.

Chen Y. 2005. *Samsung: Made in Korea*. Beijing: Enterprise Management Publishing House.

Chesbrough H. W. 2003. *Open Innovation: The New Imperative for Creating and Profiting from Technology*. Boston: Harvard Business School Press.

Chiesa V., Coughlan P. & Voss C. A. 1996. Development of a technical innovation audit. *Journal of Product Innovation Management*, 13 (2): 105–136.

Chiesa V. 1996. Managing the internationalization of R&.D activities. *IEEE Transaction on Engineering Management*, 43 (1): 7–23.

Choi T. Y., Dooley K. J. & Rungtusanatham M. 2001. Supply networks and complex adaptive systems: control versus emergence. *Journal of Operations Management*, 19: 351–366.

Christiansen J. A. 2000. *Building the Innovative Organization*. London: MacMillan Press.

Clark K. B. & Fujimoto T. 1991. *Product Development Performance: Strategy, Organization, Management in the World Auto Industry*. Boston: Harvard Business School Press.

Clark P. 2003. *Organizational Innovations*. London: SAGE Publications.

Claudia W. 2001. Knowledge and organization strategies in innovation systems. *International Journal of Innovation Management*, 5

(1): 105–127.

Collins D., Ross R. A. & Ross T. 1989. Who wants *participative management? The managerial perspective*. Group and Organizational Studies. 14: 422–455

Coombs R. & Metcalfe J. S. 2002. Organizing for innovation: co-coordinating distributed Innovation capabilities. In: Foss N. & Mahnke V. (ed.). *Competence, Governance, and Entrepreneurship*. Oxford: Oxford University Press: 209–231.

Coombs R., Harvey M. & Tether B. 2001. Analyzing distributed innovation processes: A CRIC Position Paper, 43: 1–4.

Cooper R. G. & Kleinschmidt E. J. 1997. Winning businesses in product development: the critical success factors. *The Journal of Product Innovation Management*, 14 (2): 132.

Cooper R. G. & Schmidt K. 1987. New products: what separates winner from losers. *Journal of Product Innovation Management*, 4 (3): 169–184.

Cooper R. G. 1979. The dimensions of industrial new product success and failure. *Journal of Marketing*, 43 (3): 93–103.

Cooper R. G. 1984. The strategy-performance link in product innovation. *R&D Management*, 14 (4): 247–259.

Cooper R. G. 1985. Overall corporate strategies for new product programs. *Industry Marketing Management*, 14: 179–193.

Daft R. L. 1978. A dual-core model of organizational innovation. *Academy of Management Journal*, 21 (2): 193–210.

Dai J. 2002. Analysis of self-organizing characteristics of enterprises and their effect on modern enterprise management. *Modern Management Science*, 10: 4–5.

Damanpour F., Gopalakrishnan S. 1998. Theories of organizational structure and innovation adoption, the role of environmental change. *Journal of Engineering and Technology*, 15:1–24.

Damanpour F. 1991. Organizational innovation: a meta-analysis of effects of determinants and moderators. *Academy of Management Journal*, 34: 555–590.

Damanpour F. & Evan W. M. 1984. Organizational innovation and performance: The problem of organizational lag. *Administrative Science Quarterly*, 29 (3): 392–409.

Debra A. 1998. *Innovation Strategy for the Knowledge Economy* (Business Briefcase Series). Beijing: Xinhua Press.

Dess G. & Picken J. 2000. Changing roles: Leadership in the 21st century. *Organizational Dynamics*, 28: 18–34.

Donald A. H. 2001. The financial undertow of rapid technical advance in new product development. *Journal of Engineering and Technology Management*, 18: 49–71.

Dooley K. A. 1997. Complex adaptìve systems model of organizational change. *Non-linear Dynamics, Psychology and the Life Sciences*, 1: 69–97.

Duggal S. & Revinova S. 2003. Competing in the information economy. *Proceedings of the Informing Science +IT Education (inSite) Conference*, (6): 24–27.

Dundon E. & Pattakos A. N. 2001. Leading the innovation revolution: Will the real Spartacus stand up? *Journal for Quality & Participation*, 24 (4): 48–52.

Duray R., Ward P. T. & Milligan G. W. et al. 2000. Approaches to mass customization: Configurations and empirical validation. *Journal of Operations Management*, 18 (6): 605–625.

Fan S., Li G. & Lü J. 2006. A Case study on Baosteel lean cost management. *Scientific Research Management*. 2:92.

Flombaum J. I., Santos L. R. & Hauser M. D. 2002. Neuroecology and psychological modularity. *Trends in Cognitive Sciences*, 6 (3): 106–108.

Fu Y. 1994. We must strive for the first — Revelation of the development of Samsung Group in Korea. *Tax and Business*, 6:41–42.

Galbraith J. 2002. *Designing Organizations: An Executive Guide to Strategy, Structure, and Process*. Hoboken: John Wiley & Sons Inc.

Galunic D. C. & Eisenhardt K. M. 2001. Architectural innovation and modular corporate forms. *Academy of Management Journal*, 44 (6): 1229–1249.

Gershenson J., Prasad G. & Zhang Y. 2003. Product modularity:

Definitions and benefits. *Journal of Engineering Design*, 14 (3): 295–313.

Gershenson J., Prasad G. & Zhang Y. 2004. Product modularity: Measures and design methods. *Journal of Engineering Design*, 15 (1): 33–51.

Glove S., Levy G. W., Schwartz K. M. 1973. Key factors and events in the innovation process. *Research Management*, 16: 8–15.

Greenwood W. T. 1967. *Business Policy: A Management Audit Approach*. New York: Macmillan.

Griffin A. & Hauser J. R. 1996. Integrating R&D, and marketing: A review, and analysis of the literature. *Journal of Product Innovation Management*, 13: 191.

Gronhaug K. 1988. *Innovation: A Cross-disciplinary Perspective*. Oxford: Oxford University Press.

Gundling E. 2000. *The 3M Way to Innovation: Balancing People and Profit*. Tokyo: Kodansha International.

Guo B., Xu Q. & Chen J. et al. 1997. Research on portfolio innovation of enterprise. *Studies in Science of Science*, 15 (1): 12–18.

Guo Y., Zhang S. & Guo B. et al. 2004. Practical strategies of selecting the form of strategic alliance. *Management of Scientific Research*, 5(2): 94–98.

Guo Y. 2004. Samsung Group — Competitiveness and innovation of enterprise. *World View*, 6: 63–64.

Hadley R. F. 2003. A defense of functional modularity. *Connection Science*, 15 (2/3): 95–116.

Haken H. 1984. *The Science of Structure: Synergetics*. New York: Van Nostrand Reinhold Company.

Haken H. 1989. *Advanced Synergetics*. Translated by Guo Zhian. Beijing: Science Press.

Hammer M. 1996. *Beyond Reengineering*. New York: Harper Business.

Hammer M. & Champy J. 1993. *Reengineering the Corporation*. New York: Harper Business.

Harryson S. 2004. *Japanese Technology and Innovation*

Management: From Know-How to Know-Who. Cheltenham: Edward Elgar Publishing.

Hartlaub J. 1994. Getting every employee into the (innovation) act. *Research Technology Management*, 37 (6): 41–59.

Howells J. R. 1995. Going global: the use of ICT networks in research and development. *Research Policy*, 24: 169–184.

Hospers G-J. Joseph schumpeter and his legacy in innovation studies. *Knowledge, Technology & Policy*. 2005, 18(3): 20–37.

Hu X. 2003. *Samsung President Kun-hee Lee*. Translated by Hojae Lee. Beijing: Huaxia Press.

Hu Y. 2004. *What Zhang Ruimin Says*. Hangzhou: Zhejiang People's Publishing House.

Iansiti M. & West J. 1997. Technology integration: Turning great research into great products. *Harvard Business Review*, 75 (3): 69–79.

Janssen O., Vliert E. V. D. & West M. 2004. The bright and dark sides of individual and group innovation: a special issue introduction. *Journal of Organizational Behavior*, 25 (2): 129–145.

Janszen F. 2002. *The Age of Innovation*. Translated by Ma Lewei. Kunming: Yunnan University Press.

Ji G. 2002. "Tao of Innovation" of American Enterprises. *Administrative Tribune*, 7: 72–74.

Jiang H. 2001. Integrated innovation and adaptive capability of enterprise: A case study of the core competence of Fujian Shida Computer Group. *Journal of Fujian School of Administration and Fujian Institute of Economics and Management*, 1: 23–25.

Jiang H. & Chen J. 2000. Integrated Innovation Patterns. *Science Research Management*, 21 (5): 31–39.

Jin W. 2000. Research on innovation should become a new stage of the research of philosophy of science. *Journal of Northeastern University*, 4: 257–259.

Johannessen J. A., Olsen B. & Olaisen J. 1999. Aspects of innovation theory based on knowledge-management. *International Journal of Information Management*, 19 (2): 121–139.

Kao J. 2000. *Management of Creativity: Improvisation*. Haikou:

Hainan Press.

Hughes K., Ralf M. & Michels W. 1999. *Transform Your Supply Chain*. Translated by Meng Tao and Zhang Liping. Dalian: Dongbei University of Finance Publishing House.

Kang S. 2003. Economic integration in the evolvement of economic globalization seen from the stability of system. *Journal of Systematic Dialectics*, 3:46–51.

Kaplan R. S. & Norton D. P. 1992. The balanced scorecard-measures that drive performance. *Harvard Business Review*, (1–2): 71–79.

Katz M. L. & Shapiro C. 1986. Technology adoption in the presence of network externalities. *The Journal of Political Economy*, 94: 822–841.

Katz R. 1997. *The Human Side of Managing Technological Innovation*. Cambridge, MA: Harvard Business School Press.

Kevin W. Z. 1999. Risk-pooling over demand uncertainty in the presence of product modularity. *International Journal of Production Economics*. 62 (1 –2): 75–85

Kline S. J, Rosenberg N. 1986. An overview of innovation. In: Landau R. Rosenberg N. (ed.) *The Positive Sum Strategy*. Washington: National Academy Press

Kong D. & Cui X. 2003. *Management ecology*. *Management Science in the 21st century*, 2: 8–10.

Kotter J. P. 1988. *The Leadership Factor*. New York: London: Free Press.

Kraatz M. S. & Zajac E. J. 2001. How organizational resources affect strategic change and performance in turbulent environments: Theory and evidence. *Organization Science*, 12: 632–657.

Krikke H., Le Blanc I. & Van De Velde S. 2004. Product modularity and the design of closed-loop supply chains. *California Management Review*, 46 (2): 23–39.

Lawrence P. R. & Lorsch W. 1967. *Organization and Environment*. Boston: Harvard University Business School.

Leonard W. P. 1962. *The Management Audit: An Appraisal of*

Management Methods and Performance. New Jersey: Prentice-Hall.

Leonard-Barton D. 1992. Core capabilities and core rigidities: a paradox in managing new product development. *Strategic Management Journal*, 13: 111–125.

Levin B. M. 1998. Strategic networks: the emerging business organization and its impact on production costs. *Journal of Production Economics*, 56: 397–405.

Li G., Li C. & Li L. 2005. Dynamic analysis of supply chain network structures based on CAS. *Industrial Engineering Journal*, 3: 23–27.

Li G. 2002. *Innovation-based* Corporate Culture. Beijing: Economic Management Press.

Li H. & Li J. 2003. Win by culture: Thoughts on the profound meaning of the construction of corporate culture. *Modern Enterprise Education*, 11: 51–52.

Li J. 2003. Let employees freely innovate. *Talent Outlook*, 4: 45.

Lian Y. & Ma X. 2001. Development trends evaluation of cooperation of industry, university and research institute. *China Soft Science Magazine*, 1: 54–59.

Little A. D. 1981. The strategic management of technology. European Management Forum.

Lundvall B. A. 1988. Innovation as an interactive process: From user-producer interaction to the national system of innovation. In: Dosi G., Freeman C., Nelson R. & Silverberg G. et al., (eds.) *Technical Change and Economics Theory*. London: Printer Publishers: 335–376.

Lundvrall B. A. 1992. *National Systems of Innovation*: *Towards a Theory of Innovation and Interactive Learning*. London: Pinter Publishers.

Lynn G. S. & Akgün A. E. 2001. Proiect visioning: Its components and impact on new product success. *The Journal of Product Innovation Management*, 18: 374–387.

Ma F. & Kang L. 2005. Flexible reform of elephant. *Business School*, 5: 40–41.

Magnusson T., Lindstrom G. & Berggren C. 2003. Architectural or modular innovation? Managing discontinuous product development in response to challenging environmental performance targets. *International Journal of Innovation Management*, 7 (1): 1 –26.

Maidique M. A., Zirger B. J. 1984. A study of success and failure in product innovation: the case of the US electronics industry. *IEEE Transactions on Engineering Management*, 31 (4): 192–203.

Malone T. W. & Growston K. 1994. The interdisciplinary study of coordination. *ACM Computing Surveys*, 26 (1): 87– 119.

Mao W. 2006. Total Innovation Management Competence of Firms: A Case Study of Chinese Electronic Information Industry. Zhejiang University Doctoral Dissertation.

March J. G. 1991. Exploration and exploitation in organizational learning. *Organization Science*, 2 (1): 71–87.

Martindell J. 1950. *The Scientific Appraisal of Management*. New York: Harper.

Mason Haire. 1959. *Biological Models and Empirical Histories in the Growth of Organizations in Model Organization Theory*. New York: John Wiley.

Mcgrath R. G. 2001. Exploratory learning, innovative capacity, and managerial oversight. *Academy of Management Journal*, 44 (1): 118–131.

Menke M. 2003. Total innovation management: an introduction and comparison to HP. Zhejiang University Report PPT. Zhejiang University RCID Internal Data.

Mumford M. D., Scott G. M. & Gaddis B. et al. 2002. Leading creative people: orchestrating expertise and relationships. *Leadership Quarterly*, 13: 705–750.

Nahm A. Y., Vonderembse M. A. & Koufteros X. A. 2003. The impact of organizational structure on time-based manufacturing and plant performance. *Journal of Operations Management*, 21: 281–306.

Nelson R. & Winter S. 1997. *An Evolutionary Theory of Economic Change*. Beijing: Commercial Press.

Ning M. & Luo J. 1996. Market strategy of Korean Samsung Group. *Shanghai Light Industry*, 1: 32–35.

Nishiguchi T. & Ikeda M. 1996. Suppliers innovation: Understated aspects of Japanese industrial sourcing. In: Nishiguchi T. (ed.). *Managing Product Development*. Oxford: Oxford University.

Oldham G. R. & Cummings A. 1996. Employee creativity: Personal and contextual factors at work. *Academy of Management Journal*, 39: 607–634.

Olson E. E. & Eoyang G. H. 2001. Facilitating Organization Change. San Francisco: Jossey Publishing.

Organization for Economic Co-operation and Development & EU Statistics Office. 1997. Oslo Manual. See: China Society for Science and Technology Indicators. Frascati Collection. Beijing: Xinhua Press.

Packard D. 1995. *The HP Way: How Bill Hewlett and I Built Our Company*. New York: Harper Collins Publishes

Padmore T., Schuetze H. & Gibson H. 1998. Modeling systems of innovation: An enterprise-centered view. *Research Policy*, 26 (6): 605–624.

Parker R. C. 1983. *The Management of Innovation*. New York: John Wiley&Sons Ltd.

Paterson S. J., Brown J. H. & Gsodl M. K. et al. 1999. Cognitive modularity and genetic disorders. *Science*, 286 (5448): 2355–2358.

Butler P. 1997. A revolution in interaction. *McKinsey Quarterly*, 1997, 3: 14-28.

Peng J. 2000. Historic evolution, change course and status comparison, and enlightens about technological innovation system in China. *R & D Management*, 4: 4–7.

Perrins A. C. & Tipping J. W. 1989. Global management of technology. *Research and Technology Management*, 32: 19-30.

Perrins T. 1989. Global management of technology. *Research and Technology Management*, 32: 12–19.

Peters T. 1992. Get innovative or get dead. *Engineering Management Review*, *Spring* (19): 7–14.

Peters T. 2002. *Theory of Innovation*. Beijing: Jiuzhou Press.

Porter M. 1990. *The Competitive Advantage of Nations*. New York: The Free Press.

Prahalad C. K. & Hamel G. 1990. The core competence of the corporation. *Harvard Business Review*, 5–6: 79–91.

Prescott J. E. 1986. Environments as moderators of the relationship between strategy and performance. *Academy of Management Journal*, 29: 329–346.

Radosevic S. 1998. Defining system of innovation, a methodological discussion. *Technology in Society*. 20: 75–86.

Radosevic S. 1998. The transformation of national systems of innovation in Eastern Europe: Between restructuring and erosion. *Industrial and Corporate Change*. 7 (1): 77–108.

Katz R. 1997. The Human Side of Managing Technological Innovation, a Collection of Readings. New York: Oxford University Press.

Riggs W. M. & von Hippel E. 1994. The impact of scientific and commercial values on the sources of scientific instrument innovation. *Research Policy*, 23: 459–469.

Leachman R. C., Kang J., Lin V. 2002. SLIM: Short cycle time and low inventory in manufacturing at Samsung electronics. *Linthicum*, 32 (1): 61–79.

Roberts E. 1999. *Management of Research, Development and Technology-Based Innovation*. Cambridge, MA: MIT Press.

Robertson P. L. & Langlois R. N. 1995. Innovation, networks, and vertical integration. *Research Policy*, 4 (24): 543–562.

Robinson A. G. & Sten S. 1997. Corporate Creativity: How Innovation and Improvement actually Happen. San Francisco: Berrett-Koehler Publishers.

Bean R. & Radford R. W. 2001. *The Business of Innovation, Managing the Corporate Imagination for Maximum Results*. New York: AMACOM.

Rommel G., Kluge J. & Kempis R. D. et al. 1995. *Simplicity Wins: How Germany's Mid-Sized Industrial Companies Succeed*. Boston: Harvard Business Press.

Rothwell R. & Bessant J. 1987. *Innovation, Adaptation and Growth*. Amsterdam: Elsevier Science Publishers.

Rubenstein A. H. 1980. Research and development issue in developing country, In: Bean B. et al. (ed.). *Management of Research and Innovation*. Amsterdam: North-Holland Publishing Company.

Rubinstein M. 1976. The valuation of uncertain income streams and the pricing of options. *The Bell Journal of Economics*, 7 (2): 407–425.

Rubinstein M. F. & Firstenberg I. R. 2001. The minding organization: Bring the future to the present and turn creative ideas into business solutions. Translated by Wang Shenying. Shanghai: Shanghai Jiaotong University Press.

Salvador F., Forza C. & Rungtusanatham M. 2002. Modularity, product variety, production volume and component sourcing: theorizing beyond generic prescriptions. *Journal of Operations Management*, 20 (5): 549–575.

Sanchez R. 1996. Strategic product creation: managing new interactions of technology, markets, and organizations. *European Management Journal*, 14 (2): 121–138.

Sanchez R., Collins R. P. 2001. Competing and learning in modular markets. *Long Range Planning*, 34 (6): 645–667.

Sanchez R. 1999. Modular architectures in the marketing process. *Journal of Marketing*, 63(4): 92– 111.

Sawhney M. & Prandelli E. 2000. Communities of creation. *California Management Review*, 42(4): 24–54.

Schilling M. A. 2000. Toward a general modular systems theory and its application to interfirm product modularity. *Academy of Management Review*, 25 (2): 312–334.

Schilling M. A. & Steensma H. K. 2001. The use of modular organizational forms: An industry level analysis. *Academy of Management Journal*, 44 (6): 1149–1168.

Schruijer S. G. L., Vansina L. S. 1999. Leadership and organizational change: An introduction. *European Journal of Work and Organizational Psychology*, 8 (1): 1–8.

Scott S. G. & Bruce R. A. 1994. Determinants of innovation behavior: A path model of individual innovation in workplace. *Academy of Management Journal*, 37 (3): 580–607.

Shui C., Zheng G. & Xu Q. 2004. Empirical Study on Determinant Factors of Synergetic Innovation in Large and Medium Enterprises in China. *Science of Science and Management of S&T*, 12: 44–48.

Sisodia R., Zahra H. & Matherne B. 1999. Exploiting the dynamic links between competitive and technology strategies. *European Management Journal*, 17: 188–203.

Song X. & Parry M. E. 1996. The determinants of Japanese new products success. *Journal of Marketing Research*, 34 (11): 64–76.

Song Y. 2002. Knowledge management and cultivation of enterprises' core competence. *Management World*, 8: 141–143.

Sosik J. J., Avolio B. J., Kahai S. S. 1997. Effects of leadership style and anonymity on group potency and effectiveness in a group decision support system environment. *Journal of Applied Psychology*, 82: 89–103.

Sosik J. J., Kahai S. S. & Avolio B. J. 1999. Leadership style anonymity and creativity in group decision support systems: The mediating role of optimal flow. *Journal of Creative Behavior*, 33: 1–30.

Stacey R. D. 1996. *Complexity and Creativity in Organization*. San Francisco: Berret Koehler Publishers.

Stacey R. D. 2001. *Complex Responsive Processes in Organizations: Learning and Knowledge Creation*. London and New York: Routledge.

Stalk G. Jr. 1988. Time: The next source of competitive advantage. *Harvard Business Review*, 66: 41–51.

Stalk G. Jr. & Hout T. Competing Against Time. *Research-Technology Management*. 1990, 33(2): 19–24.

Dafoe S. 2004. *HP Way: From Good Management to Outstanding Management*. Translated by Kang Yiren. Harbin. Harbin Press.

Swaminathan J. M. 2001. Enabling customization using standard operations. *California Management Review*, 43 (3): 125–135.

Tang H. K. 1998. An integrative model of innovation in organizations. *Technovation*, 18 (5): 297–309.

Teece D. J. 1996. Firm organization, industrial structure,

and technological innovation. *Journal of Economic Behavior &. Organization*, 31: 193–224.

Teece D. J., Pisano G. & Shuen A. 1997. Dynamic capabilities and strategic management. *Strategic Management Journal*, 18 (7): 509–533.

Tidd J., Bessant J. & Pavitt K. 2001. *Managing Innovation: Integrating Technological, Market and Organizational Change*. New York: John Wiley.

Tidd J. & Bessant J. 2004. *Managing Innovation: Integrating Technological, Market and Organizational Change*. Translated by Jinma Working Studio. Beijing: Tsinghua University Press.

Tornatzky L. G., Eveland J. D. & Boylan M. G. et al. 1983. The process of technological innovation reviewing the literature: productivity improvement research section, division of industrial science and technological innovation. Washington, DC: National Science Foundation.

Tornatzky L. G. & Fleischer M. 1990. *The Process of Technological Innovation: Reviewing the Literature*. Washington, DC: National Science Foundation.

Tornatzky L. G. & Fleischer M. 1990. *The Process of Technological Innovation*. Lexington, Mass.: Lexington Books.

Tucker R. B. 2002. *Driving Growth through Innovation*. San Francisco: Berrett-Koehler Publishers.

Utterback J. M., Thomas J. A. & Holloman J. H. et al. 1976. The process of innovation in five industries in Europe and Japan. *IEEE Transactions on Engineering Management*, 1 (February): 3–9.

Utterback J. M. 1999. *Mastering the Dynamics of Innovation*. Translated by Gao Jian and Li Ming. Beijing: Tsinghua University Press.

Utterback J. M. 1994. *Mastering the Dynamics of Innovation*. Boston: Harvard Business School Press.

Von Hippel E. 1988. *The Sources of Innovation*. New York: Oxford University Press.

Von Hippel E. 1997. *Source of Technology Innovation*. Translated by Liu Xielin. Beijing: Science and Technology Press.

Wang D. 2001. The knowledge application during the enterprise technical innovation process: a comparison of China and the west. *Management of Scientific Research*. 19: 1–4.

Wang W. & Xu Q. 1993. Theory of interaction between innovation and environment. *Studies in Science of Science*, 4: 24–27.

Werker C. 2001. Knowledge and organization strategies in innovation systems. *International Journal of Innovation Management*, 5 (1): 105.

Wheatley M. J. 2001. *Leading for Innovation and Organizing for Results*. San Francisco: Jossey-Bass.

Worren N., Moore K. & Cardona P. 2002. Modularity, strategic flexibility, and firm performance: A study of the home appliance industry. *Strategic Management Journal*, 23 (12):1123–1140.

Wu G. & Xie W. 1996. The concept of "user innovation" and its operation mechanism. *Management of Scientific Research*, 17 (5): 14–19.

Wu G. & Xie W. 2005. Strategic thinking of the development of Chinese technology management disciplinary, *Management of Scientific Research* 26 (6): 49–55.

Wu T. 2001. *Research on Self-organization Methodology*. Beijing: Tsinghua University Press.

Wu Y. & Guan S. 2002. Systematic construction of technology innovation system. *Journal of Dialectics of Nature*, 24 (5): 32–39.

Xu Q., Jiang J. & Zheng G. 2004. Participation of suppliers' in research on technology innovation: A case study of Baosteel Group. *Journal of China University of Geosciences* (Social Sciences Edition), 12: 6–9.

Xu Q. et al. 2000. Development of technological innovation in China: Core competence-based innovation portfolio. *Journal of Industrial Engineering and Engineering Management*, S1: 1–10.

Xu Q., Jia F. & Xie Z., et al. All-involvement innovation based on total innovation management. *Studies in Science of Science*, Z1: 252–256.

Xu Q., Liang X. & Zheng G. 2004. The evolvement of innovation management-based on the opinion of innovation degeneration. *Journal of China University of Geosciences* (Social Sciences Edition), 5: 14–18.

Xu Q., Xie Z. & Zheng G. 2004. Institutional analysis on total innovation management. *Management of Scientific Research*, 25 (3): 6–12.

Xu Q., Zheng G. & Chen J. 2006. Theoretical trace and framework of overall innovation management. *Chinese Journal of Management*, 2: 135–142.

Xu Q., Zheng G. & Yu Z. 2003. Towards Total Innovation Management (TIM): The emerging new trend of innovation management – A case study of Haier Group. *Management of Scientific Research*. 24 (5): 1–7.

Xu Q., Zhu L. & Zheng G. 2004. The way to total innovation management – A case study of technology innovation management of Haier Group. *Journal of Dalian University of Technology* (Social Science Edition), 25 (1): 6–10.

Xu Q. 2000. *Research, Development and Technology Innovation Management*. Beijing: Higher Education Press.

Yang Y. 2005. *Samsung Brand Strategy*. Guangzhou: Nanfang Daily Press.

Zeng F. 2004. Perfect integration of characteristic corporate culture and business management. *Human Resource Development*, 10: 48–49.

Zhang D. 2005. Haier and IBM: Hero worship vs. institutional building. *Market Weekly: New Logistics*. 28: 52.

Zhang L. 2006. The study of indictors system on technological innovation performance in middle and small-sized enterprises. *Economist*, 5: 176–177.

Zhang T., Sun L. & Sun H. et al. 2003. Analysis and modeling of operation mode of supply chain: Research based on CAS paradigm. *System Engineering Theory and Practice*, 11: 8–13.

Zhang W. & Wan W. 2004. A study on the incentives and models for construction of interfirm innovation networks. *R&D Management*, 16 (3):62–68.

Zhejiang University Research Center for Innovation and

Development (RCID). 2004. Investigation report of CIMC technology innovation evaluation system project.

Zhejiang University Research Center for Innovation and Development (RCID). 2005. Investigation report of CIMC technology innovation evaluation system project.

Zheng G., Chen J. & Xu Q. 1997. Research on the synergy innovation model of technology, organization and culture. *Studies in Science of Science*, 2:56–61.

Zheng G. 2003. TIM-based research on the total synergy mechanism of all the innovation agents during innovation process. Zhejiang University Doctoral Dissertation, 2004.

Zhou W. 2005. Create excellency with values. *Sino-Foreign Management*, 5: 34–36.

Zhou Y., Zheng G. & Shen W. 2004. Best practice of Chinese enterprise's technological innovation systems: The internationalized innovation systems of Haier Group. *Scientific Research Management*. 5: 75, 110–115.

Zhou Z. 2004. Samsung: Being innovation-based and taking technology as life. *Corporate Culture*. 11:10–13.

Ziman J. 2002. *Technological Innovation as an Evolutionary Process*. Translated by Sun Xijie, Zeng Guoping. Shanghai: Shanghai Technological Education Publishing House.